NATIVE AMERICAN LITERATURE

A Brief Introduction and Anthology

Gerald Vizenor
University of California, Berkeley

The HarperCollins Literary Mosaic Series
Ishmael Reed
General Editor
University of California, Berkeley

HARPERCOLLINS*COLLEGEPUBLISHERS*

Acquisitions Editor: Lisa Moore
Cover Designer: Kay Petronio
Electronic Production Manager: Eric Jorgensen
Electronic Page Makeup: Kay Spearman/The Resource Center
Printer and Binder: RR Donnelley & Sons Co.
Cover Printer: The LeHigh Press, Inc.

Native American Literature

Library of Congress Cataloging-in-Publication Data

Native American Literature: a Brief Introduction and Anthology / Gerald Vizenor
p.   cm. -- (HarperCollins Literary Mosaic Series)
Includes bibliographical references (p. 328) and index.
ISBN 0-673-46978-6
1. American Literature--Indian authors. 2. Indians of North America--Literary collections
3. American Literature--Indian authors--History and criticism. 4. Indians in literature.
I. Vizenor, Gerald Robert, 1934- . II. Series.
PS508.I5N37 1995
810.8'0897--dc20

                                                                              95-1693
                                                                              CIP

95 96 97 98   9 8 7 6 5 4 3 2

Contents

POETRY

DRAMA

Foreword

by Ishmael Reed, General Editor

I abandoned the use of textbooks early in my teaching career and developed my own "reader." I was frustrated with textbooks in which the preponderance of prose and poetry was written by people of similar backgrounds and sensibilities—the white-settler-surrounded-by-infidels-and-savages theme common to Euro-American literature. In these textbooks we seldom got information about how the Native Americans or the Africans felt. Female and minority writers were left out. There was slack inclusion of contemporary writers, and little space devoted to the popular American culture of our century. These textbooks seemed slavishly worshipful of the past, such that every mediocre line by a past "great" was treated with reverence while the present was ignored.

Of course, there are many worthwhile ideas to be gained from what in our sound-bite culture—in which complicated ideas are dumbed down for instant consumption—is referred to as "Western Civilization." But as Asian American writer Frank Chin points out when referring to the Cantonese model, after the ability of the Cantonese to absorb every culture with which they've come into contact, one doesn't have to abandon the styles of one's own tradition in order to embrace styles from other traditions. As I have mentioned elsewhere, the history of modern art would be quite different had not artists been receptive to or borrowed from the traditions of others. This creative give and take between artists of different cultures particularly characterizes the arts of the twentieth century.

Things have improved over the years, especially with the outbreak of textbooks labeled "multicultural," a term that has become a football in the struggle between the politically correct of the left and the right. However, even the new and improved multicultural texts appear to have added African American, Native American, Hispanic American, and Asian American writers as an afterthought. The same writers and the same—often unrepresentative—works show up again and again.*

The HarperCollins Literary Mosaic Series

The HarperCollins Literary Mosaic Series was created as an antidote to this version of multiculturalism whose fallibility becomes evident when talented writers, well-known and respected in their communities, are ignored. The HarperCollins Literary Mosaic Series includes not only those writers who have made it into the canon but also writers undeservedly neglected in today's crop of texts.

* *For more information on the arbitrariness of this selection process, see Michael Harper's excellent Every Shut Eye Aint Sleep.*

In his autobiographical remarks, *Asian American Literature* editor Shawn Wong makes an important point that teachers should consider when adopting texts for their ethnic literature, multiculturalism, American literature, and introductory literature courses. Wong writes that his study of Asian American literature occurred outside of the university. "At no time," he writes, "in my English and American literature undergraduate education or in my entire public school education had any teacher ever used (or even mentioned) a work of fiction or poetry by a Chinese American or any Asian American writer." Wong's observation could be made by all the editors of the HarperCollins Literary Mosaic Series: Al Young for *African American Literature*, Gerald Vizenor for *Native American Literature*, Nicolás Kanellos for *Hispanic American Literature*, and of course Shawn Wong for *Asian American Literature*. They had to go outside of the academy—which has committed an intellectual scandal by excluding these major traditions of our common American heritage.

The Series Editors: Pioneers for an Inclusive Tradition

These editors are among the architects of a more inclusive tradition. Indeed, this series is unique because the four editors are not only writers and scholars in their own right but are among the pioneers of American literature of the latter part of this century! It's hard to imagine a list of talented insiders who are as informed about the currents and traditions of their ethnic literatures as the editors of the HarperCollins Literary Mosaic Series. These texts provide teachers with an opportunity to employ material in their classrooms that has been chosen by writers who have not only participated in the flowering of their literatures but also have assisted in the establishment of a tradition for their literatures.

Al Young

Al Young is a multitalented artist who has distinguished himself as a poet, novelist, screenwriter, editor, and writing instructor. His presence is very much in demand at writing workshops and conferences. He has taught at a number of universities and colleges, including Stanford University, Crown College, the University of California at Berkeley, the University of California at Santa Cruz, Rice University, and most recently at the University of Michigan. Among his honors are a Wallace Stegner Writing Fellowship, a Joseph Henry Jackson Award, a Guggenheim Fellowship, an American Book Award, and a PEN/Library of Congress Award for Short Fiction. Al Young and I were editors of the Yardbird Reader series, which has been recognized as the first national publication of its kind devoted to presenting new multicultural literature.

Gerald Vizenor

Pulitzer Prize–winner N. Scott Momaday has said that Gerald Vizenor "has made a very significant contribution to Native American letters and also to American literature in general. He's innovative, he has the richest sense of humor of anyone I know, and in addition he's the most articulate person—he's a man to be reckoned with." Among his innovative novels are *Heirs of Columbus* and *Griever: An American Monkey King in China*. An American Book Award winner, Vizenor insists that the story of Native Americans in the United States should be told by Native Americans and not by intermediaries or translators. His *Native American Literature* anthology in the HarperCollins Literary Mosaic Series will provide students and readers with an entirely different slant on Native American literature from the one they have become accustomed to in standard texts.

Nicolás Kanellos

Author of a number of scholarly works and articles, Nicolás Kanellos is the founder and director of Arte Público Press, the oldest and largest publisher of United States Hispanic literature, as well as the *Americas Review* (formerly *Revista Chicano-Reguena*), the oldest and most respected magazine of United States Hispanic literature and art. A full professor at the University of Houston, he is a fellow of the Ford, Lilly, and Gulbenkian foundations and of the National Endowment for the Humanities. He is also the winner of an American Book Award and is a formidable essayist with an unrivaled knowledge of the intersections of African, European, and Native American cultures.

Shawn Wong

It is not surprising that Shawn Wong and Frank Chin, Lawson Inada, and Jeffery Chan have become known as "the four horsemen of Asian American literature" by both their admirers and detractors. One wonders how Asian American literature would look without their efforts. It was they who began the painstaking construction of a tradition whose existence had been denied by the academy. In *Aiiieeee! An Anthology of Asian American Writers* and its successor, *The Big Aiiieeee! An Anthology of Chinese American and Japanese American Literature,* the four editors gave permanent status to an Asian American literary tradition. Wong is also the author of *Homebase,* the first novel published in the United States by an American-born Chinese male. This novel received the Pacific Northwest Booksellers Award for Excellence and the Fifteenth Annual Governor's Writer's Day Award. Among his many other honors, Wong has also received a fellowship from the National Endowment for the Arts. He has taught writing at the University of Washington since 1984.

Remapping Our Tradition

Although the four editors are from different backgrounds, the issues raised in their introductions are those with which a few generations of multicultural scholars, writers, and artists have grappled. With *African American Literature,* Al Young has both a literary and humanistic purpose. He believes that readers and writers will be able to learn from their exposure to some of the best writing in the United States that there are experiences all of us share with the rest of humanity. Like the classic critic F. R. Leavis, Al Young believes that writing can make people better. The writers included in Gerald Vizenor's *Native American Literature* are not outsiders writing about Native Americans or colonial settlers promoting the forest as a tough neighborhood full of high-risk people, a threat to civilized enclaves, but rather works by Native Americans themselves, beginning in 1829 with William Apess's autobiography, *A Son of the Forest.* Nicolás Kanellos's *Hispanic American Literature* represents a literary tradition, part European and part African, that existed in the Americas prior to the arrival of the English. The situation in Asian American literature, one of the youngest of American literatures, is as turbulent as that of the atmosphere surrounding a new star. Shawn Wong's introduction addresses the continuing debate over issues about what constitutes Asian American literature and the role of the Asian American writer.

The books in the HarperCollins Literary Mosaic Series give a sampling of the outstanding contributions from writers in the past as well as the range of American literature that is being written today. And the anthologies in this series contain a truly representative sampling of African American, Native American, Hispanic American, and Asian American writing at the end of this century so that students can become acquainted with more than the few European and European Americans covered by traditional texts or the same lineup of token ethnic writers found in the policy issue multicultural books. It should be welcome news to instructors looking for new ways to teach that such a distinguished group committed themselves to producing three-to-five-hundred-page textbooks that can either be used as the primary text in a course, supplemented with novels, combined for a single class, or used to supplement other texts that don't have the desired coverage of ethnic literature. While each book is designed to be brief enough for flexible uses in the classroom, each volume does represent the breadth of major literary genres (autobiography, fiction, poetry, and drama) that characterizes the literary contribution of each tradition, even if—as in the case of drama—the short format of the series would accommodate only a single example. The four volumes of the HarperCollins Literary Mosaic Series constitute nothing less than a new start for those who are interested in remapping our writing traditions.

Writing for Our Lives

> The genius of the United States is not best or most in its executives or legislatures, nor in its ambassadors or authors or colleges or churches or parlors, nor even in its newspapers or inventors ... but always most in the common people. Their manners, speech, dress, friendships—the freshness and candor of their physiognomy—the picturesque looseness of their carriage ... their deathless attachment to freedom (Walt Whitman, "Leaves of Grass," 1855 Preface).

Whitman said that these qualities and others await the "gigantic and generous treatment worthy of it." Though American authors from the eighteenth century to the present day have talked about a body of writing that would be representative of these attributes of democracy, one could argue that "the gigantic and generous treatment worthy of it" is a recent and critical development because until recently many points of view have been excluded from United States literature. The Literary Mosaic Series also demonstrates that, for authors of a multicultural heritage, literature often provides an alternative to the images of their groups presented by an often-hostile media.

Of all the excellent comments made by Al Young in his introduction, one is crucial and strikes at the heart of why the writing is so varied in the HarperCollins Literary Mosaic Series. He writes,

> and if you think people are in trouble who buy the images of who they are from the shallow, deceitful versions of themselves they see in mass media, think what it must feel like to be a TV-watching African-American male. Pimp, thug, mugger, drug dealer, crackhead, thief, murderer, rapist, absentee father, welfare cheat, convict, loser, ne'er-do-well, buffoon. Think of these negative images of yourself broadcast hourly all over the globe.

When African Americans, Native Americans, Hispanic Americans, and Asian Americans write, they're not just engaging in a parlor exercise—they are writing for their lives. The twentieth century has shown that unbalanced images can cost groups their lives. That is why the HarperCollins Literary Mosaic Series came to be—to trumpet these lives, lives that are our national heritage. And once these voices have been heard, there is no turning back.

Acknowledgments

This is a series that has been taken the time, talents, and enthusiasm of its editors—Al Young, Gerald Vizenor, Nicolás Kanellos, and Shawn Wong—and I am excited that they chose to be a part of this project. In addition, the editors and I wish to thank those people who helped us prepare the series, particularly those instructors who reviewed this material in various drafts and offered their expertise and suggestions for making the books in this series even more useful to them and their students: Joni Adamson Clarke, University of Arizona; Herman Beavers, University of Pennsylvania; A. LaVonne Brown Ruoff, University of Illinois at Chicago; William Cain, Wellesley College; Rafel Castillo, Palo Alto College; Jeffrey Chan, San Francisco State University; King-Kok Cheung, University of California at Los Angeles; Patricia Chu, George Washington University; Robert Combs, George Washington University; Mary Comfort, Moravian College; George Cornell, Michigan State University; Bruce Dick, Appalachian State University; Elinor Flewellen, Santa Barbara City College; Chester Fontineau, University of Illinois at Champaign-Urbana; Sharon Gavin Levy, University of Minnesota at Duluth; Shirley Geok-Lin Lim, University of California at Santa Barbara; Tom Green, Northeastern Junior College; James Hall, University of Illinois at Chicago; Lynda M. Hill, Temple University; Lane Hirabayashi, University of Colorado; Gloria Horton, Jacksonville State University; Ketu H. Katrak, University of Massachusetts at Amherst; Josephine Lee, Smith College; Russell Leong, University of California at Los Angeles; Michael Liberman, East Stroudsburg University; Paulino Lim, Jr., California State University at Long Beach; Kenneth Lincoln, University of California at Los Angeles; Marcus "C" Lopez, Solano Community College; Shirley Lumpkin, Marshall University; Barbara McCaskill, University of Georgia; Nelly McKay, University of Wisconsin at Madison; Lucy Maddox, Georgetown University; Thomas Matchie, North Dakota State University; Joyce Middleton, University of Rochester; Alice Moore, Yakima Valley Community College; Eric Naylor, University of the South; Jon Olson, Oregon State University at Corvallis; Ernest Padilla, Santa Monica College; David Payne, University of Georgia; Joyce Pettis, North Carolina State University; David Robinson, Winona State University; Don Rothman, Oakes College, University of California at Santa Cruz; Leonard A. Slade, Jr., State University of New York at Albany; Stephen Sumida, University of Michigan; Brian Swann, Cooper Union; John Trimbur, Worcester Polytechnical Institute; Hari Vishwanadha, Santa Monica College; Marilyn Nelson Waniek, University of Connecticut; Shelly Wong, Cornell University; Jackie Valdez, Caspar College; Richard Yarborough, University of California at Los Angeles.

Introduction

Native American literatures embrace the memories of creation stories, the tragic wisdom of native ceremonies, trickster narratives, and the outcome of chance and other occurrences in the most diverse cultures in the world. These distinctive literatures, eminent in both oral performances and in the imagination of written narratives, cannot be discovered in reductive social science translations or altogether understood in the historical constructions of culture in one common name.

The name *Indian* is a convenient word, to be sure, but it is an invented name that does not come from any native language, and does not describe or contain any aspects of traditional tribal experience and literature. Used as a noun, Indian is a simulation of racialism, an undesirable separation of race in the political and cultural interests of discovery and colonial settlement of new nations; the noun does not reveal the experiences of diverse native communities. The name is unbidden, and the native heirs must bear an unnatural burden to be so christened in their own land.

The American Indian has come to mean *Indianness,* the conditions that indicate the once-despised tribes and, at the same time, the extreme notions of an exotic outsider; these conditions are advocated as *real* cultures in the world. The simulations of the outsider as the other subserve racial and cultural dominance. Race is an invention, not a noticeable genetic presence, and cultural traits are brute concoctions of the social sciences.

"The origins of racism" are obscure, but the consequences "are more tangible," wrote Richard Drinnon in *Facing West.*

> Racism defined natives as nonpersons within the settlement culture and was in a real sense the enabling experience of the rising American empire: Indian-hating identified the dark others that white settlers were not and must not under any circumstances become, and it helped them wrest a continent and more from the hands of these native caretakers of the lands.

Naturally, there were many distinct names for other tribes, names that were used in the course of trade relations, war, and other situations, but there were no common, ethnic, racial, or national names for the hundred million natives who lived in thousands of tribal communities in the Americas. The third edition of *The American Heritage Dictionary of the English Language* notes that the

> term *Indian* has always been a misnomer for the earliest inhabitants of the Americas. Many people now prefer *Native American* both as a corrective to Columbus's mistaken appellation and as a means of avoiding the romantic and generally offensive stereotypes associated with phrases such as *wild Indian* or *cowboys and Indians*.

Native American distinguishes native peoples in the Americas from the inhabitants of India.

Histories and Consequences

Some historians have understated the native presence by the millions, and conservative reductions have sanctioned the notion that colonialism and settlement dislocated a tribal population of no significance in such a vast and "unused" hemisphere. Indeed, the opposite was true. "The Americas were densely populated at the time Europeans found their way to this New World," wrote Henry Dobyns in *Native American Historical Demography*. He pointed out that recent estimates place the native hemispheric population at more than one hundred million in about 1490. Perhaps thirty million of that total number lived in what is now Mexico, and ten million natives in what is now Canada and the United States.

Old World diseases decimated tribal communities. "Smallpox became the single most lethal disease Europeans carried to the New World," wrote Dobyns. "This contagion repeatedly spread through Native American peoples, killing a high proportion of susceptible individuals not immunized by surviving a previous epidemic." Malaria, yellow fever, plague, typhus, and influenza decimated the survivors of other diseases and became the pernicious relations of colonialism.

The epidemics "weakened the Indian economic systems and dispirited the people, whose world order seemed to have collapsed in the face of unknown forces," wrote Francis Paul Prucha in *The Indians in American Society*. "Many Indians and their white friends maintained that the proper status of the Indian tribes was as small independent nations under the protection of the United States." The native economies, once based on mythic associations with the environment, were weakened by racialism, nationalism, and the politics of colonial dominance.

"Historians of Indian–white relations face the special problem of dealing with two diverse cultures," observed Prucha, "for we must understand two others, quite diverse in themselves." These others are the tribes and the "past white societies." The policies that defined the relations between the two others wavered between sovereignty, assimilation, and termination of native communities on federal reservations, established in hundreds of treaties with the tribes. These capricious policies have maintained a federal dominance over the tribes for more than a century.

"Indian Affairs were at first seen as a domestic problem, equal to and linked with the problems of war debts, western land claims, orderly expansion, and so on," wrote Dorothy Jones in *License for Empire*. "It was only after the repeated failure of attempts to handle Indian affairs as a domestic problem that United States officials were forced to consider relations *with* the Indians, rather than a unilateral policy *for* the Indians." The basis of the relations with tribes shifted from the "domestic to the diplomatic," and the treaty system became a new social order. "Outright land-grabbing was not nearly so widespread as is commonly believed. There was no need. The treaty system itself was the primary vehicle of transfer." The treaties were mentioned more often in histories than native resistance to colonial settlement and dominance.

Jones noted that when the

> English trader Alexander Henry arrived at the post of Michilimackinac in the fall of 1761, he was lectured by the Chippewa leader Minivavana: "Englishman, although you have conquered the French, you have not yet conquered us. We are not your slaves. These lakes, these woods and mountains, were left to us by our ancestors. They are our inheritance; and we will part with them to none."

The treaty system was not a course of action that honored similar or equal diplomatic powers. Native rights to the land were *inherent* and not *given* to the tribes in treaties, but the dominance of the government could not be overthrown in the absence of inseparable tribal power. Prucha writes,

> Declining from a position of prosperity and of considerable political and economic power at the beginning of the national history of the United States, the Indian tribes by the early decades of the twentieth century had become politically subordinate to and almost completely dominated by the federal government; they were economically dependent, too, upon white goods and services.

The Indian Citizenship Act of 1924 was a cruel irony of assimilation policies; native communities were hardly protected by the patent promises of a constitutional democracy. "Previously, Indians had received citizenship through a variety of haphazard means: by receipt of an allotment, by separation from one's tribe, by special permission of the Secretary of the Interior, or by service in World War I, to name a few of the more common routes taken," wrote John Wunder in *Retained by The People*. Federal citizenship, however, "did not change many things. Citizenship status theoretically gave Indians the right to vote. But this right was not protected by force or federal statutes, and it was not fully attained until several decades later." Several states prevented tribal citizens from voting. The Fifteenth Amendment, which provides that the right of citizens to vote shall not be denied or abridged by any state, "could be overcome," some states argued, "because Indians did not pay state taxes; they were still wards of the federal government, which precluded them from voting; or they were residing on lands that were not a part of the state for voting purposes."

Native American authors have presented some of these issues of inherent native rights, the duplicities of federal policies, and the burdens of racial identities in their short stories and novels. D'Arcy McNickle, for instance, an established scholar and literary artist, asserted in *Native American Tribalism* that the tribes have not accepted oblivion.

> Caught up in succeeding waves of devastating epidemics and border wars as settlement moved westward, the Indians retreated, protecting what they could, and managing to be at hand to fight another day when necessity required it. They lost, but were never defeated.

McNickle's first novel, *The Surrounded,* was published in 1936, two years after the Indian Reorganization Act was passed near the end of the Depression in the United States. This new policy ended the federal allotment of communal land to individuals and provided for the establishment of representative governments on reservations. The dire conditions in remote native communities, however, were exacerbated by the economic devastation in the nation. President Franklin Delano Roosevelt announced at the time the "only thing we have to fear is fear itself." The New Deal legislation created the Works Progress Administration and employment for millions of people in various national programs.

The "baneful effects" of the economic depression were "crushing blows to the Indian economy," wrote William Hagan in *American Indians*.

> The Depression shook the faith of many Americans in the nineteenth-century version of individualism. The hordes of unemployed seemed to demonstrate that we already had too many factory workers and too many farmers. And if the government was forced to succor college-trained white Americans, it was patently absurd to continue to talk of the average reservation Indian moving into a free, competitive society.

McNickle wrote in *Native American Tribalism* that the

> opportunities offered in the Indian Reorganization Act brought into use the capacity for social action which had never died in the Indian people, though it had been obscured. The start was slow in many instances, since the written constitutions introduced ideas and procedures which had not been part of customary practice.

Archilde, the main character in *The Surrounded*, returns to the reservation and the mistrust of his father (who is himself an outsider), the silence of his tribal mother, and the burdens of his identities. He had been away at a boarding school; now, a clever mixedblood in a white shirt and blue suit, he returns at the end of the Depression. He told his mother that he had a job. "I played my fiddle in a show house." Caught at the heart of family loyalties, burdened with the contradictions of federal policies of assimilation, and touched by tragic wisdom, he was displaced by the author in the transcendence of native reason on the reservation.

Two years earlier F. Scott Fitzgerald published *Tender is the Night*, a novel of tragic dissolution and hedonism in a culture at a great distance from the poverty on reservations. At the same time the government sponsored authors and arts programs; the proletarian themes of discovery, regionalism, and tourism were new forms of literary dominance over Native Americans.

The memories of native creation, the humor of trickster transformations, and tribal constancy were heard in a tribal enlightenment at the end of the last century. That enlightenment was associated with the first generation of students who had returned from federal and mission boarding schools to reservations and outbraved the extortion of the federal government. The next generation of mettlesome native scholars, artists, and bureaucrats outbraved in their time the Depression and the poverty of the nation.

The Indian Reorganization Act provided for democratic governments, ended the allotment program, and established a new policy that favored the employment of natives in the Bureau of Indian Affairs. These new routines, policies, and economies on reservations created new native connections and identities, and these identities were causes of native contention at the end of the Depression.

John Joseph Mathews, a prominent historian and novelist, published *Sundown* in 1934. Challenge Windzer, the main character, is an educated mixedblood in the twenties. His mother is traditional Osage. The sense of the novel is both traditional and historical, and the burdens of the protagonist are ancestral, personal, and economic; the discovery of oil on tribal land was a dangerous source of family wealth. The author and his characters were born in Indian Territory, Oklahoma.

Virginia Mathews wrote in the introduction to *Sundown* that her father was in the

> vanguard of American Indian writers who brought their education, their sophistication, and their considered pondering on a dual cultural heritage to the service of their tribes and of Indian people collectively. As a result, for more than fifty years now, Indians have been speaking on equal terms— and often on terms of significant advantage—with bureaucrats and politicians, with historians, philosophers, and other intellectuals.

Mathews created Challenge "out of what he had expunged from his own life— despair, dichotomies, the aimlessness, the uncertainties he knew when he was young— to become valuable and uniquely himself, triumphantly white and Indian."

Mathews, at the end of *Sundown*, wrote,

Mixedblood families came back to the old Agency from their homes in the mountains, in California, and elsewhere. They dropped their golf clubs and lost their homes and came back to wander aimlessly along the familiar streets. They asked with the other citizens of the town, "S'pose it'll come back?" All agreed that it would, but they wondered just the same.

McNickle, Mathews, and other authors cannot be separated from the enlightenment of their native traditions and experiences on reservations or from the national political and economic conditions of their time. McNickle attended a boarding school in Oregon. Later, he studied at the University of Montana and Oxford University. Mathews also studied at Oxford University and attended the School of International Relations in Geneva, Switzerland. These native authors endured more abstruse causes of tragic wisdom and motivation than were envisioned in the unceremonious themes of aesthetic heroism in other novels written during the Depression. Thomas Wolfe published his second novel, *Of Time and the River,* in 1935. *Tortilla Flat* by John Steinbeck appeared that same year, and his proletarian novel *The Grapes of Wrath* was published four years later. *Gone with the Wind,* the historical novel of the Civil War by Margaret Mitchell, was published in 1936.

Native American survivance is a sentiment heard in creation stories and the humorous contradictions of tricksters and read in the tragic wisdom of literature; these common sentiments of survivance are more than survival reactions in the face of violence and dominance. Tragic wisdom is the source of native reason, the common sense gained from the adverse experiences of discovery, colonialism, and cultural domination. Tragic wisdom is a pronative voice of liberation and survivance, a condition in native stories and literature that denies victimization.

Native survivance is heard in creation and trickster stories, dream songs, visions, and other presentations in thousands of native oral languages in North, Central, and South America. Some of these diverse oral narratives have been translated and published in various forms, for untold reasons, as social science evidence. The problem, of course, is that written translation, even when the languages are similar, is not a representation of oral performances, and even the best translations are scriptural reductions of the rich oral nuances.

How, for instance, could a word heard or a scene imagined in an oral story or performance have the same meaning in a written language? Moreover, how can personal dream songs or the performance of creation stories in tribal communities be understood as poems or short stories in published translations? The stories that are heard are not the same as the silence of the written word.

The many anthologies of tribal songs, dreams, and stories are beautiful images in translation, to be sure, but the original communal context of performance and other circumstances of oral expression are seldom understood in translation. Anthropologists and "folklorists, whose disciplines are not directed toward appreciation of superior artistry, usually play down, or ignore, the individual distinction of creative accomplishment in ethnographic material," Karl Kroeber pointed out in *Traditional American Indian Literatures.* The causal theories of the social sciences and the concerns of evidence have unnerved the memories of tribal stories. Too often the rich sources of native imagination and oral literary styles have been reduced in ethnographic studies to the mere evidence of culture.

The fragments of songs and oral stories published in anthologies of tribal literatures seldom have anything in common but the language of dominance. The metaphors in oral stories are mundane, abstruse, mysterious, unnameable, and more, but few collections in translation reveal the rich context of the songs and stories. For instance, was a song sacred or secular, public or private, and was the song an individual dream or a communal ceremony? How could translations of distinct tribal expressions ever be definitive or representational in another language?

The first "hermeneutical motion" of translation is "initiative trust, an investment of belief, underwritten by previous experience," George Steiner wrote in *After Babel,* his study of translation. The "demonstrative statement of understanding which is translation, starts with an act of trust."

Native American literatures have endured "acts of trust," manifest manners, and the dominance of translation for more than three centuries. Brian Swann, who edited *On the Translation of Native American Literatures,* wrote that given "the history of this hemisphere, to settle for the dignity of mystery is far preferable to any claim of definitiveness."

Some translations, however, simulate nuances, and that "initiative trust" overcasts the practices and assumes that other cultures can be represented in musical scores, registers, and scriptures. "If culture depends on the transmission of meaning across time," Steiner wrote, "it depends also on the transfer of meaning in space." The translations of tribal stories by social scientists in search of cultural evidence can be misinterpretations of tribal time, space, and the rights of consciousness. "Almost at every moment in time," Steiner observed, "notably in the sphere of American Indian speech, some ancient and rich expression of articulate being is lapsing into irretrievable silence."

The translations of tribal stories are obscure maneuvers of dominance that contribute to the simulations of *Indianness* over distinct tribal memories and stories. Moreover, translations are scriptural, and the sudden closure of oral literatures favors written texts over *heard* stories; the eternal sorrow of lost sound haunts the scriptural translation of tribal stories.

Larzer Ziff, for instance, argued in *Writing in the New Nation* that literary "annihilation, in which the representation offers itself as the only aspect of the represented that is still extant, is not, of course, physical extermination." Thomas Jefferson, James Fenimore Cooper, and thousands of others who have written about tribal cultures, have "sincerely regarded their writings as efforts at preservation." Moreover, the "process of literary annihilation would be checked only when Indian writers began representing their own culture."

Henry Rowe Schoolcraft was one of the most recognized interpreters of tribal cultures in the early nineteenth century. His translations of Anishinaabe (Chippewa or Ojibwa) songs and stories were published in *Algic Researches*. Henry Wadsworth Longfellow was influenced by this material and based his *Song of Hiawatha* on the translations of oral narratives from one tribal culture to describe another. This dubious tribal epic was a very popular poem at the time. "Hiawatha elegiacally counsels his people to abandon the old ways and adapt themselves to the coming of 'civilization,' but he does so in a verse form which only 'civilization' can provide," wrote Arnold Krupat in *For Those Who Came After*. "Longfellow derived *Hiawatha*'s trochaic meter from the Finnish epic *Kalevala*." There is no evidence of an "act of trust" in either the translations or the uses of tribal literature in this instance.

"Great translators," Steiner argued in *Language and Silence*

> act as a kind of living mirror. They offer to the original not an equivalence, for there can be none, but a vital counterpoise, an echo, faithful yet autonomous, as we find in the dialogue of human love. An act of translation is an act of love. Where it fails, through immodesty or blurred perception, it traduces. Where it succeeds, it incarnates."

Most anthologies of translated tribal literatures are "blurred perceptions" that serve dominance rather than the independence of native imagination. The inclusion of translations in anthologies of native literature, without critical mention of context, texture, and the oral nuances of performance, contributes to literary dominance.

"The Indian, becoming the province of learned groups especially organized to study him, soon was a scholarly field in himself, just like a dead language," observed Roy Harvey Pearce in *Savagism and Civilization*. The American Ethnological Society, organized in 1842, encouraged the scientific study of Indians. The Smithsonian Institute was organized four years later and "its scientists were specifically bidden to gather information on the Indian." However, as "scientists moved towards the modern study of the Indian as a normally complex and difficult human who possessed a tolerably respectable civilization of his own, they continued to think of him literally as a primitive, as one whose way of life was somehow earlier than their own."

The Turn to Autobiographies

Native Americans have published their own books since the beginning of the nineteenth century. *A Son of the Forest* by William Apess, for example, published in 1829, could be the first autobiography written by a tribal person. Professor LaVonne Ruoff, the distinguished literary historian, pointed out in *American Indian Literatures* that Apess was an orphan and that the "whites" he lived with "as a child taught him to be terrified of his own people. If he disobeyed, they threatened to punish him by sending him to the forest."

Apess was a minister, an activist for tribal rights, and a mixedblood who traced his descent to the Pequot. "His own birth and death are not documented," Barry O'Connell observed in *On Our Own Ground*. "Born to a nation despised and outcast and perhaps, to add to the stigma, not only white, a 'mulatto' or 'mixed breed,' but also part African American, a child with William Apess's history who simply made it to adulthood would be doing well."

Luther Standing Bear was one of the first tribal students at the new government school at Carlisle, Pennsylvania. "One day when we came to school there was a lot of writing on one of the blackboards," he wrote in *My People, the Sioux*. "We did not know what it meant, but our interpreter came into the room and said, 'Do you see all these marks on the blackboard? Well, each word is a white man. They are going to give each one of you one of these names by which you will hereafter be known.' "

John Rogers was born at the turn of the last century on the White Earth Reservation in Minnesota and attended the federal boarding school at Flandreau, South Dakota. "At school, if we brought in a nest or a pretty leaf, we were given much credit, and we thought we would also please Mother by bringing some to her," he wrote in *Red World and White*. "But she did not like our doing this. She would scold and correct us and tell us we were destroying something." Rogers wrote with a sense of adventure, peace, and native responsibilities in spite of the adversities of assimilation policies that he experienced on reservations. He praised his boarding school education and, at the same time, he was critical of the government.

Captain Richard Pratt, the first superintendent of the federal industrial school at Carlisle, told an annual meeting of educators, three years after the massacre at Wounded Knee, South Dakota, that

> the Indian has learned by long experience to believe somewhat that the only good white man is a dead white man, and he is just as right about it as any of us are in thinking the same of the Indian. It is only the Indian in them that ought to be killed; and it is the bad influences of the bad white man that ought to be killed too. How are these hindering, hurtful sentiments and conditions on both sides to be ended? Certainly, never by continuing

the segregating policy, which gives the Indian no chance to see, know, and participate in our affairs and industries, and thus prove to himself and us that he has better stuff in him, and which prevents his learning how wrong is his conception of the truly civilized white man.

Luther Standing Bear, John Rogers, and others of their generation were the last to hear the oral stories of natural reason in their native families before the stories were recorded and translated, and they were the first to learn how to write about their memories and experiences.

Charles Alexander Eastman was raised with a tribal name in the traditions of the Santee Sioux. He graduated with distinction from Dartmouth College and earned a degree from the Boston University Medical School. He was determined to serve native communities and became the government physician at the Pine Ridge Reservation. A few months later he treated the few survivors of the Wounded Knee massacre. The Seventh Cavalry had murdered hundreds of ghost dancers and their families on December 29, 1890.

Eastman was raised to be a traditional native leader, but that natural event would not be honored in the course of histories. Many Lightnings, his father, was imprisoned for three years in connection with the violent conflict with settlers and the Minnesota Sioux in 1862. President Abraham Lincoln commuted the death sentence. Christianity touched his father and he chose the name Jacob Eastman.

Charles was about twelve years old when he and his relatives escaped the retribution of the military. His sense of a traditional native world was never the same, and his new surname, education, and marriage were revolutions in tribal and personal identities at the time. Elaine Goodale, his wife, was a teacher on the Pine Ridge Reservation. She was from Massachusetts. He was burdened with the remembrance of the horror of the massacre at Wounded Knee.

Eastman and others of his generation, the first to be educated at federal and mission boarding schools, must have been haunted in their dreams by the atrocities of the cavalry soldiers. Wounded Knee has caused posttraumatic burdens of war in several generations because the stories of the survivors were seldom honored in the literature and histories of dominance. The second college edition of *The American Heritage Dictionary of the English Language,* for instance, notes in the geographic entries that Wounded Knee was the "site of the last major battle of the Indian Wars." Indeed, the massacre of unarmed men, women, and children is not the "last major battle." The murder of native dancers could be the end of civilization.

"Those soldiers had been sent to protect these men, women, and children who had not joined the ghost dancers, but they had shot them down without even a chance to defend themselves," wrote Luther Standing Bear in *My People, the Sioux*. He was one of the graduates of a federal school and returned to the reservation as a teacher. "The very people I was following—and getting my people to follow—had no respect for motherhood, old age, or babyhood. Where was all their civilized training?"

Eastman found and treated two wounded survivors in the snow at Wounded Knee. His composure at the time would later turn to outrage. "Trying to save the survivors of Wounded Knee had called upon all of Eastman's medical training and skill, but trauma management had not been the goal of his long preparation," wrote Frances Karttunen in *Between Worlds*. "He had intended to serve the Sioux in positive ways, especially in the field of public health."

Paula Gunn Allen convened the themes of "transformation and change" in her anthology *Voice of the Turtle,* a "comprehensive overview of Native American literature," but she is censorious of Luther Standing Bear and those children who attended and graduated from federal boarding schools. "The boys and girls at Carlisle Indian School were trained to be cannon fodder in American wars, to serve as domestics and farm hands, and to leave off all ideas or beliefs that came to them" from their communities, she wrote. "In a short time, the child comes to love and admire his captor, as Standing Bear admired and respected Richard Pratt, a not uncommon adjustment made by those taken hostage; separated from all that is familiar; stripped down, shorn, robbed of their very self; renamed."

Luther Standing Bear was educated in a new tribal enlightenment that would outbrave dominance; he never lost his sense of humor and tragic wisdom at boarding school or on the reservation. Clearly, he was never the hostage of an education, and he never reduced his various experiences to mere victimage. The simulations of academic remorse and substitutional victimization serve the literature of dominance not survivance.

"I always wanted to please my father in every way possible," Standing Bear wrote in *My People, the Sioux*.

> All of his instructions to me had been along this line: "Son, be brave and get killed." This expression had been molded into my brain to such an extent that I knew nothing else.
>
> My father had made a mistake. He should have told me, upon leaving home, to go and learn all I could of the white man's ways, and be like them....
>
> When I thought of my father, and how he had smoked the pipe of peace, and was not fighting any more, it occurred to me that this chance to go East would prove that I was brave if I were to accept it....

Now, after having had my hair cut, a new thought came into my head. I felt that I was no more Indian, but would be an imitation of a white man. And we are still imitations of white men, and the white men are imitations of the Americans.

Standing Bear graduated and worked in a department store owned by John Wanamaker in Philadelphia. He read in the newspaper that Sitting Bull, the Lakota healer, was scheduled to lecture in the city. "The paper stated that he was the Indian who killed General Custer! The chief and his people had been held prisoners of war, and now here they were to appear" in a theater.

Standing Bear visited Sitting Bull at the hotel. "He wanted his children educated in the white man's way, because there was nothing left for the Indian." The interpreter was in the room, so "I did not get a chance to tell Sitting Bull how the white man had lied about him on the stage. And that was the last time I ever saw Sitting Bull alive."

Standing Bear, to be sure, "was more fortunate" than most of the students who returned to the reservation. Some had "only a superficial education and a trade that was usually of no value," Richard Ellis wrote in *Indian Lives*. Standing Bear "had a recommendation from Pratt which led to immediate employment as an assistant teacher at a salary of three hundred dollars a year."

Standing Bear returned to teach at the government school on the Rosebud Reservation and heard the horror stories of the massacre at Wounded Knee. Later, he toured with Buffalo Bill's Wild West show in Europe. He was active in tribal rights movements, acted in several motion pictures, and wrote several books about his experiences.

Paula Gunn Allen stressed that the "survivors were fewer than victims, for boarding schools left far more dead of malnutrition, neglect, physical abuse, and epidemics than they educated." Such trenchant expediencies are celebrations of victimage and renounce the courage of native students who pursued education in the course of tribal enlightenment and survivance.

Allen, a university professor, accused the first generation of native scholars on reservations with hostage sympathies, the Stockholm syndrome. Her pretentious censure seems to be terminal, a moral bummer; the reduction of tragic wisdom to victimage. Many children died from diseases and loneliness at boarding schools, but their names would not be honored by indictments of the survivors and their narratives. The sympathies of arcane penitence over the independence of education is not the literature of survivance four generations after Wounded Knee.

"Native Americans who attended boarding schools are living archives, storehouses of memory and experience. Their memories and experiences, shaped into spoken narratives, continue to shape families, communities, and educational endeavors," wrote K. Tsianina Lomawaima in *They Called it Prairie Light: The Story of Chilocco Indian School.*

> The fact that schools often strengthened rather than dissolved tribal identity is not the only surprise tucked within alumni reminiscence. The idealized school society envisioned in federal policy often bore little resemblance to reality... [Oral and] documentary sources build an image of a boarding school culture that was created and sustained by students much more than by teachers or staff. Ironically, the practical realities of adapting to institutional life did foster self-sufficiency in many students.

No one in our time has the right of consciousness to renounce the courage and humor of native students in boarding schools at the turn of the century; no one has the right to erase the virtues and reason of their parents or the ardent manners of certain teachers. The government created the conditions that menaced native traditions, and to shame the spirit, nerve, and bravery of the students is to recant their memories. Otherwise, the students would become an aesthetic scapegoat, and the many personal letters to and from their teachers at boarding schools would be nothing more than coerced remembrance.

Native Americans have published thousands of books, stories, and poems since the nineteenth century. George Copway and Sarah Winnemucca were followed by Charles Eastman, Francis La Flesche, Gertrude Bonnin, and countless others who wrote and published their life stories, autobiographies, short stories, and novels in the twentieth century.

Christine Quintasket, for instance, was a notable author from the Colville Confederated Tribes of eastern Washington State. She was born in a canoe on the Kootenay River in Idaho. She assumed the pen name Mourning Dove and published her romantic novel *Cogewea: The Half-Blood* in 1927. "There are two things I am most grateful for in my life," she wrote in her autobiography.

> The first is that I was born a descendant of the genuine Americans, the Indians; the second, that my birth happened in the year 1888. In that year the Indians of my tribe, the Colville, were well into the cycle of history involving their readjustment in living conditions. They were in a pathetic state of turmoil caused by trying to learn how to till the soil for a living, which was being done on a very small and crude scale. It was not an easy matter for members of this aboriginal stock, accustomed to making a different livelihood, to handle the plow and sow seed for food. Yet I was born long enough ago to have known people who lived in the ancient way before everything started to change.

Janet Campbell Hale has also published novels and an autobiography. She was born in Los Angeles, California, in 1947, and is a member of the Coeur d'Alene tribe of northern Idaho. *The Jailing of Cecilia Capture,* published in 1985, is a novel that turns on the burdens of separation and racial renunciation. "I first saw the light of day in California, but the first place I remember is our home in Idaho," she wrote in *Bloodlines: Odyssey of a Native Daughter.* "For an Indian, home is the place where your tribe.... I have never heard a creation myth from my own tribe, probably because of their early conversion to Catholicism."

The Beginning of a New National Literature
Wynema by Sophia Alice Callahan, the first novel attributed to a native author, was published in 1891. *Queen of the Woods* by Simon Pokagon, published eight years later, has been cited as one of the first novels in previous studies; moreover, the actual writer of the novel may be someone other than the author.

LaVonne Ruoff has uncovered and studied the novel *Wynema*. Callahan, who was mixedblood Creek, was aware of tribal issues at the time, such as federal policies, the Ghost Dance, and Wounded Knee. She "devotes most of the novel to Indian issues," Ruoff wrote in "Justice for Indian Women" in *World Literature Today.* Callahan "also includes some strong statements about equality for women." She was born in 1868. She studied at the Wesleyan Female Institute in Virginia and taught at Muskogee's Harrell International Institute and the Wealaka School. Callahan died three years after the publication of her novel.

Since then many novels by distinguished native authors have been published and reviewed in national newspapers and journals. Some of these novels have been awarded national literary prizes. Native American authors have earned considerable recognition for dozens of novels published in the past few years.

The Surrounded by D'Arcy McNickle was published two years after the publication of *Sundown* by John Joseph Mathews. These novels, and other books by native authors, were important literary events at the time. *Wah 'Kon-Tah* by Mathews, for instance, was a selection of the Book-of-the-Month Club in 1932. Novels by McNickle, Mathews, John Milton Oskison, Todd Downing, and many others have been reissued in the past few years by university presses.

Louis Owens pointed out in *Other Destinies,* his study of Native American novelists, that *The Surrounded* was first entitled *The Hungry Generations,* a "version almost twice as long as the published manuscript, and very different in its implications." In the earlier version, Archilde, the tribal protagonist, is "allowed to travel to Paris and to experience the heady atmosphere" and milieu of the Lost Generation. He falls in love and returns to Montana. The publisher, Harcourt, Brace and Company, returned

The Hungry Generation in 1929 with a rejection letter that said the story of an Indian "wandering between two generations, two cultures" was excellent. "A new territory to be explored: ancient material used for a different end. Perhaps the beginning of a new Indian literature to rival that of Harlem." *The Surrounded,* with a more tragic closure, was published by Dodd, Mead.

N. Scott Momaday won the Pulitzer Prize for his first novel, *House Made of Dawn,* published in 1968. *Ceremony* by Leslie Marmon Silko, *Winter in the Blood* by James Welch, and many other novels followed with critical praise. *Love Medicine* by Louise Erdrich won the National Book Critics Circle Award. Wendy Rose, Maurice Kenny, Erdrich, and Gerald Vizenor have received American Book Awards, which are sponsored by the Before Columbus Foundation. Momaday, Paula Gunn Allen, and Welch have received the Native American Indian Literature Prize.

The selections in this anthology celebrate some of the most original contemporary literature by Native Americans. The selections are divided into four parts: autobiography, fiction, poetry, and drama. The anthology begins with an autobiographical selection by William Apess, continues with eight more selections from native autobiographies, choice fiction by sixteen authors and thirteen poets, and closes with two dramatic scripts. This anthology presents both established authors and several new writers, and includes short stories by Kimberly Blaeser and Evelina Zuni Lucero, and selections from first novels by Betty Louise Bell and Gordon Henry published in the American Indian and Critical Studies series at the University of Oklahoma Press.

AUTOBIOGRAPHY

William Apess

(1798–?) Pequot

William Apess announced in his autobiography that he was born January 31, 1798. He was mixedblood and traced his native descent to the Pequots in Connecticut. The date of his death has not been documented.

A Son of the Forest, one of the earliest native autobiographies, was first published in 1829. Apess was the author of five books between 1829 and 1836. In 1833 he published **The Experiences of Five Christian Indians of the Pequot Tribe.** In that same year he was one of the leaders of the Mashpee Revolt. He was arrested, fined, and sentenced to thirty days in jail for his resistance to the removal of native rights, and was one of the earliest leaders of a native rights movement.

Barry O'Connell wrote in the introduction to **On Our Own Ground** that

> Apess's people were poor laborers. By class, if not by their identity as Native Americans, these were not the people of whom the stuff of written American history has been made....

> The Pequots were more than lost or forgotten. Memory of them was deliberately suppressed. In 1637 they were the objects of the first deliberately genocidal war conducted by the English in North America. The combined forces of the Plymouth, Connecticut, and Massachusetts Bay colonies surprised the main settlement of the Pequots on the Mystic River, surrounded and set fire to it, and then slaughtered every man, woman, and child they could catch who had escaped the flames. Some Pequots survived but were compelled to sign a treaty that declared them extinct as a people and forbade the use of their name forever. Some survivors were sold into slavery in the Caribbean, the others were divided between the Mohegans and the Narragansetts who had allied with the English during the Pequot War.

Richard Drinnon wrote in **Facing West** that the "Pequot War was about extending English rule and laws, and about pacification of the countryside." The settlers were appeased by the removal of the natives. "The war established the credibility of the English will to exterminate, lessened the likelihood of 'conspiracies' to resist their rule, and established a peace based on terror that lasted more or less for four decades until the outbreak of what was called King Philip's War."

Apess was separated from his family at age four or five. He was boarded with relatives and then twice indentured to elite families. He ran away from these homes many times, enlisted in the militia as a drummer boy, and became a missionary. Apess was "bound out from age five to a series of masters," wrote LaVonne Ruoff in **American Indian Literatures**, "a common practice in dealing with orphans and foster children."

O'Connell observed that for a "Native American to command literacy required reaching across a great body of cultural difference; it also required access to all the institutions of literacy: schools, libraries, and books, newspapers, editors, and publishers." This would be very difficult for many in the early nineteenth century.

A Son of the Forest convenes the agonies and alienation of his experiences and his constant search for native identities. He became a missionary and "sought salvation for a whole people," noted O'Connell. Apess probably left the country, as no other documents mention his presence after 1838.

A Son of the Forest

Preface

In offering to the public a second edition of this work, the Author cannot but testify his gratitude for the liberal patronage bestowed upon the first edition—notwithstanding the many disadvantages under which it appeared. The present edition is greatly improved, as well in the printing as in the arrangement of the work and the style in which it is written. The first edition was hurried through the press, in consequence of which many inaccuracies occurred.

It has been carefully revised; those parts which some persons deemed objectionable have been stricken out; and in its improved form it is now submitted to the public, with the earnest prayer of the author that it may be rendered a lasting blessing to everyone who may give it even a cursory perusal.

Chapter 1

William Apess, the author of the following narrative, was born in the town of Colrain, Massachusetts, on the thirty-first of January, in the year of our Lord seventeen hundred and ninety-eight. My grandfather was a white man and married a female attached to the royal family of Philip, king of the Pequot tribe of Indians, so well known in that part of American history which relates to the wars between the whites and the natives. My grandmother was, if I am not misinformed, the king's granddaughter and a fair and beautiful woman. This statement is given not with a view of appearing great in the estimation of others—what, I would ask, is *royal* blood?—the blood of a king is no better than that of the subject. We are in fact but one family; we are all the descendants of one great progenitor—Adam. I would not boast of my extrication, as I consider myself nothing more than a worm of the earth.

I have given the above account of my origin with the simple view of narrating the truth as I have received it, and under the settled conviction that I must render an account at the last day, to the sovereign Judge of all men, for every word contained in this little book.

As the story of King Philip is perhaps generally known, and consequently the history of the Pequot tribe, over whom he reigned, it will suffice to say that he was overcome by treachery, and the goodly heritage occupied by this once happy, powerful, yet peaceful people was possessed in the process of time by their avowed enemies, the whites, who had been welcomed to their land in that spirit of kindness so peculiar to the red men of the woods. But the violation of their inherent rights, by those to whom they had extended the hand of friendship, was not the only act of injustice which this oppressed and afflicted nation was called to suffer at the hands of their white neighbors—alas! They were subject to a more intense and heart-corroding affliction, that of having their daughters claimed by the conquerors, and however much subsequent efforts were made to soothe their sorrows, in this particular, they considered the glory of their nation as having departed.

From what I have already stated, it will appear that my father was of mixed blood, his father being a white man and his mother a native or, in other words, a red woman. On attaining a sufficient age to act for himself, he joined the Pequot tribe, to which he was maternally connected. He was well received, and in a short time afterward married a female of the tribe, in whose veins a single drop of the white man's blood never flowed. Not long after his marriage, he removed to what was then called the back settlements, directing his course first to the west and afterward to the northeast, where he pitched his tent in the woods off a town called Colrain, near the Connecticut River, in the state of Massachusetts. In this, the place of my birth, he continued some time and afterward removed to Colchester, New London County, Connecticut. At the latter place, our little family lived for nearly three years in comparative comfort.

Circumstances, however, changed with us, as with many other people in consequence of which I was taken together with my two brothers and sisters into my grandfather's family. One of my uncles dwelt in the same hut. Now my grandparents were not the best people in the world—like all others who are wedded to the beastly vice of intemperance, they would drink to excess whenever they could procure rum, and as usual in such cases, when under the influence of liquor, they would not only quarrel and fight with each other but would at times turn upon their unoffending grandchildren and beat them in a most cruel manner. It makes me shudder, even at this time, to think how frequent and how great have been our sufferings in consequence of the introduction of this "cursed stuff" into our family—and I could wish, in the sincerity of my soul, that it were banished from our land.

Our fare was of the poorest kind, and even of this we had not enough. Our clothing also was of the worst description: Literally speaking, we were clothed with rags, so far only as rags would suffice to cover our nakedness. We were always contented and happy to get a cold potato for our dinners—of this at times we were denied, and many a night have we gone supperless to rest, if stretching our limbs on a bundle of straw, without any covering against the weather, may be called rest. Truly, we were in a most deplorable condition—too young to obtain subsistence for ourselves, by the labor of our hands, and our wants almost totally disregarded by those who should have made every exertion to supply them. Some of our white neighbors, however, took pity on us and measurably administered to our wants, by bringing us frozen milk, with which we were glad to satisfy the calls of hunger. We lived in this way for some time, suffering both from cold and hunger. Once in particular, I remember that when it rained very hard my grandmother put us all down in the cellar, and when we complained of cold and hunger, she unfeelingly bid us dance and thereby warm ourselves—but we had no food of any kind; and one of my sisters almost died of hunger. Poor dear girl, she was quite overcome. Young as I was, my very heart bled for her. I merely relate this circumstance, without any embellishment or exaggeration, to show the reader how we were treated. The intensity of our sufferings I cannot tell. Happily, we did not continue in this very deplorable condition for a great length of time. Providence smiled on us, but in a particular manner.

Our parents quarreled, parted, and went off to a great distance, leaving their helpless children to the care of their grandparents. We lived at this time in an old house, divided into two apartments—one of which was occupied by my uncle. Shortly after my father left us, my grandmother, who had been out among the whites, returned in a state of intoxication and, without any provocation whatever on my part, began to belabor me most unmercifully with a club; she asked me if I hated her, and I very innocently answered in the affirmative as I did not then know what the word meant and thought all the while that I was answering aright; and so she continued asking me the same question, and I as often answered her in the same way, whereupon she continued beating me, by which means one of my arms was broken in three different places. I was then only four years of age and consequently could not take care of or defend myself—and I was equally unable to seek safety in flight. But my uncle who lived in the other part of the house, being alarmed for my safety, came down to take me away, when my grandfather made toward him with a firebrand, but very fortunately he succeeded in rescuing me and thus saved my life, for had he not come at the time he did, I would most certainly have been killed. My grandparents who acted in this unfeeling and cruel manner were by my mother's side—those by my father's side were Christians, lived and died happy in the love of God; and if I continue faithful in improving that measure of grace with which God hath blessed me, I expect to meet them in a world of unmingled and ceaseless joys. But to return:—

The next morning, when it was discovered that I had been most dangerously injured, my uncle determined to make the whites acquainted with my condition. He accordingly went to a Mr. Furman, the person who had occasionally furnished us with milk, and the good man came immediately to see me. He found me dreadfully beaten, and the other children in a state of absolute suffering; and as he was extremely anxious that something should be done for our relief, he applied to the selectmen of the town in our behalf, who after duly considering the application adjudged that we should be severally taken and bound out. Being entirely disabled in consequence of the wounds I had received, I was supported at the expense of the town for about twelve months.

When the selectmen were called in, they ordered me to be carried to Mr. Furman's—where I received the attention of two surgeons. Some considerable time elapsed before my arm was set, which was consequently very sore, and during this painful operation I scarcely murmured. Now this dear man and family were sad on my account. Mrs. Furman was a kind, benevolent, and tenderhearted lady—from her I received the best possible care: Had it been otherwise I believe that I could not have lived. It pleased God, however, to support me. The great patience that I manifested I attribute mainly to my improved situation. Before, I was almost always naked, or cold, or hungry—now, I was comfortable, with the exception of my wounds.

In view of this treatment, I presume that the reader will exclaim, "What savages your grandparents were to treat unoffending, helpless children in this cruel manner." But this cruel and unnatural conduct was the effect of some cause. I attribute it in a great measure to the whites, inasmuch as they introduced among my countrymen that bane of comfort and happiness, ardent spirits—seduced them into a love of it and, when under its unhappy influence, wronged them out of their lawful possessions— that land, where reposed the ashes of their sires; and not only so, but they committed violence of the most revolting kind upon the persons of the female portion of the tribe who, previous to the introduction among them of the arts, and vices, and debaucheries of the whites, were as unoffending and happy as they roamed over the goodly possessions as any people on whom the sun of heaven ever shone. The consequence was that they were scattered abroad. Now many of them were seen reeling about intoxicated with liquor, neglecting to provide for themselves and families, who before were assiduously engaged in supplying the necessities of those depending on them for support. I do not make this statement in order to justify those who had treated me so unkindly, but simply to show that, inasmuch as I was thus treated only when they were under the influence of spirituous liquor, that the whites were justly chargeable with at least some portion of my sufferings.

After I had been nursed for about twelve months, I had so far recovered that it was deemed expedient to bind me out, until I should attain the age of twenty-one years. Mr. Furman, the person with whom the selectmen had placed me, was a poor man, a cooper by trade, and obtained his living by the labor of his hands. As I was only five years old, he at first thought that his circumstances would not justify him in keeping me, as it would be some considerable time before I could render him much service. But such was the attachment of the family toward me that he came to the conclusion to keep me until I was of age, and he further agreed to give me so much instruction as would enable me to read and write. Accordingly, when I attained my sixth year, I was sent to school, and continued for six successive winters. During this time I learned to read and write, though not so well as I could have wished. This was all the instruction of the kind I ever received. Small and imperfect as was the amount of the knowledge I obtained, yet in view of the advantages I have thus derived, I bless God for it.

Chapter II

I believe that it is assumed as a fact among divines that the Spirit of Divine Truth, in the boundless diversity of its operations, visits the mind of every intelligent being born into the world—but the time when is only fully known to the Almighty and the soul which is the object of the Holy Spirit's enlightening influence. It is also conceded on all hands that the Spirit of Truth operates on different minds in a variety of ways—but always with the design of convincing man of sin and of a judgment to come. And, oh, that men would regard their real interests and yield to the illuminating influences of the Spirit of God—then wretchedness and misery would abound no longer, but everything of the kind give place to the pure principles of peace, godliness, brotherly kindness, meekness, charity, and love. These graces are spontaneously produced in the human heart and are exemplified in the Christian deportment of every soul under the mellowing and sanctifying influences of the Spirit of God. They are the peaceable fruits of a meek and quiet spirit.

The perverseness of man in this respect is one of the great and conclusive proofs of his apostasy, and of the rebellious inclination of his unsanctified heart to the will and wisdom of his Creator and his Judge.

I have heard a great deal said respecting infants feeling, as it were, the operations of the Holy Spirit on their minds, impressing them with a sense of their wickedness and the necessity of a preparation for a future state. Children at a very early age manifest in a strong degree two of the evil passions of our nature—*anger* and *pride*. We need not wonder, therefore, that persons in early life feel good impressions; indeed, it is a fact, too well established to admit of doubt or controversy, that many children have manifested a strength of intellect far above their years and have given ample evidence of a good work of grace manifest by the influence of the Spirit of God in their young and tender minds. But this is perhaps attributable to the care and attention bestowed upon them.

If constant and judicious means are used to impress upon their young and susceptible minds sentiments of truth, virtue, morality, and religion, and these efforts are sustained by a corresponding practice on the part of parents or those who strive to make these early impressions, we may rationally trust that as their young minds expand they will be led to act upon the wholesome principles they have received—

and that at a very early period these good impressions will be more indelibly engraved on their hearts by the cooperating influences of that Spirit, who in the days of his glorious incarnation said, "Suffer little children to come unto me, and forbid them not, for of such is the kingdom of heaven."

But to my experience—and the reader knows full well that experience is the best schoolmaster, for what we have experienced, that we know, and all the world cannot possibly beat it out of us. I well remember the conversation that took place between Mrs. Furman and myself when I was about six years of age; she was attached to the Baptist church and was esteemed as a very pious woman. Of this I have not the shadow of a doubt, as her whole course of conduct was upright and exemplary. On this occasion, she spoke to me respecting a future state of existence and told me that I might die and enter upon it, to which I replied that I was too young—that old people only died. But she assured me that I was not too young, and in order to convince me of the truth of the observation, she referred me to the graveyard, where many younger and smaller persons than myself were laid to molder in the earth. I had of course nothing to say—but, notwithstanding, I could not fully comprehend the nature of death and the meaning of a future state. Yet I felt an indescribable sensation pass through my frame; I trembled and was sore afraid and for some time endeavored to hide myself from the destroying monster, but I could find no place of refuge. The conversation and pious admonitions of this good lady made a lasting impression upon my mind. At times, however, this impression appeared to be wearing away—then again I would become thoughtful, make serious inquiries, and seem anxious to know something more certain respecting myself and that state of existence beyond the grave, in which I was instructed to believe. About this time I was taken to meeting in order to hear the word of God and receive instruction in divine things. This was the first time I had ever entered a house of worship, and instead of attending to what the minister said, I was employed in gazing about the house or playing with the unruly boys with whom I was seated in the gallery. On my return home, Mr. Furman, who had been apprised of my conduct, told me that I had acted very wrong. He did not, however, stop here. He went on to tell me how I ought to behave in church, and to this very day I bless God for such wholesome and timely instruction. In this particular I was not slow to learn, as I do not remember that I have from that day to this misbehaved in the house of God.

It may not be improper to remark, in this place, that a vast proportion of the misconduct of young people in church is chargeable to their parents and guardians. It is to be feared that there are too many professing Christians who feel satisfied if their children or those under their care enter on a Sabbath day within the walls of the sanctuary, without reference to their conduct while there. I would have such persons seriously ask themselves whether they think they discharge the duties obligatory on them by the relation in which they stand to their Maker, as well as those committed to their care, by so much negligence on their part. The Christian feels it a duty imposed on him to conduct his children to the house of God. But he rests not here. He must have an eye over them and, if they act well, approve and encourage them in discreet and exemplary course of conduct while in church.

After a while I became very fond of attending on the word of God—then again I would meet the enemy of my soul, who would strive to lead me away, and in many instances he was but too successful, and to this day I remember that nothing scarcely grieved me so much, when my mind has been thus petted, than to be called by a nickname. If I was spoken to in the spirit of kindness, I would be instantly disarmed of my stubbornness and ready to perform anything required of me. I know of nothing so trying to a child as to be repeatedly called by an improper name. I thought it disgraceful to be called an Indian; it was considered as a slur upon an oppressed and scattered nation, and I have often been led to inquire where the whites received this word, which they so often threw as an opprobrious epithet at the sons of the forest. I could not find it in the Bible and therefore concluded that it was a word imported for the special purpose of degrading us. At other times I thought it was derived from the term *in-gen-uity*. But the proper term which ought to be applied to our nation, to distinguish it from the rest of the human family, is that of "*Natives*"—and I humbly conceive that the natives of this country are the only people under heaven who have a just title to the name, inasmuch as we are the only people who retain the original complexion of our father Adam. Notwithstanding my thoughts on this matter, so completely was I weaned from the interests and affections of my brethren that a mere threat of being sent away among the Indians into the dreary woods had a much better effect in making me obedient to the commands of my superiors than any corporal punishment that they ever inflicted. I had received a lesson in the unnatural treatment of my own relations, which could not be effaced, and I thought that, if those who should have loved and protected me treated me with such unkindness, surely I had not reason to expect mercy or favor at the hands of those who knew me in no other relation than that of a cast-off member of the tribe. A threat, of the kind alluded to, invariably produced obedience on my part, so far as I understood the nature of the command.

I cannot perhaps give a better idea of the dread which pervaded my mind on seeing any of my brethren of the forest than by relating the following occurrence. One day several of the family went into the woods to gather berries, taking me with them. We had not been out long before we fell in with a company of white females, on the same errand—their complexion was, to say the least, as *dark* as that of the natives. This circumstance filled my mind with terror, and I broke from the party with my utmost speed, and I could not muster courage enough to look behind until I reached home. By this time my imagination had pictured out a tale of blood, and as soon as I regained breath sufficient to answer the questions which my master asked, I informed him that we had met a body of the natives in the woods, but what had become of the party I could not tell. Notwithstanding the manifest incredibility of my tale of terror, Mr. Furman was agitated; my very appearance was sufficient to convince him that I had been terrified by something, and summoning the remainder of the family, he sallied out in quest of the absent party, whom he found searching for me among the bushes. The whole mystery was soon unraveled. It may be proper for me here to remark that the great fear I entertained of my brethren was occasioned by the many stories I had heard of their cruelty toward the whites—how they were in the habit of killing and scalping men, women, and children. But the whites did not tell me that they were in a great majority of instances the aggressors—that they had imbrued their hands in the lifeblood of my brethren, driven them from their once peaceful and happy homes—that they introduced among them the fatal and exterminating diseases of civilized life. If the whites had told me how cruel they had been to the "poor Indian," I should have apprehended as much harm from them.

Shortly after this occurrence I relapsed into my former bad habits—was fond of the company of boys—and in a short time lost in a great measure that spirit of obedience which had made me the favorite of my mistress. I was easily led astray, and, once in particular, I was induced by a boy (my senior by five or six years) to assist him in his depredations on a watermelon patch belonging to one of the neighbors. But we were found out, and my companion in wickedness led me deeper in sin by persuading me to deny the crime laid to our charge. I obeyed him to the very letter and, when accused, flatly denied knowing anything of the matter. The boasted courage of the boy, however, began to fail as soon as he saw danger thicken, and he confessed it as strongly as he had denied it. The man from whom we had pillaged the melons threatened to send us to Newgate, but he relented. The story shortly afterward reached the ears of the good Mrs. Furman, who talked seriously to me about it. She told me that I could be sent to prison for it, that I had done wrong, and gave me a great deal of wholesome advice. This had a much better effect than forty floggings—it sunk so deep into my mind that the impression can never be effaced.

I now went on without difficulty for a few months, when I was assailed by fresh and unexpected troubles. One of the girls belonging to the house had taken some offense at me and declared she would be revenged. The better to effect this end, she told Mr. Furman that I had not only threatened to kill her but had actually pursued her with a knife, whereupon he came to the place where I was working and began to whip me severely. I could not tell for what. I told him I had done no harm, to which he replied, "I will learn you, you Indian dog, how to chase people with a knife." I told him I had not, but he would not believe me and continued to whip me for a long while. But the poor man soon found out his error, as *after* he had flogged me he undertook to investigate the matter, when to his amazement he discovered it was nothing but fiction, as all the children assured him that I did no such thing. He regretted being so hasty—but I saw wherein the great difficulty consisted; if I had not denied the melon affair he would have believed me, but as I had uttered an untruth about that it was natural for him to think that the person who will tell one lie will not scruple at two. For a long while after this circumstance transpired, I did not associate with my companions.

Chapter III

About the time that I had attained my eighth year a sect called the Christians visited our neighborhood. Their hearts were warm in the cause of God—they were earnest and fervent in prayer, and I took great delight in hearing them sing the songs of Zion. Whenever I attended their meeting, which I did as often as possible, I listened to the word of God with the greatest degree of attention. It was not long before I resolved to mend my ways and become a better boy. By my strict attendance on divine worship and my orderly behavior, I attracted the notice of some of the people, who, when they discovered that I was seriously impressed, took me by the hand and strove by every possible means to cheer and encourage me. The notice thus taken of me had a very happy influence on my mind. I now determined to set about the work of repentance. On one occasion the minister addressed the people from a text touching the future state of mankind.

He spoke much on the *eternal happiness* of the righteous and the *everlasting misery* of the ungodly, and his observations sunk with awful weight upon my mind, and I was led to make many serious inquiries about the way of salvation. In these days of young desires and youthful aspirations, I found Mrs. Furman ever ready to give me good advice. My mind was intent upon learning the lesson of righteousness, in order that I might walk in the good way and cease to do evil. My mind for one so young was greatly drawn out to seek the Lord. This spirit was manifested in my daily walk; and the friends of Christ noticed my afflictions; they knew that I was sincere because my spirits were depressed. When I was in church I could not at times avoid giving vent to my feelings, and often have I wept sorely before the Lord and his people. They, of course, observed this change in my conduct—they knew I had been a rude child and that efforts were made to bring me up in a proper manner, but the change in my deportment they did not ascribe to the influence of divine grace, inasmuch as they all considered me *too young* to be impressed with a sense of divine things. They were filled with unbelief. I need not describe the peculiar feelings of my soul.

I became very fond of attending meeting, so much so that Mr. Furman forbid me. He supposed that I only went for the purpose of seeing the boys and playing with them. This thing caused me a great deal of grief; I went for many days with my head and heart bowed down. No one had any idea of the mental agony I suffered, and perhaps the mind of no untutored child of my age was ever more seriously exercised. Sometimes I was tried and tempted—then I would be overcome by the fear of death. By day and by night I was in a continual ferment. To add to my fears about this time, death entered the family of Mr. Furman and removed his mother-in-law. I was much affected, as the old lady was the first corpse I had ever seen. She had always been so kind to me that I missed her quite as much as her children, and I had been allowed to call her mother.

Shortly after this occurrence I was taken ill. I then thought that I should surely die. The distress of body and the anxiety of mind wore me down. Now I think that the disease with which I was afflicted was a very curious one. The physician could not account for it, and how should I be able to do it? Neither had those who were about me ever witnessed any disorder of the kind. I felt continually as if I was about being suffocated and was consequently a great deal of trouble to the family, as someone had to be with me. One day Mr. Furman thought he would frighten the disease out of me. Accordingly, he told me that all that ailed me was this: that the devil had taken complete possession of me, and that he was determined to flog him out. This threat had not the desired effect. One night, however, I got up and went out, although I was afraid to be alone, and continued out by the door until after the family had retired to bed. After a while Mr. F. got up and gave me a dreadful whipping. He really thought, I believe, that the devil was in me and supposed that the birch was the best mode of ejecting him. But the flogging was as poor man, found out his mistake, like many others who act without discretion.

One morning after this I went out in the yard to assist Mrs. Furman milk the cows. We had not been out long before I felt very singular and began to make a strange noise. I believed that I was going to die and ran up to the house; she followed me immediately, expecting me to breathe my last. Every effort to breathe was accompanied by this strange noise, which was so loud as to be heard a considerable distance. However, contrary to all expectation I began to revive, and from that very day my disorder began to abate, and I gradually regained my former health.

Soon after I recovered from my sickness, I went astray, associating again with my old schoolfellows and on some occasions profaning the Sabbath day. I did not do thus without warning, as conscience would speak to me when I did wrong. Nothing very extraordinary occurred until I had attained my eleventh year. At this time it was fashionable for boys to run away, and the wicked one put it into the head of the oldest boy on the farm to persuade me to follow the fashion. He told me that I could take care of myself and get my own living. I thought it was a very pretty notion to be a man—to *do business for myself and become rich*. Like a fool, I concluded to make the experiment and accordingly began to pack up my clothes as deliberately as could be, and in which my adviser assisted. I had been once or twice at New London, where I saw, as I thought, everything wonderful: Thither I determined to bend my course, as I expected that on reaching the town I should be metamorphosed into a person of consequence; I had the world and everything my little heart could desire on a string, when behold, my companion, who had persuaded me to act thus, informed my master that I was going to run off. At first he would not believe the boy, but my clothing already packed up was ample evidence of my intention. On being questioned I acknowledged the fact. I did not wish to leave them—told Mr. Furman so; he believed me but thought best that for a while I should have another master. He accordingly agreed to transfer my indentures to Judge Hillhouse for the sum of twenty dollars. Of course, after the bargain was made, my consent was to be obtained, but I was as unwilling to go now as I had been anxious to run away before. After some persuasion, I agreed to try it for a fortnight, on condition that I should take my dog with me, and my request being granted I was soon under the old man's roof, as he only lived about six miles off. Here everything was done to make me contented, because they thought to promote their own interests by securing my services. They fed me with knickknacks, and soon after I went among them I had a jackknife presented to me, which was the first one I had ever see. Like other boys, I spent my time either in whittling or playing with my dog and was withal very happy. But I was homesick at heart, and as soon as my fortnight had expired I went home without ceremony. Mr. Furman's family were surprised to see me, but that surprise was mutual satisfaction in which my faithful dog appeared to participate.

The joy I felt on returning home, as I hoped, was turned to sorrow on being informed that I had been *sold* to the judge and must instantly return. This I was compelled to do. And, reader, all this sorrow was in consequence of being led away by a bad boy: If I had not listened to him I should not have lost my home. Such treatment I conceive to be the best means to accomplish the ruin of a child, as the reader will see in the sequel. I was sold to the judge at a time when age had rendered him totally unfit to manage an unruly lad. If he undertook to correct me, which he did at times, I did not regard it as I knew that I could run off from him if he was too severe, and besides I could do what I pleased in defiance of his authority. Now the old gentleman was a member of the Presbyterian church and withal a very strict one. He never neglected family prayer, and he always insisted on my being present. I did not believe or, rather, had no faith in his prayer, because it was the same thing from day to day, and I had heard it repeated so often that I knew it as well as he. Although I was so young, I did not think that Christians ought to learn their prayers, and knowing that he repeated the same thing from day to day is, I have no doubt, the very reason why his petitions did me no good. I could fix no value on his prayers.

After a little while the conduct of my new guardians was changed toward me. Once secured, I was no longer the favorite. The few clothes I had were not taken care of, by which I mean no pains were taken to keep them clean and whole, and the consequence was that in a little time they were all "tattered and torn" and I was not fit to be seen in decent company. I had not the opportunity of attending meeting as before. Yet, as the divine and reclaiming impression had not been entirely defaced, I would frequently retire behind the barn and attempt to pray in my weak manner. I now became quite anxious to attend evening meetings a few miles off: I asked the judge if I should go and take one of the horses, to which he consented. This promise greatly delighted me—but when it was time for me to go, all my hopes were dashed at once, as the judge had changed his mind. I was not to be foiled so easily; I watched the first opportunity and slipped off with one of the horses, reached the meeting, and returned in safety. Here I was to blame; if he acted wrong, it did not justify me in doing so; but being successful in one grand act of disobedience, I was encouraged to make another similar attempt, whenever my unsanctified dispositions prompted; for the very next time I wished to go to meeting, I thought I would take the horse again, and in the same manner too, without the knowledge of my master. As he was by some means apprised of my intention, he prevented my doing so and had the horses locked up in the stable. He then commanded me to give him the bridle; I was obstinate for a time, then threw it at the old gentleman and ran off. I did not return until the next day, when I received a flogging for my bad conduct, which determined me to run away. Now, the judge was partly to blame for all this. He had in the first place treated me with the utmost kindness until he had made sure of me. Then the whole course of his conduct changed, and I believed he fulfilled only one item of the transferred indentures, and that was work. Of this there was no lack. To be sure I had enough to eat, such as it was, but he did not send me to school as he had promised.

Luther Standing Bear

(1868?–1939) Lakota

Luther Standing Bear was born Lakota, of the Teton or Western Sioux, probably in 1868. "It was a cold winter, in the month when the bark of the trees cracked, in the year of 'breaking up of camp,' that I was born," he wrote in **My People, the Sioux**, his first book, and a personal narrative published in 1928. "In those days we had no calendars, no manner of keeping count of the days; only the month and the years were observed."

Federal census and allotment records indicate that he was born a mixedblood five years earlier in 1863. Whatever the actual date of his birth, he was raised to be a hunter and warrior at the time that General George Armstrong Custer and the Seventh Cavalry were defeated on the Little Bighorn River in 1876.

Young Standing Bear, or Plenty Kill as he was known then, selected as a surname the nickname his father had earned as a warrior. The bear "will not run, but will die fighting," he wrote in **My Indian Boyhood**, his second book, published in 1931. "Because my father shared this spirit with the bear, he earned his name." Plenty Kill and other native children of his generation were among the first to bear the surnames of dominance; he was ordered to choose his first name at federal boarding school.

The Lakota were driven to encampments on reservations. The buffalo were slaughtered by the government, a barbarous policy of assimilation aimed to weaken native traditions and ensure dependencies on federal rations. They were given cattle and "issued flour, but as they did not make bread and were not instructed in the use of flour, they usually threw it away and used the sacks for shirts," noted Richard Ellis in the introduction to **My People, the Sioux**.

Standing Bear would be brave, and so he decided to leave by train with the first order of children for the federal boarding school at Carlisle, Pennsylvania, in 1879. He was eleven at the time. The train stopped at the station in Sioux City. "Many of the little Indian boys and girls were afraid of the white people," he wrote. "I really did not blame them, because the whites acted so wild at seeing us. They tried to give the war-whoop and mimic the Indian and in other ways got us all wrought up and excited, and we did not like this sort of treatment."

The natural reason of these students was transmuted overnight by uncomfortable clothes, short hair, and the given names of dominance. Native languages were silenced as one of the wicked means of assimilation by decree in a constitutional democracy. The children contravened these heinous censures with some humor, to be sure, but they were burdened with the shadow distance of their native memories and solace. Many children died from various diseases, as infections were the major cause of death in the world at that time. Medical care was minimal, but the institutional meals at boarding schools were better than the nutrition on most reservations.

Standing Bear was hired as an assistant teacher at the government school on the Rosebud Reservation in South Dakota. He owned a ranch, served as an assistant to a minister, and traveled with Buffalo Bill's Wild West Show in Europe. He published four books, the first when he was more than fifty years old. **Land of the Spotted Eagle (1933)**, his third book, is about native customs and philosophies. **Stories of the Sioux**, his last book, was published in 1934.

Richard Ellis noted that Standing Bear became an actor and activist in the Native American community in Los Angeles. He had "many friends, both Indian and white. Those who studied with him remember him fondly and mourned his passing in 1939 while he was working on the film **Union Pacific**.*"*

My People, the Sioux

Preface

The preparation of this book has not been with any idea of self-glory. It is just a message to the white race; to bring my people before their eyes in a true and authentic manner. The American Indian has been written about by hundreds of authors of white blood or possibly by an Indian of mixed blood who has spent the greater part of his life away from a reservation. These are not in a position to write accurately about the struggles and disappointments of the Indian.

White men who have tried to write stories about the Indian have either foisted on the public some bloodcurdling, impossible 'thriller'; or, if they have been in sympathy with the Indian, have written from knowledge which was not accurate and reliable. No one is able to understand the Indian race like an Indian.

Therefore, I trust that in reading the contents of this book the public will come to a better understanding of us. I hope they will become better informed as to our principles, our knowledge, and our ability. It is my desire that all people know the truth about the first Americans and their relations with the United States Government.

First Days at Carlisle

At last the train arrived at a junction where we were told we were at the end of our journey. Here we left the train and walked about two miles to the Carlisle Barracks. Soon we came to a big gate in a great high wall. The gate was locked, but after quite a long wait, it was unlocked and we marched in through it. I was the first boy inside. At that time I thought nothing of it, but now I realize that I was the first Indian boy to step inside the Carlisle Indian School grounds.

Here the girls were all called to one side by Louise McCoz, the girls' interpreter. She took them into one of the big buildings, which was very brilliantly lighted, and it looked good to us from the outside.

When our interpreter told us to go to a certain building which he pointed out to us, we ran very fast, expecting to find nice little beds like those the white people had. We were so tired and worn out from the long trip that we wanted a good long sleep. From Springfield, Dakota, to Carlisle, Pennsylvania, riding in day coaches all the way, with no chance to sleep, is an exhausting journey for a bunch of little Indians.

But the first room we entered was empty. A cast-iron stove stood in the middle of the room, on which was placed a coal-oil lamp. There was no fire in the stove. We ran through all the rooms, but they were all the same—no fire, no beds. This was a two-story building, but we were all herded into two rooms on the upper floor.

Well, we had to make the best of the situation, so we took off our leggins and rolled them up for a pillow. All the covering we had was the blanket which each had brought. We went to sleep on the hard floor, and it was so cold! We had been used to sleeping on the ground, but the floor was so much colder.

Next morning we were called downstairs for breakfast. All we were given was bread and water. How disappointed we were! At noon we had some meat, bread, and coffee, so we felt a little better. But how lonesome the big boys and girls were for their far-away Dakota homes where there was plenty to eat! The big boys seemed to take it worse than we smaller chaps did. I guess we little fellows did not know any better. The big boys would sing brave songs, and that would start the girls to crying. They did this for several nights. The girls' quarters were about a hundred and fifty yards from ours, so we could hear them crying. After some time the food began to get better; but it was far from being what we had been used to receiving back home.

At this point I must tell you how the Carlisle Indian School was started. A few years previously, four or five tribes in Oklahoma had some trouble. They were Cheyennes, Arapahoes, Comanches, and Wichitas. There was another tribe with them, but I have forgotten the name. The Government arrested some braves from these various tribes and took them to Virginia as prisoners. Captain Pratt was in charge of them. He conceived the idea of placing these Indians in a school to see if they could learn anything in that manner. So they were put into the Hampton School, where negroes were sent. They were good-sized young men, having been on the war-path already, but old as they were, they were getting on splendidly with their studies.

That gave Captain Pratt another idea. He thought if he could get some young Indian children and educate them, it would help their people. He went to the Government officials and put the proposition up to them, and asked permission to try the experiment. They told him to go ahead and see what he could do, providing he could get any Indians to educate. Captain Pratt was not at all sure he could do this.

He had nothing prepared to start such a school, but the Government gave him the use of some empty buildings at Carlisle, Pennsylvania. He brought some of the Indian prisoners from Virginia with him, and they remained in the Carlisle Barracks until Captain Pratt could go to Dakota and return with his first consignment of "scholars." Carlisle School had been a soldiers' home at one time; so at the start it was not built for the education of the Indian people.

I had come to this school merely to show my people that I was brave enough to leave the reservation and go East, not knowing what it meant and not caring.

When we first arrived at Carlisle, we had nothing to do. There were no school regulations, no rules of order or anything of that sort. We just ran all over the school grounds and did about as we pleased.

Soon some white people began to come in from nearby towns to see us. Then we would all go up on the second floor and stand against the railings to look down at them. One of our boys was named Lone Hill. He watched the people closely, and if he saw a negro in the crowd he would run inside and put his war-shirt on. Then he would come out and chase the negro all over the grounds until he left. How the people laughed at this!

For some time we continued sleeping on the hard floor, and it was far from being as comfortable as the nice, soft beds in our tipis back home. One evening the interpreter called us all together, and gave each a big bag. He said these were to be our mattresses, but that we would have to fill them ourselves with straw. He said, "Out behind the stable is a large haystack. Go there and fill these bags all full."

So we all ran as fast as we could to the haystack and filled our sacks as quickly as possible, pushing and scuffling to see who would get finished first. When the bags were all full, we carried them to one of the big rooms on the second floor. Here the bags were all laid out in a row. We little fellows certainly did look funny, lugging those great bags across the yard and upstairs.

That night we had the first good sleep in a long time. These bags were sewed all around, and in the center there was a slit through which they were filled with the straw; but there was nobody to sew the slit up after the bag was filled. We had no sheets and no extra blankets thus far—nothing but the blankets we had brought from the reservation.

The next day we played back and forth over these bags of straw, and soon it began to filter out through the slits. Presently it was scattered all over the floor, and as we had no brooms with which to sweep it up, you can imagine the looks of the room at the starting of our school!

Although we were yet wearing our Indian clothes, the interpreter came to us and told us we must go to school. We were marched into a schoolroom, where we were each given a pencil and slate. We were seated at single desks. We soon discovered that the pencils made marks on the slates. So we covered our heads with our blankets, holding the slate inside so the other fellow would not know what we were doing. Here we would draw a man on a pony chasing buffalo, or a boy shooting birds in a tree, or it might be one of our Indian games, or anything that suited our fancy to try and portray.

When we had all finished, we dropped our blankets down on the seat and marched up to the teacher with our slates to show what we had drawn. Our teacher was a woman. She bowed her head as she examined the slates and smiled, indicating that we were doing pretty well—at least we interpreted it that way.

One day when we came to school there was a lot of writing on one of the blackboards. We did not know what it meant, but our interpreter came into the room and said, "Do you see all these marks on the blackboard? Well, each word is a white man's name. They are going to give each one of you one of these names by which you will hereafter be known." None of the names were read or explained to us, so of course we did not know the sound or meaning of any of them.

The teacher had a long pointed stick in her hand, and the interpreter told the boy in the front seat to come up. The teacher handed the stick to him, and the interpreter then told him to pick out any name he wanted. The boy had gone up with his blanket on. When the long stick was handed to him, he turned to us as much as to say, 'Shall I—or will you help me—to take one of these names? Is it right for me to take a white man's name?' He did not know what to do for a time, not uttering a single word—but he acted a lot and was doing a lot of thinking.

Finally he pointed out one of the names written on the blackboard. Then the teacher took a piece of white tape and wrote the name on it. Then she cut off a length of the tape and sewed it on the back of the boy's shirt. Then that name was erased from the board. There was no duplication of names in the first class at Carlisle School!

Then the next boy took the pointer and selected a name. He was also labeled in the same manner as Number One. When my turn came, I took the pointer and acted as if I were about to touch an enemy. Soon we all had the names of white men sewed on our backs. When we went to school, we knew enough to take our proper places in the class, but that was all. When the teacher called the roll, no one answered his name. Then she would walk around and look at the back of the boys' shirts. When she had the right name located, she made the boy stand up and say "Present." She kept this up for about a week before we knew what the sound of our new names was.

I was one of the "bright fellows" to learn my name quickly. How proud I was to answer when the teachers called the roll! I would put my blanket down and half raise myself in my seat, all ready to answer to my new name. I had selected the name "Luther"—not "Lutheran" as many people call me. "Lutheran" is the name of a church denomination, not a person.

Next we had to learn to write our names. Our good teacher had a lot of patience with us. She is now living in Los Angeles, California, and I still like to go and ask her any question which may come up in my mind. She first wrote my name on the slate for me, and then, by motions, indicated that I was to write it just like that. She held the pencil in her hand just so, then made first one stroke, then another, and by signs I was given to understand that I was to follow in exactly the same way.

The first few times I wrote my new name, it was scratched so deeply into the slate that I was never able to erase it. But I copied my name all over both sides of the slate until there was no more room to write. Then I took my slate up to show it to the teacher, and she indicated, by the expression of her face, that it was very good. I soon learned to write it very well; then I took a piece of chalk downstairs and wrote 'Luther' all over everything I could copy it on.

Next the teacher wrote out the alphabet on my slate and indicated to me that I was to take the slate to my room and study. I was pleased to do this, as I expected to have a lot of fun. I went up on the second floor, to the end of the building, where I thought nobody would bother me. There I sat down and looked at those queer letters, trying hard to figure out what they meant. No one was there to tell me that the first letter was "A" the next "B" and so on. This was the first time in my life that I was really disgusted. It was something I could not decipher, and all this study business was not what I had come East for anyhow—so I thought.

How lonesome I felt for my father and mother! I stayed upstairs all by myself, thinking of the good times I might be having if I were only back home, where I could ride my ponies, go wherever I wanted to and do as I pleased, and, when it came night, could lie down and sleep well. Right then and there I learned that no matter how humble your home is, it is yet home.

So it did me no good to take my slate with me that day. It only made me lonesome. The next time the teacher told me by signs to take my slate to my room, I shook my head, meaning "no." She came and talked to me in English, but of course I did not know what she was saying.

A few days later, she wrote the alphabet on the blackboard, then brought the interpreter into the room. Through him she told us to repeat each letter after her, calling out "A," and we all said "A"; then "B," and so on. This was our real beginning. The first day we learned the first three letters of the alphabet, both the pronunciation and the reading of them.

I had not determined to learn anything yet. All I could think of was my free life at home. How long would these people keep us here? When were we going home? At home we could eat any time we wished, but here we had to watch the sun all the time. On cloudy days the waits between meals seemed terribly long.

There soon came a time when the church people fixed up an old building which was to be used as our dining-room. In it they placed some long tables, but with no cover on. Our meals were dished up and brought to each plate before we entered. I very quickly learned to be right there when the bell rang, and get in first. Then I would run along down the table until I came to a plate which I thought contained the most meat, when I would sit down and begin eating without waiting for anyone.

We soon "got wise" when it came to looking out for the biggest portion of meat. When we knew by the sun that it was near dinner time, we would play close to the dining-room, until the woman in charge came out with a big bell in her hand to announce that the meal was ready. We never had to be called twice! We were right there when it came meal-time!

After a while they hung a big bell on a walnut tree near the office. This was to be rung for school hours and meals. One of the Indian boys named Edgar Fire Thunder used to sneak around the building and ring the bell before it was time to eat. Of course we would all rush for the dining-room, only to find the doors locked. Nobody seemed to object to this boy playing such pranks, but we did not like it.

We were still wearing our Indian clothes. One of the Indian prisoners was delegated to teach us to march in to the dining-room and to school. Some of the boys had bells on their leggins, which helped us to keep time as we stepped off.

One day we had a strange experience. We were all called together by the interpreter and told that we were to have our hair cut off. We listened to what he had to say, but we did not reply. This was something that would require some thought, so that evening the big boys held a council, and I recall very distinctly that Nakpa Kesela, or Robert American Horse, made a serious speech. Said he, "If I am to learn the ways of the white people, I can do it just as well with my hair on." To this we all exclaimed "Hau!"—meaning that we agreed with him.

In spite of this meeting, a few days later we saw some white men come inside the school grounds carrying big chairs. The interpreter told us these were the men who had come to cut our hair. We did not watch to see where the chairs were carried, as it was school time, and we went to our classroom. One of the big boys named Ya Slo, or Whistler, was missing. In a short time he came in with his hair cut off. They then called another boy out, and when he returned, he also wore short hair. In this way we were called out one by one.

When I saw most of them with short hair, I began to feel anxious to be "in style" and wanted mine cut, too. Finally I was called out of the schoolroom, and when I went into the next room, the barber was waiting for me. He motioned for me to sit down, and then he commenced work. But when my hair was cut short, it hurt my feelings to such an extent that the tears came into my eyes. I do not recall whether the barber noticed my agitation or not, nor did I care. All I was thinking about was that hair he had taken away from me.

Right here I must state how this hair-cutting affected me in various ways. I have recounted that I always wanted to please my father in every way possible. All his instructions to me had been along this line: "Son, be brave and get killed." This expression had been moulded into my brain to such an extent that I knew nothing else.

But my father had made a mistake. He should have told me, upon leaving home, to go and learn all I could of the white man's ways, and be like them. That would have given a new idea from a different slant; but Father did not advise me along that line. I had come away from home with the intention of never returning alive unless I had done something very brave.

Now, after having had my hair cut, a new thought came into my head. I felt that I was no more Indian, but would be an imitation of a white man. And we are still imitations of white men, and the white men are imitations of the Americans.

We all looked so funny with short hair. It had been cut with a machine and was cropped very close. We still had our Indian clothes, but were all "bald-headed." None of us slept well that night; we felt so queer. I wanted to feel my head all the time. But in a short time I became anxious to learn all I could.

Next we heard that we were soon to have white men's clothes. We were all very excited and anxious when this was announced to us. One day some wagons came in, loaded with big boxes, which were unloaded in front of the office. Of course we were all very curious, and gathered around to watch the proceedings and see all we could.

Here, one at a time, we were "sized up" and a whole suit handed to each of us. The clothes were some sort of dark heavy gray goods, consisting of coat, pants, and vest. We were also given a dark woolen shirt, a cap, a pair of suspenders, socks, and heavy farmer's boots.

Up to this time we had all been wearing our thin shirts, leggins, and a blanket. Now we had received new outfits of white men's clothes, and to us it seemed a whole lot of clothing to wear at once, but even at that, we had not yet received any underwear.

As soon as we had received our outfits, we ran to our rooms to dress up. The Indian prisoners were kept busy helping us put the clothes on. Although the suits were too big for many of us, we did not know the difference. I remember that my boots were far too large, but as long as they were "screechy" or squeaky, I didn't worry about the size! I liked the noise they made when I walked, and the other boys were likewise pleased.

How proud we were with clothes that had pockets and with boots that squeaked! We walked the floor nearly all the night. Many of the boys even went to bed with their clothes all on. But in the morning, the boys who had taken off their pants had a most terrible time. They did not know whether they were to button up in front or behind. Some of the boys said the open part went in front; others said, "No, it goes at the back." There is where the boys who had kept all their clothes on came in handy to look at. They showed the others that the pants buttoned up in front and not at the back. So here we learned something again.

Another boy and I received some money from home. His name was Waniyetula, or Winter, and he was my cousin. We concluded we might as well dress up like white men; so we took all our money to the interpreter and asked him if he would buy us some nice clothes. He promised he would.

We did not know the amount of money which we handed over to him, but we gave him all we had received, as we did not know values then. He took the money and went to town. When he returned he brought us each a big bundle. We took them and went into an empty room to dress up, as we did not want the other boys to see us until we had the clothes on. When we opened the bundles, we were surprised to see how many things we had received for our money. Each bundle contained a black suit of clothes, a pair of shoes and socks, stiff bosom shirt, two paper collars, a necktie, a pair of cuffs, derby hat, cuff buttons, and some colored glass studs for our stiff shirt fronts.

We were greatly pleased with our purchases, which we examined with great curiosity and eagerness. As it was nearly time for supper, we tied the bundles together again and took them into one of the rooms where an Indian prisoner was staying, asking him to keep the bundles for us until the next day. We had to talk to him in the sign language, as he was from a different tribe. The sign language, by the way, was invented by the Indian. White men never use it correctly.

We felt very proud of our new purchases and spent most of that evening getting off by ourselves and discussing them. We found out later that our wonderful clothes cost all together about eleven dollars. The interpreter had bought the cheapest things he could get in the town of Carlisle.

All the next day we were together. We kept our eyes on our disciplinarian, Mr. Campbell, because we wanted to see how he put on his collar. We were studying not very far away from him and we watched him constantly, trying to figure out how he had put that collar on his shirt.

When evening came at last, we carried our bundles up to the second floor where we could be alone. Here we opened the things up and started to dress up. While we were thus engaged, in came the prisoner with whom we had left the bundles the night before. We were glad, in a way, that he had come in, because he knew more about how the clothes ought to be worn than we did, and he helped us dress.

Just as we were through, the bell rang for supper. The other boys were already in line. We came down the outside stairway, and when they observed us, what a war-whoop went up! The boys made all kinds of remarks about our outfits, and called us "white men." But our teachers and the other white people were greatly pleased at our new appearance.

We had only two paper collars apiece, and when they became soiled we had to go without collars. We tried our best to wear the ties without the collars, but I guess we must have looked funny.

It was now winter and very cold, so we were supplied with red flannel underwear. These looked pretty to us, but we did not like the warmth and the "itching" they produced. I soon received some more money from my father, and another boy named Knaska, or Frog, and I bought us some white underwear. This was all right, but we did not dare let any one else know it, as the rules were that we had to wear the red flannels. So every Sunday morning we would put the red ones on, because they held inspection on Sunday morning. Captain Pratt and others always looked us over that day very carefully; but as soon as the inspection was through, we would slip into our white underclothes and get ready to attend Sunday School in town.

All the boys and girls were given permission to choose the religious denomination which appealed to them best, so they were at liberty to go where they pleased to Sunday School. Most of us selected the Episcopal Church. I was baptized in that church under the name of Luther.

In our room lived a boy named Kaici Inyanke, or Running Against. While not exactly bad, he was always up to some mischief. His father's name was Black Bear, so when the boy was baptized he took his father's name, while his Christian name was Paul. He is yet living at Pine Ridge Agency, South Dakota. More than once Captain Pratt had to hold Paul up. He would play until the very last minute and then try to clean his shoes and comb his hair, all at once seemingly. On this particular Sunday Paul rushed in and was so busy that he did not get half finished. He had combed his hair, but had applied too much water, which was running down his face, while one of his shoes was cleaned and the other was dirty.

We had been taught to stand erect like soldiers when Captain Pratt, Dr. Givens, and others entered the room for inspection. First, Captain Pratt would "size us up" from head to foot, notice if we had our hair combed nicely, if our clothes were neatly brushed, and if we had cleaned our shoes. Then he would look the room over to see if our beds were made up right, often lifting the mattresses to see that everything was clean underneath. Often they would look into our wooden boxes where we kept our clothes, to see that everything was spick and span.

Paul Black Bear had not been able—as usual—to finish getting ready for inspection, and when Captain Pratt looked at his feet, Paul tried to hide the shoe that was not polished, by putting it behind the other one. Captain Pratt also noticed the water running down his face. We all expected to see Paul get a "calling down," but Captain Pratt only laughed and told Paul to do better next time.

At Carlisle it was the rule that we were not to be permitted to smoke, but Paul smoked every time he had a chance. One day he made a "long smoke" and stood by one of the big fireplaces, puffing away very fast. All at once he got sick at the stomach and fainted. We had to drag him out of the fireplace and pour water on him.

One day our teacher brought some wooden plates into the schoolroom. She told us they were to paint on. She gave me about half a dozen of them. We each received a small box of watercolors. I painted Indian designs on all my plates. On some of them I had a man chasing buffalo, shooting them with the bow and arrow. Others represented a small boy shooting at birds in the trees. When I had them all painted, I gave them back to the teacher. She seemed to be well pleased with my work, and sent them all away somewhere. Possibly some persons yet have those wooden plates which were painted by the first class of Indian boys and girls at Carlisle.

About this time there were many additions to the school from various tribes in other States and from other reservations. We were not allowed to converse in the Indian tongue, and we knew so little English that we had a hard time to get along. With these other tribes coming in, we were doing our best to talk as much English as we could.

One night in December we were all marched down to the chapel. When the doors were opened, how surprised we were! Everything was decorated with green. We all took seats, but we could not keep still. There was a big tree in the room, all trimmed and decorated. We stretched our necks to see everything. Then a minister stood up in front and talked to us, but I did not mind a thing he said—in fact, I could not understand him anyway.

This was our first Christmas celebration, and we were all so happy. I saw the others were getting gifts from off that tree, and I was anxious to get something myself. Finally my name was called, and I received several presents, which had been put on the tree for me by the people for whom I had painted the plates. Others were from my teacher, Miss M. Burgess, and some from my Sunday School teacher, Miss Eggee. I was very happy for all the things I had received.

I now began to realize that I would have to learn the ways of the white man. With that idea in mind, the thought also came to me that I must please my father as well. So my little brain began to work hard. I thought that some day I might be able to become an interpreter for my father, as he could not speak English. Or I thought I might be able to keep books for him if he again started a store. So I worked very hard.

One day they selected a few boys and told us we were to learn trades. I was to be a tinsmith. I did not care for this, but I tried my best to learn this trade. Mr. Walker was our instructor. I was getting along very well. I made hundreds of tin cups, coffee pots, and buckets. These were sent away and issued to the Indians on various reservations.

After I had left the school and returned home, this trade did not benefit me any, as the Indians had plenty of tinware that I had made at school.

Mornings I went to the tin shop, and in the afternoon attended school. I tried several times to drop this trade and go to school the entire day, but Captain Pratt said, "No, you must go to the tin shop—that is all there is to it," so I had to go. Half school and half work took away a great deal of study time. I figure that I spent only about a year and a half in school, while the rest of the time was wasted, as the school was not started properly to begin with. Possibly you wonder why I did not remain longer, but the Government had made an agreement with our parents as to the length of time we were to be away.

A short time later, some boys, myself among the number, were called into one of the schoolrooms. There we found a little white woman. There was a long table in front of her, on which were many packages tied in paper. She opened up one package and it contained a bright, shining horn. Other packages disclosed more horns, but they seemed to be different sizes.

The little white woman picked up a horn and then looked the boys over. Finally she handed it to a boy who she thought might be able to use it. Then she picked out a shorter horn and gave it to me. I learned afterward that it was a B-flat cornet. When she had finished, all the boys had horns in their hands. We were to be taught how to play on them and form a band.

The little woman had a black case with her, which she opened. It held a beautiful horn, and when she blew on it it sounded beautiful. Then she motioned to us that we were to blow our horns. Some of the boys tried to blow from the large end. Although we tried our best, we could not produce a sound from them. She then tried to talk to us, but we did not understand her. Then she showed us how to wet the end of the mouthpiece. We thought she wanted us to spit into the horns, so we did. She finally got so discouraged with us that she started crying.

We just stood there and waited for her to get through, then we all tried again. Finally, some of the boys managed to make a noise through their horns. But if you could have heard it! It was terrible! But we thought we were doing fine.

So now I had more to occupy my attention. In the morning I had one hour to practice for the band. Then I must run to my room and change my clothes and go to work in the tin shop. From there I had to run again to my room and change my clothes and get ready for dinner. After that, I had a little time to study my lessons.

Then the school bell would ring and it was time for school. After that, we played and studied our music. Then we went to bed. All lights had to be out at nine o'clock. The first piece of music our band was able to play was the alphabet, from "a" to "z." It was a great day for us when we were able to play this simple little thing in public. But it was a good thing we were not asked to give an encore, for that was all we knew!

After I had learned to play a little, I was chosen to give all the bugle calls. I had to get up in the morning before the others and arouse everybody by blowing the morning call. Evenings at ten minutes before nine o'clock I blew again. Then all the boys would run for their rooms. At nine o'clock the second call was given, when all lights were turned out and we were supposed to be in bed. Later on I learned the mess call, and eventually I could blow all the calls of the regular army.

I did these duties all the time I was at Carlisle School, so in the early part of 1880, although I was a young boy of but twelve, I was busy learning everything my instructors handed me.

One Sunday morning we were busy getting ready to get to Sunday School in town. Suddenly there was great excitement among some of the boys on the floor below. One of the boys came running upstairs shouting, "Luther Standing Bear's father is here!" Everybody ran downstairs to see my father. We had several tribes at the school now, many of whom had heard of my father, and they were anxious to see him.

When I got downstairs, my father was in the center of a large crowd of the boys, who were all shaking hands with him. I had to fight my way through to reach him. He was so glad to see me, and I was delighted to see him. But our rules were that we were not to speak the Indian language under any consideration. And here was my father, and he could not talk English!

My first act was to write a note to Captain Pratt, asking if he would permit me to speak to my father in the Sioux tongue. I said, "My father is here. Please allow me to speak to him in Indian." Captain Pratt answered, "Yes, my boy; bring your father over to my house."

This was another happy day for me. I took my father over to meet Captain Pratt, who was so glad to see him, and was very respectful to him. Father was so well dressed. He wore a gray suit, nice shoes, and a derby hat. But he wore his hair long. He looked very nice in white men's clothes. He even sported a gold watch and chain. Captain Pratt gave father a room with Robert American Horse, in the boys' quarters. He allowed the boys to talk to him in the Indian tongue, and that pleased the boys very much. Here Father remained for a time with us.

John Rogers

(1890–?) Anishinaabe

John Rogers was born on the White Earth Reservation in northern Minnesota in 1890. He attended the federal boarding school at Flandreau, South Dakota. The memories of his childhood on the reservation and at school were first published privately as **A Chippewa Speaks** in 1957. He was sixty-seven years old at the time he wrote about his experiences at boarding school. Sixteen years later his autobiographical stories were published as **Red World and White: Memories of a Chippewa Boyhood** by the University of Oklahoma Press (1973).

In spite of his adverse experiences in a racist nation, Rogers wrote with a sense of peace about the changes he observed on his return to the reservation. He was rightly suspicious at times, dubious of the promises made by the government, but his memories as an elder were not bitter or consumed with hatred of white people. He praised nature as a spiritual teacher, and his resistance to institutional knowledge is similar to the conflicts voiced by native students today. "Perhaps," he wrote, "there were advantages that would make up for what I had left behind!"

Joseph Whitecotten, in the foreword to the last edition, wrote that the book "focuses on his boyhood, and depicts the thinking and learning processes of a youth caught between two cultural worlds" (1987). Rogers was six years old when he left the reservation for boarding school and twelve when he returned. He learned that his parents were separated and his mother was living alone in a wigwam. After six years of education his mother was right to ask him if he "would be happy gathering birch bark, tobacco, and wood? I was pleased to feel that I would grow into a strong young brave, and so I tried very hard to please her and to learn once more the Chippewa language."

The Chippewa are the Anishinaabe in the oral language of the tribe. The plural is Anishinaabeg. Many tribes are known by at least two names: one name is traditional and oral, and the second is written in English. The native names in oral languages are seldom recorded in dictionaries. John Nichols, a linguist, pointed out that "although the English name Chippewa is commonly used both for the people and their ancestral language in Michigan, Minnesota, North Dakota, and Wisconsin, in the language itself the people are the Anishinaabeg and the language is called Anishinaabemowin.

Rogers remembers tribal names in an oral language, and there are variations in the transcription of these words in names and stories. The sound of words is regional and one transcription does not represent the absolute sound; written words, for that matter, are heard with regional variations. Way Quah Gishig, his native name, for instance, he translates as dawn of day. Bishop Baraga in **A Dictionary of the Otchipwe Language**, first published in 1878, records the translation of dawn as bidaban. More recent dictionaries translate dawn, or the dawn approaches as biidaaban and it is dawn, or daybreak as waaban. Day is giihig or gijig. Perhaps his descriptive name means end of the day rather than dawn. Waiekwa is used to mean the end of something. Way Quah Gishig could be a variation of waiekwa gijig and mean the end of the day. The word manito used in his autobiography means spirit in the context of spirits that animate the natural world.

Rogers mentions the towns of Mahnomen and Beaulieu on his return to the reservation. Mahnomen or manoomin *is a native word that means wild rice. Beaulieu is a town and a surname traced to the first fur traders.*

Return to White Earth

Way quah Gishing was six years old when my two sisters, Bishiu and Min di, accompanied me to Flanreau, South Dakota, to attend an Indian boarding school.

It was very difficult for me at first, for students at the school were not allowed to speak the language of the Indians. At that time I understood nothing else.

Neither did I like to be forced to remain with my sisters in the girls' building instead of being assigned to the quarters occupied by the boys.

I was as shy and timid as the young buck in the forest and clung very closely to my sisters. But soon I learned to speak and understand a little of the white man's language; and gradually the boys began coaxing me to play with them. At first I wore my hair in two braids, Indian fashion, but at last my sisters gave in and allowed it to be cut so that I would be like the other boys.

My many happy years at the school have no place in this volume, so I will begin at the time Min di, Bishiu, and I took the train to return home. Min di, who at school was given the name of Caroline, was tall and slender as the sapling pine. Her eyes as soft and innocent as a doe's. She wore her raven black hair loose, hanging down her back, and tied with a buckskin string.

We got off the puffing, snorting train at Mannheim. There was a man named John Carr who met us. He put us in his light wagon. Min di sat on the seat beside him, and Bishiu and I alternately stood or lay down in the rear.

With ever widening interest we stared off at the passing landscape. The road wound along ahead of us, turning and curling like a slithering serpent.

I was anxious to see my mother and be home again, but even this strong desire could not keep me awake for many hours, and finally Weetig, the sleep spirit, settled down over me.

We stopped briefly at the town of Beaulieu, where we got out and stretched our legs and had lunch. When we started out again, the scene was changed. We came into wooded places, where trees seem to tower upward to the sky and cast deep dark shadows on the fallen leaves encircling them.

Finally Min di turned and exclaimed, "Look, Way quah!" She pointed toward the north.

There in the distance I saw the sparkle of water and the ripple of waves as the sun was reflected back through the trees. This I knew was home!

Coming to a halt near a wigwam, the driver got down and helped us out.

"Here we are, children. Over there is your mother."

He did not mention my father, and I wondered about him.

Mother was seated on the ground, working on some fish nets. She was heavy and broad, but her hands and feet were small. Her hair, straight and black, was tied with a red string. She wore a full-skirted blue calico dress, with long blousey sleeves, a low neck, and tight-fitting waist. Her waist was encircled by a fringed belt with red, yellow-green, and blue figures in it.

I learned later that mother had to keep very busy making linen-thread fish nets to sell—for now she had extra mouths to feed.

She looked up from her work, and we children made a mad scramble toward her. As she stood up with outstretched arms her eyes sparkled as does the sun on laughing waters.

What a reunion that was! She endeavored to gather us all into her arms at once. She started talking joyously, but we couldn't understand very well what she said, for we had forgotten much of the Indian language during our six years away from home.

But all that mattered was we were welcome here in mother's wigwam—the home of our birth.

After supper that evening Mother took us back to where the nets were, and there was our baby brother, Ahmeek. I had known nothing about him until then. But there he was, lying in his cradle which looked something like a white man's hammock strung between two trees. It was situated conveniently so that mother could reach out as she sat making nets and swing him back and forth, and croon to him to the accompaniment of the wind that rustled in the towering pines.

I stood staring down at my baby brother, and suddenly he looked up at me with his pretty dark eyes, raised his chubby little hands, and gurgled happily. To me he was saying, "Aren't you proud of your new little brother?"

His hair was straight and dark. He wore a little red and white checked calico dress.

Bishiu, now fourteen years of age, came up to me. She was tall for her age, but shorter and heavier than Min di. She had teasing brown eyes and was very pretty. She still wore the uniform of the school—a white blouse and blue skirt, with high-buttoned shoes and black stockings. She always liked the dress of the white people.

Bishiu bent over the cradle and held out her arms to her new baby brother. "Min di said I should bring him to the wigwam," she said, "and you are to help Mother straighten out her nets."

Mother, who sat nearby, shook her head.

"No, we will go into the wigwam now."

She picked up her pipe and kinnikinic (Indian tobacco), and we all went into the wigwam. It was about the size of a large room in a white man's dwelling. In the center was a fireplace, and above in the middle of the roof was an opening for light and for the smoke to escape. Suspended from a framework over the fire were two kettles almost full of water.

On one side of this large room I saw a bedframe made of poles. Over these were laid boughs to make a smooth, springy couch about the size of a double bed. The bedding consisted of deer pelts and, when not in use, could be folded back to the wall and serve as a back-rest.

Along the east wall was mother's workshop, and opposite the door the kitchen equipment was kept. On the west side was a place for the man's workshop. Over at the opposite wall was the pit used for storing and the wood pile. The storage pit was a hole dug in the ground, and this was overlaid with hay, on top of which was some birch bark. Here were potatoes, carrots, corn, onions, and any canned or dried fruits that had accumulated from the gather of fruits and berries.

I wondered where I was to sleep during that first night at home, for I could see but one bed. After awhile I questioned Min di, and she answered in Indian fashion:

"For the time, while our earth mother is still warm, you will sleep outside under the trees. But later, when the thunder clouds bring the rains, you will have another bed on the opposite side of the room."

I was then instructed what to do to prepare the outside bed. They told me to get four poles and place them upright in the ground. From the four corners thus formed a netting was draped down over the sides to protect me from mosquitoes and other insects during the time when darkness reigned and man dwelt under the spell of the sleep spirit.

During the days that followed we had a happy time getting acquainted after those long years of separation. Mother kept saying what a big help I was going to be. She asked whether I thought I would be happy gathering birch bark, tobacco, and wood? I was pleased to feel that I would grow into a strong young brave, and so I tried very hard to please her and to learn once more the Chippewa language. Min di was the only one who could speak both the Chippewa and English tongues, so for a time she interpreted all that mother said to Bishiu and me.

Mother promised to teach me the ways of the forest, rivers, and lakes—how to set rabbit snares and deadfalls, how to trap for wolves and other wild animals that roamed this land of the Chippewas.

While we sat around the fire talking and planning, Mother told my oldest sister to explain that she wanted us to be called by our Indian names. She insisted that we start at once to use them. So Min di told us not ever to use our school names any more. And so we became Min di and Bishiu, my two sisters, and Ahmeek, which meant "beaver" (the baby). My own Indian name, Way Quah, meant "dawn of day" and at school I was known as John.

At the time of my homecoming I was twelve years old and quite tall for my age. I was straight as a pine. My hair was black and wavy, and my eyes sharp and brown.

I generally kept very quiet when in the presence of people.

Mother was very clever and direct in teaching me the Indian way of things. One day she called out abruptly: "Way quah, get those rocks and floats out by the tree. They are tied with wegoob."

Wegoob is the green inner bark from the basswood tree. This I got immediately, as mother watched me. I picked the rocks she wanted, which were about the size of a wild-duck egg, and the floats, which were made of cedar. I carried them into the wigwam and Mother and Min di arranged them on the nets.

"And now," said Mother approvingly, "get a hatchet and come with me down the beach to our nearest neighbor. There we will borrow a canoe to use for setting the nets."

As we walked along, she pointed to some red willow. She cut some of this to show me how, and took it along with us.

I shall never forget the experience in the borrowed canoe. This was my first ride in a boat made of birch bark. Mother put me in front, and we paddled back to our landing.

Mother frequently smoked a pipe, and I wondered where she got it and whether I could make one like it. So I asked her, and she explained that when a young girl she had gone with Chief Bay mi chig gah nany (meaning "Long Lake"), and he it was who had given the pipe to her. It had been handed down from chief to chief, until it finally came to him and he then told her that it was now hers.

"And so, Way quah," she said, "when you have grown to be a strong young brave, this pipe shall be yours." And to this day I have it among my prized possessions.

The peace pipe is made of black stone, and has a round bowl on a square base. It is inlaid with red stone and lead. The stem is made from the ash tree that grows in the swamps.

Often when Mother and all of us would sit around the fire, she would tell us stories of the Chippewas and about our brother and sister who were away at school in Morris, Minnesota; a brother and sister I would see again after the robin returned and the sun began once more to melt the snows and warm the earth.

This was the first time I knew I had two brothers and three sisters. I envisioned the fun we would all have playing on the shore of the lake and swimming in its smiling, rippling waters.

In Mother's stories were many interesting facts about our Grandmother. Mother promised we would go to her for a visit before many more suns. She hadn't seen us since we left for school.

It was early morning of a day in the following week that we started on this visit.

We took with us some mosquito netting and enough food to last for a few days. This was quite a load for us to pack, for we also had little Ahmeek to carry, and Grandmother's house was some six miles distant on a different trail.

We traveled slowly, but enjoyed every step of the way. The call of the birds and the voices of other wild things were like music to my ears. It seemed that the trees and shrubs were whispering messages and that the Great Spirit hovered very near on this trail where the shadows were deep. Now and then we would see a deer or a rabbit, or perhaps, it would be a squirrel that would scamper up the tree and scold us for intruding upon his peaceful domain.

Coming at last to the house, we dropped our packs outside. Mother's sister came to the door and greeted us with open arms. Grandma's face lighted up when she saw who it was. She seemed to be a very happy person, and she had been blessed with a very long life. She opened her heart to us instantly and made us feel at home while we remained in her dwelling.

When at last we were ready for the return trip through the forest trail, Mother's sister offered to drive us home. Mother and Min di were never idle. They fashioned many useful articles with strips of birch bark peeled from nearby trees. From the sweet grass various roots and bulrushes were obtained. Then there were mats, baskets, and little birch-bark canoes.

In the gathering of rushes, Mother made us go out into the deep water where we would dive for the longer rushes. The longer the better, she told us; for the longer ones made larger and finer mats. Articles she made this way could be traded for flour, sugar, and other food supplies.

Now the time of the melting snows had come and gone. Soft, gentle winds warmed the earth. Summer was well along. We gathered birch bark for Mother, and with this she would make containers and dishes for our winter supplies. To remove this bark from the trees required skill in order not to harm the bark. If we cut too deeply it would leave a scar, for the new bark would not again grow out smooth.

Mother was careful to teach us just how it was done. With a sharp knife we would cut through the inner bark only. Indeed, it seemed that the Great Spirit had placed it there to let us know just how deeply to cut. It was our code never to destroy anything that Nature had given us. If we took care in stripping the bark, more would be provided on the same tree.

At the coming of the robin was the best season for getting the bark, but since Mother had time now, in the fall, to teach us, she felt there was no need to wait.

While the leaf was still brown on the forest trees and the cold north wind had yet to bring the snow to our village, a young brave named Wa goosh came to our wigwam and asked Mother to come to the church of the white man, for a prayer meeting.

Mother looked upon Wa goosh with favor. He seemed to be always about when needed and always willing to help.

When Wa goosh first saw my sister Min di, it was plain that he liked her and it was the beginning of a beautiful friendship.

Wa goosh (meaning "fox") was tall and strong. He was the typical Chippewa brave. His shirt was tan and of buckskin, open at the throat with long sleeves and beautifully beaded cuffs. His trousers were dark and soft as the forest moss. Knotted about his throat he wore a colored silk handkerchief. But he wore no hat and no earrings. Usually there was just a band about his forehead and his hair hung in two braids.

I learned that Wa goosh was a hunter, a farmer, and a blacksmith, and would gather herbs beneficial to the sick. For these he would never accept pay, saying that those who were helped in their sickness could pay him with gifts if they chose to do so.

One morning Wa goosh asked Mother:

"Have the children ever seen a squaw dance?" "No, Wa goosh, they haven't," she answered.

"Then at the time of the next dance you are all to go with me."

"We will come," Mother promised.

Thus it was when the Indians next gathered for this great occasion of the dance, we went with Wa goosh. We had heard that he was counted as one of the best solo dancers on the White Earth reservation. In his beautiful costume the young brave made the heart of every Indian maiden beat with desire to win his favor. But apparently he was most pleased when Min di joined him in the dance.

It is the custom at the squaw dance for the male to offer a gift to the girl with whom he wishes to perform, such as a handkerchief or goods for a new dress or maybe an article of food she would like. If she accepts, then she dances with him; and if she desires another dance with him, she gives him something in return. This might be a pair of beaded gloves or beaded cuffs. Or perhaps any beaded article that she owns and believes may please the young brave of her choice.

Here at the dance it was also the custom to exchange articles. If one wanted a pony that would pair with one he owned, he would offer his costume in exchange. The arrangement is made through one of his people, and they too join in the dance.

After a time they sit at the edge of the circle. Next comes the solo dance—without partners. Single dancers weave in and out and around one another, always circling the drummers, who are in the center. Only the men take part in this, and it is very rhythmic and beautiful. Then, after a time, he who has received the costume arises to announce that he will give his pony for it.

I shall never forget that first squaw dance that I attended. I never missed another one.

And so the long white winter passed. The snows melted from field and forest. Birds appeared in the budding trees and their song gladdened the hearts of all who heard.

While playing with Ahmeek one morning, Bishiu and I were swinging him in his cradle when we heard a wagon deep in the forest. A little later it came into view, bringing a man, a woman, and two children. We ran into the wigwam to our sister, Min di, and asked her who it could be. She and mother came out.

"Why, it's your brother and sister—Mah ni do mi naince and Osh kin nah way!" exclaimed Mother.

They were back from school. We boys stood there and admired each other's coats. Boylike, we compared them and found them very much alike, both having brass buttons and buttoned right up to the neck. The rest of Osh kim nah way's costume was a lot like mine too—blue gray short trousers, high shoes, and black stockings.

He was ten years old, short and chubby, with black hair and brown eyes. He was very bashful. We called him Osh kin for short.

Mah ni do mi naince was twelve, tall and slender, but not very strong. She had long dark hair, braided to fall in front and tied with a red ribbon. Her eyes were brown. Her uniform was a jumper skirt of blue and a white blouse, high shoes, and black stockings. We called her Mah ni.

Neither could talk Indian. So I felt sorry for them. They would have to learn the Indian tongue all over again, the same as Bishiu and I had to do. I felt I could be of much help to them.

The four of us children would make birch-bark baskets and take them out to fill with berries. There were strawberries, raspberries, high bush cranberries, wild grapes, and blueberries, for it was the time of their ripening.

If we had more than we could eat, Mother would dry them out in the sun, then put them away for use when the cold, icy days of the winter came.

Soon came the time for the leaves to turn brown and yellow and gold. The forest was beautiful and the wind rustled the dry leaves. We just couldn't resist the temptation to gather those beautiful colored leaves and the empty birds' nests.

At school, if we brought in a nest or a pretty leaf, we were given much credit, and we thought we would also please Mother by bringing some to her. But she did not like our doing this. She would scold and correct us and tell us we were destroying something—that the nests were the homes of the birds and the leaves were the beauty of the forest.

I loved to lie on my back under the trees and watch the clouds forming and moving. Sometimes it seemed they were so swift in their movements I would wonder where they were going. And then at other times they would just hang there, like great white doves.

With the coming of night, Mother would teach us how to make dishes out of birch bark. When we went on camping trips, having no horses, we were able to take only the necessary pots and supplies, so it was urgent that we understood how to make our own dishes.

These we fashioned as we needed them, for always did we carry birch bark with us. Sometimes we had soup, and this would call for deeper dishes. The dishes were always burned after each meal—no washing and nothing left around to attract bugs or flies.

We had so much to learn. Mother taught us how to get larger strips of birch bark, up to eighteen or thirty-six inches. This had to be taken from a tree about six inches through making a strip some eighteen inches wide and as long as we wanted to strip them. They were sewed together to make a strip about twelve to eighteen feet long and thirty-six inches wide. The raw edges were in thirty-six-inch widths and bound with cedar and sewed with basswood bark. This prevented breaking and tearing when rolled. Ten or twelve sheets like this were sufficient to cover a wigwam.

The rolls were very light in weight. The wigwam frame was made by pushing long poles into the ground about sixteen inches apart and bending and tying them together at the top with basswood bark. These were covered with birch-bark strips, starting at the bottom by the door opening and working around the bottom and upwards.

There is always an opening about three by five feet right in the center of the top, as we were taught that light which came directly down from the abode of the Great Spirit was better for us. It served as an outlet for the smoke from our fires also.

In order to keep the fires burning with the least trouble, Mother taught us the kind of wood to gather that would not throw off sparks and set our clothing or bedding on fire while we slept. The logs were cut larger and greener for the base of the fire, to keep the ashes and hot coals together. The night fire was always made with hardwood limbs, oak or ash, as these burned slower and had no flame and not much smoke. We never expected the fire to last all night, but it would keep the base of the fireplace warm so it wouldn't take long to heat up and allowed a good hearth of coals for baking a fish or fowl for the noonday meal.

The way we prepared fish for baking in the ashes of an open fire was to clean and dress them, cutting out the gills and slitting down the back from the head, leaving the head and scales on and taking out the insides. The fish were then carefully packed in clay, about the thickness of a child's hand, and buried quite deep near the base of the coals. The fire must not be too hot.

It required about half a morning or more to bake them. But when they were taken from the fire and clay, the scales would cling to the clay, so the fish were all ready to eat. And, oh, how delicious they were!

The manner of cooking partridges and ducks was a little different. After cleaning and dressing them, they were packed in clay and buried in the ashes head down, with rocks between them and the fire, so the feet would not burn off. When the feet, if jerked gently, would pull away, the fowl was done.

Mother had accepted the kind offer of Wa goosh to take us to the rice beds. So she made for Osh kin and me "rice moccasins." These were made to fit higher and snugger around the foot and ankle, to prevent the rice husks from getting in.

Finally we were ready to go. It was quite a job getting everything from the wigwam down to the lake shore, a job for us children.

It was decided that Mother and Wa goosh would first take all of the supplies in the canoe, heading towards the river, up the river, across the lake, up another river, and then into the rice bed.

They found the place where Mother wanted to camp and then came back for us. This took from sun to sun.

The first night we slept under the stars, for we had no time to make a wigwam before darkness fell. We thought this was a lot of fun.

With the first morning light Wa goosh took us two boys out to cut down about thirty long poles for the wigwam. We dragged them to the location of the camp. Min di, Mother, and Wa goosh set them up. Then Mother and Min di took the birch bark, which was light, and covered the poles. They tied the bark firmly around the poles so the wind could not easily blow it off.

Our next chore was to get wood for the fires. We gathered enough to last three or four days.

It was the dark of the moon, so Wa goosh suggested that Mother and he go on a fire hunt. This meant he would have to return to his home and get the canoe to be used for the hunt. It was smaller and would be much better for the rice beds too, for the smaller the canoe the less parting in the rice grains. Four could sit in it easily, but even six could ride.

Like all children we begged to go along, and finally Wa goosh consented. We had made little paddles of our own and were dying to use them. Running to get these, we came back and sat in the middle of the canoe and in our rather futile way helped to paddle.

Back over the lake we glided, then down the river into another lake, the waters of which were like glass. But it was beautiful, and we could see the reflection of the shoreline all around. It seemed that we actually skimmed over the water, it was so smooth.

At last we arrived at the lake near Wa goosh's home. He pulled the big canoe up on shore and covered it with twigs and boughs. He told us he wanted us to come up to meet his Mother and Father. This we did as well as snooping around his place. We discovered many interesting things and were astonished at the different kinds of tools he had. I decided with a workshop like this I could build a canoe as graceful as a swan—and sometime I would!

We came down again to the shore where Wa goosh uncovered the smaller canoe and pushed it into the water. The difference in size was as that of a mother swan and her young.

By this time the wind had risen and the lake was getting rough, as though the water manito were displeased. Min di and Wa goosh went to the shore.

"Maybe it won't be too bad," they said, "for the wind is blowing in the right direction to be in our backs."

As they came down to get in the canoe, Wa goosh had a box on a pole. It looked like a reflector. This he put in the canoe with us. Sister told us this was what he was going to use in his fire hunt.

Wa goosh and Min di were well trained at the paddles and so the water's roughness did not bother us. We crossed the lake in good time, then into the river again. While paddling along, Wa goosh told Sister that he would teach us how to make bows and arrows—and might one day take us out for a hunt.

When we got back to the wigwam, Mother's face was like storm cloud. She didn't like to have us always wanting to do everything Wa goosh planned. He was a man and we were still little fellows.

After our evening meal around the fire, Mother told Min di she wanted to relate a story about our father. This was in the Indian language, and Min di had to translate it to us in English. We were much excited. Mother started off:

"Your Father was a very brave hunter and a good provider. He knew the woods and lakes, and the habits of different animals. We made our canoe ready by placing a box like a reflector on a pole four feet long. This was placed in the bow of the canoe, so he could sight the game. A lantern was set in the boxlike structure throwing the light forward."

"He rowed over to the location where we might sight some deer, and then I took over the paddle. My task was to keep the canoe headed toward shore, so the light would attract the deer. Then he would be prepared to shoot when he saw the two fiery eyes."

"I guess I'm very good at this, for the least ripple from a paddle or the scraping of the paddle on the canoe would scare the animals and cause them to dart into the safety of the forest."

"Suddenly we heard a strange noise. It didn't sound like a deer or a large animal. I stopped paddling. Never had we heard anything like it, and Father turned his head quickly. Neither one of us spoke—just listened, wondering what it was."

"Finally Father motioned for me to pull closer to the shore. I obeyed, and as we advanced I saw that the object was a porcupine—probably just coming down to drink. Father and I looked at one another. We both knew that meeting a porcupine at night was not a good omen. Should we catch him or let him go? Finally Father whispered: 'Let's get him and put him in the canoe. I want to get some venison. We'll take a chance on our good luck.' "

"Your Father got out on the shore, seized a club and prepared to kill the porcupine. This accomplished, he loaded it into the canoe, and we continued paddling around looking for a deer."

"Before long we heard a splashing sound. Your Father looked at me. I shook my head and nodded. He pointed out the direction toward which I should paddle the canoe. As we approached I had to be very careful the light didn't move from side to side nor flicker. We both sat very still. He had put his paddle in the bottom of the canoe and was ready with his gun. Then we saw that it was a great moose."

As Mother talked, we children forgot all about what we were so eager to hear, about the trouble that had made Mother and Father forget the love that had once brought them together. We listened eagerly to know what would happen next in the story.

"I wondered why your father didn't shoot," continued Mother. "Then he whispered that he must get close enough to kill it with one shot, for the gun was loaded with buckshot."

"Finally we got close enough, and he took a shot at the moose and almost at the same instant put out the light. He thought at first he had killed the moose with one shot, but now we heard it coming our way. We realized we were in for a fight."

"I turned the canoe around quickly and headed it out to deeper water. But the beast, being wounded, made a lunge and came right out after us. He lashed the canoe to pieces, and we were both thrown into the lake. Luckily the beast didn't mangle us. We swam to shore while the moose turned to go back. But he bled to death before he could make it."

"We returned home, but the next day we borrowed a canoe and went back to where the moose had died. The lake was like glass and at the bottom of it we could see the gun, the sack of cartridges, and the lantern. We pulled the moose from the water and dressed him, then loaded him into the canoe. Father retrieved the gun and dried it out and as he looked at the shells, he saw that instead of buckshot the gun was loaded with fine shot, suitable for smaller game."

" 'No wonder we met the porcupine,' he said to me. 'We were not prepared with the right shot. Surely the Great Spirit was watching over us.' "

Mother stopped in her story to be sure that we understood if anything out of the ordinary ever happened, like meeting a porcupine, we must be sure to take warning.

Mother went on to tell how they got the meat home, but before she had finished, sleep had made our eyes heavy.

The next morning we awoke to see a deer strung up in a tree. It was then that Wa goosh told us how, in the dead of the night, he and Mother had gone out on the fire hunt. He had used his box, and when they got to the location, Mother kept the canoe pointed to shore, sliding along until the light attracted the deer. It was then Wa goosh had a chance to shoot. By good luck he had killed a big buck. Mother and he loaded it into the canoe and rowed it home. It was two o'clock in the morning by then, and before going to sleep they had been forced to skin it and dress it.

Later that day we built a fire out of doors. Over this we fashioned a rack to hang the rice kettles on. Higher over this was another rack on which the deer meat could be dried.

While Wa goosh was cutting the venison, Osh kin and I were very alert, watching him. We noticed how he cut it up into long strips, as thick as a good steak and as long as he could cut them. The smoke kept the flies away. These strips were hung over the poles to dry in the sun and to absorb the heat from the fire and sun. The meat shrank a lot. This worried me, because I thought it would become tough. But Mother explained:

"It will be good for your teeth, having to chew the food well. It will make your teeth stronger and you can use them longer."

N. Scott Momaday

(b. 1934) Kiowa

N. Scott Momaday was born at Lawton, Oklahoma, in 1934. The initial N in his name designates Natachee, his mother's given name. His father was Kiowa and his mother mixedblood Cherokee. His parents were teachers at several federal schools in native communities.

"My father's people are arrogant and set in their ways," Momaday wrote in **The Names***. "I like this in them, for it gives them a certain strength of character, a color and definition of their own. But it means that they are hard to suffer, too. This distemper of theirs was a very serious matter to my mother about the time of her marriage. She came warily among the Kiowas."*

Momaday, as a youth, lived at Jemez, New Mexico, the source of his formative memories as a writer.

> *I existed in that landscape, and then my existence was indivisible with it. I placed my shadow there in the hills, my voice in the wind that ran there, in those old mornings and afternoons and evenings. It may be that the old people there watch for me in the streets; it may be so.*

Momaday graduated from a private military academy, studied at the University of New Mexico, and earned his doctorate in literature at Stanford University in 1963. He has taught at several universities and is now at the University of Arizona. He is a member of the Kiowa Gourd Dance Society and a fellow of the American Academy of Arts and Sciences.

His first novel, **House Made of Dawn***, was published in 1968 and won the Pulitzer Prize. Overnight, this eloquent scholar and author of extraordinary vision and precision became a celebrated literary figure. The international recognition of a native author and the critical responses to a distinct but unconsidered literature have been an inspiration to hundreds of other native authors. "I have been called 'the man made of words,' a phrase that I myself coined some years ago in connection with a Kiowa folktale," he wrote in his recent collection of stories and poems* **In the Presence of the Sun***. "It is an identity that pleases me. In a sense, a real sense, my life has been composed of words."*

Momaday honored the memories and imagination of his grandmother in **The Way to Rainy Mountain** *published in 1969. Aho "lived out her long life in the shadow of Rainy Mountain, the immense landscape of the continental interior lay like memory in her blood. I wanted to see in reality what she had seen more perfectly in the mind's eye." His grandmother heard the oral stories of her ancestors on a migration that had lasted five centuries; she heard and imagined the landscape, the certain shadows of a native remembrance, and yet she had never been out of sight of Rainy Mountain, Oklahoma.*

*"***The Way to Rainy Mountain** *is a compelling work, but one most difficult to talk about, for at every turn it reaches beyond its powerfully felt and meticulously observed world and invites the reader to participate in what is ultimately a visionary experience beyond the reach of language," wrote Helen Jaskoski in* **Approaches to Teaching**

Momaday's "The Way to Rainy Mountain," *edited by Kenneth Roemer. The voices in the book search in the silence of creation. Some readers are not at ease in silence. "Sometimes I ask students in a class to close their eyes, put down anything they are holding, and quietly observe the darkness for two or three minutes before listening to a passage. Hearing in this posture makes a difference."*

His second novel continues a vision of ritual journeys and spiritual healing in his literature. **The Ancient Child** *was published in 1989. Grey, the main character,*

> *dreamed of sleeping with a bear. The bear drew her into its massive arms and licked her body and her hair. It hunched over her, curving its spine like a cat, until its huge body seemed to have absorbed her own. Its breath which bore a deep, guttural rhythm like language, touched her skin with low, persistent heat.*

Set is an orphan, separated from his native origins on the reservation, who returns with the spiritual power of his ancestors.

> *Set took the medicine bundle in his hands and opened it. The smell of it permeated the whole interior. When he drew on the great paw, there grew up in him a terrible restlessness, wholly urgent, and his heart began to race. He felt the power of the bear pervade his being, and the awful compulsion to release it.*

N. Scott Momaday published his memoir **The Names** *in 1976. He honors in his memoir that sense of presence in imagination and shows how the landscape is inherent and the names are remembered in native identities. His parents were teachers at federal schools and he lived most of his youth at Jemez, New Mexico.*

"At Jemez I came to the end of my childhood," he wrote.

> *In the seasons and among the people of the valley I was content. My spirit was quiet there. The silence was old, immediate, and pervasive, and there was great good in it. The wind of the canyons drew it out; the voices of the village carried and were lost in it. Much was made of the silence; much of the summer and winter was made of it.*

Momaday wrote in **The Names** *that children*

> *trust in language. They are open to the power and beauty of language, and here they differ from their elders, most of whom have come to imagine that they have found words out, and so much of magic is lost upon them. Creation says to the child: Believe in this tree, for it has a name....*

> *The names at first are those of animals and of birds, of objects that have one definition in the eye, another in the hand, of forms and features on the rim of the world, or of sounds that carry on the bright wind and in the void. They are old and original in the mind, like the beat of rain on the river, and intrinsic in the native tongue, failing even as those who bear them once in the memory, go on, and are gone forever.*

The Way to Rainy Mountain

A single knoll rises out of the plain in Oklahoma, north and west of the Wichita Range. For my people, the Kiowas, it is an old landmark, and they gave it the name Rainy Mountain. The hardest weather in the world is there. Winter brings blizzards, hot tornadic winds arise in the spring, and in summer the prairie is an anvil's edge. The grass turns brittle and brown, and it cracks beneath your feet. There are green belts along the rivers and creeks, linear groves of hickory and pecan, willow and witch hazel. At a distance in July or August the steaming foliage seems almost to writhe in fire. Great green and yellow grasshoppers are everywhere in the tall grass, popping up like corn to sting the flesh, and tortoises crawl about on the red earth, going nowhere in the plenty of time. It is an aspect of the land. All in the plain are isolated; there is no confusion of objects in the eye, but one hill or one tree or one man. To look upon that landscape in the early morning, with the sun at your back, is to lose the sense of proportion. Your imagination comes to life, and this, you think, is where Creation was begun.

I returned to Rainy Mountain in July. My grandmother had died in the spring, and I wanted to be at her grave. She had lived to be very old and at last infirm. Her only living daughter was with her when she died, and I was told that in death her face was that of a child.

I like to think of her as a child. When she was born, the Kiowas were living the last great moment of their history. For more than a hundred years they had controlled the open range from the Smoky Hill River to the Red, from the headwaters of the Canadian to the fork of the Arkansas and Cimarron. In alliance with the Comanches, they had ruled the whole of the southern Plains. War was their sacred business, and they were among the finest horsemen the world has ever known. But warfare for the Kiowas was preeminently a matter of disposition rather than of survival, and they never understood the grim, unrelenting advance of the U.S. Cavalry. When at last, divided and ill-provisioned, they were driven onto the Staked Plains in the cold rains of autumn, they fell into panic. In Palo Duro Canyon they abandoned their crucial stores to pillage and had nothing then but their lives. In order to save themselves, they surrendered to the soldiers at Fort Sill and were imprisoned in the old stone corral that now stands as a military museum. My grandmother was spared the humiliation of those high gray walls by eight or ten years, but she must have known from birth the affliction of defeat, the dark brooding of old warriors.

Her name was Aho, and she belonged to the last culture to evolve in North America. Her forebears came down from the high country in western Montana nearly three centuries ago. They were a mountain people, a mysterious tribe of hunters whose language has never been positively classified in any major group. In the late seventeenth century they began a long migration to the south and east. It was a journey toward the dawn, and it led to a golden age. Along the way the Kiowas were befriended by the Crows, who gave them the culture and religion of the Plains. They acquired horses, and their ancient nomadic spirit was suddenly free of the ground. They acquired Tai-me the sacred Sun Dance doll, from that moment the object and symbol of their worship, and shared in the divinity of the sun. Not least, they acquired the sense of destiny, therefore courage and pride. When they entered upon the southern Plains they had been transformed. No longer were they slaves to the simple necessity of survival; they were a lordly and dangerous society of fighters and thieves, hunters and priests of the sun. According to their origin myth, they entered the world through a hollow log. From one point of view, their migration was the fruit of an old prophecy, for indeed they emerged from a sunless world.

Although my grandmother lived out her long life in the shadow of Rainy Mountain, the immense landscape of the continental interior lay like memory in her blood. She could tell of the Crows, whom she had never seen, and of the Black Hills, where she had never been. I wanted to see in reality what she had seen more perfectly in the mind's eye, and traveled fifteen hundred miles to begin my pilgrimage.

Yellowstone, it seemed to me, was the top of the world, a region of deep lakes and dark timber, canyons and waterfalls But, beautiful as it is, one might have the sense of confinement here. The sky line in all directions is close at hand, the woods and deep cleavages of shade. There is a perfect freedom in the mountains, but it belongs to the eagle and the elk, the badger and the bear. The Kiowas reckoned their stature by the distance they could see, and they were bent and blind in the wilderness.

Descending eastward, the highland meadows are a stairway to the plain. In July the inland slope of the Rockies is luxuriant with flax and buckwheat, stonecrop and larkspur. The earth unfolds and the limit of the land recedes. Clusters of trees, and animals grazing far in the distance, cause the vision to reach away and wonder to build upon the mind. The sun follows a longer course in the day, and the sky is immense beyond all comparison. The great billowing clouds that sail upon it are shadows that move upon the grain like water, dividing light. Farther down, in the land of the Crows and Blackfeet, the plain is yellow. Sweet clover takes hold of the hills and bends upon itself to cover and seal the soil. There the Kiowas paused on their way; they had come to the place where they must change their lives. The sun is at home on the plains. Precisely there does it have the certain character of a god. When the Kiowas came to the land of the Crows, they could see the dark of light on the grain shelves, the oldest deity ranging after the solstices. Not yet would they veer southward to the caldron of the land that lay below; they must wean their blood from the northern winter and hold the mountains a while longer in their view. They bore Tai-me in procession to the east.

A dark mist lay over the Black Hills, and the land was like iron. At the top of a ridge I caught sight of Devil's Tower upthrust against the gray sky as if in the birth of time the core of the earth had broken through its crust and time and motion of the world was begun. There are things in nature that engender an awful quiet in the heart of man; Devil's Tower is one of them. Two centuries ago, because they could not do otherwise, the Kiowas made a legend at the base of the rock. My grandmother said: *Eight children were there at play, seven sisters and their brother. Suddenly the boy was struck dumb; he trembled and began to run upon his hands and feet. His fingers became claws, and his body was covered with fur. Directly there was a bear where the boy had been. The sisters were terrified; they ran, and the bear after them. They came to the stump of a great tree, and the tree spoke to them. It bade them climb upon it, and as they did so it began to rise into the air. The bear came to kill them, but they were just beyond its reach. It reared against the tree and scored the bark all around with its claws. The seven sisters were borne into the sky, and they became the stars of the Big Dipper.*

From that moment, and so long as the legend lives, the Kiowas have kinsmen in the night sky. Whatever they were in the mountains, they could be no more. However tenuous their well being, however much they had suffered and would suffer again, they had found a way out of the wilderness.

My grandmother had a reverence for the sun, a holy regard that now is all but gone out of mankind. There was a wariness in her, and an ancient awe. She was a Christian in her later years, but she had come a long way about, and she never forgot her birthright. As a child she had been to the Sun Dances; she had taken part in those annual rites, and by then she had learned the restoration of her people in the presence of Tai-me. She was about seven when the last Kiowa Sun Dance was held in 1887 on the Washita River above Rainy Mountain Creek. The buffalo were gone. In order to consummate the ancient sacrifice—to impale the head of a buffalo bull upon the medicine tree—a delegation of old men journeyed into Texas, there to beg and barter for an animal from the Goodnight herd. She was ten when the Kiowas came together for the last time as a living sun dance culture. They could find no buffalo; they had to hang an old hide from the sacred tree. Before the dance could begin, a company of soldiers rode out from Fort Sill under orders to disperse the tribe. Forbidden without cause the essential act of their faith, having seen the wild herds slaughtered and left to rot upon the ground, the Kiowas backed away forever from the medicine tree. That was July 20, 1890, at the great bend of the Washita. My grandmother was there. Without bitterness, and for as long as she lived, she bore a vision of deicide.

Now that I can have her only in memory, I see my grandmother in the several postures that were peculiar to her: standing at the wood stove on a winter morning and turning meat in a great iron skillet; sitting at the south window, bent above her beadwork, and afterwards, when her vision failed, looking down for a long time into the fold of her hands; going out upon a cane, very slowly as she did when the weight of age came upon her; praying. I remember her most often at prayer. She made long, rambling prayers out of suffering and hope, having seen many things. I was never sure that I had the right to hear, so exclusive were they of all mere custom and company. The last time I saw her she prayed standing by the side of her bed at night, naked to the waist, the light of a kerosene lamp moving upon her dark skin. Her long, black hair, always drawn and braided in the day, lay upon her shoulders and against her breasts like a shawl. I do not speak Kiowa, and I never understood her prayers, but there was something inherently sad in the sound, some merest hesitation upon the syllables of sorrow. She began in a high and descending pitch, exhausting her breath to silence; then again and again—and always the same intensity of effort, of something that is, and is not, like urgency in the human voice. Transported so in the dancing light among the shadows of her room, she seemed beyond the reach of time. But that was illusion; I think I knew then that I should not see her again.

Houses are like sentinels in the plain, old keepers of the weather watch. There, in a very little while, wood takes on the appearance of great age. All colors wear soon away in the wind and rain, and then the wood is burned gray and the grain appears and the nails turn red with rust. The windowpanes are black and opaque; you imagine there is nothing within, and indeed there are many ghosts, bones given up to the land. They stand here and there against the sky, and you approach them for a longer time than you expect. They belong in the distance; it is their domain.

Once there was a lot of sound in my grandmother's house, a lot of coming and going, feasting and talk. The summers time were full of excitement and reunion. The Kiowas are a summer people; they abide the cold and keep to themselves, but when the season turns and the land becomes warm and vital they cannot hold still; an old hove of going returns upon them. The aged visitors who came to my grandmother's house when I was a child were made of lean and leather, and they bore themselves upright. They wore great black hats and bright ample shirts that shook in the wind. They rubbed fat upon their hair and wound their braids with strips of colored cloth. Some of them painted their faces and carried the sears of old and cherished enmities. They were an old council of warlords, come to remind and be reminded of who they were. Their wives and daughters served them well. The women might indulge themselves; gossip was at once the lie mark and compensation of their servitude. They made loud and elaborate talk among themselves full of jest and gesture, fright and false alarm. They went abroad in fringed and flowered shawls, bright beadwork and German silver. They were at home in the kitchen, and they prepared meals that were banquets.

There were frequent prayer meetings, and great nocturnal feasts. When I was a child I played with my cousins outside, where the lamplight fell upon the ground and the singing of the old people rose up around us and carried away into the darkness. There were a lot of good things to eat, a lot of laughter and surprise. And afterwards, when the quiet returned, I lay down with my grandmother and could hear the frogs away by the river and feel the motion of the air.

Now there is a funeral silence in the rooms, the endless wake of some final word. The walls have closed in upon my grandmother's house. When I returned to it in mourning, I saw for the first time in my life how small it was. It was late at night, and there was a white moon, nearly full. I sat for a long time on the stone steps by the kitchen door. From there I could see out across the land; I could see the long row of trees by the creek, the low light upon the rolling plains, and the stars of the Big Dipper. Once I looked at that moon and caught sight of a strange thing. A cricket had perched upon the handrail, only a few inches away from me. My line of vision was such that the creature filled the moon like a fossil. It had gone there, I thought, to live and die, for there, of all places, was its small definition made whole and eternal. A warm wind rose up and purled like the longing within me.

The next morning I awoke at dawn and went out on the dirt road to Rainy Mountain. It was already hot, and the grasshoppers began to fill the air. Still, it was early in the morning, and the birds sang out of the shadows. The long yellow grass on the mountain shone in the bright light, and a scissortail hid above the land. There, where it ought to be, at the end of a long and legendary way, was my grandmother's grave. Here and there on the dark stones were ancestral names. Looking back once, I saw the mountain and came away.

The Names

There was at Jemez a climate of the mind in which we, my parents and I, realized ourselves, understood who we were, not perfectly, it may be, but well enough. It was not our native world, but we appropriated it, as it were, to ourselves; we invested much of our lives in it, and in the end it was the remembered place of our hopes, our dreams, and our deep love.

My father looked after the endless paper work that came down from the many levels of the Bureau of Indian Affairs. In innumerable ways he worked with the people of the village and was their principal contact with the Government of the United States. When a boy or girl wanted to apply for admission to the Santa Fe Indian School or the Albuquerque Indian School, or when a man wanted to find work, or a woman to use the telephone to talk to her daughter in California, it was to my father that the petition was made. But first of all he was the man of the family. It was he who got up before daylight and went out to get wood and coal for the fires on winter mornings; it was he who dealt with the emergencies, great and small, of those years: and it was he who taught me such responsibilities as I learned then. One of these was to myself, and it was to dream. On winter evenings before the fire, or on summer nights on the porch, our home of Jemez was a place to dream, and my father dreamed much of his youth. He told me the stories of the coming-out people, of Mammedaty and of Guipagho, of Saynday, who wandered around and around. And very softly, as to himself, he sang the old Kiowa songs. And in all he went on with his real work, the making of paintings. He saw wonderful things, and he painted them well.

My mother has been the inspiration of many people. Certainly she has been mine, and certainly she was mine at Jemez, when inspiration was the nourishment I needed most. I was at that age in which a boy flounders. I had not much sense of where I must go or of what I must do and be in my life, and there were for me moments of great, growing urgency, in which I felt that I was imprisoned in the narrow quarters of my time and place. I wanted, needed to conceive of what my destiny might be, and my mother allowed me to believe that it might be worthwhile. We were so close, she and I, when I was growing up that even now I cannot express the feelings between us. I have great faith in words, but in this there are no words at last; there is only a kind of perfect silence—the stillness of a late autumn afternoon in the village and the valley—in which I listen for the sound of her voice. In a moment she will speak to me; she will speak my name.

One day my mother burned her hand. In a way it was my fault, for I had got in her way when she was carrying a hot pan to the table. It was a strange moment. She made a little cry, and I looked to see what was the matter. I stepped out of the way at once, but her hand was already burned. My mother said nothing about it—that was what seemed strange to me—but I had seen the pain in her face.

Many times she called me to the kitchen window to see something of interest—horses running on the road, a hen with new chicks in the Tosa's garden, a storm gathering in San Diego Canyon, a sunset. At night we talked about innumerable things at the kitchen table, the innumerable things of our world and of our time. We laughed often together, and we saw eye to eye on the larger issues of our lives. The words we had were the right ones; we were easy and right with each other, as it happened, natural, full of love and trust. "Look," one of us would say to the other, "here is something new, something that we have not seen together." And we would simply take delight in it.

In the seasons and among the people of the valley I was content. My spirit was quiet there. The silence was old, immediate, and pervasive, and there was great good in it. The wind of the canyons drew it out; the voices of the village carried and were lost in it. Much was made of the silence; much of the summer and winter was made of it.

At Jemez I came to the end of my childhood. There were no schools within easy reach. I had to go nearly thirty miles to school at Bernalillo, and one year I lived away in Albuquerque. My mother and father wanted me to have the benefit of a sound preparation for college, and so we read through many high school catalogues. After long deliberation we decided that I should spend my last year of high school at a military academy in Virginia.

The day before I was to leave I went walking across the river to the red mesa, where many times before I had gone to be alone with my thoughts. And I had climbed several times to the top of the mesa and looked among the old ruins there for pottery. This time I chose to climb the north end, perhaps because I had not gone that way before and wanted to see what it was. It was a difficult climb, and when I got to the top I was spent. I lingered among the ruins for more than an hour, I judge, waiting for my strength to return. From there I could see the whole valley below, the fields, the river, and the village. It was all very beautiful, and the sight of it filled me with longing.

I looked for an easier way to come down, and at length I found a broad, smooth runway of rock, a shallow groove winding out like a stream. It appeared to be safe enough, and I started to follow it. There were steps along the way, a stairway, in effect. But the steps became deeper and deeper, and at last I had to drop down the length of my body and more. Still it seemed convenient to follow in the groove of rock. I was more than halfway down when I came upon a deep, funnel-shaped formation in my path. And there I had to make a decision. The slope on either side was extremely steep and forbidding. And yet I thought that I could work my way down on either side. The formation at my feet was something else. It was perhaps ten or twelve feet deep, wide at the top and narrow at the bottom, where there appeared to be a level ledge. If I could get down through the funnel to the ledge, I should be all right; surely the rest of the way down was negotiable. But I realized that there could be no turning back. Once I was down in that rocky chute I could not get up again, for the round wall which nearly encircled the space there was too high and sheer. I elected to go down into it, to try for the ledge directly below. I eased myself down the smooth, nearly vertical wall on my back, pressing my arms and legs outward against the sides. After what seemed a long time I was trapped in the rock. The ledge was no longer there below me: it had been an optical illusion. Now, in this angle of vision, there was nothing but the ground, far, far below, and jagged boulders set there like teeth. I remember that my arms were scraped and bleeding, stretched out against the walls with all the pressure that I could exert. When once I looked down I saw that my legs, also spread out and pressed hard against the walls, were shaking violently. I was in an impossible situation: I could not move in any direction save downward in a fall, and I could not stay beyond another minute where I was. I believed then that I would die there, and I saw with a terrible clarity the things of the valley below. They were not the less beautiful to me. It seemed to me that I grew suddenly very calm in view of that beloved world. And I remember nothing else of that moment. I passed out of my mind, and the next thing I knew I was sitting down on the ground, very cold in the shadows, and looking up at the rock where I had been within an eyelash of eternity. That was a strange thing in my life, and I think of it as the end of an age. I should never again see the world as I saw it on the other side of that moment, in the bright reflection of time lost. There are such reflections, and for some of them I have the names.

Gerald Vizenor

(b. 1934) Anishinaabe

Gerald Vizenor was born in Minneapolis, Minnesota, in 1934. His father was from the White Earth Reservation, and his mother, the granddaughter of immigrants, was from the city. When his father was murdered he lived with his grandmother in a crowded tenement in Minneapolis. Later his mother placed him in foster homes. He served in the military in Japan, where he was inspired by haiku poetry and the similarities of haiku to native dream songs.

"The woodland dream songs and trickster stories that would bear the humor and tragic wisdom of tribal native experiences were superseded in the literature of dominance," he wrote in "The Envoy to Haiku," an autobiographical essay published in the **Chicago Review**. "The Anishinaabe, my ancestors of the woodland, were named the Chippewa. The oral stories and dream songs of the tribes were translated and compared as cultural evidence; scarcely with wisdom, humor, or eminence."

He is the author of five books of haiku and several studies of dream songs and stories of the Anishinaabe. **Summer in the Spring: Anishinaabe Lyric Poems and Stories** was published in 1993. "The presence of haiku, more than other literature, touched my imagination and brought me closer to a sense of tribal consciousness," he wrote.

Vizenor studied at New York University and the University of Minnesota. He is professor of Native American literature at the University of California, Berkeley. He has published narrative histories, critical studies of literature, and five novels. **The People Named the Chippewa** was published in 1984. **Manifest Manners**, a collection of essays, and **Shadow Distance: A Gerald Vizenor Reader**, were published in 1994. His first novel, **Bearheart: The Heirship Chronicles**, was published in 1978. **Griever: An American Monkey King in China** won the American Book Award in 1988.

Interior Landscapes: Autobiographical Myths and Metaphors was published in 1990. LaVonne Ruoff noted in **American Indian Literatures** that "by turns poignant, sprightly, and satiric," the author writes about his ancestry and

> his uneasy relationship with his mother; and his eventual love of his stern stepfather, whom his mother abandoned and who died shortly thereafter in an accident at work. In the third grade, Vizenor began to escape into the world of his imaginative trickster friend Erdupps McChurbbs, where dreams became stories and tricksters raised him in imagination. The motif of the personal and tribal trickster runs through the book as it does Vizenor's other words.

His autobiography begins with the native creation of the earth, presents his ancestors and families in the fur trade and on the reservation, and then displays his own crossblood presence in stories. He celebrates the native inheritance of natural reason, chance, imagination, and the crane, one of the original five totems of the Anishinaabe. Tribal tricksters created the earth in stories, he asserts, and the stories of native creation are heard in the myths, metaphors, and ideas of each generation.

"Clement William Vizenor, my father, was a crane descendant," he wrote in **Interior Landscapes**.

> *He was born on the reservation and murdered twenty-six years later on a narrow street in Minneapolis. My tribal grandmother and my father were related to the leaders of the crane; that succession, over a wild background of cedar and concrete, shamans and colonial assassins, is celebrated here in the autobiographical myths and metaphors of my imagination, my crossblood remembrance. We are cranes on the rise in new tribal narratives.*
>
> *My father died in a place no crane would choose to dance, at a time no tribal totem would endure. One generation later the soul of the crane recurs in imagination; our reversion, our interior landscapes.*

Measuring My Blood

Alice Beaulieu, my grandmother, told me that my father was a tribal trickster with words and memories; a compassionate trickster who did not heed the sinister stories about stolen souls and the evil gambler. Clement William must have misremembered that tribal web of protection when he moved to the cities from the White Earth Reservation.

Nookomis, which means grandmother, warned her trickster grandson that the distant land he intended to visit, in search of his mother who had been stolen by a wind spirit, was infested with hideous humans, "evil spirits and the follower of those who eat human flesh." Naanabozho was the first tribal trickster on the earth. He was comic, a part of the natural world, a spiritual balance in a comic drama, and so he must continue in his stories. "No one who has ever been within their power has ever been known to return," she told her grandson. "First these evil spirits charm their victims by the sweetness of their songs, then they strangle and devour them. But your principal enemy will be the great gambler who has never been beaten in his game and who lives beyond the realm of darkness." The trickster did not heed the words of his grandmother.

Naanabozho paddled by canoe to the end of the woodland and took a path through the swamps and over high mountains and by deep chasms in the earth where he saw the hideous stare of a thousand gleaming eyes. He heard groans and hisses of countless fiends gloating over their many victims of sin and shame. The trickster knew that this was the place where the great gambler had abandoned the losers, the spirits of his victims who had lost the game.

The trickster raised the mat of scalps over the narrow entrance to the wiigiwaam. The evil gambler was inside, a curious being, a person who seemed almost round; he was smooth, white, and wicked.

"So, Naanabozho, you too have come to try your luck," said the great gambler. His voice was horrible, the sound of scorn and ridicule. Round and white, he shivered. "All those hands you see hanging around the wiigiwaam are the hands of your relatives who came to gamble. They thought as you are thinking, they played and lost their lives in the game. Remember, I demand that those who gamble with me and lose, give me their lives. I keep the scalps, the ears, and the hands of the losers; the rest of the body I give to my friends the wiindigoo, the flesh eaters, and the spirits I consign to the world of darkness. I have spoken, and now we will play the game."

Clement William Vizenor lost the game with the evil gambler and did not return from the cities. He was a house painter who told trickster stories, pursued women, and laughed most of his time on earth. He was murdered on a narrow street in downtown Minneapolis.

"Giant Hunted in Murder and Robbery Case," appeared as a headline on the front page of the *Minneapolis Journal,* June 30, 1936. The report continued: "Police sought a giant Negro today to compare his fingerprints with those of the rifled purse of Clement Vizenor, 26 years old, found slain yesterday with his head nearly cut off by an eight-inch throat slash.

"Vizenor, an interior decorator living at 320 Tenth Street South, had been beaten and killed in an alley.... He was the second member of his family to die under mysterious circumstances within a month. His brother, Turban Vizenor, 649 Seventeenth Avenue Northeast, was found in the Mississippi river June 1, after he had fallen from a railroad bridge and struck his head.

"Yesterday's slashing victim, who was part Indian, had been employed by John Hartung, a decorator. One pocket had been ripped out of the slain man's trousers. His purse lay empty beside him. Marks in the alley showed his body had been dragged several feet from the alley alongside a building."

The *Minneapolis Tribune* reported that the arrest of a "Negro in Chicago promised to give Minneapolis police a valuable clue to the murder of Clement Vizenor, 26-year-old half-breed Indian, who was stabbed to death in an alley near Washington Avenue and Fourth street early June 27. Vizenor's slaying was unsolved." The murder was never solved, and no motive was ever established. Racial violence was indicated in most of the newspaper stories, but there was no evidence in the investigations that race was a factor in the murder. My father could have been a victim of organized crime. There was no evidence of a struggle; he had not been robbed; the police would not establish a motive for the crime. There were several unsolved homicides at that time in Minneapolis.

The picture of my father published in the newspaper was severed from a photograph that shows him holding me in his arms. This is the last photograph, taken a few weeks before his death, that shows us together. Clement wore a fedora and a suit coat; he has a wide smile. We are outside, there is a tenement in the background; closer, a heap of used bricks. I must remember that moment, my grandmother with the camera, our last pose together.

The *Minneapolis Tribune* reported later that the police had "arrested a half-breed Indian in a beer parlor near Seventh Avenue South and Tenth Street and are holding him without charge for questioning in connection with the slaying, early Sunday, of Clement Vizenor.... The man who, according to police, was drunk, was picked up after making statements that indicated he might know who Vizenor's assailant was. He is alleged to have claimed knowledge of who Vizenor's friends were, and of many of the murdered man's recent activities. The murder was blamed by police upon any one of a growing number of drunken toughs roaming the Gateway district almost nightly, armed with knives and razors.

The killing of Vizenor climaxes a series of violent assaults upon Gateway pedestrians in recent weeks by robbers who either slugged or slashed their victims."

In another report, the police "sought the husband of a former New York showgirl for questioning in connection with the knife murder of Clement Vizenor. The man sought is believed to be the same who left with Vizenor from a cafe at 400 Tenth Street South about five hours before the murder. Alice Finkenhagen, waitress at the Tenth Street cafe, gave police a good description of the man who called Vizenor to come outside. Detectives partially identified the showgirl's husband as that man. Also they learned this man had resented Vizenor's attentions to his showgirl wife.

"Vizenor was called from the cafe at about 12:30 a.m. Sunday. Later he appeared at his home, then left again. His body was found at 5:30 a.m., his throat slashed, in an alley near Washington and Fifth Avenues South. Police also were holding three half-breed Indians for questioning in the case. Vizenor was a half-breed."

The report continues: "A former New York showgirl and her husband were released by Minneapolis police Thursday after questioning failed to implicate them as suspects in the knife murder.... Police learned that Vizenor's attentions to the showgirl had been resented by her husband. But that difference was amicably settled long ago, detectives found out."

The *Minneapolis Tribune* reported later that "Captain Paradeau said he was convinced Clement had been murdered but that robbery was not the motive. The slain youth was reported to have been mild tempered and not in the habit of picking fights. Police learned he had no debts and, as far as they could ascertain, no enemies."

THE LAST PHOTOGRAPH
clement vizenor would be a spruce
on his wise return to the trees
corded on the reservation side
he overturned the line
colonial genealogies
white earth remembrance
removed to the cities at twenty three

my father lived on stories
over the rough rims on mason jars
danced with the wounded shaman
low over the stumps on the fourth of july

my father lied to be an indian
he laughed downtown
the trickster signature to the lights

clement honored tribal men at war
uniforms undone
shadows on the dark river
under the nicollet avenue bridge

tribal men burdened with civilization
epaulets adrift
ribbons and wooden limbs
return to the evangelists
charities on time

catholics on the western wire
threw their voices
treaties tied to catechisms
undone in the woodland

reservation heirs on the concrete
praise the birch
the last words of indian agents
undone at the bar

clement posed in a crowded tenement
the new immigrant
painted new houses pure white
outback in saint louis park
our rooms were leaded and cold
new tribal provenance
histories too wild in the brick
shoes too narrow

clement and women
measured my blood at night

my father holds
me in the last photograph
the new spruce
with a wide smile
half white
half immigrant
he took up the cities and lost at cards

Clement Vizenor was survived by his mother, Alice Beaulieu; his wife, LaVerne
Peterson; three brothers, Joseph, Lawrence, and Everett; two sisters, Ruby and Lorraine;
and his son, Gerald Robert Vizenor, one year and eight months old. When my father
was murdered, I was living with my grandmother, aunts, and uncles in a tenement at
320 Tenth Street South in Minneapolis.

Twenty-five years later I met with Minneapolis police officials to review the
records of their investigation. I was, that summer, the same age as my father when he
was murdered.

There was some resistance, some concern that my intentions were not personal
but political; the police must be defensive about crimes they have never solved. A thin
folder was recovered from the archives. The chief of detectives was surprised when
he examined the file; he saw his name on a report and remembered that he was the
first officer called to investigate the crime. He explained that he was a new police
officer then and defended his trivial report. "We never spent much time on winos and
derelicts in those days.... Who knows, one Indian vagrant kills another."

"Clement Vizenor is my father."

"Maybe your father was a wino then," he said, and looked to his watch. "Look
kid, that was a long time ago. Take it on the chin, you know what I mean?"

I knew what he meant and closed the investigation on an unsolved homicide. The detective must have been the same person who told my mother to move out of town and forget what had happened. She tried to forget and left me with my grandmother in the tenement. Later, my mother placed me in several foster homes.

I hear my father in that photograph and imagine his touch, the turn of his hand on my shoulder, his warm breath on my cheek, his word trickeries, and my grandmother behind the camera. My earliest personal memories are associated with my grandmother and my bottle. She would hide my bottle to wean me in the trickster manner because, she said later, I carried that bottle around all day clenched between my front teeth. She reconsidered the trickster method, however, when I learned the same game and started to hide her bottles of whiskey. She might have forgotten where she placed the bottles, mine and hers, and then told stories, compassionate reunions of our past. I remember the moment, the bottles, and the stories, but not the camera. My father and that photograph hold me in a severed moment, hold me to a season, a tenement, more than we would remember over the dark river.

Alice Beaulieu continued her career in a tenement, poor but never lonesome. She was in her sixties when she married a blind man in his forties. I was eighteen, home on leave from the military at the time, and proud to wear my new uniform to a reception. My grandmother was in the kitchen, in the arms of her new husband. "He's a lusty devil," she whispered to me, "and he thinks I'm beautiful, so don't you dare tell him any different." She was a lover, favored in imagination, and she was plump and gorgeous that afternoon.

Alice and Earl Restdorf lived in a narrow dark apartment on LaSalle Avenue near Loring Park. Earl was pale, generous, and sudden with his humor. He repaired radios, a sacrament to sound, and collected radios that needed repair. Cabinets, chassis, tubes, and superheterodynes were stacked at the end of the small dining room. My grandmother would sit on the side of a double bed, because she had never had a secured, private bedroom in the tenement, and chew snuff when she was older. Earl did not approve of her tobacco habits. Alice stashed soup cans in secret places to catch her brown spit; she pretended that her husband could not smell the snuff or hear the juice. He smiled, folded in a chair near his radios.

My grandmother paid my son a dollar each time we visited to hold her pinches of snuff a secret. Robert was two and three years old when he learned the pleasures of secrets. She loved to tease and praise children, her grandchildren and great-grandchildren, and when she laughed on the side of the bed her cheeks bounced and her stomach leapt under the worn patch pockets on her plain print dresses. Alice Beaulieu was gorgeous. Robert has never told a soul about her juice cans at the side of the bed.

Maria Campbell

(b. 1940) Cree

Maria Campbell was born "during a spring blizzard" in northern Saskatchewan in 1940. She was born a "halfbreed," a descendant of poor "road allowance" families who had been denied native rights. Native women who married white men, at that time, lost their treaty rights and land in Canada.

Campbell endured the separation of native communities, and the denials and desperation of mixedblood or Métis identities. She was sustained in spirit and humor by the natural reason and "gift of second sight" of her great-grandmother Cheechum. She was "my very best friend and confidante." Cheechum smoked a clay pipe, and refused to sleep on a bed or eat at a table.

Halfbreed was first published in Canada when Maria was thirty-three years old. "I write this for all of you, to tell you what it is like to be a Halfbreed woman in our country," she wrote in the introduction. "I want to tell you about the joys and sorrows, the oppressing poverty, the frustration and the dreams.... I hurt because in my childhood I saw glimpses of a proud and happy people. I heard their laughter, saw their dance, and felt their love."

Cheechum was a hundred and four years old when she died in an accident. "She waited all her life for a new generation of people who would make this country a better place to live in," Maria wrote at the end of **Halfbreed**. "I have brothers and sisters, all over the country, I no longer need my blanket to survive."

Campbell, the activist, collaborated with Linda Griffiths, the playwright, in the play **Jessica**. They published a narrative of their work together in **The Book of Jessica: A Theatrical Transformation**. The play, inspired by the autobiography but not an adaptation of **Halfbreed**, opened at the Theatre Passe Muraille in Toronto in 1986. The book was published three years later.

"Halfbreed people flirt a lot, not like they want to come on to you, but like there's so much in the world to be happy about," Maria wrote in **The Book of Jessica**. Maria is not bitter or burdened with racialism. The activist and author flirts in native communities and in her persuasive autobiography.

Campbell does not think of herself as a writer "bumping around all over reading and talking about 'great literature.'... My work is in the community," she said in an interview published in **Contemporary Challenges**. "I get quite embarrassed when I have to speak from the point of view of a writer, because I really don't know what that is."

Kate Vangen wrote in her essay in **The Native in Literature** that the

> world the half-breed inhabits is the same world in which Euro-Canadians live; yet, the frustrations and heart-breaks they experience, even today, arise from the invisibility which is culturally and legally imposed upon them. By owning the term 'half-breed' and defiantly claiming its full history and sprinkling it with a good measure of humor, Campbell becomes one of the leaders of her people who Cheechum predicted would one day come.

Agnes Grant pointed out in "Contemporary Native Women's Voices in Literature," published in **Canadian Literature**, that the recurrent "allusions to love, peace, beauty, and *happiness indicate that Métis are not hopelessly caught between two cultures. But Maria's life is devoid of this warmth and sense of belonging as she leaves home. She is manipulated by people who are strangers to her and her way of life.*

The original handwritten manuscript was more than two thousand pages long. One section of the book was removed because it was incriminating, at the time, to the Royal Canadian Mounted Police. Maria said she would rewrite **Halfbreed**, *but "I don't think I'd make changes. What I would do with the book is, I would only put in that piece that was taken out."*

The Little People

I was born during a spring blizzard in April of 1940. Grannie Campbell, who had come to help my mother, made Dad stay outside the tent, and he chopped wood until his arms ached. At last I arrived, a daughter, much to Dad's disappointment. However this didn't dampen his desire to raise the best trapper and hunter in Saskatchewan. As far back as I can remember Daddy taught me to set traps, shoot a rifle, and fight like a boy. Mom did her best to turn me into a lady, showing me how to cook, sew and knit, while Cheechum, my best friend and confidante, tried to teach me all she knew about living.

I should tell you about our home now before I go any further. We lived in a large two-roomed hewed log house that stood out from the others because it was too big to be called a shack. One room was used for sleeping and all of us children shared it with our parents. There were three big beds made from poles with rawhide interlacing. The mattresses were canvas bags filled with fresh hay twice a year. Over my parents' bed was a hammock where you could always find a baby. An air-tight heater warmed the room in winter. Our clothes hung from pegs or were folded and put on a row of shelves. There were braided rugs on the floor, and in one corner a special sleeping rug where Cheechum slept when she stayed with us, as she refused to sleep on a bed or eat off a table.

I loved that corner of the house and would find any excuse possible to sleep with her. There was a special smell that comforted me when I was hurt or afraid. Also, it was a great place to find all sorts of wonderful things that Cheechum had—little pouches, boxes, and cloth tied up containing pieces of bright cloth, beads, leather, jewelry, roots and herbs, candy, and whatever else a little girl's heart could desire.

The kitchen and living room were combined into one of the most beautiful rooms I have ever known. Our kitchen had a huge black wood stove for cooking and for heating the house. On the wall hung pots, pans, and various roots and herbs used for cooking and making medicine. There was a large table, two chairs and two benches made from wide planks, which we scrubbed with homemade lye soap after each meal.

On one wall were shelves for our good dishes and a cupboard for storing everyday tin plates, cups, and food.

The living-room area had a homemade chesterfield and chair of carved wood and woven rawhide, a couple of rocking chairs painted red, and an old steamer trunk by the east window. The floor was made of wide planks which were scoured to an even whiteness all over. We made braided rugs during the winter months from old rags, although it often took us a full year to gather enough for even a small rug.

There were open beams on the ceiling and under these ran four long poles the length of the house. The poles served as racks where furs were hung to dry in winter. On a cold winter night the smell of moose stew simmering on the stove blended with the wild smell of the drying skins of mink, weasels, and squirrels, and the spicy herbs and roots hanging from the walls. Daddy would be busy in the corner, brushing fur until it shone and glistened, while Mom bustled around the stove. Cheechum would be on the floor smoking her clay pipe and the small ones would roll and fight around her like puppies. I can see it all so vividly it seems only yesterday.

Our parents spent a great deal of time with us, and not just our parents but the other parents in our settlement. They taught us to dance and to make music on the guitars and fiddles. They played cards with us, they would take us on long walks and teach us how to use the different herbs, roots, and barks. We were taught to weave baskets from the red willow, and while we did these things together we were told the stories of our people—who they were, where they came from, and what they had done. Many were legends handed down from father to son. Many of them had a lesson but mostly they were fun stories about funny people.

My Cheechum believed with heart and soul in the little people. She said they are so tiny that unless you are really looking for them you will never find them; not that it matters, because you usually only see them when they want you to.

The little people live near the water and they travel mostly by leaf boats. They are a happy lot and also very shy. Cheechum saw them once when she was a young woman. She had gone to the river for water in the late afternoon and decided to sit and watch the sun go down. It was very quiet and even the birds were still. Then she heard a sound like many people laughing and talking at a party. The sounds kept coming closer and finally she saw a large leaf floating to shore with other leaves following behind. Standing on the leaves were tiny people dressed in beautiful colours.

They waved to her and smiled as they came ashore. They told her that they were going to rest for the evening, then leave early in the morning to go further downstream. They sat with her until the sun had gone down and then said good-bye and disappeared into the forest. She never saw them again, but all her life she would leave small pieces of food and tobacco near the water's edge for them which were always gone by morning. Mom said it was only a fairy tale but I would lie by the waters for hours hoping to see the little people.

Cheechum had the gift of second sight, although she refused to forecast anything for anyone. Once in a while if someone had lost something she would tell them where to find it and she was always right. But it was something over which she had no control.

Once, when we were all planting potatoes and she and I were cutting out the eyes, she stopped in the middle of a sentence and said, "Go get your father. Tell him your uncle is dead." I ran for Dad, and I can remember word for word what she told him. "Malcolm shot himself. He is lying at the bottom of the footpath behind your mother's house. I'll prepare the others. Go!" (Malcolm was Dad's brother-in-law.) Dad took off, with me right behind him. When we reached Grannie Campbell's no one was home. While Dad went to the door I sped down the footpath. Just as Cheechum had said, my uncle's body was lying there just as if he was sleeping.

Another time, late at night, Cheechum got up and told Dad that an aunt of ours was very sick and that he should go for Grannie Campbell as there was no time to waste. They arrived a few minutes before the aunt died.

She often had this kind of foresight and would tell Mom and Dad days before someone died or something happened. I wanted to be able to see things as she did, but she would reply that it was a sad thing to know that people who are close to you are going to die or have bad fortune—and to be unable to do anything to help them because it is their destiny. I am sure that she could see what was in store for me but because she believed life had to take its course she could only try to make me strong enough to get through my difficulties.

Qua Chich was Dad's aunt, Grannie Campbell's older sister, a widow, and a strange old lady. She had married Big John when she was sixteen. He had come to the Sandy Lake area before it was made a reserve. He brought with him two yoke of oxen, an axe, and a beautiful saddle horse. He settled beside the lake, built himself a large cabin, and broke the land. After the first year there was a home, a crop, a garden, and the addle horse had a colt. He traded one ox for a cow and a calf, the other for another horse, and then went hunting for a wife.

He visited all the nearby families and looked over their daughters, finally settling on Qua Chich because she was young and pretty, strong and sensible. Some years later, when the treaty-makers came, he was counted in and they became treaty Indians of the Sandy Lake Reserve instead of Halfbreeds. Then the great flu epidemic hit our part of Saskatchewan around 1918 and so many of our people died that mass burials were held. Big John went first and a week later his two children.

Qua Chich never remarried; half a century later she still wears widow's clothes: long black dresses, black stockings, flat-heeled shoes, and black petticoats and bloomers. She even wore a black money-bag fastened with elastic above her knee, as I discovered one day when peeking under the tent flaps. A small black bitch, blind in one eye from age, went everywhere with her. She scolded it continually, calling it bitch in Cree and accusing it of running around shamelessly with the other dogs.

She was considered wealthy by our standards as she owned many cows and horses as well as a big two-story house full of gloomy black furniture. She was stingy with money and if someone was desperate enough to ask for help she would draw up formal papers and demand a signature.

Qua Chich visited her poor relations, the Halfbreeds, every year in early May and late September. She would drive up to our house in a Bennett buggy pulled by two black Clydesdales and set up her own tent for a week. The first afternoon she would visit Mom and Dad. Her black eyes never missed anything and when she focused them on us we would fairly shrink. Sometimes I would catch her watching me with a twinkle in her eye but she would quickly become her usual self again.

The second day of her visit she would rouse Dad and my uncles out of bed early so that they could take her horses to plough and rake our large gardens. In the fall we could haul our supply of wood for the winter. When this was done, she would rest the horses for a day and then go on to visit other relatives. Our people never had strong horses and few had good ploughs, so this was her way of helping. When one of the family married she gave them a cow and a calf, or a team, but the calf was usually butchered the first year and the cow often suffered the same fate. The horses just ended up as Halfbreed horses—fat today, skinny tomorrow.

Once a year we all went to Qua Chich's house, usually when the cows came fresh. She would line the young ones all around the table and bring a pudding from her oven made from the first milking. She would say a prayer in Cree before we ate that awful pudding, and then we were not allowed to talk or make a sound all day, which was very difficult for us noisy, rowdy children. Dad said he had to do this too when he was little.

Once the old lady told me never to look at animals or people when babies were being made or else I would go blind. Of course, this was repeated with great authority among the rest of the kids. About a week later one of my boy cousins looked at two dogs and screamed that he was blind. By the time we helped him to the house we were all hysterical. Cheechum finally calmed us down and found out what happened. She told us to be quiet and said, "No one goes blind from seeing animals make babies. It is a beautiful thing. Now stop being so foolish and go and play."

When World War II broke out many of our men were sent overseas. The idea of traveling across Canada was unbelievable enough, but the sea was frightening for those who had to let loved ones go. Many of our men never returned, and those who did were never the same again. Later on, I'd listen to them talk about the far-off places I'd read about in Mom's books, but I never heard any of them talk about the war itself.

Daddy signed up but was rejected, much to his disappointment and everyone's relief, especially Cheechum's. She was violently opposed to the whole thing and said we had no business going anywhere to shoot people, especially in another country. The war was white business, not ours, and was just between rich and greedy people who wanted power.

We also acquired some new relatives from the war: war brides. Many of our men brought home Scottish and English wives, which of course didn't go over very well with our people. They marry either their own kind or Indians. (It's more common among Indians to marry a white.) However, these women came and everyone did their best to make them welcome and comfortable.

What a shock it must have been for them to find themselves in an isolated, poverty-stricken native settlement instead of the ranches and farms they had believed they were coming to!

Two of the war brides I remember very well. One was a very proper Englishwoman. She had married a handsome halfbreed soldier in England believing he was French. He came from northern Saskatchewan's wildest family and he owned nothing, not even the shack where a woman and two children were waiting for him. When they arrived, his woman promptly beat the English lady and gave her five minutes to get out of her sight, and told the man she'd do what the Germans didn't do (shoot him) if he didn't get his ass in the house immediately. Mom brought the woman home and because she had no money and too much pride to write home and ask for some, the people in the settlement got together and collected enough money to pay her way to Regina, where they were sure the government would help her. She wrote Mom a letter from England a year later and was fine.

The other bride was a silly blonde. She married a sensible hard-working man who provided well for her, but she drank and ran around, and was so loud and bawdy that she shocked even our own women. In spite of everything she was kindhearted and likeable, and eventually settled down to raise a large family.

I grew up with some really funny, wonderful, fantastic people and they are as real to me today as they were then. How I love them and miss them! There were three main clans in three settlements. The Arcands were a huge group of ten or twelve brothers with families of anywhere from six to sixteen children each. They were the musicmakers, and played the fiddles and guitars at all the dances. We always knew, when arriving at a party, if there was an Arcand playing. They were loud, noisy, and lots of fun. They spoke French mixed with a little Cree. The St. Denys, Villeneuves, Morrisettes and Cadieux were from another area. They were quiet, small men and spoke more French than English or Cree. They also made all the home brew, of which they drank a lot. They were *ak-ee-top* (pretend) farmers with great numbers of poor skinny horses and cows. Because they intermarried a great deal years ago, they looked as scrubby as their stock.

The Isbisters, Campbells, and Vandals were our family and were a real mixture of Scottish, French, Cree, English, and Irish. We spoke a language completely different from the others. We were a combination of everything: hunters, trappers, and *ak-ee-top* farmers. Our people bragged that they produced the best and most fearless fighting men—and the best looking women.

Old Cadieux was always having visions. Once he saw the Virgin Mary in a bottle when he was pouring home brew, and prayed for a week and threw all his booze out, much to everyone's dismay. The priest had given his daughter a bottle with the Virgin inside to try to scare him out of making home brew and she had put it beside the other empty bottles. Poor old Cadieux! He was very religious and never missed Mass, but he was back making booze again in a week. He made what we called *schnet* from raisins, yeast bran, old bannock and sugar. He kept it in his cellar where we once saw a swollen rat floating in it. He just scooped it out and strained the brew. His wife was a French woman who spoke no English and was almost too fat to move. One daughter, Mary, was tiny, with one of the most beautiful faces I ever saw. She was very religious and wanted to become a nun. In the Cadieux family was Chi-Georges, son of Old Cadieux. He was short and round with extra-long, skinny arms. He was near-sighted and slow-witted and always drooled. He walked everywhere because he didn't trust horses, and wherever he went he had a bannock under his arm. When he got tired he would climb up a tree, sit on a branch and eat his bannock. If someone asked what he was doing up there he would say, "Hi was jist lookin' 'round to see hif hi could spot a hindian. Don't trust dem hindians!" It was nothing out of the ordinary to go somewhere and see Chi-Georges up in a tree.

He died some years ago after a party with his father. He had been missing for six days when Pierre Villeneuve, out setting rabbit snares, came running to the store all bug-eyed and screaming in French, "He's laughing at me!" The men in the store followed him and found Chi-Georges lying on a footpath with his head on a fallen tree, his eyes and mouth pecked off by birds. His whole body was moving with maggots. Poor Pierre, who was the local coward, prayed for months, and if he had to go anywhere at night he always carried a rosary, a lantern, a flashlight, and matches so he would have a light. He was afraid Chi-Georges would haunt him.

Then there were our Indian relatives on the nearby reserves. There was never much love lost between Indians and Halfbreeds. They were completely different from us—quiet when we were noisy, dignified even at dances and get-togethers. Indians were very passive—they would get angry at things done to them but would never fight back, whereas Halfbreeds were quick-tempered—quick to fight, but quick to forgive and forget.

The Indians' religion was very precious to them and to the Halfbreeds, but we never took it as seriously. We all went to the Indians' Sundances and special gatherings, but somehow we never fitted in. We were always the poor relatives, the *awp-pee-tow-koosons*. They laughed and scorned us. They had land and security, we had nothing. As Daddy put it, "No pot to piss in or a window to throw it out." They would tolerate us unless they were drinking and then they would try to fight, but received many sound beatings from us. However, their old people, our "Mushooms" (grandfathers) and "Kokums" (grandmothers), were good. They were prejudiced, but because we were kin they came to visit and our people treated them with respect.

Grannie Dubuque's brother was chief on his reserve and as they loved me, I often stayed with them. Mushoom would spoil me, while Kokum taught me to bead, to tan hides and in general to be a good Indian woman. They had plans for me to marry the chief's son from a neighbouring reserve when we grew up. But the boy was terrified of me and I couldn't stand him.

They took me to pow-wows, Sundances and Treaty Days, and through them I learned the meanings of those special days. Mushoom would also take me with him to council meetings which were always the same: the Indian agent called the meeting to order, did all the talking, closed it, and left. I remember telling Mushoom, "You're the chief. How come you don't talk?" When I expressed my opinion in these matters, Kokum would look at Mushoom and say, "It's the white in her." Treaty Indian women don't express their opinions, Halfbreed women do. Even though I liked visiting them, I was always glad to get back to the noise and disorder of my own people.

Louis Owens

(b. 1948) Choctaw/Cherokee

Louis Owens was born in 1948. He traces his descent from Choctaw, Cherokee, and Irish ancestors, and was raised in Mississippi and California. He has been a wilderness ranger and fire fighter for the United States Forest Service. Later, he earned his doctorate in literature at the University of California at Davis. He has taught creative writing and comparative literature at the University of California at Santa Cruz, and is now a professor at the University of New Mexico.

Owens is the author of both fiction and esteemed critical studies of literature. **American Indian Novelists**, *an annotated critical bibliography with Tom Colonnese, and his first critical study,* **John Steinbeck's Re-Vision of America**, *were published in 1985. Four years later he published his second study of Steinbeck's novels,* **The Grapes of Wrath: Trouble in the Promised Land**. *He received a National Endowment for the Arts creative writing fellowship in 1989. His most important critical study,* **Other Destinies: Understanding the American Indian Novel**, *was published in 1992.*

"What is this thing that so compels us to thus organize and articulate the world?', he asks at the end of his autobiographical essay. "It is all in the way family stories when nothing is written down become the same kind of moonless dance I recall from that Mississippi night so long ago, the motion of fire and form."

Motion of Fire and Form

Memory is the most unreliable narrator, so perhaps I should begin by at least trying to get a few things straight: I was born in prison. I grew up in Mississippi and California. I have lived a great deal in the outdoors. I am not a real Indian. I have eight brothers and sisters. My mother walked barefoot across half of Texas. My father killed and ate another man's pig. The world is dangerously literal. Autobiography contains too many "i's." Were they to read what follows, and undoubtedly they will, my family would surely remember our life differently. But since nothing has been written down, I must put things together from the scraps of stories in my memory and imagination beginning with Mississippi, where everything begins.

How to evoke that feeling of a Mississippi mud road, late at night forty years ago in the middle of nowhere on the way home from my Granma and Grampa's house which at one time had been a small church and still had a steeple and cotton fields that came sneaking up from the woods on all sides? The black bones of trees, what now after a college education I call deciduous, on both sides of the road because it must have been winter and probably there was ice in the ruts and in the muddy stream beside the road and no moonlight at all that I can remember. The winter air frozen cold and thick as Karo syrup. A big car, probably a forty-something Chevy or Ford, one of those cars that make your parents say repeatedly, "Now don't you go to sleep back there," because of carbon monoxide that would maybe kill you if you went to sleep with any or all of your eight brothers and sisters piled on top of each other. The same kind of car we'd drive back and forth to California, across all that desert with canvas water bags hanging and dripping from every sharp projection of mirror, hood ornament, and door handle. Big and solid and perfectly crafted for pig killing on a dark Mississippi night.

Dinner had been possum, I think, a greasy, strong-flavored, stringy meat my grandparents loved, and probably hominy, since there was always hominy at their house, and cornbread because there was always cornbread. There is the odor of wood smoke, kerosene, and rusty pump-water, and in my memory a too-long farewell in the car. Out in the bare, hard-packed dirt yard, my Grampa's two bony bluetick hounds lying in the lantern light of the porch. Then the sullen comfort of too many kids tangled and tired on the wide back seat—although we weren't nine yet, but only five. The Yazoo River with its brown, impenetrable water was off there in the dark, and perhaps I remember being six years old and sensing its presence not far away through the woods, maybe remember imagining that I heard the alligators barking the way I sometimes did at night in our plank-walled shotgun shack with its tar-paper sides and tin roof while our father was out there across the river hunting coons and, I now strongly suspect, poaching alligators. Our cabin stood a couple hundred yards from the river, facing the same mud road we were driving, with a big pecan tree across the road before the river jungle began, the tree underneath which I truly believe I saw one Black woman cut another Black woman with her straight razor one afternoon so that the cut one bled and died later and even at five years old I knew or heard someone in the crowd of Black people and Indians say it was " man trouble." Muscadines grew on vines in the thick woods by the river, and the river mud flaked in big cracks by the leaky rowboat I pushed us off in so we almost drowned trying to get to the other side which was where they said Indians lived. Large, hidden things lived in the river—alligators, snapping turtles, water moccasins, catfish big enough to swallow a dog, needle-toothed shadowy things just waiting for a foolish child. Across the river was a world I wondered about and dreamed about but never saw. Out of that world came the panther that followed my father back from hunting one night, crying, he said, like a woman in pain. On the roof of our cabin, the black cat walked furiously, screaming and terrifying us kids before it knocked the tin chimney off and leapt away into the night. Into that world my father disappeared when darkness came each evening.

Rainwater collected in a barrel on the front porch. At night there would be the acrid smell of my father's carbide hunting lamp, and by daylight there would be coon skins nailed to the shed wall and dark men and women coming to take away the bodies of naked flesh. In the fields I dragged a child-size cotton bag and the Black cotton pickers laughed as they filled it for me and then carried me back to the shade of the trailers when I grew sleepy. All around me were relatives.

Born in prison because my father ran away from home when he was fifteen and lied to join the Army during World War II and then went awol from the paratroops just before he was about to be shipped out for some invasion. His sharecropper parents were alone in Mississippi, and both got pneumonia at the same time and needed help to stay alive and get the cotton picked. When the Army wouldn't give him emergency leave to help, he just left anyway and took care of them until they were better and then came back to turn himself in. So they threw him out of the paratroops and for punishment made him a policeman at the military prison in Lompoc, California, "the Valley of Flowers," where he was walking down the street one day and saw Ida Brown, dark-eyed and beautiful Oklahoman with long black hair already at age twenty married and divorced twice and the mother of a boy and girl, waitressing in a cafe and said to his buddy, "Hey, that's an Indian girl" and claimed later that he also said, "And I'm going to marry her." So I was born in the military prison hospital to which my mother was brought because she had left what she and my grandmother, Nora Bailey Brown— a more-than-half-Cherokee woman who bore my mother at age thirteen and was descended from a Cherokee mother who disappeared and left her to be raised by a grandmother named Storm and an absent mixedblood father named John Bailey said in family myth to have been an "Indian Scout" who guided wagon trains had left what she and my grandmother called the "Nation" in Oklahoma and come out to California to work in the shipyards during the war and somehow drifted to Lompoc where her sister married—to an Italian family from near Pisa (the grandmother of which never did learn to speak English) and was working in a Chinese-owned American-style cafe when a cocky, nineteen-year-old fellow named Hoey Owens whose mother was a Choctaw-Cajun woman from the Choctaw Strip in Catahoula Parish, Louisiana and whose father was a dirt-poor Irish sharecropper across the river in Mississippi came walking by and decided to marry her. "Indian Scout" because, I suspect, he guided those "Sooner" land thieves into Indian Territory before reservations were allotted and legally thrown open to white settlement. A Judas Scout, maybe.

Nobody saw the pig, but everybody heard it. In the headlights it was huge and dead with its throat cut by the time we kids were out looking and shivering in the cold night, the black blood spurting and pooling in front of the radiator. And then it was in the trunk of the car and we were home and a pit was dug beneath the big walnut tree behind the cabin and fire and neighbors from other cabins in the woods who today, more than forty years later, form a dancing, strutting tableau of mostly angular shadows around the corpse of the pig hanging over the fire from a big branch. Perhaps I remember staring through the rusty screen door of the kitchen at the gyrating, laughing, pig-eating men and women, and wandering through the mess of shadows made by fire and fired people. By morning the pig is gone, and today I know, somehow, that it belonged to the rich white man "up the road" and my father almost went to jail for it. And it's funny how a lot of years turn memories into that kind of thing, the way family stories when nothing is written down become the same kind of moonless dance and wild dream.

California because that was where we settled more or less for good when I was about seven. In my immediate memory, I always leap to the belief that we moved first to the oak-and-pine coast range of the Santa Lucia Mountains miles up a dirt road behind the serious ranching town of Paso Robles. I remember that place with a feeling I can only define as love—remember the texture of the dry earth and rustle of prickly oak leaves, the heat of summer on wild oats and manzanita, the taste of a spring hillside when the world seemed startled with new grass. But it isn't true that we moved there first. We had already made at least one failed move to the state of my birth, initially to California's great Central Valley, where we lived in a small tent "city" on the outskirts of Delano while my father got work in the fields nearby. I recall now that our A-frame tent had a wooden floor and contained the chocolate cake of my fifth birthday. We lived there a few months (or weeks?) until my father was promoted and we moved into a little house on the "ranch" where he worked. It was there that he made slingshots for my brother and me, rock-hard oak forks with red rubber bands from old tire inner tubes. From that point on, we would always seek out the red "real" rubber from World War II as the best slingshot material, seldom finding it again. It was also here that I lurked just inside the kitchen door listening to my father explain to my mother that he had been called a "goddamn Indian" and fired by the field foreman, my very firm concrete awareness that to be Indian was a bad thing. Only later, after we had returned to Mississippi in our shambles of a car, did I learn that somewhere before or after that exchange he had punched the foreman. Still an amazingly powerful man today, at age sixty-five, my father has only struck two people in my lifetime, as far as I know: the foreman who cursed him and my mother's brother, bad Uncle Bob.

During that wandering time in California, we camped farther down the Central Valley, near the potato sheds at Shafter where for a while we gleaned potatoes after the fields were harvested, and then we moved to Paso Robles, into the county "Housing

Project" where our low-income apartment was surrounded by a paradise of mown grass and wild children. The Project is still there today, seeming unchanged after so many years. Driving south from San Francisco on U.S. 101, I glance to my right and see the dull brown buildings and recall those months as a very happy time. It was in the Project that a beautiful Border collie appeared magically during one of our games and remained with us for the next nine years—Rex, the wonder dog. Still there between the freeway and the Project are the train tracks, where my brother and I would lay wire in the path of the Southern Pacific so that the wire would be flattened to razor-sharp blades. With the unflattened part wrapped around a stick, these were lethal weapons capable of beheading flowers, lizards, or anything with a low survival quotient in a kid's world.

And then we were abruptly gone from the Project and living in Mississippi on a place still known in family stories as the "Hog Ranch," a time that has coalesced into a single image of a gray winter day and a mule with his head down against a muddy barn. I assume there were also hogs, but hogs do not populate my memories there. Then just as abruptly we were headed back to California, a trip that remains vivid because of a flash flood that swept like a mirage across the desert somewhere in New Mexico or Arizona, citing the highway and leaving us stranded for some time—one day, two days?

Nine of us moved into a small house with flaking white paint set deep in the Santa Lucia Mountains west of Paso Robles, so remote that a bear came onto our porch one night and mountain lions left tracks in the yard. That was a secure and private world, where my older brother, Gene, looked up at me from deep in the cave we were digging and said, "Look at these Indian things," and we sat together in the sun to study two lovely arrow points and a tiny white stone doll dug from six feet down in the shaley earth. Who were those Indians, I wondered, finding it impossible to imagine real Indians amidst all that light. Why had they set such things so carefully in the earth, and where were those people now? And then, just before my fifth-grade year, we moved ten miles away to the crumbling bank of the Salinas River which was not a river at all but a lovely, wide sand-and-brush-and-cottonwood world filled with the rabbits and quail and doves and pigeons and deer we hunted.

California was a world as different from Mississippi as day from night, where a river was white sand rather than brown water and the hillsides were golden grain and shiny oaks rather than the black tangle of that Yazoo country. A world where my nine-year-old self had sat dreaming on a remote wild-oat ridge not far from the ocean and foolishly believed for a long time that everything was visible, nothing hidden. Where I followed after my brother as we learned from our father and Uncle Bob how to catch fish by putting crushed unripe black walnuts in a sack and dropping that sack into a pool so that the fish rose stunned and could be scooped out; how to turn a hollow log into a box trap for rabbits, possums, and, most often, pack rats; how to grapple with our hands for fish in stream and tidepool; and how to set deadfalls that never worked for small game. We graduated from slingshots to twenty-two, shotgun, and thirty-ought-six-hunting everything from squirrels to deer.

California was a world in which on a strange kind of absent-minded automatic pilot I became the second after my brother (and today still only the second) in the history of our whole extended family to graduate from high school. And then, while my brother served three tours of duty in Vietnam, I drifted from high school to work in a can factory in Hayward, California and then to a junior college and then, to my amazement and the astonishment of everyone who paid attention, on to the University of California at Santa Barbara. So that now for almost twenty years I have lived in a world incalculably different from that of everyone else in my family. In troubled lives scattered across America, from Oregon to Arkansas they see my name on books and shadows of themselves in the same books and they tell me with great tact how proud they are.

Not a real, essential Indian because I'm not enrolled and did not grow up on a reservation. Because growing up in different times I naively thought that Indian was something we were, not something we did or had or were required to prove on demand. Listening to my mother's stories about Oklahoma, about brutally hard lives and dreams that cut across the fabric of every experience, I thought that was Indian. We were "part Indian" she said, and my Uncle Bob, out of jail temporarily and strutting in new hundred-dollar, un-paid-for cowboy boots, would be singing about "way down yonder on the Indian nation" and boasting that only a Cherokee could be as handsome as he. No one but a Choctaw, I thought, could be a beautiful as my father's mother, or as great a hunter as my father, and though in California I was embarrassed by our poverty and bad grammar, I was nonetheless comfortable with who we were. The only other Indian I knew in California was my best friend and hunting-and-fishing companion, an Osage with blond hair and light eyes. He was enrolled and somewhat smug about that fact, though it meant little to me then.

Now I know better, and in life's mid-passage I have learned to inhabit a hybrid, unpapered, Choctaw-Cherokee-Welsh-Irish-Cajun mixed space in between. I conceive of myself today not as "Indian," but as a mixedblood, a person of complex roots and histories. Along with my parents and grandparents, brothers and sisters, I am the product of liminal space, the result of union between desperate individuals on the edges of dispossessed cultures and the marginalized spawn of invaders. A liminal existence and a tension in the blood and heart must be the inevitable result of such crossing. How could it be otherwise? But tension can be a source of creative power—

as such brilliant writers as Gerald Vizenor and Leslie Silko have taught me. This is an "other" territory which I, too, have claimed, like those early Choctaws who migrated westward across the Mississippi River, reversing the direction from which their ancestors had come carrying bones, to hunt and live and remain in Louisiana, I am descended from those people, but I am not those people, just as I bear the blood of the Trail of Tears and of an enormous Owens clan that reunites periodically somewhere in Kentucky or Tennessee, but I am not those people either. The descendant of mixedblood sharecroppers and the dispossessed of two continents, I believe I am the rightful heir of Choctaw and Cherokee storytellers and of Shakespeare and Yeats and Cervantes. Finally, everything converges and the center holds in the margins. This, if we are to go on.

My paternal grandmother, Mahala Jobe Owens, whose name is not written down and no one in my family is certain of spelling correctly, is sixteen years old in a photograph. She is Choctaw and Cajun, my mother tells me, and her hair is thick and black and falls straight to the floor. Her white dress is buttoned at the neck and descends to her feet. She is extraordinarily beautiful, somber and dark-eyed, slim and proud-looking, or so I remember, for I haven't seen the photograph in at least fifteen years. Like so much in our family, it has been lost, is perhaps hidden and forgotten somewhere in a box or suitcase. The photo was taken in Louisiana, I think, probably in Catahoula Parish where she was born, and probably just before she ran away with the gambler down the Mississippi River. And her father tracked them down in New Orleans with a gun and brought her back and forced her to marry the son of Welsh-Irish sharecroppers next door. Or so the family story goes. The story says my grandfather, my father's father, was her punishment as was a lifetime of sharecropping in Mississippi before my father borrowed money to move his parents to California, to live on a chicken ranch in a converted barn outside of Paso Robles, when I was in third grade. All of this is picture and story without text.

I believe that she never cut her hair. When I was young I'd watch her take it down at night and brush it, and just as in the photograph it touched the floor when she stood, but now it was silver instead of black. And almost as soon as they were in California, it seems in my memory, she was killed in an automobile accident and Grampa moved back to Mississippi.

I recall no photographs of my mother's mother, who finally drank herself to death when I was twenty. But I lived with her for a whole year once, and I remember her well. She was the one who was but thirteen and scarcely five feet tall when she bore my mother, the first of her three children. It was she who, already husbandless, gave her children away to a farmer who admired them at an Oklahoma country dance.

After two years of beatings and worse abuse, my mother dreamed of little people who foretold the farmer's death. Three days after the dream, the man died from a snakebite and my grandmother returned to claim her children. My grandmother who had been left by her own mother—through death or abandonment—shortly after birth and who had been raised by her grandmother in what she persisted in calling the "Nation" until her death. It was she who went through men by the score and whose postcards I discovered in my mother's papers after my mother died, each postcard from a different place in America—Boston, Albuquerque, Laramie, Seattle, San Diego, Tulsa, Little Rock, Las Vegas. What was she doing, that little half-Cherokee wild woman on the run in America? "Miss you. Wish you were here." Almost as though the Removal had buried a seed that drove her just as it would drive her only son, my smooth-talking Uncle Bob, from state to state and in and out of prison all his short, hard-drinking life until he was finally murdered in a Texas oilfield—but not before he totaled my thirty-six Chevy.

There are pieces of story, tantalizing fragments. Such as my mother's account of walking across half of Texas all of one long frozen winter, barefoot with her mother, little brother and sister, living in the woods or abandoned barns, eating roots, stealing food from gardens and chicken houses, living for two luxurious weeks in an empty rail car. They were going back to Oklahoma, I know, but I never found out why they were walking or where they were really headed. In retrospect, I believe I could see the marks of that journey in my mother's face all the years I knew her.

Not long ago my mother's sister, Aunt Betty, wrote to ask if I could find out who she was. The only surviving member of her family, my aunt—like my mother, uncle, and grandparents—has no birth certificate but only stories growing more distant each year. Born at home, in different homes, none of them had the luxury of a recorded birth. For fifty years she has lived in an Italian-American world where her dark skin and hair fit perfectly, but now that she's old, she has begun to wonder, begun apparently to desire a record of her existence, unwilling to remain unwritten. She told me the names of her mother's father and mother, my great-grandparents, and I dutifully took the names to the National Archives. Sure enough he was there in the 1910 census for Oklahoma, in the Indian section, and there also on the Dawes Roll. John Bailey, a Cherokee mixedblood. But her fullblood grandmother's name wasn't anywhere on paper and remains, therefore, unreal, without essence.

My sister's son, a father himself now and in the Army, writes from Germany to tell her he wants to enroll his own infant son. He's thinking of college scholarships, an admirably far-sighted young man. My good Osage friend from childhood keeps a copy of his enrollment card taped to the wall above his computer, where he is active on an Indian internet line. I imagine a vast new tribe of Internet Indians.

For seven years I worked seasonally for the U.S. Forest Service, building trails, being a wilderness ranger, fighting fires on a hotshot crew. I watched Rookie cut his big toe off with a double-bit axe and be packed out by mule, saw Mick laid out in an emergency room with his right hand severed at the wrist from a fireline accident, and watched my friend Joe fell a tree the wrong way in a hard wind so that he turned and sprawled full-length on his running chainsaw. I climbed glaciated peaks to radio in reports of frozen lakes far below, and wandered the high country of the North Cascades when it was under ten feet of hardpacked snow, alone above timberline for days and weeks at a time in the most beautiful place in the world. I stumbled across a surly wolverine when there weren't supposed to be any in that country, and one morning I watched a mountain lion walk slowly across the zenith of a snowfield, outlined by the bluest sky I have ever seen. I fought fires in Washington, Arizona, and California, watching a project fire crown-out in hundred-foot walls of flame that raced from ridge to ridge one night near Winslow, Arizona, and dodging flaming yucca balls at midnight in a steep canyon outside of Tucson. I learned to drink great quantities of beer and climb granite faces as a sawyer on the Prescott Hotshots, which they told us was the only technical rock-climbing fire crew in America. I careened through burning mountains in helicopters driven by mad Vietnam vets, and I listened to a phone call telling me that two friends had been killed in such a helicopter after I'd quit to return to school.

Seven years of that, and then in the fall of 1990, as a newly appointed full professor at the University of California, Santa Cruz, I returned to the Northwest with my old journals, determined, twenty years after first seeing the Cascades, to retrace familiar routes with the vague idea of writing another book. The third day out, I found myself alone on the edge of a glacier and looking across a high route to the summit of Glacier Peak, a mountain called *Dakobed* by the Salishan people born there. The edge of the glacier was a steep icefield covered by a few inches of snow with a run-out ending thousands of feet down in a glacial river. On the other side of the first slope a series of crevasses began, their blue mouths opening to the black depths of the mountain. My ice axe firmly buried, I hesitated. The world was suddenly unfamiliar and very threatening, and I had decided to turn back and retrace my route down the rocks when I saw a shadow move on the ice. Looking up, I watched a golden eagle banking off an updraft close overhead. When I looked back at the glacier, I saw the tracks. A fresh, clear set of coyote prints began near where I stood and continued out onto the glacier. Hesitating no longer, I began to follow coyote, crossing the steep slope easily, remembering even that it is fun to slide down a glacier. Where coyote leapt across the narrow end of a crevasse, I leapt full pack and all. Where he strolled across an icebridge, I did the same. Together our tracks emerged onto the rock crest on the other side of the glacier, and as I stood there in a tearing wind and looked out at what seemed a thousand miles of Cascade peaks, I imagined coyote doing the same. Why else would he be on a mountain of ice and rock except for the pure pleasure of it? As I cut across a snowfield to finish the high route, the eagle circled endlessly. Alone, as I would continue to be for the next ten days, thousands of miles from the Yazoo and Salinas Rivers, I had never felt so at home in my life. Home had become a much bigger place, and the book I had imagined writing seemed unimportant.

Perhaps I began to write novels as a way of figuring things out for myself. I think my works are about the natural world and our relations with that world, with one another, and, most crucially, with ourselves. Though each of my works begins and ends with place itself, the mysteries of mixed identity and conflicted stories, both the stories we tell ourselves and the stories others tell about us and to us, are what haunt my fiction. In a novel called *Wolfsong*, I wrote of a young Indian coming home to a valley in the North Cascades, wondering who and where he is meant to be. In that novel, set in the Glacier Peak Wilderness, the omniscient narrator says, "Sometimes at night, when he lay in bed and tried to figure it out, he felt as if he were descended from some madman's dream. Indians rode spotted horses over golden plains. They lived in the light of the sun, where nothing was hidden and earth rose up to sky. They sat on horseback against the infinite horizon. Those were the Indians they studied in school." In a second novel, called *The Sharpest Sight*, a work moving between Mississippi and California and drawing heavily upon my own family, I wrote of a young Choctaw-Cherokee-Irish mixedblood who must learn who he is and how to balance a world that has led his brother to madness and destroyed him, a world of stories in deadly conflict. I needed my father's name, Hoey, and my Grandfather's name, Luther, in that novel, and I created an old Choctaw lady named Onatima whom I modeled upon what I remembered and imagined of my Grandma Onatima, who too, ran away with a gambler on the great river. I also based a major character in that novel on my brother, Gene, who had come back from three tours in Vietnam with such pain that he became one of the psychological casualties who disappeared into the Ozark Mountains of Arkansas. For me it had been as if he never came back from the war, and that is how I wrote the novel. Later, after emerging from long familial isolation, he would jokingly say to our sister, "Gee, first he put me in a mental hospital and then he killed me. What's he going to do to me next?" Because I wanted to explore mixed and relational identity—the liminal landscape of the mixedblood—more fully, I also included in *The Sharpest Sight* a young mestizo named Mundo Morales who discovers in his own blood an inextricable web of inherited identities.

In a third novel, *Bone Game*, published in 1994, I reentered the life of Cole McCurtain from *The Sharpest Sight*, and the lives of his family, in order to examine imprints of evil left upon the American landscape by the European invader's destructive violence. In that novel I delved further into my grandma's story—Onatima's story—imagining the feelings that must have driven her to flee with her gambler, and the pain of returning home to marriage. In this third novel Cole McCurtain, twenty years after going home to Mississippi in *The Sharpest Sight*, is still uncertain as to who he is. Maybe the message is that certainty is not a condition mixedbloods can know.

Every work is a different gamble and exploration. Every work teaches me a great deal. As a university professor, I watch students bring me their stories, even their novels, and I marvel again and again at the force that drives us to so make and remake the world. I imagine a world crowded with stories that jostle one another and war for space, a world in which pigs are killed and eaten by dancing shadows and a young boy imagines that he watches and then carries that imagining with him for forty years. Stories that carry us from the muddy waters of the Yazoo River to a tent in California and a glacial world of sheerest blue and frozen light. What is this thing that so compels us to thus organize and articulate the world? It is all in the way family stories when nothing is written down become the same kind of moonless dance I recall from that Mississippi night so long ago, the motion of fire and form.

Wendy Rose

(b. 1948) Hopi/Miwok

Wendy Rose was born in Oakland, California, in 1948. She is mixedblood and traces her native ancestors to the Hopi of Arizona and the Miwok of California. "I have heard Indians joke about those who act as if they had no relatives," she wrote in "Neon Scars," an autobiographical essay in **I Tell You Now**. *"I wince, because I have no relatives. They live, but they threw me away—so, I do not have them. I am without relations. I have always swung back and forth between alienation and relatedness."*

Rose is a mighty poet, a serious and invincible native voice in literature, and she is a notable painter. She studied anthropology at the University of California at Berkeley, and now teaches at Fresno City College in California. Her poems have appeared in numerous anthologies, and she has published at least ten books. **The Halfbreed Chronicles** *was published in 1985.*

Rose told Laura Coltelli in an interview published in **Winged Words** *that her*

> *father is a full-blood Hopi from Arizona. He lives on the reservation. My mother is mostly Scots and Irish, but also Miwok.... I've always thought in terms of being a half-breed because that is the way that both sides of the family treated me. The white part of the family wanted nothing to do with her.... The Hopi side of my family is more sympathetic to my situation, but our lineage is through the mother, and because of that, having a Hopi father means that I have no real legitimate place in Hopi society. I am someone who is from that society in a biological sense, in what I like to think is a spiritual sense, and certainly in an emotional sense, but culturally I would have to say I'm pretty urbanized: an urban, Pan-Indian kind of person.*

Rose is an artist. She pointed out that nobody "bothered to tell me until I was an adult that there was anything wrong with being both a visual and a verbal artist," she told Joseph Bruchac in an interview published in **Survival This Way**.

> *I think that's the only reason why that isn't the case with more people, and I think that's the reason why it is the case for so many Native American people. Look at the number of Native American authors who illustrate their own work and who illustrate other people's work. There is a tremendous number. There is nothing unusual about it among Native American people at all.*

Bruchac asked why death seems to be very important in her work. Rose responded that she did not know.

> *I never really thought of it as being important to the work. I guess if I really think about it, yeah, I've got a lot of bones rattling around in there. I guess there's a sense of feeling—sometimes I feel like I'm dead. Like I'm a ghost. Similarly, sometimes I feel that I'm alive but there are ghosts all around me, so that's part of it. But as far as the symbols go, of things like the bones for instance, I think maybe it's argument against death. Maybe what I'm saying is that the bones are alive.*

Neon Scars

I hate it when other people write about my alienation and anger. Even if it's true. I'm not proud of it. It has crippled me, made me sick, made me out of balance. It has also been the source of my poetry.

Writing this autobiographical essay has been the most difficult, most elusive task I have faced as a writer. I worked hard to be less self-involved, less self-centered, less self-pitying. As readers and listeners have noted the angry or somber tone of my poems, I have struggled to lessen these things or, at least, kept them in proportion. I work toward balance and attempt to celebrate at least as often as I moan and rage. Everything I have ever written is fundamentally autobiographical, no matter what the topic or style; to state my life now in an orderly way with clear language is actually to restate, simplified, what has already been said. If I could just come right out and state it like that, as a matter of fact, I would not have needed the poetry. If I could look my childhood in the eye and describe it, I would not have needed to veil these memories in metaphor. If I had grown up with a comfortable identity, I would not need to explain myself from one or another persona. Poetry is both ultimate fact and ultimate fiction; nothing is more brutally honest and, at the same time, more thickly coded.

When I speak of bruises that rise on my flesh like blue marks, do you understand that these are real bruises that have appeared on my flesh? Or has the metaphor succeeded in hiding the pain while producing the fact, putting it in a private place just for those readers and listeners who know me well enough to have seen the bruises? I live with ghosts and like anyone who lives with ghosts, I am trapped inside their circle. I long for someone to siphon off the pain, someone to tell it all to, someone to be amazed at how well I have survived. There is both a need for and a revulsion from pity. More than pity, I have needed respect. More than respect, I have needed to be claimed by someone as their own, someone who is wanted. I have survived—and there is pride in the fact—but is my survival of any value? Is my survival different from the millions of survivals in the world? Or is its kinship with them the truth of the matter—that we are growing, reproducing, living together as relations? Is my survival the final proof I have needed that I belong here after all? Will I be missed someday?

When I was first approached for this essay, my response (which lasted for several months) was simply to insist that the editor take some body of my poetic work and let it speak for me. I must have decided that there is some reason to make my pain public, although I am enough of a coward to keep the greatest pain (and the greatest pleasure) to myself. Would releasing the secrets let loose a passion so great and so uncontrolled that it would destroy the poetry? I am told that I take risks. When I am told that, the tellers mean I take risks artistically, in style or technique, in placing the words on the page just so in a way that other poets would have the sense or the training not to do. It is usually meant as a compliment.

> Do you know what is the greatest risk of all? Someday I may be forced to see myself as in a sweat vision, wide open to the world. I may find that I am only that one I saw in the vision, no more, no less. I am only what you see. The vision is naked and cannot be tampered with. Is it enough? Will the voices that have always said I am not good enough be quiet? Is this worth the pain and the poetry? Will you be satisfied?

Facts: May 7, 1948. Oakland. Catholic hospital. Midwife nun, no doctor. Citation won the Kentucky Derby. Israel was born. The United Nations met for the first time. It was Saturday, the end of the baby boom or the beginning. Boom. Stephen's little sister. Daughter of Betty. Almost named Bodega, named Bronwen instead. Little brown baby with a tuft of black hair. Baptized in the arms of Mary and Joe. Nearly blind for ten years. Glasses. Catholic school. Nuns with black habits to their ankles. Heads encased in white granite. Rosary beads like hard apricots—measuring prayers, whipping wrists. Paced before the blackboard. Swore in Gaelic. Alone. Alone at home. Alone in the play yard. Alone at Mass. Alone on the street. Fed, clothed in World War II dresses, little more. Mom too sick to care; brother raised by grandparents. Alone. Unwatched. Something wrong with me; everyone knows but me. They all leave me alone. No friends. Confirmation. Patron Francis of Assisi. He understands. Public high school. Drugs, dropping out. Finally friends. Getting high, staying high. Very sick, hospital. No more drugs, no more friends. Alone again. Married at eighteen. Tried to shoot me. Lasted three months. Again at nineteen. Lived in basement, then in trailer. Worked in Yosemite. Sold Indian crafts. Went on display. Drinking, fighting, he tried to burn down the house; he gave me the name Rose. Starved in Nevada; nearly died. Home. Eating again; got fat. College. Graduated in ten years. Went to grad school. Alone again. Met Arthur. Fell in love, still happy. Another ten years. Live in a nice house. Fresno. Have a swimming pool. Air conditioning. Have an old cat. Rent a typewriter. Teach. Work on doctorate. Two of us now. Moved to another planet, home.

Healing.

I am probably my mother. She bears my face but is lighter in complexion, taller, long-legged. She was thin enough as a girl to have been teased for it. Her eyebrows each come to a point in the center, little tepees at the top of her face. My brother inherited these, while I got her upturned nose and hair that thins at the temple. From my father I have coarse dark hair, a flatness of face and mouth, no waist, a body made of bricks. At different times, I have resembled each of them. I see myself in old photographs of my mother as a short, stocky, dark version of her, and others have seen my father in me, thinner, younger, lighter, female.

> As much as I have come from them, the two of them threw me away. I am the part of them they worked long and hard to cut off. I have never depended on them. I have floated into the distance, alone.

I have heard Indians joke about those who act as if they have no relatives. I wince, because I have no relatives. They live, but they threw me away—so, I do not have them. I am without relations. I have always swung back and forth between alienation and relatedness. As a child, I would run away from the beatings, from the obscene words, and always knew that if I could run far enough, then any leaf, any insect, any bird, any breeze could bring me to my true home. I knew I did not belong among people. Whatever they hated about me was a human thing; the nonhuman world has always loved me. I can't remember when it was otherwise. But I have been emotionally crippled by this. There is nothing romantic about being young and angry, or even about turning that anger into art. I go through the motions of living in society, but never feel a part of it. When my family threw me away, every human on earth did likewise.

> I have been alone too much. I have been bitter too long. This part of me is not in balance. It has made me alien. This is something to pray about.

There is only one recent immigrant in my family. Sidney, my mother's father, came from England around the turn of the century. I don't know his father's name, but his mother was Christine. Early pictures of Sidney show a serious English schoolboy intent on his economic future. What he did in America was learn photography and operate a small studio in Berkeley for the rest of his life. He took misty portraits of young girls and babies, Victorian still-lifes, and sweeping panoramas of San Francisco Bay.

> I don't remember being touched by Sidney at all, but he was my brother's greatest influence. Even today there is a British clip to my brother's speech. When I was in his house, Sidney was always on the other side of some door. I have wondered, too, why his middle name was "Valdez." And how he came to be so dark and brooding as a young man, so gray when old. Why did he leave England? Where did he meet Clare, the mountain girl from Mariposa, who would give birth to my mother?

Clare was born thirty years after the Gold Rush, in Bear Valley. Bear Creek branches from the Merced River near there, just down the mountain from Yosemite, rippling through oak-wooded grassy hills and bull-pines. Her mother and father were born there also; he was raised in a house that belonged to John C. Fremont. Their people had ridden wagons west across the plains or had sailed around the Horn to find prosperity in a land newly claimed from Mexico. Clare's father, Maurice, was the son of German immigrants who had traveled from Missouri in a wagon train; there is a story told by his mother, Margaret, of how one night Indians came to steal the babies. Clare's mother, Elizabeth, had a noble and well documented lineage. Her people were known by name all the way back to the eighth century on the Scottish side and to the Crusades on the Irish. The dominant thread in her ancestry crossed into Britain with William the Conqueror, part of the family rumored to have been related to him through one of his brothers. The Normans of my mother's background are very well documented and include the modern Lord Dunboyne, although our branch of the Dunboynes split from his during the seventeenth century. This Norman part of the family included Butlers and Massys, Barretts and Percys, Le Petits and de Berminghams—names that fiercely colonized Ireland and settled on stolen land. Among the parts of Ireland that they stole were certain women: O'Brien of Thomond, McCarthy Reagh, Carthach of Muskerry, all representing royal native Irish families. Another thread can be followed to the Scottish Highlands and to royal Celtic and Pictish families via the clans MacInnes and Drummond.

> By the time Clare was born in the 1880s, the family had included an Indian man, most probably Miwok. Clare's blond hair and transparently blue eyes belied that less well known (and probably involuntary) heritage, but the native blood reappeared in my mother. How many almost-comic photographs do I have of the sharp-faced blond and delicate lady who sits before the long-faced mustached Englishman and, between them, holds the chubby little girl with the dark round face, that little Indian baby.

Late in the summer of 1984, I received a package from my mother's cousin Joe, who is also my godfather, although I had not seen him for more than thirty years. He was both black sheep and bachelor in the family, a mystery man of whom I have no clear memories. Now I am laughing at myself. I have always searched for my place and my people, focusing that search on my father. His Hopi people have been sympathetic but silent; they trace their lineage through the mother and I could never be more than the daughter of a Hopi man. How ironic and unexpected Joe's package was! It contained diary excerpts, lists of names and dates, and newspaper clippings about my mother's family. She had always refused to answer my questions about ancestry, citing the melting pot as her excuse. My interest in our heritage was, in her eyes, just an aberration which—like slipping away from the Church—would someday be fixed. Yet the package with its precious communication came to me.

> Now why didn't Joe send it to my brother? My brother is what they wanted. He is white-looking, with brown hair and green eyes; he has maintained his ties to home and hearth, even while in the Army. He has expressed great interest in his European blood, has dabbled in Druidic and neo-pagan rites, and looks like them. His hair and beard are long, his clothing covered with mystic symbols. The package did not go to him. I gave him and my mother copies of everything; they were as surprised as I that Joe chose me.

I learned that the Normans who stole Irish land went bankrupt, lost their land, and booked passage in 1830 for Quebec. The MacInnes clan, near that time, was forbidden to wear the tartan and fled Scotland to preserve their heritage. The weekend after Joe's package arrived, Highland Games were held in Fresno. In no other year would it have occurred to me to attend, but Arthur and I walked onto the grounds to search for my roots, he Japanese and I wearing all my turquoise for courage. It may have looked funny to all those Scots to see an Indian looking for a booth with her clan's name on it. The first booth was Irish; I showed my list of ancestral names to the man there, and he pointed to certain ones and said they had stolen his castle. I apologized to all of Ireland on behalf of John Bull and returned his castle to him, I suspect it would not hold up in Parliament and, anyway, they were the ancestors who had gone bankrupt. This is not the heritage I would have picked—to be the daughter of the invaders. It is not where my sympathies lie. Searching the grounds, I found my clan:

> Great-great-grandmother Henrietta MacInnes, who came to California for gold from Quebec, you have given me what my own father could not. I learned that I am entitled to wear your tartan, your symbol of strong arm pointing to the sky with a bow in its hand. I also learned that you were the natives of Scotland, descended from the Pictish kind, Onnus, and lent strength to my apology for Ireland. The colonizer and the colonized meet in my blood. It is so much more complex than just white and just Indian. I will pray about this, too.

This year Sidney and Clare, Grandad and Nana, are turning real for me. They have been dead twenty-five years but my thoughts go to them as I continue to listen to my mother's jokes about their embarrassment. Clare got so angry sometimes! Like when people would ask what racial mixture her little girl, my mother, was. Or when that little girl shared a room with a Jew in college. Or when that little girl, who had bobbed her hair and hung out with flappers, married a man with Indian blood and rural background. Clare knew who to blame. My mother told me of her mother's peculiar habit of taking my brother into her home when he was sick to nurse him back to health and, when I was sick, taking my brother into her home so he wouldn't catch what I had. She was amused by this.

> Nana! I'm afraid you'll see me cry! I have never been able to cry in front of you, of anyone. Any strong emotion is dangerous, as people are dangerous. Poetry has been the safest way to cry in public. I bristle when people say I'm cold and unfriendly, but they're right. I can't tell you straight out how I feel without putting it into a poem. And I have written some for you, safely cloaked in metaphor or masked by a persona. I hope you understand that the poetry is the only way I can love you. I *do* love. But you are dangerous. Does mom know how much it hurts when she tells me about the way you turned from me? Does she know how much it hurts for me to know that it could have gone unsaid?

I am turning numb. I have been educated to put a name to the things that my parents did, but the child within has no such knowledge. I recall that every dirty word I ever knew was my first heard from my father's lips, from the man who raised me as he struck over and over. As an adult, I take this apart and study it. I suppose it was a kind of rape for him to talk like that in the middle of his violence, to name the parts of my body he intended to mutilate or cut away. I recall lying in my bed, hearing him scream at my mother that he wanted to kill me; and I recall that he tried, more than once. Symbolic of what he wanted to do to me, he smashed my toys. My mother's memories float in and out of those scenes; at times she denies everything, but I remember it was she who pulled him away as he tried to choke me on my bed. There was no media hype about abuse in those days, no public awareness; I begged the police to put me in a foster home, but I was always sent back. Eventually I learned that I was to blame for all of this, just as I was to blame for my parents' unhappiness.

> I embarrassed them. They tell me their marriage began to be bad when I was born, although they never divorced. He lived in one room, she in another. How much it must embarrass them for me to say these things to strangers! I would say something else, be someone else, act some other way—but there is no way I can twist my genes around. There is no sugar sweet enough to smear on the story of our household. These are ghosts that will never leave, the ghosts of knowing how I destroyed their lives. They sent me to social workers and psychiatrists, to priests, to people whose roles or professions I never knew. They told me I was sick, and must try to get better so that my family could mend. Everything, they said, depended on me. I just wanted to get out so that the beatings, the obscene language

about my body, and the constant knowledge of his hatred would be far away. Didn't they believe what I told them? Couldn't they see the scars? I didn't know that such scars never heal up. It's probably lucky that my nature is a fighting one; otherwise I would have died.

I will just talk about being different, as if I were talking about someone else. My mother said I was born different.

Her mother said she was born different. No one ever said what the difference was all about, but everyone knew it when they saw it. They avoided it as if it burned them. And so she was always alone and not just alone, but thrown away. They made sure she knew she was being thrown away. They told her so, over and over, through action and word, until she could see it in no other way. And so she knew she was rejected and she knew she was rejectable. She learned to worship her difference, whatever it was, and this empowered her. She rejected them.

Or, I could try this. I'll make up a story about my childhood and see if anyone believes it. I will tell about happy summer days with all my friends. Us girls are trying on makeup, combing each other's hair, comparing lies about boyfriends. The boys all want to date me, but I can only choose one at a time. I hate to hurt the others. I have been riding my beautiful stallion on the mountain; alongside is my healthy young collie. I know that when I go home, my parents will be glad to see me; they'll hug me, and kiss me and hold me. They know all about me, what my interests are, what I did that day. I have been placed in the gifted program at school and will be high school valedictorian. I have been skipping grades because everyone thinks I'm so smart. I'm pretty, too. I will enter college at seventeen with an enormous scholarship. I will receive gold jewelry or a diamond for my graduation. My father will kiss me on the cheek and take my picture.

I don't want to lie to you, but I don't want to tell the truth. The dirty laundry flaps in the wind, yet the alternative is to go on wearing it. How do you admit in public that you were abused, that the only time your parents ever touched you—that you can remember—was in anger, that your cousins probably don't know that you exist, that your own grandparents have no use for you? How do you acknowledge that you were left so alone you never learned to brush your teeth or fix your food? How do you reveal that you were a bag lady at fourteen, having been turned out of the house, or that when you ran away no one looked for you? How do you expect anyone to believe how hungry you were at times, how you nearly died from starvation twice when they can plainly see how fat you are now? How do you explain that you dropped out of high school, were classified as retarded but educable, and were not allowed to take college prep classes? How do you reconcile being an "Indian writer" with such a non-Indian upbringing? It is not the Indian way to be left so alone, to be alienated, to be friendless, to be forced to live on the street like a rat, to be unacquainted with your cousins. It would certainly be better for my image as an Indian poet to manufacture something, and let you believe in my traditional, loving, spiritual childhood where every winter evening was spent immersed in storytelling and ceremony, where the actions of every day continually told me I was valued.

Today I live about fifty miles from Bear Valley. As I write, it is early August and the days are valley-hot, the nights thickly warm and filled with crickets. Although last winter was dry, this summer has found an explosion of toads in my yard. To uncover the memories, I have peeled back layers of scar tissue. I have invoked the ghosts and made them work for me. Is that the answer? To keep them busy? There is nothing authentic or nice about my past; I am sure that I would be a great disappointment to anthropologists. But then, you know—now—why I write poetry; being Indian was never the reason. I have agonized for months about writing this essay, and now that it is finished I am afraid of it. I am mortified and embarrassed. I am certain I said too much, whined perhaps, made someone squirm. But there is no way I can change the past and the literal fact is that I have tried to forget what is unforgettable, there are few happy moments that I recall or perhaps, as I have succeeded in forgetting the bad, the good has also been forgotten. Perhaps the editor and the readers will forgive me for using that as an exorcism.

My father told me, when I took Arthur down to meet him, that Hopi earth does contain my roots and I am, indeed, from that land. Because the roots are there, I will find them. But when I find them, he said, I must rebuild myself as a Hopi. I am not merely a conduit, but a participant. I am not a victim, but a woman.

I am building myself.
There are many roots.
I plant, I pick, I prune.
I consume.

FICTION

John Joseph Mathews

(1894–1979) Osage

John Joseph Mathews was born at the Osage Agency, Oklahoma, in 1894. He was mixedblood Osage and raised at Pawhuska. He graduated from the University of Oklahoma. Trained as a pilot, he served in France during World War I and later studied at Oxford and Geneva. He lived in California for a time, but when his marriage ended he moved back to Pawhuska and built a cabin in the blackjack oaks region.

Mathews published his first novel, **Sundown**, in 1934. Challenge Windzer, the main character, inherits the burdens of racialism and the politics of identities in two nations: one, the tribal interior traditions and subversions of descent; and the other, anomalous, reductive, and duplicitous.

Louis Owens wrote in **Other Destinies** that

> **Sundown** seems to offer a quintessential postcolonial scenario, as described by the authors of **The Empire Writes Back**: "A valid and active sense of self may have been eroded by dislocation, resulting from migration, the experience of enslavement.... Or it may have been destroyed by cultural denigration, the conscious and unconscious oppression of the indigenous personality and culture by a supposedly superior racial or cultural model." Like others in such a postcolonial drama, including nearly all Native Americans, Mathews's characters are beset by 'a pervasive concern with ... identity and authenticity."

Challenge is born in the blackjack region, "into the easily recognizable postcolonial and modernist position of deracination, alienation, and confusion."

LaVonne Ruoff noted in **American Indian Literatures** that Challenge's mother is a traditionalist and his father a mixedblood, who is

> an assimilationist and a strong advocate of allotment. Windzer is a passive hero who rejects his ancestral past without feeling at home in the white-dominated present. His white education has cut him off from his Indian roots; his cultural separation is completed by a brief stint at the University of Oklahoma and service with the armed forces during World War I.

Virginia Mathews wrote in the introduction to the University of Oklahoma edition of **Sundown** that the novel reflects so much of her father's

> personal experience, feeling, observation, conflict, and complexity, it is thought of as autobiographical, and of course, in a sense, it is. But there are important differences between the author and his protagonist.

> Like Chal Windzer in **Sundown**, John Joseph Mathews was of mixed Indian and white blood ... he was born in Indian Territory in 1894, also roamed the hills and prairies with horse and dog, a boy full of dreams and wonderings. Even then the tug of his Indian heritage was strong, and he spent time in the camps of the elder fullbloods, listening to their tales. Like Chal, he observed the coming of statehood in 1906, when the Osage Nation became part of the state of Oklahoma. Like Chal,

he went off to the University of Oklahoma, played football, and joined a fraternity, popular because of his good looks, his brains, and his athletic skill but always feeling himself to be a bit of an outsider. Mathews interrupted his college career to enlist in the army. He chose the cavalry, but because of his exceptional night vision, he was soon transferred to the aviation branch of the Signal Corps and served as an instructor in night flying and as an aviator in France during World War I.

Unlike the fictional character Chal, Mathews returned to the University of Oklahoma and was graduated Phi Beta Kappa in 1920, with a degree in geology. He refused the offer of a Rhodes Scholarship and went to Oxford on his own.

Mathews and D'Arcy McNickle, both mixedblood scholars and novelists, studied at Oxford University.

Mathews "toured Europe and North Africa on a motorbike, did a reporting stint for an American newspaper, married an American girl in Geneva, Switzerland, lived in California, and fathered two children before returning to his Osage hills in 1929." He was eighty-four years old at the time of his death in 1979.

The Birth of Challenge

The god of the great Osages was still dominant over the wild prairie and the blackjack hills when Challenge was born.

He showed his anger in fantastic play of lightning, and thunder that crashed and rolled among the hills; in the wind that came from the great tumbling clouds which appeared in the northwest and brought twilight and ominous milk-warm silence. His beneficence he showed on April mornings when the call of the prairie chicken came rolling over the awakened prairie and the killdeer seemed to be fussing; on June days when the emerald grass sparkled in the dew and soft breezes whispered and the quail whistled; and in the autumnal silences when the blackjacks were painted like dancers and dreamed in the iced sunshine with fatalistic patience. And perhaps on moon-silvered nights when the leaves of the blackjack were like metal and the insects chorused from the grass roots; when from the fantastic shadows came the petulant cry of the whippoorwill. But not on tranquil, dreamy nights when the screech owl screamed tremulously like a disillusioned soul, like the homeless spirit of a dead warrior. The screech owl carried the evil spirit.

On this birthnight the red, dim light which shone from the narrow window of the room where his mother labored, seemed faint and half-hearted in the brilliant moonlight; faint as though it were a symbol of the new order, yet diffident in the vivid, full-blooded paganism of the old; afraid, yet steady and persistent, and the only light in the Agency on this tranquil, silver night of silence. Not even an Indian dog barked.

Sometimes the reddish gleam of the eye under the oaks would be obliterated as one of the people in the room moved, then shine out again in its feeble persistence.

Then a door slammed. It was like a gunshot on the stillness. John Windzer came out onto the little porch, caught hold of a post and looked up at the postoaks.... An old setter came around the corner of the house and walked up to him. Half crouching with his tail lowered, he apologetically licked John's hand. John paid no attention to him but stood looking; looking up at the treetops, or over them at the faintly showing stars. With a quick movement he jumped from the porch and walked out under the trees. The setter followed him; the rise of hope for some sort of activity, or at least some recognition, was indicated by the slight raising of his tail.

John stopped at the picket gate and leaned on it, looking out on the dusty road; dust fetlock deep, and the wagon ruts casting long moon shadows like parallel black ribbons, cut into here and there by the ragged, black shadows of the oaks.

At the sound of his master's voice the setter brought his tail up and cocked his ear, then moved quickly and looked up into his face, eager but uncomprehending. The master's face was still turned toward the tops of the trees, and the voice sounded in a sort of rhythm:

> "And now I'm in the world alone
> Upon the wide wide sea;
> But why should I for others groan
> When none will sigh for me?"

Again the silence. Then a feeling sprang up in John; a pleasant, warm feeling of victory, and he felt that he had conquered, but he didn't know just what—anyway he was happily vindictive. He felt like a great orator standing there in the bright light, and that all the imaginary calumnies that had been heaped upon him were proved false, and he had emerged as a hero; a conqueror, not only by his sword but by ringing words, and this little patch of the world under the oaks, unresisting and tranquil in this savage valley, was symbolic of the world that had ignored him and taken special trouble to persecute him. The setter raised his paw and scratched tentatively at John's leg. He looked down, then raised his hand to the silent, patient trees, and said in a louder voice with a special tone which he believed to be an imitation of William Jennings Bryan, his hero:

> "Perchance my Dog will whine in vain
> Till fed by stranger hands;
> But long ere I come back again
> He'd tear me where he stands."

He hesitated, then, "But I live as a challenge." However, his thoughts were not clear; he didn't know what he challenged. As a matter of fact it had never been definite, and his confused mind tonight could not formulate words. This inability caused a slight annoyance. He moved away from the gate and started toward the house, stepping off the flagged walk once, but righting himself and walking on with shoulders straight and a quick animal-like movement into the house, slamming the door behind him. The door popped like a gun; like a crack under the strain of the heavy silence.

He fumbled in the dark kitchen, then with the aid of the broad shafts of moonlight coming through the windows found the bottle of Rock and Rye where he had left it. His hand stuck to the neck as he turned the bottle up to his wide mouth. He set it heavily on the table and said, "Hagh." He stood a moment, then went with light but unsteady steps into the room where the dim red light shone.

The government doctor was ready to leave, and the wrinkled old woman who was John's mother-in-law was smiling broadly. The doctor said, "Well, John, a boy all right and a daisy." John looked at the hump under the crazy patterned quilts, then at the straight black hair flowing over the pillow. He could see the quilts move gently as his wife breathed.

Again the ecstatic feeling came over him, and he said oratorically as the thought presented itself for the first time, "He shall be a challenge to the disinheritors of his people. We'll call him Challenge." The doctor looked at him with a quizzical expression, then smiled with tolerant amusement, which changed to seriousness when John looked at him. The old mother-in-law padded here and there in her moccasins, her stomach and her flat breasts shaking. As the doctor put his hand on the door knob, she sat down in the only chair, and with her forefinger twisted a strand of iron gray hair over each ear, but remained silent.

"Well, good night," said the doctor. "Challenge is a good name."

John was up early. He went to the kitchen and kindled the fire in the stove, brushed the shavings and pieces of bark off the top with a wild turkey wing. He went to the barn and fed the team, and his buckskin saddle-horse. When he came back to the kitchen the white girl was up and preparing breakfast. He took a glass, put sugar in it, then filled it with hot water from the kettle, then poured in some of the straight rye whiskey, carried the mixture to the front porch and sat down to await breakfast.

At ten o'clock he went into his wife's room and looked at the baby. The little fellow was wrinkled and very red, with a surprising shock of very black hair.

John left the room without saying anything to his wife. He brushed his suit carefully before putting it on, then arranged his large black cravat, and fastened in it the diamond horseshoe stickpin which Le Chateau had brought him from Washington. When he was dressed he went to the barn, saddled the buckskin, and swung up the dusty road in the crisp air of early autumn.

It was only a short distance from his small frame house to the center of the Agency where the Council House and the traders' stores were, but he always rode the buckskin, tied him to the hitching rack at the side of the store. All day the little pony stood, patiently stamping to shake the flies from his forelegs. Sometime another pony would be hitched to the rack near him, and he would squeal his displeasure, lowering his ears flat to his skull, and showing his yellow teeth.

The benches in front of the trader's store were filled as John walked up. The red and white striped blankets of the fullbloods shone conspicuously among the drab suits of the mixedbloods. He said, "How," to the bench-sitters in general, and receiving a lazy response, walked into the store. The trader looked up from behind the counter, his hands black and greasy from handling the shiny harness which he had just hung up on some pegs behind him.

"Well!" he smiled, "Ready for them cigars this mornin'?"

"Reckon I am."

"Sure 'nough, now?"

"Yeah."

"Tain't a boy, surely?"

"Guess so this time."

"Say, now, that's purty fine. I tell yuh." The trader went to the glass showcase, which was profusely specked by flies, and brought out a box which had been opened, in fact the only box of cigars in the store. "Here," he said, " 'bout half full, but reckon they's enough to go 'round." He handed the box to John and went over to the desk to make an entry in a large book.

Soon the smoke from the cheap cigars was curling around the broad-rimmed Stetsons, both black and light ones, and eddying around the eagle feathers sticking in the scalplocks of the fullbloods. The air was so still that the smoke hung in little clouds around the heads of the sitters. A forlorn, nondescript Indian dog got up from the cool shade at the side of the bench, stretched, yawned vocally, as though there had been some painful disturbance on his inside, looked up at the silent men with profound sadness, then trotted dejectedly across the dusty road.

The shade in front of the store became narrower as the sun climbed over the quiet valley, and the shade of the postoaks, which rose with great dignity above the dusty area, drew closer and closer around their roots.

A wagon came down the street, creaking, and with hubs knocking on the axles; the hoofs of the horses and the rasping of the tires were muted in the deep dust. A tall blanketed figure sat straight and regal on the front seat, and in the bed a fat woman sat with a baby-board across her lap. Suddenly there was a sharp, inquisitive bark from the shade of the blackjacks across the road, then a medley of excited barking, and lean shapes of all colors and blends imaginable rushed out and ran toward the wagon. The three dogs following the wagon stopped and their hair stood erect on their backs and along their spines. Then there was a medley of short barks, growls, whining and sharp, shrill yelps. The fat woman shouted in a shrill, menacing voice, but her words were drowned in the terrific din. The tall man seemed not to notice. He drove on to a hitching rack under a tall oak, threw the reins out on each side, slowly climbed down and hitched his team. The woman climbed out, still scolding, although the dogs that had followed the wagon were running for shelter across the road with the others in pursuit.

The tall Indian came up to the group on the bench and stopped; his wife, who had thrown the baby-board on her back, went into the store. A "how" was exchanged, then Charlie Bienvenue, a mixedblood, said with shining black eyes, "How, my little son," in Osage. Everyone laughed. This was a joke, as Red Feather, the tall Indian, was a man of great dignity and much older than Bienvenue. When the laughter had died, one of the blanketed figures said, "It is good to see you." After a long silence, John reached down under the bench and pulled out the box of cigars. As he offered it to Red Feather he said, "My father, I want you to smoke this—a son has come to my house." Wrinkles came to the corners of Red Feather's eyes as he smiled. "Good," he said. "For long time I thought that you did not have strong juices in your body, but now since you have son I know that you have good juices." John was slightly embarrassed as he looked down and smiled guiltily. The others laughed. Red Feather continued, "They say it is good that son should come to lodge after many girls have come. I believe it is better since these girls have gone away."

One by one the fullbloods stood up, pulled their blankets about them, and walked off down the road. Soon, only John and three mixedbloods were left. Bienvenue threw the butt of his cigar away, then said to no one in particular, "Looks like the guv'mint's gonna play hell with the Frazer lease—'s talkin' with Jim the other day and he said he thought the Council 'ud have to go to Washin'ton this winter."

"Ain't the Frazer lease all right?" asked John. "Whatta they wantta monkey 'round about it for?"

"That's what I say," spoke up Pilgrim, and he spat tobacco juice out into the dust, as though freeing his tongue for action. "But of course the Reservation Oil and Gas is gonna try to git in somehow and—they tell me they're purty powerful—tell me the guv'mint's fer 'em too."

The Bienvenue said, "Hell, that 'ud ruin the Nation, if they ever let them fellas git a finger in."

Ed Caldwell had not spoken. Suddenly he reached in his pocket and pulled out a great gold watch to which a fob with an onyx ornament was attached. "Noon," he announced. "I tell yu they's a nigger in the woodpile somewhur. They's a few fellas in the Department itself actin' funny about the whole thing. I ain't gonna call no names. We'd better play clost to the chest up there. If they's any oil in the Nation, why we wantta get the benefit of it—if they ain't, well, they won't be nobody hurt."

"The guv'mint won't allow the Reservation Oil and Gas not to do only what's fair," said John. Ed got up and kicked each leg of his pants down, then winked at Bienvenue, "Jist come in from Elgin last night—let's go down to the barn and see what we can find." The sitters rose eagerly. "Ha ha ha HEY!" said John. "Ha ha ha HEY!" echoed the others, and they followed Ed's tall form across the dusty road to the government barn.

D'Arcy McNickle

(1904–1977) Salish

D'Arcy McNickle was born on the Flathead Reservation in Montana in 1904. He attended mission schools; the boarding school at Chemawa, Oregon; and studied at the University of Montana, Oxford University, Columbia University, and the University of Grenoble.

McNickle was a notable scholar, novelist, and historian and an active intellectual in the formation of native organizations and federal policies. Dorothy Parker reported in **A Biography of D'Arcy McNickle** *that he "served as an administrator in the Bureau of Indian Affairs under John Collier" and he was a professor of anthropology at the University of Saskatchewan. Moreover, he was the first director of the Center for American Indian History at the Newberry Library in Chicago. In 1983, six years after his death, the center was renamed in his honor the D'Arcy McNickle Center for the History of the American Indian.*

McNickle was the author of three novels, one a posthumous publication. **The Surrounded** *was first published in 1936.* **Runner in the Sun: A Story of Indian Maize**, *a novel for younger readers, appeared in 1954.* **Wind from an Enemy Sky**, *a story of family conflict over the development of sacred tribal land, was published one year after his death. All three novels have been reprinted by university presses.*

The Surrounded *was first submitted to publishers with the title* **The Hungry Generation**. *The original manuscript was a much longer narrative that included a romance in France. McNickle was then known as D'Arcy Dahlberg, the assumed surname of his stepfather. He was never adopted and restored his birth name in 1933.*

"On April 6, 1929, Harcourt, Brace and Company rejected a novel manuscript by D'Arcy Dahlberg entitled **The Hungry Generations**, *" wrote Louis Owens in* **Other Destinies**.

> *Addressed to "Miss Dahlberg," the rejection letter quoted a confidential reader's report: "The story of an Indian, wandering between two generations, two cultures; excellent.... A new territory to be explored: ancient material used for a different end. Perhaps the beginning of a new Indian literature to rival that of Harlem." More than five years later, with the novel entirely rewritten, McNickle would receive another editor's manuscript report even more favorable.*

But the novel was rejected. Finally the novel was published by Dodd, Mead in 1936.

The Surrounded *begins as Archilde Leon returns to his home on the Flathead Reservation in Montana. Archilde, like the author, had been away at a boarding school in Oregon. "Archilde's venturing forth into the 'other' world outside of Salish culture resembles a 'wandering time' or vision quest common to Native American cultures," wrote Louis Owens.*

> *Such a journey—requiring temporary separation from community—is a search for identity, for a profound understanding of one's place within the world, and, if the quest is successful, results in a newly forged sense of intimate relationship with the.... Archilde, however returns home with the appearance of being both assimilated and disoriented, dressed in a blue suit, his shoes polished, and his attitude toward his Indian past one of indifference bordering on embarrassment. The disjuncture between worlds is emphatic: "When you came home to your Indian mother," McNickle writes, "you had to remember that it was a different world."*

Dorothy Parker pointed out in **A Biography of D'Arcy McNickle** *that Catherine, Archilde's mother, "conveys the traditional Salish culture throughout the novel, and her estrangement" from her Spanish husband, Max Leon, who is an outsider, "provides one element of the story's basic conflict. Even more significant is her eventual estrangement from the church. Although she confesses her role in the murder of the game warden, the church's absolution fails to give her the peace of mind she seeks." Archilde bears the burdens of silence and natural reason; he honors his mother as he would native traditions, and chooses not to own his innocence as a witness in the prosecution of his mother.*

"Max stopped and looked down at his Indian wife," wrote McNickle. "When he talked to her he had to use her tongue, since if he tried to use English, which she knew perfectly, she would pretend not to understand. He had to try to overcome her obstinacy by never talking to her." Max spoke to her in Salish.

Catherine had been his wife for forty years, and "she had borne him eleven children, and he had come no closer to her than that. She would not tell him what he knew she knew. She did not trust him. That was something to make a man reflect on the meaning and purpose of his life."

Max "spat and walked away. He entered his house through the kitchen. It was as well furnished as any white man's house." Indeed, and there is one more metaphor of the distance between families and cultures.

A Different World

Archilde Leon had been away from his father's ranch for nearly a year, yet when he left the stage road and began the half-mile walk to the house he did not hurry. When he emerged from behind a clump of thornbush and cottonwood and caught his first glimpse of the cluster of buildings before him, he looked once, and that was all.

He avoided the front of the big house, where his father would most likely be sitting, and made for the dirt-roofed log cabin which occupied lower ground, down toward the creek. Two dogs, one yellow and one black and white, leaped and howled, but they were the only ones to meet him.

He walked past the big house, which was his father's, and went to the cabin, his mother's. There she was, as he knew she would be, sitting in the shade. If she heard him she did not look up at once. But she was a little deaf and a little blind—perhaps she had not sensed his approach. He let the heavy suitcase slip from his sweating hand.

Then she looked up. A sigh escaped her and a quick smile multiplied the many fine lines in her wrinkled brown face.

Here he was, the best of her sons, and the youngest, home again after a year—but would he stay? She had only a faint idea of where he had been; the world out that way was so unlike Sniél-emen; she had even less of an idea of what he did when he went away. But never mind. Here he was again. She smiled quickly, a little at a distance; she did not wish to embarrass him with her attention.

"So you have come back," she said.

"Yes, I am here." He turned his suitcase over on its side for a seat.

"Where have you been this time?"

"To Portland. That's where the stinking water is."

She let the word echo in her ears, saying nothing herself, but it had no meaning. If he had said he had been down toward the mouth of the Supoilshi (Columbia) River, she would have known what he meant. But Portland! Her red-rimmed eyes gazed toward the timber which came down to the far bank of the creek. Two boys were splashing in the water down there.

"You have been gone a long time."

"I had a job. I played my fiddle in a show house. I can always get a job now any time I go away."

She looked at him quickly, taking him in. He wore a blue suit and a white shirt and his tan shoes were new and polished. So he could go away any time now? He did not have to be fed at home?

"They paid me this money. Look!" She barely glanced at the offered money. It was all strange, she could not make it into a picture. An Indian boy, she thought, belonged with his people.

They sat in silence for some time. It was useless to speak of fiddle playing, and for a while Archilde could think of nothing that was not equally useless. When you came home to your Indian mother, you had to remember that it was a different world. Anyhow you had not come to show your money and talk about yourself. There would be fishing, riding, climbing a mountainside—those things you wanted to do one more time. Why talk of fiddle-playing?

The heat of the afternoon lingered. The three horses in the pasture below the house were bothered by the flies. They had been in the timber across the creek since midday and had come out only a short while before. As they ate, they moved along, stopping now and then to rub their muzzles on their forelegs or to kick themselves under the belly.

His gaze returned to his mother. How did she look after a year? No different. He had not expected her to look any different. Her eyes, which were getting weaker each year, were watery slits in the brown skin. She wore a handkerchief around her head and her calico dress was long and full and held in at the waist by a beaded belt. Her buckskin moccasins gave off a pungent odor of smoke. Nothing was any different. He knew it without looking. He had not come all the way from Portland to these mountains in Montana to satisfy himself on that score.

"No one fishes when you are away. My bones groan so loud when I walk the fish stay under their rocks."

It seemed impossible that no one cared to fish. The creek was full of swift, cunning trout. He got excited just thinking about it. Tomorrow he would cut himself a pole and try it.

The old lady was saying something else. "I will have some people here. We will make a feast and my friends will see you again."

That was something he had forgotten to include in his visit—the old lady and her feasts! You gorged yourself on meat until you felt sick, and a lot of old people told tiresome stories. He frowned. He ought to refuse. He had not come for a feast. She ought to be told that. But it was a small matter. His mother was old. It was a small matter.

"How is everybody?" He had begun to smoke a cigarette which he took ready rolled out of a package.

The question made the old lady sigh. Eheu! It was bad!

"Louis stole some horses last week. I think no one knows it yet. He's in the mountains."

"He'll go to pen if they find him."

"He'll go to hell!"

Already he was hearing the old stories—quarreling, stealing, fighting. His brothers knew nothing else. And his mother knew nothing but the fear of hell, for herself and for her sons.

A small girl, his niece, came to the corner of the cabin. Her hair was braided, with white strings tied to the end of each braid. She was bashful and kept her chin on her breast.

"Gran'pa wants to see you," she announced when she was still a dozen paces away.

"Come and shake hands, Annie!"

She looked at him but hugged the cabin wall.

Archilde got to his feet and stretched himself. He looked toward the mountains in the east, and then upward to the fleckless sky. Nowhere in the world, he imagined, was there a sky of such depth and freshness. He wanted never to forget it, whatever he might be in times to come. Yes, wherever he might be!

Down by the creek his two nephews were standing uncertainly and watching the house. They had just seen Archilde. Their shouts died away and they went behind the brush to dress.

As Archilde picked up his suitcase and walked toward the house he realized all of a sudden that he dreaded meeting his father, Max Leon, the Spaniard. That dread was something which went back a long time, and Archilde, who was growing into a man now, was disturbed by it. It ought not to be.

His father had just awakened from his afternoon nap and was sitting on the front porch, his gray hair tousled and matted. Every afternoon on awakening he drank a whisky eggnog. A half-empty glass stood on the table at his elbow. He stretched out his hand.

It was a thin, bony hand. Archilde looked down at it with some surprise. This was his father's hand.

"Sit down, my *son!*" With what sarcasm he could utter that word! "Agnes said you were here. Where have you been this time?" His voice was deep and its least variation gave strong emphasis to his words. He handled his voice like a whip.

"In Portland."

"Portland, I suppose, is a busy city. They make you work to live. And what did you do? I see you have good clothes."

"I played in an orchestra."

"Yes? What do you play—the accordion, or mouthharp?"

"The fiddle."

"Really? I've never heard you. You never play for your people at home."

Archilde sat down then and looked at his Spanish father. He was of middle size and build, of stocky limbs. His face sagged into pouches and under the stubble of gray whiskers the skin looked oily. He had a high forehead and a long nose. It was not a weak face, and not a commonplace one. What was it in that face that could so dominate one who was no longer a child? Archilde gazed steadily at his father and tried not to show his irritation.

"Some day you must play for me," his father was saying.

"I have no fiddle now. I gave it to a friend."

"In a card game, perhaps?" There was a slight smile.

"No, it was a present."

"But don't you play cards?"

"No."

"What kind of Indian are you, then?"

Archilde shrugged his shoulders. His confidence was failing him. It was just as it had always been in recent years; after a few more thrusts from Max he would be helpless before him. He had thought it would never happen again.

"You haven't many answers. But tell me this, have you any money after working, as you say?"

Archilde showed his money. He wanted to refuse, out of defiance, but he showed the money.

"You better let me put it in the bank for you."

"No, I'll keep it."

"So! You have learned nothing! You will blow your money on a good time and then go on living off me!"

It was more than Archilde could stand. He had to speak out in anger and so confess his helplessness.

"I didn't come to live off you, God damn it! I came to see my mother, not you, and in a few days I'm going again. Keep your stinking money!" He knew it was the answer of a child.

Old Leon laughed. "I see you're getting a good opinion of yourself." He said it insultingly, and yet his eyes looked closely at the boy. At least he had not slunk away like a whipped dog.

A horseman appeared in the lane, riding swiftly, a cloud of dust hanging like a plume in the still air. The rider, a rancher from the flatlands of the valley, tied his horse and entered the front gate.

"You're riding fast on a hot day," Max called out. "Come up in the shade!"

"That's fine grain you got down by the road. On the flat we're burned out."

"So I've heard. No doubt you're thirsty. Here, Agnes! Bring water to Emile Pariseau!"

Agnes, his daughter, kept his house. Her fullblood husband had had his head kicked in by a horse, and Max, though he spoke profanely of her husband, brought her and her three children to live with him. She appeared on the porch with a pail of water and a long-handled dipper.

Max scowled. "Where's the pitcher? You're not bringing water to an Indian!"

The rancher was good-natured. "I never drink out of a pitcher—this is all right." Seeing Archilde standing off to one side Pariseau spoke to him.

"How long you been away, Arsheel?"

When the question was answered another was asked. "Have you seen your brother Louis?" The rancher avoided Max's eyes.

"No. I've just come."

"Are you looking for Louis?" Max asked. "God knows where he is, Pariseau. I probably know less about my family than you do."

"That's what I come to see you about."

Archilde went inside. He had waited to be dismissed but Max appeared to ignore him.

Pariseau stopped to roll a cigarette, saying nothing meanwhile. When he had finished he looked up.

"What I come to tell you is this. Louis stole some horses from me. We got the goods on him. Somebody seen him with the horses."

Max's face went cold. "What's that got to do with me?"

"Well, we used to be neighbors—I wanted to tell you. If we catch him it'll have to go hard. There's too damn much horse stealing by these young fellows—"

"Good!" Max cut in on him. "Send 'em up to pen, hang 'em—but what's it got to do with me?"

"Well, I dunno. I just thought I'd tell you. Then you could tell him to lay low— or you could maybe tell me where to find him." The rancher grinned.

"I see none of these sons of bitches unless they come here to eat—and they never stay long. I don't know where you'll find him. His mother's relations are everywhere. Don't ask me."

In a little while the rancher rode away, having heard Max Leon curse his sons up one side and down the other, as they say.

He sat motionless for several minutes, watching the rider disappear behind a cloud of dust. His eyes had been alert before the rancher came; now they looked dull. He was slow and heavy in getting to his feet. His legs were slightly bowed from many years of riding. He walked toward his wife's cabin.

She was sitting as Archilde had left her an hour before. The shadow of the cabin had lengthened. Max stopped and looked down at his Indian wife. When he talked to her he had to use her tongue, since if he tried to use English, which she knew perfectly, she would pretend not to understand. He had tried to overcome her obstinacy by never talking to her. That was some years ago. He had not been able to keep it up, there were occasions when he had to speak, and in the end he had decided that it was better to get an answer than to fight an endless battle. So he spoke her Salish.

"Where's Louis?"

"How should I know!"

"Have you heard about him?"

"I hear nothing. My sons are scattered."

"He stole some horses."

She was silent, gesturing slightly with her hand.

"A friend has come to warn me. He said the police would hang him. If you know where he is tell me."

"I know nothing. My sons are afraid to come here."

"I'll send a rider to warn him."

A silence.

He had been married for forty years to this woman, she had borne him eleven children, and he had come no closer to her than that. She would not tell him what he knew she knew. She did not trust him. That was something to make a man reflect on the meaning and purpose of his life.

He spat and walked away. He entered his house through the kitchen. It was as well as furnished as any white man's house. A stove with nickel trimmings, a linoleum covering on the floor, a white enameled kitchen cabinet against the wall, a well stocked pantry—no white man with a white woman for a wife had more.

Agnes sat on the floor by the window peeling potatoes. Max took a drink from the water bucket.

"Where's Louis?" he asked as he stood drinking.

"Perhaps in town, I don't know."

He stood there for a moment on the point of asking another question, but scowled and walked away. To Archilde, who was drinking coffee at the kitchen table, he motioned to follow him to the porch.

"What does your mother say about Louis?"

Archilde appeared to reflect. "His name wasn't mentioned. Did Pariseau want him?"

"He's been stealing horses. You didn't know about that, eh?"

Archilde didn't know.

Max was wrathful, his face deeply colored. "So! You're going to be like the rest! Lying to me already and you're not home an hour! I'm telling you this for Louis' good. If they catch him they'll hang him! Tell the old lady yourself, if you won't take my word. I'll save his damn neck; I'll do that much. Understand?"

Archilde started to walk away.

"Don't let her know I talked to you about this."

That was how matters always stood in Max Leon's family. There was always this distrust, this welfare.

He was a tall youth, just short of six feet, and built with a slim waist and swinging limbs. He had a long head, much like his father's, and his face was distinguished by thinness of lips, fineness of nostrils and alert eyes.

He had not walked far when he observed through the tail of his eye someone moving in a clump of willows near the creek. He kept his eyes lowered as he walked along and appeared to take no notice. He waited until he had gone a little way past, then he whirled quickly in his tracks.

His two small nephews, taken unawares, were caught in the act of running to cover. They had been following him down the creek, too bashful to come out in the open. They started to run but stopped when he called.

"Hey, there! Mike and Narcisse! Wait a minute! I've got a cigarette here!"

They kept their heads lowered as he came up to them. When he gave them cigarettes their eyes sparkled.

"Now tell me, why do you run like rabbits?"

Neither answered at once; then the older, a boy of twelve, the one who was called Narcisse, found his nerve.

"Let's see your money!"

Archilde laughed. "Just look!"

"Where you steal that?" asked Mike, younger by three years.

"I didn't steal it! I worked for it!" He scowled. "Who tells you about stealing?" Such a question pained Mike. He did not have to be told such things.

The boys flopped down in the grass beside their uncle. They were no longer shy.

"Where's Louis?" he asked. They looked at each other and did not answer.

"Don't look stupid like a calf. The old lady told me already. Don't tell Max anything if he asks."

"That's what the old lady said," Narcisse remarked.

"How many horses did he steal?"

"About fifty, I guess," Mike said proudly.

"Big liar!" Narcisse pushed him over in the grass. "The old lady said six big mares. He came last week and got meat. I guess he's in the mountains."

"Last week I shot a grouse," Mike bragged.

"You shot him on the ground! I shot him out of the tree!" Narcisse was scornful.

"Pouf! Your shot just tickled him. Me, I killed him!"

"Neither of you catch fish, the old lady tells me."

"We got no hooks," Narcisse explained.

"Make a spear then."

"You talk crazy!" Mike said. "You got to have a hook to make a spear!"

"That shows what empty heads you got. All you need is a piece of wire."

"Buy us hooks! Who wants to fish with wire?"

"All right. But tell me, how was it in school?"

"Huh. Those Fathers don't know much!" Mike would not explain further what he meant but he was positive about meaning what he said. Narcisse had to explain.

"They call him Little Lord Jesus in school because he won't cut his hair. He thinks he'll be a chief if he don't cut it off."

"No sir!" Mike kicked out at his brother and they rolled over together in the grass. Archilde stopped the fight.

"I'll take you to the barber, Mike. He'll put nice smell in your hair."

"Then I'll smell like a skunk cabbage."

"No, like a horse's poop!" Again the boys tangled.

"Stop fighting! It's supper time." They were on their feet in an instant and were racing across the meadow.

Archilde followed more slowly. He had been home just these few hours and he was wishing to God that he had stayed away. But perhaps he would know enough next time. Tomorrow he would go fishing. He would look at the sky some more. He would ride his horse. Then wherever he might go, he would always keep the memory of these things.

Elizabeth Cook-Lynn

(b. 1930) Dakota

Elizabeth Cook-Lynn was born in the government hospital at Fort Thompson, South Dakota, in 1930. She is a member of the Crow Creek tribe. The Crow Creek Reservation is located southeast of Pierre, South Dakota, on a bend in the Missouri River.

She studied at South Dakota State College and has taught at several universities. **Wicazo Sa Review**, *a notable native journal of literary and historical studies, was founded and edited by her when she was an associate professor at Washington State University in Cheney.*

Cook-Lynn is the author of poetry, short stories, and a novel. **Then Badger Said This** *was her first book, a collection of poems and narratives published in 1978.* **Blue Cloud Quarterly** *published* **Seek the House of Relatives**, *a collection of poems, five years later. Her poems have appeared in numerous journals and anthologies, including* **Prairie Schooner** *and* **The Remembered Earth**. *She celebrates the honorable conditions of tribal sovereignty and survivance in her novel* **From the River's Edge**, *published in 1991.*

"Ever since I learned to read, I have wanted to be a writer," she wrote in her autobiographical essay "You May Consider Speaking about Your Art...." Cook-Lynn read everything from **Faust** *to* **The Scarlet Letter** *and the Sears catalog. "Reading, if it is not too obvious to say so, precedes writing, though I teach college students today who are examples of an apparently opposing point of view. They have read nothing." Anger*

> *is what started me writing. Writing, for me, then, is an act of defiance born of the need to survive. I am me. I exist. I am a Dakotan. I write. It is the quintessential act of optimism born of frustration. It is an act of courage, I think. And, in the end, as Simon Ortiz says, it is an act that defies oppression.*

Cook-Lynn pointed out that in her early days she had a need to write and to survive

> *in a world in which the need to write was not primary. The need "to tell," however, was. And so I listened and heard about a world that existed in the flesh and in the imagination, too, and in the hearts and minds of real people. In those days I thought the world was made up of "Siouxs" and "Wasichus."*

Wasichus are white people.

> *"Seeing the Missouri River country of the Sioux is like seeing where the earth first recognized humanity and where it came to possess a kind of unique internal coherence about that condition," she wrote in* **From the River's Edge**.

A Good Chance

I

When I got to Crow Creek I went straight to the Agency, the place they call "the Fort," and it was just like it always has been to those of us who leave often and come home now and then: mute, pacific, impenitent, concordant. I drove slowly through the graveled streets until I came to a light blue HUD house.

"I'm looking for Magpie," I said quietly to the little boy who opened the door and looked at me steadily with clear brown eyes. We stood and regarded one another until I, adultlike, felt uncomfortable and so I repeated, "Say, I'm looking for Magpie. Do you know where he is?"

No answer.

"Is your mother here?"

After a few moments of looking me over, the little boy motioned me inside.

"Wait here," he said.

He went down the cluttered hallway and came back with a young woman wearing jeans and a cream-colored ribbon shirt and carrying a naked baby covered only with rolls of fat. "I'm Amelia," she said. "Do you want to sit down?"

The small, shabby room she led me into was facing east and the light flooded through the window making everything too bright, contributing to the uneasiness we felt with each other as we sat down.

"I need to find Magpie," I said. "I've really got some good news for him, I think," and I pointed to the briefcase I was carrying. "I have his poems and a letter of acceptance from a University in California where they want him to come and participate in the Fine Arts Program they have started for Indians."

"You know then that he's on parole, do you?" she asked, speaking quickly with assurance. "I'm his wife but we haven't been together for a while." She looked at the little boy who had opened the door, motioned for him to go outside and, after he had left she said softly, "I don't know where my husband is but I've heard that he's in town somewhere."

"Do you mean in Chamberlain?"

"Yes, I live here at the Agency with his sister and she said that she saw him in town, quite a while ago."

I said nothing.

"Did you know that he was on parole."

"Well, no, not exactly," I said hesitantly, "I haven't kept in touch with him but I heard that he was in some kind of trouble. In fact, I didn't know about you. He didn't tell me that he was married though I might have suspected that he was."

She smiled at me and said, "He's gone a lot. It's not safe around here for him, you know. His parole officer really watches him all the time and so sometimes it is just better for him not to come here. Besides, " she continued, looking down, absent-mindedly squeezing the rolls of fat on the baby's knees, "we haven't been together for a while."

Uncomfortably, I folded and refolded my hands and tried to think of something appropriate to say. The baby started to cry as though, bored with all this, he needed to hear his own voice. It was not an expression of pain or hunger. He rolled his tongue against his gums and wrinkled his forehead but when his mother whispered something to him he quieted immediately and lay passive in her lap.

"But Magpie would not go to California," she said, her eyes somehow masking something significant that she thought she knew of him. "He would never leave here now even if you saw him and talked to him about it."

"But he did before," I said, not liking the sound of my own defensive words. "He went to the University of Seattle."

"Yeah, but... well, that was before," she said, as though to finish the matter.

"Don't you want him to go?" I asked.

Quickly, she responded, "Oh, it's not up to me to say. He is gone from me now." She moved her hand to her breast, "I'm just telling you that you are in for a disappointment. He no longer needs the things that people like you want him to need," she said positively.

When she saw that I didn't like her reference to "people like you" and the implication that I was interested in the manipulation of her estranged husband, she stopped for a moment and then put her hand on my arm. "Listen," she said, "Magpie is happy now, finally. He is in good spirits, handsome and free and strong. He sits at the drum and sings with his brothers: he's okay now. When he was saying all those things against the government and against the council, he became more and more ugly and embittered and I used to be afraid for him. But I'm not now. Please, why don't you just leave it alone now?"

She seemed so young to know how desperate things had become for her young husband in those days and I was genuinely moved by her compassion for him and for a few moments neither of us spoke. Finally, I said, "But I have to see him. I have to ask him what he wants to do. Don't you see that I have to do that?"

She leaned back into the worn, dirty sofa and looked at me with cold hatred. Shocked at the depth of her reaction, I got up and went outside to my car. The little boy who had opened the door for me appeared at my elbow and, as I opened the car door, asked, "If you find him, will you come back?"

"No," I said, "I don't think so."

I had the sense that the little boy picked up a handful of gravel and threw it after my retreating car as I drove slowly away. When I pulled around the corner I glanced over my shoulder and saw that he was still standing there, watching my car leave the street: he was small, dark, closed in that attitude of terrible resignation I recognized from my own childhood and I knew that resignation to be the only defense, the only immunity in a world where children are often the martyrs. That fleeting glimpse of my own past made me even more certain that Magpie had to say yes or no to this thing himself, that none of us who knew and loved him could do it for him.

II

"Home of the Hunkpati," proclaimed a hand-lettered sign hanging over the cash register at the cafe. It could not be said to be an inaccurate proclamation, as all of us who perceived the movement of our lives as emanating from this place knew, only an incomplete one. For as surely as the Hunkpati found this their home, so did the Isianti, the Ihantowai, even the Winnebagoes briefly, and others. Even in its incompleteness, though, it seemed to me to be *ne plus ultra,* the super-structure of historiography which allows us to account for ourselves, and I took it as an affirmation of some vague sort. In a contemplative mood now, I sat down in a booth and ordered a cup of what turned out to be the bitterest coffee I'd had since I left Santa Fe: "A-a-a-eee-e, pe juta sapa," I could hear my uncle saying.

I thought about the Hunkpati and all the people who had moved to this place and some who were put in prison here as great changes occurred, as they strove to maintain an accommodation to those changes. The magic acts of white men don't seem to work well on Indians, I thought, and the stories they tell of our collective demise have been "greatly exaggerated" or, to put it into the vernacular of the myth-tellers of my childhood, "Heh yela owi hake"—this, the appropriate ending to the stories which nobody was expected to believe anyway.

I was thinking these things so intently I didn't notice the woman approaching until she was standing beside the booth saying, "They gave me your note at the BIA office. You wanted to see me?"

"Yes," I said from the great distance of my thoughts, having nearly forgotten my search for the young poet I wished to talk to about his great opportunity. As I looked up into her sober intent face, it all seemed unimportant and for a moment I felt almost foolish.

Remembering my mission, I said solicitously, "Thank you for coming," and asked her to sit down across the table from me.

"Are you Salina?"

"Yes."

"This place here didn't even exist when I was a child," I told her. "The town that we called 'the Fort' in those days lay hidden along the old creek bed and the prairie above here was the place where we gathered to dance in the summer sun."

"I know," she said. "My mother told me that we even had a hospital here then, before all this was flooded for the Oahe Dam. She was born there in that hospital along the Crow Creek."

We sat in thoughtful remembrance, scarcely breathing, with twenty years difference in our ages, and I thought: yes, I was born there too, along that creek bed in that Indian hospital which no longer exists, in that Agency town which no longer exists except in the memories of people who have the capacity to take deeply to heart the conditions of the past. And later my uncle offered me to the four grandfathers in my grandmother's lodge even though it was November and the snow had started, and I was taken into the bosom of a once-larger and significant, now dwindling family, a girl-child who in the old days would have had her own name.

Abruptly, she said, "I don't know where Magpie is. I haven't seen him in four days."

"I've got his poems here with me," I said. "He has a good chance of going to a Fine Arts school in California, but I have to talk with him and get him to fill out some papers. I know that he is interested."

"No, he isn't," she broke in. "He doesn't have those worthless, shitty dreams anymore."

"Don't say that, Salina. This is a good chance for him."

"Well, you can think what you want," she said and turned her dark eyes on me, "but have you talked to him lately? Do you know him as he is now?"

"I know he is good. I know he has such talent."

"He's Indian," she said, as though there were some distinction I didn't know about. "And he's back here to stay this time."

She sat there all dressed up in her smart gray suit and her black shiny fashion boots, secure in her GS-6 Bureau secretarial position, and I wondered what she knew about "being Indian" that accounted for the certainty of her response. Was it possible that these two women with whom I had talked today, these two lovers of Magpie, one a wife and the other a mistress, could be right about all of this? Is it possible that the drama of our personal lives is so quiescent as to be mere ceremony whose staging is unpredictable? Knowable? In the hands of those who love us, are we mere actors mouthing their lines? Magpie, I thought, my friend, a brother to me, who am I and who are they to decide these things for you?

Near defeat in the face of the firm resolve of these two women, almost resigned with folded hands on the table, I looked out the window of the cafe and saw the lines of HUD houses row upon row, the design of government bureaucrats painted upon the surface of this long-grassed prairie, and I remembered the disapproving look of the little boy who threw gravel at my car and I found the strength to try again.

"Would you drive into Chamberlain with me?" I asked.

She said nothing.

"If he is Indian as you say, whatever that means, and if he is back here to stay this time and if he tells me that himself, I'll let it go. But Salina," I urged, "I must talk to him and ask him what he wants to do. You see that, don't you?"

"Yes." she said finally. "He has a right to know about this, but you'll see..."

Her heels clicked on the brief sidewalk in front of the cafe as we left, and she became agitated as she talked. "After all that trouble he got into during that protest at Custer when the courthouse was burned, he was in jail for a year. He's still on parole and he will be on parole for another five years—and they didn't even prove anything against him! Five years! Can you believe that? People these days can commit murder and not get that kind of a sentence."

She stopped to light a cigarette before she opened the car door and got in.

As we drove out of "the Fort" toward town, she said, "Jeez, look at that," and she pointed with her cigarette to a huge golden eagle tearing the flesh from some carcass which lay in the ditch alongside the road.

I thought as many times as I've been on this road in my lifetime. I've never seen an eagle here before. I've never seen one even near this place . . . ma tuki.

III

Elgie was standing on the corner near the F & M Bank as we drove down the main street of Chamberlain, and both Salina and I knew without speaking that this man, this good friend of Magpie's, would know of his whereabouts. We looked at him as we drove past and he looked at us, neither giving any sign of recognition. But when we went to the end of the long street, made a U-turn and came back and parked the car, Elgie came over and spoke. "I haven't seen you in a long time," he said as we shook hands.

"Where you been?" he asked as he settled himself in the back seat of the car. "New Mexico?"

"Yes."

"I seen the license plates on your car," he said as if in explanation. There might have been more he wanted to say but a police car moved slowly to the corner where we were parked and the patrolmen looked at the three of us intently and we pretended not to notice.

I looked down at my fingernails, keeping my face turned away and I thought: this is one of those towns that never changes. You can be away twenty minutes or twenty years and it's still the same as ever. I remembered a letter that I had read years before written by a former mayor of this town, revealing his attitude toward Indians. He was opposing the moving of the Agency, flooded out by the Ft. Randall Power Project, to his town:

> April 14, 1954
>
> Dear U.S. Representative:
>
> I herewith enclose a signed resolution by the city of Chamberlain and a certified copy of a resolution passed by the Board of County Commissioners of Brule County, So. Dak. The County Commissioners are not in session so I could not get a signed resolution by them.
>
> As I advised you before, we have no intentions of making an Indian comfortable around here, especially an official. We have a few dollar diplomats that have been making a lot of noise and trying to get everyone that is possible to write you people in Washington that they wanted the

Indians in here, but the fact is 90 percent of the people are strongly opposed to it and will get much more so, if this thing comes in. Anybody who rents them any property will have to change his address and I wouldn't want the insurance on this building. We do feel that this town should be ruined by a mess like this and we do not intend to take it laying down irregardless of what some officials in Washington may think.

(Signed H.V.M. Mayor)

That same spring, my uncle Narcisse, thirty-seven years old, affably handsome with a virtuous kind of arrogance that only Sioux uncles can claim, was found one Sunday morning in an isolated spot just outside of town with "fatal wounds" in his throat. This city's coroner and those investigating adjudged his death to be an "accident," a decision my relatives knew to be ludicrous and obscene: Indians killing and being killed did not warrant careful and ethical speculation, my relatives said bitterly.

The patrol car inched down the empty street and I turned cautiously toward Elgie. Before I could speak, Salina said, "She's got some papers for Magpie. He has a chance to go to a writer's school in California."

Always tentative about letting you know what he was really thinking, Elgie said, "Yeah?"

But Salina wouldn't let him get away so noncommittally. "Ozela," she scoffed. "You know he wouldn't go!"

"Well, you know," Elgie began, "one time when Magpie and me was hiding out after that Custer thing, we ended up on the Augustana College Campus. We got some friends there. And he started talking about freedom and I never forget that, and then after he went to the pen it became his main topic of conversation. Freedom. He wants to be free and you can't be that, man, when they're watching you all the time. Man, that freak that's his parole officer is some mean watch-dog."

"You think he might go for the scholarship?" I asked, hopefully.

"I don't know. Maybe."

"Where is he?" I asked.

A truck passed and we waited until it had rumbled on down the street. In the silence that followed, no one spoke.

"I think it's good that you come," Elgie said at last, "because Magpie, he needs some relief from this," he waved his hand. "This constant surveillance, constant checking up, constant association. In fact, that's what he always talks about. 'If I have to associate with wastchus,' he says, 'then I'm not free: there's not liberty in that for Indians.' You should talk to him now." Elgie went on earnestly, eyeing me carefully,

"He's changed. He's for complete separation, segregation, total isolation from the wastchus."

"Isn't that a bit too radical? Too unrealistic?" I asked.

"I don't know," he said, hostility rising in his voice, angry perhaps that I was being arbitrary and critical about an issue we both knew had no answer. "Damn if I know—is it?"

"Yeah," said Salina, encouraged by Elgie's response. "And just what do you think it would be like for him at that university in California?"

"But it's a chance for him to study, to write. He can find a kind of satisfying isolation in that, I think."

After a few moments, Elgie said, "Yeah, I think you're right." A long silence followed his conciliatory remark, a silence which I didn't want to break since everything I said sounded too argumentative, authoritative.

We sat there, the three of us, and I was hoping we were in some kind of friendly agreement. Pretty soon Elgie got out of the back seat, shut the door and walked around to the driver's side and leaned his arms on the window.

"I'm going to walk over the bridge," he said. "It's about three blocks down there. There's an old, white two-story house on the left side just before you cross the bridge. Magpie's brother, he just got out of the Nebraska State Reformatory and he's staying there with his old lady, and that's where Magpie is."

At last! Now I could really talk to him and let him make this decision for himself.

"There's things about this though," Elgie said. "Magpie shouldn't be there, see, because it's a part of the condition of his parole that he stays away from friends and relatives and ex-cons and just about everybody. But Jeez, this is his brother."

"Wait until just before sundown and then come over," he directed. "Park your car at the service station just around the block from there and walk to the back entrance of the house and then you can talk to Magpie about all this."

"Thanks, Elgie," I said.

We shook hands and he turned and walked down the street, stopping to light a cigarette, a casual window shopper.

IV.

Later, in the quiet of the evening dusk, Salina and I listened to our own breathing and the echoes of our footsteps as we walked toward the two-story house by the bridge where Elgie said we could find Magpie. We could see the water of the Missouri River, choppy and dark as it flowed in a southwesterly direction, and the wind rose from the water, suddenly strong and insistent.

The river's edge, I knew, was the site of what the Smithsonian Institute had called an "extensive" and "major" archaeological "find" as they had uncovered the remains of an old Indian village during the flooding process for the Oahe Dam. The "find" was only about a hundred yards from the house which was now Magpie's hiding place. The remains of such a discovery, I thought, testify to the continuing presence of ancestors, but this thought would give me little comfort as the day's invidious, lamentable events wore on.

Salina was talking, telling me about Magpie's return to Crow Creek after months in exile and how his relatives went to his sister's house and welcomed him home. "They came to hear him sing with his brothers," she told me, "and they sat in chairs around the room and laughed and sang with him."

One old uncle who had taught Magpie the songs felt that he was better than ever, that his voice had a wider range, was deeper, more resonant, yet high-pitched, sharp and keen to the senses at the proper moments. "This old uncle," said Salina, "had accepted the facts of Magpie's journey and his return home with the knowledge that there must always be a time in the lives of young men when they move outward and away and in the lucky times they return."

As she told me about the two great-uncles' plans for the honor dance, I could see that this return of Magpie was a time of expectation and gratitude. Much later, I would see that this attitude of expectancy, a habit of all honorable men who believe that social bonds are deep and dutiful, was cruelly unrealistic. For these old uncles and for Magpie, there should have been no expectation.

Several cars were parked in the yard of the old house as we approached, and Salina, keeping her voice low, said, "Maybe they're having a party. That's all we need."

But the silence which hung about the place filled me with apprehension, and when we walked in the back door which hung open, we saw people standing in the kitchen. I asked carefully, "What's wrong?"

Nobody spoke but Elgie came over, his bloodshot eyes filled with sorrow and misery. He stood in front of us for a moment and then gestured us to go into the living room. The room was filled with people sitting in silence, and finally Elgie said, quietly, "They shot him."

"They picked him up for breaking the conditions of his parole and they put him in jail and ... they shot him."

"But why?" I cried. "How could this have happened?"

"They said they thought he was resisting and that they were afraid of him."

"Afraid?" I asked, incredulously. "But ... but ... was he armed?"

"No," Elgie said, seated now, his arms on his knees, his head down. "No, he wasn't armed."

I held the poems tightly in my hands, pressing my thumbs, first one and then the other, against the smoothness of the cardboard folder.

N. Scott Momaday

(b. 1934) Kiowa

N. Scott Momaday received the Pulitzer Prize in 1969 for his novel **House Made of Dawn**. *"The Rise of the Song" is a selection of two chapters at the end of the novel. Abel, the main character, had returned to the Southwest. "The town lay huddled in the late winter noon, the upper walls and vigas were stained with water, and thin black columns of smoke rose above the roofs, swelled, and hung out against the low ceiling of the sky."*

Momaday evokes the haunted scenes of the adobe town in a few words, as in the oral tradition and the memories of death on the landscape, the "streets were empty," and there was "no telling of the sun, save for the one cold, dim, and even light that lay on every corner of the land and made no shadow, and the silence was close by and all around and the bell made no impression upon it. There was no motion to be seen but the single brief burst and billow of the smoke." We read the last words and memories of his grandfather. Francisco's

> *voice was thin and the words ran together and were no longer words. The fire was going out. He got up and struck a match to the lamp. The white walls moved in upon him, and the objects in the room stood out; shadows leaped out upon the white walls, and the windows were suddenly black and opaque, terminal as mirrors to the sight. The old man had spoken six times in the dawn, and the voice of his memory was whole and clear and growing like the dawn."*

Momaday turns the characters in his stories back to the memories of creation and native ceremonies. Abel, at the end of the novel, is running in the snow. "He was running, and under his breath he began to sing. There was no sound, and he had no voice; he had only the words of a song. And he went running on the rise of the song. House made of pollen, house made of dawn, Qstsedaba.*"*

Susan Scarberry-Garcia noted in **Landmarks of Healing**, *a study of* **House Made of Dawn**, *that the title means "the earth" and*

> *comes from one of the healing songs in the Navajo night chant. The title of the novel makes it clear that the world is conceived of in Navajo terms through the exertion of language on place. Jemez Pueblo, the major tribal setting for the events of the story, can then be thought of not only in terms of its own worldview, but also in relation to this concept of an extended Navajo universe.*

Momaday begins the novel with the word Dypaloh *and closes the stories with the word* Qtsedaba. *These are words of native observance that embrace stories at Jemez Pueblo. "Through this device," wrote Scarberry-Garcia, "Momaday stresses the importance of language acts as he establishes the bond between narrator and audience or writer and reader." He exercises "Pueblo and Kiowa traditions for the novel's design, but he primarily structures the novel around Navajo healing patterns."*

Momaday told Charles Woodard in an interview in **Ancestral Voices** *that many "things happen in* **House Made of Dawn** *that I can't explain in a logical way. They are based upon insights which I think are valid, but those insights are not fully conscious. That is, they weren't consciously developed. They exist beneath the level of everyday consciousness, but they are nonetheless real."*

The Rise of the Song

The river was dark and swift, and there were jagged panes of ice along the banks, encrusted with snow. The valley was gray and cold; the mountains were dark and dim on the sky, and a great, gray motionless cloud of snow and mist lay out in the depth of the canyon. The fields were bare and colorless, and the gray tangle of branches rose up out of the orchards like antlers and bones. The town lay huddled in the late winter noon, the upper walls and vigas were stained with water, and thin black columns of smoke rose above the roofs, swelled, and hung out against the low ceiling of the sky. The streets were empty, and here and there were drifts of hard and brittle snow about the fence posts and the stones, pocked with soil and cinders. There was no telling of the sun, save for the one cold, dim, and even light that lay on every corner of the land and made no shadow, and the silence was close by and all around and the bell made no impression upon it. There was no motion to be seen but the single brief burst and billow of the smoke. And out of the town on the old road southward the snow lay unbroken, sloping up on either side to the rocks and the junipers amid the dunes. A huge old black rabbit bounded across the hillside in a blur of great sudden angles and settled away in the snow, still and invisible.

Father Olguin was at home in the rectory. He was alone and busy in the dark rooms, and in seven years he had grown calm with duty and design. The once-hectic fire of his spirit had burned low, and with it the waste of motion and despair. He had aged. He thought of himself not as happy (for he looked down on that particular abstraction) but in some real sense composed and at peace. In the only way possible, perhaps, he had come to terms with the town, and that, after all, had been his aim. To be sure, there was the matter of some old and final cleavage, of certain exclusion, the whole and subtle politics of estrangement, but that was easily put aside, and only now and then was it borne by a cold and sudden gust among his ordinary thoughts. It was irrelevant to his central point of view, nothing more than the fair price of his safe and sacred solitude. That safety—that exclusive silence—was the sense of all his vows, certainly; it had been brought about by his own design, his act of renunciation, not the town's. He had done well by the town, after all, he had set an example of piety, and much in the way of good works were accrued to his account. Once in a great while he took down from a high hidden shelf the dusty journal of Fray Nicolás. He regarded it now with ease and familiar respect, a kind of solemn good will. It lay open in his hands like a rare and wounded bird, more beautiful than broken, and with it he performed the mild spiritual exercise that always restored him to faith and humility.

Abel sat in the dark of his grandfather's house. Evening was coming on, and the bare gray light had begun to fail at the window. He had been there all day with his head hanging down in the darkness, getting up only to tend the fire and look in the old man's face. And he had been there the day before, and the day before that. He had been there a part of every day since his return. He had gone out on the first and second days and got drunk. He wanted to go out on the third, but he had no money and it was bitter cold and he was sick and in pain. He had been there six days at dawn, listening to his grandfather's voice. He heard it now, but it had no meaning. The random words fell together and made no sense.

The old man Francisco was dying. He had shivered all morning and complained of the cold, though there was a fire in the room and he lay under three blankets and Abel's gray coat. At noon he had fallen into a coma again, as he had yesterday and the day before. He revived in the dawn, and he knew who Abel was, and he talked and sang. But each day his voice had grown weaker, until now it was scarcely audible and the words fell together and made no sense: "Abelito ... kethá ahme ... Mariano ... frío ... se dió por ... mucho, mucho frío ... vencido ... aye, Porcingula ... que blanco, Abelito ... diablo blanco ... Sawish ... Sawish ... el hombre negro ... sí ... muchos hombres negros ... corriendo, corriendo ... frío ... rápidamente ... Abelito, Vidalito ... ayempah? Ayempah!"

Abel waited, listening. He tried to think of what to do. He wanted earlier, in the dawn, to speak to his grandfather, but he could think of nothing to say. He listened to the feeble voice that rose out of the darkness, and he waited helplessly. His mind was borne upon the dying words, but they carried him nowhere. His own sickness had settled into despair. He had been sick a long time. His eyes burned and his body throbbed and he could not think what to do. The room enclosed him, as it always had, as if the small, dark interior, in which this voice and other voices rose and remained forever at the walls, were all of infinity that he had ever known. It was the room in which he was born, in which his mother and his brother died. Just then, and for moments and hours and days, he had no memory of being outside of it.

The voice was thin and the words ran together and were no longer words. The fire was going out. He got up and struck a match to the lamp. The white walls moved in upon him, and the objects in the room stood out; shadows leaped out upon the white walls, and the windows were suddenly black and opaque, terminal as mirrors to the sight. His body ached even with the motion of getting up and crossing the room, and he knelt down to place wood on the fire. He waited until the wood caught fire and he could see the slender pointed flames curling around the wood, and the wood began to crackle and the bright embers flew against the black earthen corner of the box and out upon the hearth. Then the farther walls began faintly to glow and vibrate with ripples of yellow light, and the firelight fell and writhed upon the bed and the old man's face and hair. And the old man's breathing was rapid and deep. The vague shape of his body rose and fell, and the voice rattled on, farther and farther away, and the eyes darted and roved.

Abel smoothed the coat and drew it up to his grandfather's throat. The old man's face was burning, and his lips were cracked and parched. Abel dipped a cloth in water and pressed it gently to his grandfather's mouth. He wanted to sponge the eyes, but they were open and roving and straining to see, and he laid it on the brow instead. There was nothing more to do, and he sat down again at the table and hung his head. The walls quivered around him and the fire began to hum and roar and a thin steam grew up on the cold black windows. There was a dull glint upon the empty bottles that stood on the table, and, through the glass, a distortion of lines upon the ancient oilcloth. The kerosene was low in the green glass well of the lamp, and now and then the merest black wisp of smoke rose out of the globe. It was growing late, and he dozed. Still he could hear the faintest edge of his grandfather's voice on the deep and distant breathing, out of sight, going on and on toward the dawn . . . another— one more dawn. The voice had failed each day, only to rise up again in the dawn. The old man had spoken six times in the dawn, and the voice of his memory was whole and clear and growing like the dawn.

They were old enough then, and he took his grandsons out at first light to the old Campo Santo, south and west of the Middle. He made them stand just there, above the point of the low white rock, facing east. They could see the black mesa looming on the first light, and he told them there was the house of the sun. They must learn the whole contour of the black mesa. They must know it as they knew the shape of their hands, always and by heart. The sun rose up on the black mesa at a different place each day. It began there, at a point on the central slope, standing still for the solstice, and ranged all the days southward across the rise and fall of the long plateau, drawing closer by the measure of mornings and moons to the lee, and back again. They must know the long journey of the sun on the black mesa, how it rode in the seasons and the years, and they must live according to the sun appearing, for only then could they reckon where they were, where all things were, in time. There, at the rounder knoll, it was time to plant corn; and there, where the highest plane fell away, that was the day of the rooster race, six days ahead of the black bull running and the little horse dancing, seven ahead of the Precos immigration; and there, and there, and there, the secret dances, every four days of fasting in the kiva, the moon good for hoeing and the time for harvest, the rabbit and witch hunts, all the proper days of the clans and societies; and just there at the saddle, where the sky was lower and brighter than elsewhere on the high black land, the clearing of the ditches in advance of the spring rains and the long race of the black men at dawn.

These things he told to his grandsons carefully, slowly and at length, because they were old and true, and they could be lost forever as easily as one generation is lost to the next, as easily as one old man might lose his voice, having spoken not enough or not at all. But his grandsons knew already; not the names or the strict position of the sun each day in relation to its house, but the larger motion and meaning of the great organic calendar itself, the emergency of dawn and dusk, summer and winter, the very cycle of the sun and of all the suns that were and were to come. And he knew they knew, and he took them with him to the fields and they cut open the earth and touched the corn and ate sweet melons in the sun.

He was a young man, and he rode out on the buckskin colt to the north and west, leading the hunting horse, across the river and beyond the white cliffs and the plain, beyond the hills and the mesas, the canyons and the caves. And once, where the horses could not go because the face of the rock was almost vertical and unbroken and the ancient handholds were worn away to shadows in the centuries of wind and rain, he climbed among the walls and pinnacles of rock, adhering like a vine to the face of the rock, pressing with no force at all, his whole mind and weight upon the sheer ascent, running the roots of his weight into invisible hollows and cracks, and he heard the whistle and moan of the wind among the crags, like ancient voices, and saw the horses far below in the sunlit gorge. And there were the caves. He came suddenly upon a narrow ledge and stood before the mouth of a cave. It was sealed with silver webs, and he brushed them away. He bent to enter and knelt down on the floor. It was dark and cool and close inside, and smelled of damp earth and dead and ancient fires, as if centuries ago the air had entered and stood still behind the web. The dead embers and ashes lay still in a mound upon the floor, and the floor was deep and packed with clay and glazed with the blood of animals. The chiseled dome was low and encrusted with smoke, and the one round wall was a perfect radius of rock and plaster. Here and there were earthen bowls, one very large, chipped and broken only at the mouth, deep and fired within. It was beautiful and thin-shelled and fragile-looking, but he struck the nails of his hand against it, and it rang like metal. There was a black metate by the door, the coarse, igneous grain of the shallow bowl forever bleached with mean, and in the ashes of the fire were several ears and cobs of corn, each no bigger than his thumb, charred and brittle, but whole and hard as wood. And there among the things of the dead he listened in the stillness all around and heard only the lowing of the wind ... and then the plummet and rush of a great swooping bird—out of the corner of his eye he saw the awful shadow which hurtled across the light—and the clatter of wings on the cliff, and the small, thin cry of a rodent. And in the same instant the huge wings heaved with calm, gathering up the dead weight, and rose away.

All afternoon he rode on toward the summit of the blue mountain, and at last he was high among the falls and the steep timbered slopes. The sun fell behind the land above him and the dusk grew up among the trees, and still he went on in the dying light, climbing up to the top of the land. And all afternoon he had seen the tracks of wild animals and heard the motion of the dead leaves and the breaking of branches on either side. Twice he had seen deer, motionless, watching, standing away in easy range, blended with light and shadow, fading away into the leaves and the land. He let them be, but remembered where they were and how they stood, reckoning well and instinctively their notion of fear and flight, their age and weight.

He had seen the tracks of wolves and mountain lions and the deep prints of a half-grown bear, and in the last light he drew up in a small clearing and made his camp. It was a good place, and he was lucky to have come upon a bed of rock; it was clear of the damp earth and the leaves, and the wood made an almost smokeless fire. The timber all around was thick, and it held the light and the sound of the fire within the clearing. He tethered the horses there in the open, as close to the fire as he could, and opened the blanket roll and ate. He slept half sitting against the saddle, and kept the fire going and the rifle cocked across his waist.

He awoke startled to the stiffening of the horses. They stood quivering and taut with their heads high and turned around upon the dark and nearest wall of trees. He could see the whites of their eyes and the ears laid back upon the bristling manes and the almost imperceptible shiver and bunch of their haunches to the spine. And at the same time he saw the dark shape sauntering among the trees, and then the others, sitting all around, motionless, the short pointed ears and the soft shining eyes, almost kindly and discreet, the gaze of the gray heads bidding only welcome and wild goodwill. And he was young and it was the first time he had come among them and he brought the rifle up and made no sound. He swung the sights slowly around from one to another of the still, shadowy shapes, but they made no sign except to cock their heads a notch, sitting still and away in the darkness like a litter of pups, full of shyness and wonder and delight. He was hard on the track of the bear; it was somewhere close by in the night, and it knew of him, he had been ahead of him for hours in the afternoon and evening, holding the same methodical pace, unhurried, certain of where it was and where he was and of every step of the way between, keeping always and barely out of sight, almost out of hearing. And it was there now, off in the blackness, standing still and invisible, waiting. And he did not want to break the stillness of the night, for it was holy and profound; it was rest and restoration, the hunter's offering of death and the sad watch of the hunted, waiting somewhere away in the cold darkness and breathing easily of its life, brooding around at last to forgiveness and consent; the silence was essential to both, and it lay out like a bond between them, ancient and inviolable. He could neither take nor give any advantage of cowardice where no cowardice was, and he laid the rifle down. He spoke low to the horses and soothed them. He threw fresh wood upon the fire and the gray shapes crept away to the edge of the light, and in the morning they were gone.

It was gray before the dawn and there was a thin frost on the leaves, and he saddled up and started out again, slowly, after the track and into the wind. At sunrise he came upon the ridge of the mountain. For hours he followed the ridge, and he could see for miles across the land. It was late in the autumn and clear, and the great shining slopes, green and blue, rose out of the shadows on either side, and the sunlit groves of aspen shone bright with clusters of yellow leaves and thin white lines of bark, and far below in the deep folds of the land he could see the tops of the black pines swaying. At midmorning he was low in a saddle of the ridge and he came upon a huge outcrop of rock and the track was lost. An ancient watercourse fell away like a flight of stairs to the left, the falls broad and shallow at first, but even more narrow and deep farther down. He tied the horses and started down the rock on foot, using the rifle to balance himself. He went slowly, quietly down until he came to a deep open funnel in the rock. The ground on either side sloped sharply down to a broad ravine and the edge of the timber beyond, and he saw the scored earth where the bear had left the rock and gone sliding down, and the swath in the brush of the ravine. He thought of going the same way; it would be quick and easy, and he was close to the kill, closing in and growing restless. But he must make no sound of hurry. The bear knew he was coming, knew better than he how close he was, was even now watching him from the wood, waiting, but still he must make no sound of hurry. The walls of the funnel were deep and smooth, and they converged at the bank of the ravine some twenty feet below, and the ravine was filled with sweet clover and paintbrush and sage. He held the rifle out as far as he could reach and let it go; it fell upon a stand of tall sweet clover with scarcely any sound, and the dull stock shone and the long barrel glinted among the curving green and yellow stalks. He let himself down into the funnel, little by little, supported only by the tension of his strength against the walls. The going was hard and slow, and near the end his arms and legs began to shake, but he was young and strong and he dropped from the point of the rock to the sand below and took up the rifle and went on, not hurrying but going only as fast as the bear had gone, going even in the bear's tracks, across the ravine and up the embankment and through the trees, unwary now, sensible only of closing in, going on and looking down at the tracks.

And when at last he looked up, the timber stood around a pool of light, and the bear was standing still and small at the far side of the break, careless, unheeding. He brought the rifle up, and the bear raised and turned its head and made no sign of fear. It was small and black in the deep shade and dappled with light, its body turned three-quarters away and standing perfectly still, and the flat head and the small black eyes that were fixed upon him hung around upon the shoulder and under the hump of the spine. The bear was young and heavy with tallow, and the underside of the body and the backs of its short, thick legs were tufted with winter hair, longer and lighter than the rest, and dull as dust. His hand tightened on the stock and the rifle bucked and the sharp report rang upon the walls and carried out upon the slopes, and he heard the sudden scattering of birds overhead and saw the darting shadows all around. The bullet slammed into the flesh and jarred the whole black body once, but the head remained motionless and the eyes level upon him. Then, and for one instant only, there was a sad and meaningless haste. The bear turned away, and lumbered, though not with fear, not with any hurt, but haste, slightly reflexive, a single step, or two, or three, and it was overcome. It shuddered and looked around again and fell.

The hunt was over, and openly then could he hurry; it was over and well done. The wound was small and clean, behind the foreleg and low on the body, where the fur and flesh were thin, and there was no blood at the mouth. He took out his pouch of pollen and made yellow streaks above the bear's eyes. It was almost noon, and he hurried. He disemboweled the bear and laid the flesh open with splits, so that the blood should not run into the fur and stain the hide. He ate quickly of the bear's liver, taking it with him, thinking what he must do, remembering now his descent upon the rock and the whole lay of the land, all the angles of his vision from the ridge. He went quickly, a quarter of a mile or more down the ravine, until he came to a place where the horses could keep their footing on the near side of the ridge. The blood of the bear was on him, and the bear's liver was warm and wet in his hand. He came upon the ridge and the colt grew wild with its eyes and blew, pulling away, and its hoofs clattered on the rock and the skin crawled at the roots of its mane. He approached it slowly, talking to it, and took hold of the reins. The hunting horse watched, full of age and indifference, switching its tail. There was no time to lose. He held hard to the reins, turning down the bit in the colt's mouth, and his voice rose a little and was edged. Slowly he brought the bear's flesh up to the flaring nostrils of the colt and smeared the muzzle with it.

And he rode the colt back down the mountain, leading the hunting horse with the bear on its back, and, like the old hunting horse and the young black bear, he and the colt had come of age and were hunters, too. He made camp that night far down in the peneplain and saw the stars and heard the coyotes away by the river. And in the early morning he rode into the town. He was a man then, and smeared with the blood of a bear. He shouted, and the men came out to meet him. They came with rifles, and he gave them strips of the bear's flesh, which they wrapped around the barrels of their guns. And soon the women came with switches, and they spoke to the bear and laid the switches to its hide. The men and women were jubilant and all around, and he rode stonefaced in their midst, looking straight ahead.

She was the child of a witch. She was wild like her mother, that old Pecos woman whom he feared, whom everyone feared because she had long white hair about her mouth and she hated them and kept to herself. But the girl was young and beautiful, and her name was Porcingula. The women of the town talked about her behind her back, but she only laughed; she had her way with their sons, and her eyes blazed and gave them back their scorn.

It was a warm summer night, and she waited for him by the river. He came upon the sand in the cut of the bank and did not see her. He stood looking around and called her name. There was no answer, and the river ran in the moonlight and the leaves of the cottonwood were still and black against the sky. And at last she came out of hiding, laughing and full of the devil. "Well, you were early after all," she said, "and Mariano had not done with me." "Come," he said, and he took her breasts in his hands and moved against her and kissed her mouth. But first she must have her way, playful and mocking. Was he not a sacristan now? Francisco was his name, and had he not been sired by the old consumptive priest? Had he not been told by his father who she was? So she went on, would go on for a while, keeping him on a string, but he stroked her body and she grew quiet and supple with hunger. And she drew him down upon the sand and placed his hands on her naked flesh, the warm curve of her belly and the long dark hollows of her thighs, pressing the tips of his fingers to the tendons and the angle of the hair, into the hot wet flesh that sucked open and closed and quickened to his touch. And then she was wild and on fire and she opened her thighs and he came upon her suddenly and hard and deep, and she writhed under him, pleading and cursing and catching at her breath, and she made small hard hooks of her hands and heels and set them with all her strength into his shoulders and his back, holding the awful swerve of his force down and upon her, into the back of her loins.

She laughed and wept and carried his child through the winter, and as her time drew near she became more and more beautiful. The wild brittle shine fell away from her eyes and the hard high laughter from her voice, and her eyes were sad and lovely and deep, and she was whole and small and given up to him. But he was wary; the women of the town whispered among themselves, and the old priest hid away and stared at his back. And sometimes in the night, when she lay close beside him, he thought of who she was and turned away. The child was stillborn, and she saw that the sight of it made him afraid, and it was over. The shine came again upon her eyes, and she threw herself away and laughed.

"Abelito! Andale, muchacho!"

He would go soon to the fields, but first there was something he must do, and he sent Vidal ahead in the wagon. He put his younger grandson in front of him on the horse, they rode out a little way north from the town. They crossed the broad Arroyo Bajo which ran south and east from Vallecitos and came to the cinch of the valley. There in the plain, between the blue hills and the low line of the red cliffs, was the round red rock. As they approached it from the south, it seemed only a grade, a gentle rise in the plain, but when they came upon it the land fell away. He took the boy down from the horse, and they stood on the edge of the rock, facing north, and the deep red face of the rock dropped under them forty feet to the plain. The neat fields lay out below, and they could see across a hundred hills to the mouth of the canyon. "Listen," he said, and they stood perfectly still on the edge of the rock. The sun took hold of the valley, and a morning breeze rose out of the shadows and the long black line of the eastern mesa backed away. Far below, the breeze ran upon the shining blades of corn, and they heard the footsteps running. It was faint at first and far away, but it rose and drew near, steadily, a hundred men running, two hundred, three, not fast, but running easily and forever, the one sound of a hundred men running. "Listen," he said. "It is the race of the dead, and it happens here."

It was November. The long line of wagons lay out on the road, and there was a low roar of fires and voices on the town. All morning the sky had been gray, and the gray haze of the smoke lay still above the roofs, and pale squadrons of geese flew south on the river. But at noon the smoke rose away and the sky cleared. Then the weather was clear and cold, and a sudden burst of colors came out upon the land. The walls deepened into gold and the fires ran into the glowing earth and the sun struck fire upon the scarlet pods that bled from the vigas. The squash clan came from the kiva, and he with them, standing apart with the drum. The dancers took their places, and he waited; it seemed a long time before they were ready, and he waited. He had never carried the drum before, and he was self-conscious and afraid. The old men, the singers and officials, would watch him, were watching him now. He wore white pants and a borrowed silver belt. The queue of his hair was wrapped around with a bright new cloth, and there was a rust-colored rouge under his eyes. He tried to think ahead to the songs, to all the dips and turns of the dancers, the rattle of the gourds, to all the measured breaks in the breath and the skipping beat of the drum, but it all ran together in his mind, and he waited under the eyes of the elders, fidgeting and full of dread. The chant began low and away, and the two dancers at the heads of the lines moved out, and one after another the others followed, so that a perfect chain of motion ran slowly upon the lines from front to back and the lines drew slowly out and sound swelled upon them. The drums rolled like thunder in his hand, and he had no memory of setting the deep sound upon it. It had happened, and he no longer had fear, not even any thought of fear. He was mindless in the wake of the dancers, riding high like the gourds on the long bright parallels of motion. He had no need of seeing, nor did the dancers dance to the drum. Their feet fell upon the earth and his hand struck thunder to the drum, and it was the same thing, one motion made of sound. He lost track of the time. An old man came beside him with another drum, larger and warm from the fire. He waited, going on, not counting, having no fear and waiting for the pass, only nodding to the beat. And the moment came in mid-motion, and he crossed the stick to the heated drum and the heavy heated drum was in his hand and the old man turned—and nothing was lost, nothing; there had been nothing of time lost, no miss in the motion or the mind, only the certain strange fall of the pitch, the deeper swell of the sound on the warm taut head of the drum. It was perfect. And when it was over, the women of the town came out with baskets of food. They went among the singers and the crows, throwing out the food in celebration of his perfect act. And from then on he had a voice in the clan, and the next year he healed a child who had been sick from birth.

There was a moment in which he knew he could not go on. He had begun at the wrong pace, another and better man's pace, had seen the man come almost at once to the top of his strength, hitting his stride without effort, unlimbering and lining out and away. And like a fool he had taken up the bait, whole and at once, had allowed himself to be run into the ground. In the next instant his lungs should burst, for now they were burning with pain and the pain crowded out the last and least element of his breath, and he should stumble and fall. But the moment passed. The moment passed, and the next and the next, and he was running still, and still he could see the dark shape of the man running away in the swirling mist, like a motionless shadow. And he held on to the shadow and ran beyond his pain....

Abel was suddenly awake, wide awake and listening. The lamp had gone out. Nothing had awakened him. There was no sound in the room. He sat bolt upright, staring into the corner where his grandfather lay. There was a deep red glow on the embers, and the soft light opened and closed upon the walls. There was no wind outside, nor any sound; only a thin chill had come in from the night and it lay like the cold of a cave on the earthern floor. He could see no movement, and he knew that the old man was dead. He looked around at the windowpanes, those coal-black squares of dim reflection. There was nothing. It was a while still before the dawn, before the first light should break in advance of the seventh dawn, and he got up and began to get ready. There was no need for the singer to come; it made no difference, and he knew what had to be done. He drew the old man's head erect and laid water to the hair. He fashioned the long white hair in a queue and wound it around with yarn. He dressed the body in bright ceremonial colors: the old man's wine velveteen shirt, white trousers, and low moccasins, soft and white with kaolin. From the rafters he took down the pouches of pollen and of meal, the sacred feathers and the ledger book. These, together with ears of colored corn, he placed at his grandfather's side after he had sprinkled meal in the four directions. He wrapped the body in a blanket.

It was pitch black before the dawn, and he went out along the corrals and through the orchards to the mission. The motor turned and, one after another, the lights went on upstairs and in the stair well and in the hall, and Father Olguin threw open the door.

"What is God's name—?" he said.

"My grandfather is dead," Abel said. "You must bury him."

"Dead? Oh ... yes—yes, of course. But, good heavens, couldn't you have waited until—"

"My grandfather is dead," Abel repeated. His voice was low and even. There was no emotion, nothing.

"Yes, yes. I heard you," said the priest, rubbing his good eye. "Good Lord, what time is it, anyway? Do you know what time it is? I can understand how you must feel, but—"

But Abel was gone. Father Olguin shivered with cold and peered out into the darkness. "I can understand," he said. "I understand, do you hear?" And he began to shout. "I understand! Oh God! I understand—I understand!"

Abel did not return to his grandfather's house. He walked hurriedly southward along the edge of the town. At the last house he paused and took off his shirt. His body was numb and ached with cold, and he knelt at the mouth of the oven. He reached inside and placed his hands in the frozen crust and rubbed his arms and chest with ashes. And he got up and went hurriedly to the road and south on the wagon road in the darkness. There was no sound but his own quick, even steps on the hard crust of the snow, and he went on and on, far out on the road.

The pale light grew upon the land, and it was only a trick of the darkness at first, the slow stirring and standing away of the night; and then the murky, leaden swell of light upon the snow and the dunes and the black evergreen spines. And the cast deepened into light above the black highland, soft and milky and streaked with gray. He was almost there, and he saw the runners standing away in the distance.

He came among them, and they huddled in the cold together, waiting, and the pale light before the dawn rose up in the valley. A single cloud lay over the world, heavy and still. It lay out upon the black mesa, smudging out the margin and spilling over the lee. But at the saddle there was nothing. There was only the clear pool of eternity. They held their eyes upon it, waiting, and, too slow and various to see, the void began to deepen and to change: pumice, and pearl, and mother-of-pearl, and the pale and brilliant blush of orange and of rose. And then the deep hanging rim ran with fire and the sudden cold flare of the dawn struck upon the arc, and the runners sprang away.

The soft and sudden sound of their going, swift and breaking away all at once, startled him, and he began to run after them. He was running, and his body cracked open with pain, and he was running on. He was running and there was no reason to run but the running itself and the land and the dawn appearing. The sun rose up in the saddle and shone in shafts upon the road across the snow-covered valley and the hills, and the chill of the night fell away and it began to rain. He saw the slim black bodies of the runners in the distance, gliding away without sound through the slanting light and the rain. He was running and a cold sweat broke out upon him and his breath heaved with the pain of running. His legs buckled and he fell in the snow. The rain fell around him in the snow and he saw his broken hands, how the rain made streaks upon them and dipped soot upon the snow. And he got up and ran on. He was alone and running on. All of his being was concentrated in the sheer motion of running on, and he was past caring about the pain. Pure exhaustion laid hold of his mind, and he could see at last without having to think. He could see the canyon and the mountains and the sky. He could see the rain and the river and the fields beyond. He could see the dark hills at dawn. He was running, and under his breath he began to sing. There was no sound, and he had no voice; he had only the words of a song. And he went running on the rise of the song. House made of pollen, house made of dawn. Qtsedaba.

Gerald Vizenor

(b. 1934) Anishinaabe

Gerald Vizenor has published five novels and numerous short stories. **Bearheart: The Heirship Chronicles**, *his first novel, was published in 1978.* **Griever: An American Monkey King in China** *combines the persona of a native trickster with that of the elusive and wise Chinese Monkey King. This, his third novel, won the American Book Award in 1988.* **The Heirs of Columbus** *is an ironic novel; the discoverer is a crossblood trickster in search of his homeland.* **Dead Voices: Natural Agonies in the New World** *pursues the consciousness of various creatures in the voices of a native woman in the city.*

"At the heart of Vizenor's fiction lies a fascination with what it means to be of Indian and European heritage in the contemporary world—in Vizenor's terminology, a 'crossblood,'" wrote Louis Owens in **Other Destinies: Understanding the American Indian Novel**. *"And out of this fascination arises the central and unifying figure in Vizenor's art: the trickster. In Vizenor's work the mixedblood and the trickster become metaphors that seek to balance contradictions and shatter static certainties."*

Not only the characters and tricksters but the scenes in his stories overturn the static reductions of native identities with chance and natural reason, otherwise heard as common sense. "Heartlines," for instance, is imagined as a real landscape, with historical documents, and the characters seem believable at first, but their interaction is given over to chance transformations. The outcome, in this sense, is as real as the presence of dreams, chance, and natural reason.

Gesture Browne, the acudenturist, is a "trickster of precise memories" and the "founder of the first reservation railroad." The point is that the denturist is the acupuncturist of the teeth. Gesture is armed to the teeth with his trickster stories. Once the scenes are set with contradictions and chance, the tricksters are the source of natural reason in the story. "The Naanabozho Express lurched out of the lonesome casino station on the last wild run from the White Earth Reservation to the White House in Washington." The White Earth Reservation is located in northern Minnesota. In the past decade many reservations have established casinos, the postindian wave of economic development. Naanabozho is the name of the trickster in the language of the Anishinaabe.

"The mixedblood trickster as liberator, observer, or entrepreneur is a dominant theme in Vizenor's work," observed LaVonne Ruoff in **American Indian Literatures. The Trickster of Liberty**, *for instance, contains a whole family of such tricksters, who rebel against conventional systems, establish their ingenious enterprises, and tell trickster stories at such places as White Earth, Berkeley, and China."*

Heartlines

The acudenturist:

Lake Namakan never hides the natural reason of our seasons. The wind hardens snow to the bone, cements over the cedar ruins, and hushed currents weaken the ice under the wild reach of our winter.

Overnight, the wild heirs are in the birch, the chase of wise crows. Higher in the distance, the bald eagles brace their nests once more with wisps of white pine, the elusive censers of the summer.

Everywhere, silence is unnatural in our seasons. Listen, the rivers cut massive stones to the ancient heartlines. Memories are more precise on the borders of reservations, nations, and the turns of creation. Trickster stories are the hidden currents of the seasons, the natural reason of our independence.

Gesture Browne is a trickster of precise memories, an esteemed tribal acudenturist, and the founder of the first reservation railroad. He was born in the summer, on an island near the international border, at the same time that Henry Ford established a modern assembly line to build automobiles. That industrial gesture, the coincidence of his birth, and his railroad adventures as an acudenturist were cause to mention the course of natural reason in trickster stories.

Lake Namakan, the memories of our seasons, the crows and bald eagles, the creation of reservations, and the revolution of automobiles were connected in a common vision of unrest and mobility. Gesture reasoned, as he probed a carious lesion in a molar, that the assurance of tribal independence was not a crown decoration of discoveries and treaties, but a state of natural motion. He shouted out, as his father had done from the water tower on the reservation, that sovereignties were moveable stories, never the inactive documents of invented cultures.

The treatment:

Gesture told me that trickster stories come out of the heart, not the mouth. "My heart hears the silence in stones, but teeth rot in the mouth, and what does a wimpy smile mean that covers rotten teeth?" His words warmed the air and brushed my cheek as he leaned over me in the dental chair. He smiled as he leaned, but never showed his teeth. Later, he revealed his crown.

Gesture was an acudenturist in motion, an acute denturist with a singular practice on his very own railroad. The dental chair was located at the end of the train, at the back of the luxurious parlor car. The train had been built for a rich banker who traveled on weekends to his country estate near Lake Namakan.

The banker, by chance of an abscessed tooth and a wild storm on the lake, gave his entire private railroad to the acudenturist and created an endowment to sustain the operation of the train on the reservation.

Gesture was born on Wanaki Island in Lake Namakan. He could have been a child of the wind and natural reason. The otters heard his stories on the stones in the spring, and he was more elusive in the brush than cedar waxwings. The islands were heard in the stories of the seasons, and seen in the everlasting flight of tribal memories. His relatives and the shamans come to the island in summer and winter to hear stories, to hear the stones and heal their presence in humor. His father was exiled and never returned to the reservation.

Ashigan, his father, was born on an island near the border. Six years later his family was removed by treaty to a federal exclave, and then the unscrupulous agents ordered him to leave forever the White Earth Reservation. The order was a paradox; banished, as it were, back to the very islands his family had been removed from eleven years earlier. The sentence was truly ironic, as he had removed the United States Indian Agent for crimes against tribal sovereignty, and held him hostage in a water tower. He told his son that "one removal must beget another in a stolen nest."

Ashigan shouted out the names of the criminal agents and told trickster stories on tribal independence several times a day for three weeks. Some people listened under the tower, others laughed and waited for the agents to shoot him down. He was a scarce silhouette on the tower, smaller for his age than anyone in his family, but his mouth was enormous, and his loud voice had been hired more than once to announce the circus and wild west shows. He was no more than seventeen at the time of the removal and had earned the nickname "big mouth bass" for his stories about the heinous incursions, assaults, larcenies, and murders on the reservation by the federal government.

Big Mouth Bass moved to the border islands and never mentioned the removal, the wicked agents, the twisted mouths of missionaries, or those tribal emissaries who had weakened his revolution in the water tower. The islands were sacred stones in his stories, and the avian shadows his natural solace, but he never shouted about anything ever again. At last, in his eighties, he returned to the reservation with his son, at the controls of their own train. He said the tribal railroad, *ishkodewidaabaan,* or the fire car in translation, was his "island in motion."

Since then tribal people with terminal teeth, some of them with abscesses bigger than the one drained on the banker, drank wild rice wine in the lounge and watched the landscape rush past the great curved windows. They waited in the sovereignty of the parlor car to have their teeth repaired by their very own acudenturist.

"So, lucky for you this is not heart surgery," he said and then leaned over me, the side of his thick hand on my right cheek bone. Lucky indeed, were my very thoughts, but my heart was in my molars that morning. The silence was ironic. No one else has ever had permission to enter my mouth with various instruments, inflict pain, and then ask me questions that were not answerable. No silence could be more sorely heard than the mute responses of a crossblood journalist to the intrusions of an acudenturist, his unanswerable queries of me in a dental chair on a tribal railroad.

Gesture poked and scratched with a dental probe at the ancient silver in my molars. Closer, his breath was slow, warm, and seductively sweet with a trace of clove and commodity peanut butter. The leather chair clicked, a clinical sound, leaned to the side, and shivered as the train rounded a curve over the river near the border of the reservation. "Loose here, and there, there, there, can you feel that?" He pounded on my molars and we nodded in silence on the curve. Then, with a straight chisel he scraped the rough edges of the silver. I could taste the metal, the cold instruments, and his warm bare fingers in my mouth.

"Tribal independence is motion, stories to the heartlines, not the mere sentences and silences of scripture, not the cruelties of dead words about who we might have been in the past to hear our presence," he said and we nodded as the train leaned in the other direction. "Museums iced our impermanence, and the cold donors measure our sovereignty in the dead voices of their own cultures." He snorted and then explained that he would not be able to use an anesthetic because he was an acudenturist, "not a drugstore doctor." The silver was already too loose in my molars to wait on a licensed dentist at the end of the line.

"Instead, here are some scents of the seasons on the islands," he said, and turned a narrow cone toward my face. The rush of air was moist and cool, a the first scent was a thunderstorm, then wet wool, a dog, and later on the essence of sex, but that must have come from generations of sweat on the leather chair in the parlor car.

We nodded in silence and he turned the dental chair from the curved windows and the landscape to the power instruments. The other patients in the lounge turned with me from the rush of birch and white pine to the instrument. He started the mechanical dental engine. The drill was archaic, but the sound of the drive cables created a sense of contentment, the solace of an acudenturist in his own trickster stories. He drilled and cleaned the lesion, and then pounded real gold into the central grooves of my molars.

"Now, you are truly worth more than you were last night on the reservation, and we are both still free," said the acudenturist as he turned the chair back toward the curved windows.

The abscessed banker:

I was born on the reservation but my father moved to the city in search of work. I quit school, bounced around for years, served in the military, and finally landed as a journalist for a large daily newspaper, the *Twin Cities Chronicle*. Naturally, the editors named me Big Cheep, a nickname they learned from me. A nickname based on the way Ishi, the Yahi man who lived in a museum at the University of California, said the word Chief, a personal reference to the anthropologist Alfred Kroeber.

I was assigned to cover any story that had the slightest hint of tribal presence, as if no one else could cover such events without a genetic connection to a reservation. For all that, and even the heartless celebration of essentialism over racial deverbatives, such as drinkers, drummers, and dancers, no one in my crossblood generation had a more exciting job. I would have it no other way, and was more than pleased to write about the unnameable tribes and such unbelievable characters as the acudenturist Gesture Browne.

My editors, however, as much as they liked my work from the unknown and exotic headwaters of the reservations, were never certain if my stories were true or not. The other reporters shouted out their rough humor in the newsroom when one of my stories landed on the front page. I heard their playful envy, to be sure, and the ironies of what was sold as daily news, but I would have laughed anyway at such racial quibbles as, "You need tribal fishing rights to believe this story," or "The second coming of Christ is worth a page and a half, unless she's an Indian."

In the end, the distinctions between fact and fiction never seemed to really matter much to the editors or readers and surely that must be the reason why tribal humor and trickster stories have endured the most outrageous abuses by missionaries, government agents, and above all other cruelties, the dominance of dead letter anthropologists.

The city editor often said that my stories about tribal people on the reservation "may not be the truth, but his stories are truer than what we publish day after day about elected politicians all the way to the White House."

My editor bought the truth of the banker with the abscess who was lost in a thunderstorm, and he ran my story as a feature on the front page, but he would not believe the stories about my golden molars. These stories, and the leather dental chair in a parlor car, were not convincing. He even looked in my mouth, poked the bright molar with a pencil, and then shouted, "fool's gold on a tribal railroad, now that is believable!"

He smiled, and then we nodded in silence.

Gesture never hides the natural reason of a thunderstorm on the islands at Lake Namakan. He waits on the massive stones for a burst of creation. I know, because when he hears that certain wind, the crash of thunder in the distance, he is transformed by the power of the storm. He told me that the most natural death is to be struck by lightning, "a crash of thunder and the human remains are a thunderstone."

Ashigan and his son were healed by the power of the west wind, the rush of water over the massive stones. Gesture looks at least ten years younger when he faces a thunderstorm. And it was a storm, one ferocious thunderstorm over the islands, that changed his life forever. Indeed, he was out in the wild wind, but he was struck by a banker, not lightning, in the end.

Cameron Williams, the wealthy banker, was out in a canoe that very afternoon, a chance to show his grandson the bald eagles near the international border. The banker had no sense of natural reason and, distracted by the rise of the eagles on the wind, he drifted on the rough water over the border and was lost in the many bays and islands on Lake Namakan.

Gesture saw a canoe turnover on the waves near the island. The banker was lucky that such a tribal man would stand in a storm and watch the lake catch the wind. The canoe tumbled on the waves, and then he saw the blue face of a child in the water, the faces that haunted him in dreams, the blue faces beneath the ice near the mouth of the river. He tied a rope to the tree and swam out to the canoe. The lightning hissed overhead, and the water was wicked on the rise in the wind. The child was ashen, blue around his eyes and mouth, and his ancient blue hands were closed on a miniature plastic paddle. The banker trembled, he was too scared to shout, but he held onto the canoe.

Gesture tied the rope to the canoe and towed the child to shore. Cameron nodded, the waves crashed over them, and lightning crashed in the trees on the island. Later, the child recovered near the fire, but the banker weakened, his eyes were swollen and lost color. The storm passed overnight, but the wind howled and the waves crashed on the stones for two more days. They could not paddle against the high waves.

Cameron was weakened because he had a canine abscess that distended his right cheek and ear, and closed one eye. The swollen banker was delirious on the second night. He cursed women and the weather for his condition, and then he started to wheeze, his breath was slower, strained, and his thin hands turned inward to the silence.

Gesture heard the last stories in the old man. The lake was thunderous, and the waves were too high for a canoe, so he decided to operate on the banker, then and there on the island, and drain the abscess. That night he built a small sweat lodge and warmed the old man near the stones, and moistened his swollen mouth with willow bark soaked in hot water.

The next morning he moved the banker out to the boulders on the shore, turned his head to the sun, and told the child to hold his swollen mouth open with a chunk of driftwood. The child nodded in silence, and then he wound a thin wire several times around the base of the canine, and with a wooden lever, braced in the seam of a stone, he wrenched the poison tooth from his mouth.

Purulence and marbled blood oozed out around the tooth, ran down his chin and neck, and stained the stone. Then pure putrid mucus gushed from the hole of the abscessed canine. He choked and gurgled, but in minutes he could see. His swollen eye opened, and he turned to his side on the stone and moaned as the infection drained from his head. The child cried over the color of the poisoned blood, and then he gathered water and washed the pus from the stone.

Later, the child touched the dark hollow abscess with his fingers. That afternoon the banker laughed and said his mistake in navigation was "not much better than

Columbus." Perched on the warm stones he told stories about his childhood, and took great pleasure in his missing tooth, the natural imperfection of his weathered smile.

Gesture paddled the banker and the child in their canoe back to their vacation home on the luxurious western reach of the lake, a great distance on the other side of the border. The water was calm in the narrows, and the sun bounced over the scant waves. The eagles teased the wind and then circled closer and closer to the shallow water on the shoreline.

The feature story:

I was a journalist and convinced at the time that my stories created a sense of the unusual in a real world, even more in feature stories. Alas, the politics of the real are uncertain, and stories of natural reason and survivance in the tribal world were scarcely heard, and seldom recorded as sure historical documents.

Cameron Williams was one of my real features, a banker in the blood who reared his own documents and caused histories that touched on natural reason and tribal survivance. I was a reservation crossblood with a shadow of chance and the sound of oral stories in my ears, and he was a rich banker with several vacation homes and his own railroad. He was a serious stockholder in the very newspaper that employed me, and he traced his ancestors to the founding families of puritan New England.

My editors at the *Twin Cities Chronicle* were too liberal for the banker, so it was even more difficult for me to track down any good information about the extraction of his abscessed canine in a thunderstorm. One of his assistants told me that he would not be interviewed for any story, and "certainly not about his exodontist."

I think it was my simple savings account at one of his banks that opened the door the first time. He was a pragmatist, to be sure, and he must have judged me by my documents, a savings account in this instance. Later, however, it would take more than my meager savings to overcome his suspicion of crossbloods. He told me that my genes were "enervated" and the "inheritance of a racial weakness has never been an honorable birthright." Crossblood or not, my recognition of one of his distant relatives earned an invitation to travel with him on his plane and train.

Cameron was a descendant of John Williams, a minister at the turn of the eighteenth century in Deerfield, Massachusetts. His family was captured one winter night, and his daughter turned to the tribes and never returned. Eunice Williams renounced the dominance of her puritanical father and married a tribal man, and that historical document could not be denied by enervation. Twelve generations later the banker is an heir to that crossblood union of Puritans and Kahnawakes in Canada.

"Sir, at our best we are crossbloods."

"At your best, you are a listener," said the banker.

"Indeed, and the abscess is your story."

"So, this is what you want to see, the hole," said the banker. He removed a false canine with his fingers and then smiled to show the hole. "The first thing my grandson did was touch the bloody hole, and he still does it when we tell the story together."

"How does an abscess become a reservation railroad?"

"Pack for an overnight and meet me in three hours at the entrance to the garage," he said and waved me out of the conference room. The scent of mint, an executive insinuation of nature in the carpets, lingered on my clothes for several hours.

Cameron was silent in the limousine to the airport. He only gestured at scenes out the window as we flew in his private jet over the lakes and landed at the airport near his vacation home. From there we boarded a pontoon plane and flew close to the peaks of red pines, circled the many islands, and then landed on the smooth sheltered bay near Wanaki Island.

Gesture should have been there to meet the seaplane. How could he not hear the engines, and how often does company arrive by air? There was no dock on the island so we waded over the massive boulders to shore.

"We were caught in a vicious storm and rolled over right out there," said the banker. "And here, on this very stone, a stranger saved my life, and he asked nothing for his trouble."

Gesture was reading in his cabin, a precise response to the curiosities and uncommon praise of a banker. Not even his mongrels were moved to denounce our presence on their island. 'We never challenge bears or humans," he told me later.

The modern cabin was constructed mostly with metal, not what we expected to find in the remote pristine wilderness of the border islands. There were other surprises, such as skylights, a toilet that generated methane, and water heated by solar panels.

Gesture explained that the modern accommodations were a contradiction of tribal rights and federal wilderness laws. He had the aboriginal right to live on the islands, but he could not crap on the land or cut the trees to build a house. "Not because the trees have rights, that would be natural reason, but because the trees are on a pristine reservation," he told me. "So, we can live here in a natural museum."

Gesture and his father, their wives and several children, saved their money from treaty settlements, and income as guides for fishing parties, to buy modular ecological homes that were airlifted to the island in large sections and assembled in less than a week.

"I tried several times to remember what your house looked like, but my memory lost the picture," said the banker. The mongrels sniffed his ankles and sneezed several times.

High Rise, the white mongrel with the short pointed ears, moaned and rolled over at the feet of the banker. He rubbed his wet jowls on his shoes and ankles. He raised his trousers, and reached down with one hand to touch his head, to push him aside, but the mongrel moaned louder and licked his hand.

Poster Girl, the mottled brown mongrel that looked like a cat, was very excited by the scent of the banker and the moans of High Rise. She barked and ran around the banker in tiny circles. Her nails clicked on the wooden floor, an ecstatic dance. The banker was not amused by the mongrels.

"High Rise must have a nose for bankers," said the banker.

"Maybe, but he goes for the scent of mint," said Gesture.

"Yes, lingering from the executive carpets."

"Gesture, could we get down to some business?"

"You mean the mongrels?"

"Would you like a paid scholarship to dental school?"

"Dental school?" asked Gesture.

"Yes, an even chance to turn a mere instinct into a real profession, and you could be the very first dentist in your entire tribe," said the banker. His manner was earnest, but the invitation was an obscure pose of dominance.

"You flew way out here to send me to dental school?"

"A measure of my respect," said the banker.

"The measure is mine," said Gesture. He pointed to the books stacked near the wooden bench and the mongrels moved in that direction. There were several novels and a book on dental care and hygiene. "You see, out here we are denturists with no natural reason to be dentists, our teeth are never the same, but denturists never turn mouths into museums."

"You saved my life," pleaded the banker.

"Maybe," said Gesture.

"You owe me the courtesy to recognize my everlasting debt to you," said the banker. "My grandson admires you more than anyone else in the family right now, he thinks you are the dentist of the islands."

"Denturist, and you had the abscess not me."

"You are an original," said the banker. He moved to the bench and read the titles of books in several stacks. High Rise nosed his ankles, and Poster Girl posed beside him on the bench. There were new novels by Gordon Henry, Betty Louise Bell, Louis Owens, and Randome Browne, and older novels by Franz Kafka, Herman Melville, and Yasunari Kawabata. He was distracted by a rare book, the *Manabosho Bestiary Curiosa,* the very first tribal book, published in the middle of the seventeenth century. The anonymous tribal curiosa of human and animal sexual transformations was discovered a century later at an auction of rare books in France.

"Gesture, this is a very rare book," said the banker.

"Poster Girl is a healer," said Gesture.

"What does she heal?" asked the banker.

"Whatever you want?"

"What do *you* want?" shouted the banker.

"What do you have?" shouted Gesture.

High Rise raised her head at the tone of his voice and sniffed the distance in the air. Poster Girl watched the banker on the bench. He was distracted more by the curiosa than the mongrels.

"Basically, it comes down to this," said the banker. He laid the curiosa on the stack of books, leaped from the bench, and turned to the window. "What would you accept that would make me feel better about this?"

"Make me an offer," said Gesture.

"Come with me and see," shouted the banker. He turned and marched across the room to the door. The mongrels followed him out. He ordered the pilot to make room for one more passenger, but not the mongrels.

"Would you consider a scholarship to study at the university?" asked the banker. The pontoon plane bounced several times and then lifted slowly from the water.

"Why the university?"

"Say, to study literature," said the banker.

"I already do that," said Gesture.

"Anthropology then."

"Anthropology studies me."

"You have a point there," said the banker.

"Natural reason is the point."

"You could be a pilot, and have your own business on the lakes," said the banker. The plane circled the islands near the border. The late sun shivered in wide columns on the water.

"Do you have a railroad?" asked Gesture.

"Yes, my own private line."

"Give me that, and we have a deal," said Gesture. He gestured with his lips toward the shoreline. Bald eagles turned their shadows over and over on Lake Namakan.

"Great idea, the first tribal railroad in the history of the nation," said the banker. He raised his hands and shouted nonsense in the air. "Did you hear that mister crossblood, this is the return of the noble train."

The trickster express:

The Naanabozho Express, a seven coach train, lurched out of the casino station on the White Earth Reservation and thundered into the sacred cedar on the last wild run to the White House in Washington.

Gesture Browne, the founder of the tribal railroad, or *ishkodewidaabaan,* in the memories of the elders, negotiated with the national native art museum the installation of a mobile cultural exhibition on the train, and then he summoned his heirs to declare motion a tribal island, a natural sovereign tribal state.

The trickster express ran on borrowed rails with a new museum, a parlor dental car, an acudenturist, a nurse with several nicknames, and the crystal trickster of tribal parthenogenesis. The express train was natural reason in motion, a nomadic survivance from a woodland reservation to the national capital.

Gesture never surprised anyone on the reservation with his uncommon transactions. His words rushed and bounced, one over the other with no connections or closure, but with that visual sense of transformations in his stories. Natural reason never ended, never in trickster stories, and never in his natural invectives. He was a wind in the best seasons, and his humor healed those who heard his stories on the trickster train. The man who conceived the first railroad on the reservation would not be caught unaware by his heirs on a wise run to tribal sovereignty.

The others, the educated canons on the bungee lines of reason, were astonished that an old man, who said he was once a woman, had stolen the sacred treasures of his own culture from a museum. The curators, on the other hand, were the dead voices of native museums, burdened with their obsessions, discoveries, heartless recoveries, and their mean manners of terminations and postindian tenancies.

Gesture reassured me that motion is autonomous, that natural reason and memories are motion, and motion can never be stolen. Bones and blankets are stolen, motion is a natural sovereignty. The museum commodities on the train had been removed, silenced, and unseen, as the tribes had been removed to reservations. He repeated that the museum was not stolen, but in motion. "The absurdities of museums are so cruel, that the sacred objects in the collection were stolen and are more secure than tribal families on reservations. The museums are dead and we dance at the treelines."

The crystal trickster:

Cozie Browne heard that the west wind was lost, an ominous situation to consider that winter on the reservation. She heard the crows too, and rushed outside to warn the birch near the river. The ice waited in silence, hardhearted on the blue summer mire, and even the cedar waxwings were uncertain over the late turn of the seasons. She overheard these stories as a child, and no one has ever been the same in her memories.

Notice of the lost wind was delivered by her cousin who lived in a cold basement apartment in the city. She was nine years old at the time and enticed by his wild urban manners. The mere mention of cities, that sense of distance and urban vengeance, molded the seasons in her memories. He was older and wiser about obscure tribal traditions and the enchanted stories of creation, and avowed that he could hear stories on the weave and wander of the wind.

Cozie was born in the summer at the same time that the first nuclear powered submarine sailed under fifty feet of polar ice. The wind touched her head at birth with an ovate bunch of blond hair, a sign that tribal elders were reborn in their children. She learned to hear the bald eagles and to carry a sprig of white pine. She mourned in the presence of spirits, not humans, and no one but tricksters dared cross her trail to the fire.

Trickster stories tease a tribal presence, a chance to be heard between the reservations and the cities; otherwise, unseen, she would have shivered in silence over the insinuations of natural reason. Her uncle rushed the thunderstorms on the islands, a wise man of motion, but the stories she heard would mend the absence not the presence of the west wind that winter.

Cozie earned four memorable nicknames in the natural service of the seasons. One name at birth, the second was shortened and secular, and much later she secured two more names as the first permanent night nurse at the public health clinic on the White Earth Reservation.

Gesture Browne named his niece *minomaate* when she was born, a tribal word that means a good smell, like "something burning" in the language of the *anishinaabe*. The shorter version of her name was *mino,* a word that means *good,* and that was translated as *cozy* by the missionaries. The two time release nicknames, the first such postindian names on the reservation, were given when she became the night nurse.

Cozie is her heartline name, a trace to the ancestors, but the two other nicknames are essential in the stories of those who heard the seasons and were healed by *oshkiwiinag,* the crystal trickster in the dead of night.

She is touched by the sound of the wind, the distance of shadows, that rare presence of creation as the dew rises over memories, and the natural ecstasies of ancient rivers. Later, she is morose as the sun haunts the ruins of the night. She hears the tricksters of creation overnight, not in the bright light.

Sour is her nickname at first light, and later, seen closer to the sunset, she is summoned as Burn. The dawn and sunset determine the mood and manner of her timeworn names in the clinic on the reservation. Sour in the morning. Burn as the night nurse.

Sour was summoned one morning to the clinic. "Some sort of emergency," the director said on the telephone. She was not pleased, but there was a reported medical crisis on the reservation at Camp Wikidin near Bad Medicine Lake. The girl scouts had been ravished and were rumored to be in posttraumatic ecstasies.

"To be sure, the bitter light of day is on me," she said and leaned over his polished desk for instructions. Sour covered her eyes and told him to close the blinds.

"Sour, you know we would never bother you in the morning, but it might cloud over and rain, so we thought you could bear partial light and examine the campers," said the director. "Who else could answer the emergency?" He closed the blinds very slowly.

"Heat rash?"

"No, more serious," said the director.

"Poison ivy?"

"No, more serious than that, it seems."

"Hornets in the shower," said Sour.

"No, more serious, some sort of ecstatic hysteria brought on by something they ate, some allergic reaction, or whatever," said the director. "The camp leader said it might have something to do with the discovery of a statue."

"What statue?"

"No, no, this is not that myth of the trickster who transformed all the tribal women one summer in ancient memory," he said and then raised his hands to resist the rest of the story. "No, no, this is not one of those trickster diseases, these are young white girl scouts from the city."

"Why not?"

"No, the trickster in that story was made out of crystal."

"The *oshkiwiinag* and plenty more," said Sour.

"Right, hundreds of women were pregnant that summer."

"My grandmother told me those stories."

"Never mind, get out to the camp," said the director.

"My uncle said the crystal trickster was a man and a woman at a circus that summer, and somehow, he teased, the population doubled in one year on the reservation," said Sour.

Sour packed a medical case with calamine, ammonia, baking soda, various antihistamines, and epinephrine. She drove the shortest route over unpaved backroads to the girl scout camp. The first giant drops of rain burst in the loose sand, and the black flies wavered in the slipstream. Splendid foliage leaned over the road, a natural arbor that reduced the light north of Bad Medicine Lake.

Camp Wikidin was built on stolen tribal land, a sweetheart concession to the scouts on land that had been ascribed to the tribes in treaties. "Maybe the scouts are allergic to the reservation," she muttered on the last turn. The camp director and two anxious assistant scout leaders were waiting in the parking lot.

"This thing is sexual," shouted one leader. Her checks were swollen and bright red, her gestures were uncertain, and she watched the shadows at the treeline in the distance.

"Wait a minute," said Sour.

"Really, some kind of sexual thing" she insisted.

"No, no, stand back and let me park the car."

"Dark windows," said the other leader.

"I hate the light," said Sour.

"Allergic?" asked the camp director.

"No, just hate what the bright light does to faces and the play of shadows," said Sour. "So, now about that sexual thing, where are the girls who need some medical attention?"

"We locked the girls in the main cabin to protect them for now," said the camp director. "We thought it best, as they had the very same symptoms."

"Why?" asked Sour.

"Because, this thing *could* be sexual," said the director.

"Do you mean a man?"

"Something very sinister has happened here."

"Doctor Sour...."

"Nurse Cozie Browne," said Sour.

"Nurse Browne, we thought you would be a doctor."

"Perhaps you need a surgeon from the city," said Sour.

"Never mind, we have all been touched by something overnight," said the camp director. She turned toward the nurse, her face was narrowed by one wide crease down the center of her forehead. She turned the loose wedding ring on her finger. She was worried, but not frightened. "Something that *could* be sexual, but we cannot believe our own words."

The assistants were closer to panic than the director. Their hands were unclean and trembled out of control. The assistant with the big red cheeks chewed on her knuckles. She could not determine if the "sexual thing" was the beginning or the end of her career as a girl scout leader.

Sour moaned at the last turn to the main cabin. The campers were at the windows, their bright red faces pressed on the panes. Their sensuous bodies had overheated the building and a wave of moist warm air rushed out when the director unlocked the door.

Sour examined every camper in a private office with pictures of prancing horses on the walls. She soothed the girls with gentle stories about nature, images of lilacs, pet animals, and garden birds, but could not detect any allergies, infections, or insect bites. Most of the campers were shied by the heat of their own bodies, and mentioned their dreams, the unnatural sensations of soaring over water.

Barrie, one of the campers, had the sense at last to consider what had changed in their lives that might have caused such ecstasies. The girl described, with unintended irony, their habits and activities over the past few days, and then she revealed the secret of the scouts, that the campers had not been the same since they discovered a statue buried on the other side of the lake.

Later, when the campers gathered to clean and examine the figure, their secret tribal treasure, some of the girls swooned and fainted right at the table. The emotions were so contagious that the campers buried the statue and worried that they were being punished by some demon of the tribal land who hated outsiders from the cities. These were signs of posttraumatic ecstasies.

Barrie, who was a senior scout, drew a very detailed map of the secret burial site. She blushed as she marked the trail to the burial near a cedar tree. Then she fanned her cheeks with the map. The mere thought of the trickster statue caused her breath to shorten.

Cozie located the crystal trickster in a shallow grave. She bound the statue in a beach towel, and returned to the clinic. She was ecstatic on the backroads, certain that the treasure was the very crystal trickster that had transformed the mundane in so many tribal stories on the reservation.

She locked the trickster in a laboratory and reported to the director that there were no diseases to treat at the camp, nothing but blushes, short breath, and mild posttraumatic histaminic ecstasies. Later, the camp leaders reported that the girls were much better and that a cookout was being prepared. The scouts swore that they would never reveal the stories of the crystal trickster.

Burn unbound the trickster that night when she had finished her rounds in the clinic. The room was dark with an examination light on the statue. She soaked the trickster in warm water and as the mire washed away the pure crystal seemed to brighten the laboratory.

The crystal trickster was named *oshkiwiinag* in the stories she heard on the islands and the reservation. The ancient statue warmed her hands and face. The crystal was smoother than anything she had ever touched. Smoother than a mountain stone, human flesh, otter hair, smoother than ice cream.

The *oshkiwiinag* was about seventeen inches high and each part of the crystal anatomy was polished with precision. The arms, legs, head, torso, and penis were perfect interlocking parts. For instance, the bright head could not be removed unless both arms were raised, and the arms could not be removed with the head attached. The pure crystal penis was the most precise and intricate part of the trickster. She could not determine how to remove the penis from the crystal body.

Burn polished each part with such pleasure that she lost her sense of time and place. She carried the shrouded trickster home in the front seat of her car and placed the statue in a locked closet. She would consider how to present the trickster to her uncle and grandparents at Wanaki Island.

Cozie and the thirteen girl scouts who had touched the *oshkiwiinag* were pregnant, and nine months later their trickster babies were born at almost the same hour. The coincidence became a scandal in the media, and hundreds of reporters roamed the reservation in search of wicked tricksters. The tribal government was cursed with nonfeasance, and the clinic was sued for malpractice by several mothers of the trickster babies. Cozie was portrayed as a tribal witch on several radio and television shows, a nurse who hated the light and caused those innocent girl scouts to become pregnant.

Cozie was forced to leave the only job she ever loved at night. At the same time she had a clever daughter and an incredible trickster who could conceive a child with a crystal touch. She trusted that *oshkiwiinag* was the real father of her child, because she had not been with a man for three years, two months, and nineteen days. Her uncle taught her to be precise with memories, and he would say the trickster babies were natural reason. Several months later the state medical examiners concluded in their report that the conceptions were curious cases of parthenogenesis. There is medical evidence that ecstasies and even terror have been the occasions of innocent conceptions. Such trickster stories were heard in tribal communities centuries before the medical examiners were overcome by the coincidence of parthenogenesis.

Gesture invited his niece to dinner in the parlor car. The trickster express was at the station near the clinic overnight. Cozie told him about *oshkiwiinag* and the investigations on the reservation. He insisted that she establish her own clinic on the train and practice trickster conceptions to women who would rather not bear the sensations and tortures of sexual intercourse. She moved to the train that very night and painted an announcement on the side of the parlor car that read, "Parthenogenesis on the Naanabozho Express," and in smaller letters, "Conceptions in Motion with No Fears or Tears."

The trickster express circled the reservation for several months, and in that time thousands of people had their terminal teeth repaired free by the one and only acudenturist in motion, and even more women boarded the train for a short time to touch *oshkiwiinag* and conceive a child without sex. Some women had their teeth renewed and touched the trickster at the same time, ecstasies on one end and a better smile on the other. The crystal trickster soothed those who would fear the pain of dental instruments.

Gesture is precise about memories and his mission to show the nation that tribal independence is truer in motion than in the hush of manners, that natural reason is heard in the stories of chance and coincidence, not in the cultural weave and wash of silence. The Naanabozho Express lurched out of the lonesome casino station on the last wild run from the White Earth Reservation to the White House in Washington.

Paula Gunn Allen

(b. 1939) Laguna Pueblo

Paula Gunn Allen was born in Albuquerque, New Mexico, in 1939. She traces her maternal descent to the Sioux and Laguna Pueblo. Her father was Lebanese. She studied at the University of New Mexico and is now a professor of English at the University of California at Los Angeles.

"I always knew I was Indian," she wrote in "The Autobiography of a Confluence," in **I Tell You Now**.

> *I was never told to forget it, or deny it. Indians were common in the family, at least on my mother's side. In fact, unlike many people I meet who are claiming they're "Indian" or reluctantly revealing it, far from being denied, my relationship to the pueblo down the line was reinforced in a number of ways. I was told over and over, "Never forget that you're Indian."*

> *I grew up on the Cubero Land Grant, in New Mexico. I grew up with wilderness just up the road, with civilization much farther away....My life is history, politics, geography. It is religion and metaphysics. It is music and language. For me the language is an old brand of English, mostly local, mostly half-breed spoken by the people around me, filled with elegance and vulgarity side by side.*

Allen is the author of seven books of poetry and many collections of essays and stories. **The Woman Who Owned the Shadows,** *her novel, was published in 1983.* **The Sacred Hoop: Recovering the Feminine in American Indian Tradition,** *a collection of essays, was published in 1986.* **Skin and Bones** *is a book of poetry published two years later.* **Grandmothers of the Light: A Medicine Woman's Sourcebook** *was published in 1991.*

Louis Owens pointed out in **Other Destinies** *that the*

> *postmodern insistence upon the fragmented sense of self finds its reflection in the radically deracinated mixed blood of much Indian fiction—figures such as Abel in* **House Made of Dawn,** *Ephanie in* **The Woman Who Owned the Shadows** *and many others—characters who truly find themselves between realities and wondering which world and which life might be theirs.*

*"***The Woman Who Owned the Shadows** *focuses on the journey toward spiritual rebirth of the central character, [Ephanie] Atencio, a half-blood who feels at home neither in the Southwest nor in San Francisco," wrote LaVonne Ruoff in* **American Indian Literatures**. *"In the course of her psychological and spiritual journey toward emergence as a shaman, [Ephanie] searches her memory to recall both childhood experiences that reveal the sources of her adult fears and the Kertes myths that are the base of her Indian heritage."*

Allen coined the word cosmogyny *in* **Grandmothers of the Light**. *The stories in the sourcebook "connect us to the universe of medicine." The crystal skull, carved from rock crystal, is thought to be Aztec. The origin of the carving, however, has not been established by archaeologists or historians.*

"The Crystal Skull, the amazing crystallized remains of the immortal I have called Crystal Woman, was found in Mopán country early this century." Allen envisioned and "channeled information" from Crystal Woman in her story "Someday Soon." She wrote that the "events as they have unfolded to this time are uncannily parallel to events described in traditional myths and legends of the Maya and other Native Americans."

Allen told Joseph Bruchac in an interview published in **Survival This Way** *that she "fell in love with Gertrude Stein" when she was in high school. "My mother bought me everything she could find, everything that was available, and I read Stein and tried to copy her, tried to write like her. Then I gave up for a while. But the earliest work I ever wrote, which no one will ever see because I lost it, is noticeably Stein."*

Someday Soon

In 1986 two American men went to Belize (formerly British Honduras) to make a video travelogue to help Belize become better known to American tourists. One of the men was Native American. The other, a spiritual seeker of Middle Eastern Christian descent was curious about what had happened to the Maya; he was also interested in finding the lost continent of Atlantis, which he thought might be beneath the Caribbean Sea, as many seekers have believed. In the process of making their film, they became acquainted with a Maya who took them to the Maya homelands in Belize. What transpired over the next two or three years is recorded in "Someday Soon."

The Mopán Maya, among whom the two men moved for many months in that and following years, are said to be the oldest of the various Maya groups. Scholars are coming to believe that they are the original Maya, from whom the others derived. The Crystal Skull, the amazing crystallized remains of the immortal I have called Crystal Woman, was found in Mopán country early this century. Studied by archaeologists, visited by seekers, and filmed by the men who quested among the Maya and discovered the Skull in the process, this being (I can't call her an artifact!) is a powerful and beautiful presence. I was honored to have channeled information from her when I visited her home in Canada in the summer of 1987. Much of what she told me is included in this story.

The events as they have unfolded to this time are uncannily parallel to events described in traditional myths and legends of the Maya and other Native Americans. This account is offered as a demonstration that the immortals are still among us, even among people who rely on high-tech equipment, jet planes, and hotel accommodations during their quests.

The Mopán Maya of Belize say that the new age will begin in 2012, when an era of harmony, peace, and renewal will be ushered in.

Long ago, Crystal Woman. Before the human beings, before the five-fingered beings. She standing there in the southwest. In the southeast, standing. In the mountains on the edge of the world, before the world became as we know it, there she stood. There she waited for the time to be ripe.

She was a priestess, a shaman, a medicine woman. She was an adept trained in the seven arts and the thirteen ways. In the ways of the immortals one of whom she was. It was in the time of the end, of the transformation from this, that she was, to another thing. It was their work, the work of the thirteen of them, to become all that was possible to become, to know all it was possible to know. To put that knowledge into their being-bodies. To infuse their cell and bone with all they knew. Only thus could they be sabías, women of knowledge. There were twelve who were younger, and an old woman who was wise in the ways of the sacred. She they called Mother, and she would in later days be called Mother of the Gods.

There in the Cave of Knowing they practiced their art. There they became all they knew. There in the cave in the west where the crystals now grow. The place reached by river, by boat, by crawling on hands and knees and slithering like serpents, under the mountain, they were. They entered. And so they became. Over many days, they became. Over centuries, thirteen times fifty-two bundles of years, they became. And then they were very old. The Ancient of Days they were known then. The Women of Wisdom. The Crones.

Scores of them had come to their place of learning from the east. In the east they had begun. With the dawn they had touched land, from the waters of the void, from the waters of emptiness, they had come forth and there they had remained. The waters returned in a rush, and the lands they had left were drowned.

There they remained for many years. Then they were young and shaken by the cataclysm, but they persevered. They there grew in age and wisdom. They had been priestesses in the days before. The days before their land had failed, the seas had drawn away from their shores, the depths of the waters had stood empty around them.

Then they had seen that the time of their youth was at an end. That they must leave the island of the childhood and find their way to a new land. Then they had gone west, and emerged as dawn touched the eastern shore from the dry ocean bed of their journey. Then they had slept, and the waters had been restored.

When they had gone to the west, their sisters had gone to the east. Thus they say that the lost sister will return. For the sisters will be united and their knowing will be whole in the ripeness of completion.

Long they had stayed there, learning the ways of the spirit and the mystery. Long they had stayed, waiting for Huracán, Gucumatz, to tell them their way. Long they tended the land they had entered, making it full of life, of plants and birds, of beasts and reptiles, of insects and beings so small they cannot be seen. There they planted corn. There they planted tobacco. There they stayed, learning and growing, making the world in the ways it would need to be.

In the fullness of time, the thirteen removed themselves to the west. They raised the mountains there to cover their abode. They hollowed out caves where they could live undisturbed over ages, to do the work it was given them to do next.

In that time, they infused their cells, all their flesh and bone, with the knowing. In that time, those periods, they danced and chanted, chanted and danced; they entered the heart of heaven, the heart of earth, the greenness of the fire that flickers between this world and the other one. In those long years, they perfected their skills and made into flesh every word they said.

And then at last it was finished, all but the sacrifice was done. They lay still and deep within their bodies, quiet and at rest within their sacred flesh. They lay as though sleeping, without thought, without movement, without breath. Long they lay there, unmoving. Long they lay at rest.

And as they lay there, their flesh became stone. It became hardened and rigid. Each cell became mineral, became hard, was petrified. They slowly over this time abstracted their being, their consciousness, from their flesh. They entered another kind of being that mortals call air, fire, spirit. They entered the world that surrounds this world, the world that interpenetrates this world. In this time, as the old stories say, they left the world and went to another world, the world of the spirits, the world of the supernaturals, the world of the immortals, the world of the gods. The immortals they became. The spirits they became. The supernaturals they became. The holy people they became. The gods they became.

And the stone they flew from like birds. Rising as heat from the fire, they retained all they knew, all they took with them, all they had left behind. Saying, when it is time, when it is time, when it is time, they shall come, the human beings, and take these crystallizations to their homes. There they shall smoke them, they shall sing them, they shall dance them into gleaming purity, translucence, clarity. Then they shall polish them, court them, honor them. Then they shall use them to speak to us in our place of abiding. Thus they shall learn the ways of the universe, the dance of the stars, the beginning and end of all things.

In later times, long after the gods had gone away, the priestesses and the shamans came to the hills. They entered the channel to the place of the crystals beneath the peaks. They moved along the river, they crawled on their knees, they slithered like serpents, until they entered the cave of being and found the thirteen bodies made of stone laid out perfectly, their limbs ordered in alignment, their heads to the west.

In that place where thousands of crystals grew, some as large as boulders, some tiny and new, the priestesses found the fire of life burning. Behind it grew the ten-branched tree of life. Upon each branch hung a disk, and each disk was made of gold.

Carefully they removed one body. Carefully they wrapped it in skins and softened bark. Gently they moved it from the cave of its sleeping to the place of becoming. The citadel they had made for the work they would do. The room cleansed by sacred smoke. The place cleansed by clear, pure flame. The place cleansed by water. The place made of stone, whose floor was of packed earth. Into this place they brought the stone woman, and in this place they removed her head.

And for generations after, unceasingly night after night, they sang and smoked the head until all traces of flesh had vanished, leaving only image of bone, until all smokiness within was banished, and the mineral was clear as pure water, sweet as spring. Women and men, they smoked her. Women and men, they sang. The priests all sang, and all bathed the head in the sacred mist, the smoke infused with life.

The head only they made sacred. Two rounded eye sockets, below it the bony ridge of the nose and wide grinning mouth, upper and lower jaw filled each with its row of perfect teeth. The lower jaw was separated from the skull in the final period, for a priest of the last generations to sing her into crystal grasped it and tore it from the head, though the two fit snugly when matched together. In this way, he thought to compel the goddess within to answer whenever they had need. Her head only they made sacred, wrapping the rest of the figure in leaves, skin, and bark, they reserved them.

For generations, they used what they had prepared to gain knowledge and to see to the needs of the people. For generations, they walked the path the immortals had set for them and left sleeping beneath the mountains until the people were ripe.

In time, they fell into conflict. In time, the world was much changed. In time, they began to walk by themselves. Halting, stumbling, they took their first steps alone, along the path marked by a soft, clear, glowing green light.

In time, as the days wheeled and turned, the temples fell and were buried beneath the proliferation of green. In time, the priests and priestesses faded into the forests, the writings fell to the fires, the statues were stolen, the people continued to survive. In the forests they lived. In the paths of the holy ones they lived. In the shadow of the immortals, they lived. And all the knowing seemed to sleep.

The skull lay hidden in the deep rubble of its house. From time to time, a wise one would come to her, take her for a time, restore the link between the world of the immortals and the world of the human beings. And time sunk deeper into the green.

And then one day, more than seventy years ago, a maiden was out walking. This maiden had no parents, or they had died. She did not know. Her father who adopted her was from a land far away from the jungle, far, far away from the green. But he knew of the old ones, the Ancient of Days. He had come to the forest, seeking, and had left his daughter behind to be raised by the Indians while he sought further, sought the green, sought the teachings, sought the way that seemed lost to him long before.

On the day she was wandering, he had been gone for seven years and then had returned. There was much activity around the old temples. The lost cities of the lost tribes. The Indians were hired to do the digging. They were not asked much, they did not say much. And on the day she went walking, the child, whose name means Daughter of Dawn Light, or Daughter of Corn, looked down. From among the vines that grew thick and tangled over the stones of the ruined temple, she saw a small but unmistakable flash of light.

She went to her father and told him. He went to see for himself, but the light did not beckon him with its brightness. He saw only vines and rubble. He saw only darkness within the interstices. He saw only holes.

But this chief was a wise man, wise enough to follow a maiden, his adopted child. He ordered the men to clear away the stones, to make an opening sufficiently large that they could climb down into the room below.

After many weeks, the floor was uncovered. An opening large enough was cleared, and enough rock moved so that they could climb down into the room below.

After many weeks, the floor was uncovered. An opening large enough was cleared, and enough rock moved so that there was no danger. Then he called his daughter, Dawn Light Girl, and said, "You found it. You go down and bring it up."

So Dawn Light Girl entered the cave they had made together, the builders of the old times and the workers of the new, and she brought the skull out of the room and gave it to her father. Only the head was there. The lower jaw was found later, lying a few feet away from the place where the skull had lain.

It is said the Indians were joyful. They danced and sang for days. They erected a brush shelter and for miles around they came to pay homage. "Our Grandmother is restored to us," they said.

It is said they were unhappy, stricken that their crystal was thus exposed, that they came for days to bid her good-bye.

In time the headman from far away left the region. He took his daughter and the skull away. It is said the people tried to keep it, but the white man refused. "I must take it for safekeeping," he told them.

It is also said the headman said to the people, "I cannot take this with me. You must keep it because it is yours." But the people demurred, saying, "No. It was found by your daughter, Sun Woman. It must stay with her." And so saying, they parted, the man, his daughter, and the immortal woman's bones went north, went east. The people, the forests, and the fallen temples stayed.

Years passed. In the year 1987, C.E., two men made their way south to the coastal city a few hundred miles to the north of the place where the skull had been found. By then the world was changing. It was the days of the beginning. It was the days of the end. They went to seek answers to an old, old question: Where were the

Mayas? Where was the lost world? Did anyone know of the calendar that told the end of the days? Like the heroes of old, they were seeking. Like the old heroes, they had traveled great distances in short time.

They were led by a wise one into the forest, and there bemused by the green light the foliage and the sun together cast upon them, they climbed the old temples and sat in the house of the gods, looking out at the forest below. Many days they spent in the wilderness, learning the ways of the people, the ways of the forest, the ways of the gods.

In the fullness of time, they found the place where the skull had come to light, and after a time they discovered its present home. They made their way far to the north, to the crisp, suburban home of Sun Woman, Daughter of Light. She and her companion, both old women now, greeted them warmly and asked them in.

In the weeks and months that followed, they strengthened their bonds with the people to the south and the women in the north. Over that time, Sun Woman entrusted them more and more with the crystal. Over time the wise men in the south taught them the old ways, the dances, and the ascent of the tree of life. They took the men to the place of the beginnings, and they remembered the old times for the two men's sakes.

As was proper, the two men brought gifts and food to the south on their journeys, taking care of the people as the people took care of them. As was proper, the two men paid their respects to Old Sun Woman and her companion, and aided them as they could.

It is said that at the time of the beginning, the Goddess will return in the fullness of her being. It is said that the Mother of All and Everything, the Grandmother of the Sun and the Dawn, will return to her children and with her will come harmony, peace, and the healing of the world. It is said that time is coming. Soon.

James Welch

(b. 1940) Blackfoot/Gros Ventre

James Welch was born in Browning, Montana, in 1940. He is mixedblood, a descendant of the Blackfoot and Gros Ventre. He studied at the University of Montana and has taught writing and literature at the University of Washington and Cornell University.

Riding the Earthboy 40, his first collection of poems, was published in 1971. Winter in the Blood, his first novel, was published three years later. The Death of Jim Loney, his second novel, followed in 1979. Fools Crow was published in 1986. The historical novel won the American Book Award and was named Book of the Year by the Los Angeles Times. The Indian Lawyer, his most recent novel, was published in 1990.

Winter in the Blood "is a tale told in the first person by a narrator whose name we never learn," wrote Louis Owens in Other Destinies. "The nameless narrator is frozen in time, caught in a wintry dormancy as he moves tentatively and torturously toward a glimmer of self-knowledge and a tenuous unification of past, present, and future."

The narrator has an intense presence without a name, and at the same time the author creates the "airplane man," an ironic other with a descriptive name. "In the tall weeds of the borrow pit, I took a leak and watched the sorrel mare, her colt beside her, walk through burnt grass to the shady side of the log-and-mud cabin." The scenes in the first few sentences of the novel introduce the mood and manner and the narrator.

Owens noted that a

> *borrow pit is an excavation from which earth has been taken for use elsewhere, earth appropriated or "borrowed." We will learn later in the novel that the narrator's father, First Raise, has been found frozen to death in this same borrow pit, "pointing toward home."*

LaVonne Ruoff wrote in American Indian Literatures that

> *Welch realistically depicts reservation life and creates vivid characterizations, especially of women. Using a spare style, he combines tragedy with scenes of Faulknerian humor. The novel also reflects the influence of Emilio Vittorini's In Sicily in its use of a nameless hero who returns home to learn about his family.*

Laura Coltelli asked Welch about the "airplane man" in an interview published in Winged Words. "Well, I don't know," he responded, "I don't think there is any terrific significance attached to him. You know, in one way I just wanted him as a kind of comic relief character.... And also he represents a kind of escape, the airplane man does."

Welch was then asked about the sense of winter in his novel. He said that winter was "very treacherous. You're always aware of how vulnerable you are during the winter months.... The winter, I suppose, of Winter in the Blood has to do mostly with the character's feeling of distance," the distance of space, a "distance from his mother, distance from his grandmother, distance from the girl that he brought home."

The Earthboy Place

In the tall weeds of the borrow pit, I took a leak and watched the sorrel mare, her colt beside her, walk through burnt grass to the shady side of the log-and-mud cabin. It was called the Earthboy place, although no one by that name (or any other) had lived in it for twenty years. The roof had fallen in and the mud between the logs had fallen out in chunks, leaving a bare gray skeleton, home only to mice and insects. Tumbleweeds, stark as bone, rocked in a hot wind against the west wall. On the hill behind the cabin, a rectangle of barbed wire held the graves of all the Earthboys, except for a daughter who had married a man from Lodgepole. She could be anywhere, but the Earthboys were gone.

The fence hummed in the sun behind my back as I climbed up to the highway. My right eye was swollen up, but I couldn't remember how or why, just the white man, loose with his wife and buying drinks, his raging tongue a flame above the music and my eyes. She was wild, from Rocky Boy. He was white. He swore at his money, at her breasts, at my hair.

Coming home was not easy anymore. It was never a cinch, but it had become a torture. My throat ached, my bad knee ached and my head ached in the even heat.

The mare and her colt were out of sight behind the cabin. Beyond the graveyard and the prairie hills, the Little Rockies looked black and furry in the heat haze.

Coming home to a mother and an old lady who was my grandmother. And the girl who was thought to be my wife. But she didn't really count. For that matter none of them counted; not one meant anything to me. And for no reason. I felt no hatred, no love, no guilt, no conscience, nothing but a distance that had grown through the years.

It could have been the country, the burnt prairie beneath a blazing sun, the pale green of the Milk River valley, the milky waters of the river, the sagebrush and cottonwoods, the dry cracked gumbo flats. The country had created a distance as deep as it was empty and the people accepted and treated each other with distance.

But the distance I felt came not from country or people; it came from within me. I was as distant from myself as a hawk from the moon. And that was why I had no particular feelings toward my mother and grandmother. Or the girl who had come to live with me.

I dropped down on the other side of the highway, slid through the barbed-wire fence and began the last two miles home. My throat ached with a terrible thirst. . . .

Lame Bull had decided the night before to give me a ride into Dodson. From there I could catch the bus down to Malta. We left early, before the gumbo flat could soak up enough rain to become impassable. The pickup slipped and skidded through the softening field as the rain beat down against the windshield. There was no wiper on my side and the landscape blurred light brown against gray. Patches of green relieved this monotony, but suddenly and without form. I had placed a piece of cardboard in my side window—the glass had fallen out one night in town last winter—to keep out the rain. I could have been riding in a submarine. At last we spun up the incline to the highway, and now I made out the straight ribbon of black through the heart of a tan land.

"Looks pretty good, huh?"

Lame Bull was referring to the rain and the effect it would have on the new growth of alfalfa.

"Not bad," I said. I didn't even want to think about haying again, not after we had struggled through that last field of bales.

"You know it." He hunched forward over the steering wheel. "I think we need a new rig, pal—the windshield wiper is slowing down on this one."

We passed Emily Short's fields, which were the best in the valley. They had been leveled by a reclamation crew from the agency. Emily was on the tribal council.

"Looky there!" Lame Bull slowed down.

Through his side window, I could see a figure in black shoveling a drain in one of the shallow irrigation ditches. A lonely moment—that man in the green field, the hills beyond and the gray sky above. His horse stood cold and miserable, one back leg cocked, the others ankle-deep in mud.

"Poor sonofabitch . . . "

When we got to Dodson, we went straight to Wally's. Lame Bull bought me a whiskey, then made out a check to me for thirty dollars. The bartender cashed it and brought another drink, including one for himself. He took the amount out of my check.

Out of habit, I decided to check for mail. As I hurried through the rain, my leg began to ache—not bad, just a dull pressure around the knee. Though it had been operated on twice, they had never managed to take away the stiffness or the ache that predicted endless dissatisfactions as surely as Teresa predicted lightning storms with her holy water.

The interior of the post office was dark and mahogany; rows of box windows reflected the gray beyond the larger gold-lettered window that looked out on the only street in town. I turned the combination dials to the numbers I had known since a child. Mose and I used to fight to see who got to open this box. There was a letter to Teresa from the priest in Harlem, a perfectly white envelope with his name stamped in silver in the corner. I started to put it back, but on second thought, more likely on no thought, I stuck it in the breast pocket of my Levi jacket. On my way out, I glanced at the men staring into the gloom of the post office from the wanted posters. They were the same faces I had memorized so many years before. Only the names were different.

I had another whiskey with Lame Bull. I thought of the hours my father had put in here, joking with the white men, the farmers from out north, the cattlemen to the east, the men from the grain elevator—they were acquaintances; they had bought me beers on those few occasions First Raise dragged me in. But they were foreign— somehow their lives seemed more orderly, they drank a lot but left early, and they would be back at work in the morning, while First Raise . . .

Now, except for the bartender and us, the place was empty. I said goodbye to Lame Bull and walked down to the cafe to wait for the bus. Then I walked back to the drugstore to buy a toothbrush. . . .

The bus was two hours late. The driver, a small man with tufts of black hair sticking out his ears, took my money, then sat down to a cup of coffee. I picked up my paper sack, which contained clean underwear and socks and an extra shirt, and walked out to the bus. It had gotten noticeably darker, though it was early afternoon. I sat across from a young woman and listened to the rain drum against the roof. The driver climbed aboard, shut the door and announced that we were headed for Malta. I stared at the woman's white legs and tried to imagine what she looked like under the purple coat, but I fell asleep.

An hour later we were in Malta. I stuffed the sack up under my jacket and hurried down the street to Minough's. Dougie, my girl's brother, was sitting at the bar. Beside him a large white man dozed, his head resting on his freckled forearms. His hat was pushed back almost to his shoulders. A cigarette smoldered in the ashtray next to his curly red hair.

I set the sack on a table behind me.

"I'm looking for your sister," I said.

"How come?"

"A personal matter."

"How come?" Dougie took a comb out of his shirt pocket and blew flecks of dandruff from it. "What are you going to do when you find her?"

"That's up to her, I guess."

"You going to beat her up?" He ran the comb through his hair, fluffing the wave with his other hand.

"I don't know, maybe . . . " I tried to keep my voice down.

"What did she do to you?"

"She took some things that don't exactly belong to her," I mumbled.

He laughed. "That's her, that's the way she operates ..." He punched me on the shoulder. "Man, you're lucky you got any nuts left—do you?" He made a sudden grab for my crotch. I flinched away. He leaned over and whispered: "See this guy here?"

"Is he the guy she's been running around with?"

"He drives a big-ass Buick."

"Where is she?"

"Help me get him back to the can and we'll see how much money he has on him. He drives a big Buick."

"You mean he used to—she probably stole it."

"No, hell, it's parked right outside—we been riding around all day. Come on, give me a hand."

"Then you'll tell me where she is?"

"Sure."

"What if he wakes up?"

"Shit, this guy's so far gone he wouldn't know it if a cow pissed in his eye."

We dragged the big man back into the toilet. He was half a foot taller than I was. Dougie was lost under the other armpit, but he already had the man's wallet in his hand. We sat him down on the toilet.

"How much is in the wallet?" I said.

"Nothing. The sonofabitch is empty."

But I saw Dougie's small hand sneak a wad of bills into his pocket.

"Wait a minute—give me some of that."

"Bullshit. The deal was I was just going to tell you where my sister is. We never said anything about any money." He turned to the urinal and peed.

"But I didn't think we were going to find anything," I whined. "Besides, it would be compensations for what your sister took."

"I'm not her goddamn keeper."

"But my gun alone ..."

"Look, do you want to know where my sister is or not?" He buttoned his pants indignantly.

Just then the white man toppled off the seat, banging his head against the washbowl. He slid to the floor, his hat upside down in the basin.

"We been drunk for practically a week." Dougie grinned, disappearing out the door.

I looked down at the pale sleeper's face. His red hair seemed strangely out of place among the white fixtures. I placed the hat over his eyes to shield them from the glare.

Dougie was not in the bar. I ran to the door and looked up and down the street, but he was not in sight. A big yellow Buick was parked at the curb. It was covered with mud, the only clean part the windshield where the wipers had fanned their trails.

Although I knew it would be useless, I searched all the bars and cafés in town, even the hotel and movie house. I paid seventy-five cents to walk up and down the aisle until the usher, a young bald man, told me to either sit down or leave. Bewildered, I sat down and looked at the screen but nothing made sense. I recognized Doris Day. She was drunk and had gotten her toe stuck in a bottle. Then I remembered the Buick. I ran down to Minough's, but the car was gone.

The rain continued to fall. My shoulders slumped under the weight of my soaked jacket and my leg ached. In the gray light of dusk, the sidewalk glistened beneath Minough's neon sign. . . .

"Nothing to be done about it," the man said. He dabbed his cigar into the bottom of the ashtray. "Happens all the time—hell, you're not unique. Happened to me plenty of times."

We were sitting at the bar of the Pomp Room, which was connected to the Regent's Roost Hotel. The man was from New York. He had shown me his credit cards when I said I didn't believe him.

"Well, you take me—do I look like the sort who would run out on a wife and two beautiful daughters? Hell, by your standards, I was a rich man!"

"You look rich enough to me," I said, and he did. He had on one of those khaki outfits that African hunters wear. I thought of McLeod and Henderson in the *Sports Afield*. His outfit was crisp, with a flowery handkerchief tied around his neck.

"Well, that's another story . . . we're trying to solve your problems."

Problems?

"Of course."

The only problem I had now was trying to stay out of the way of the man I had helped Dougie roll. That was the only problem that was still clear to me. The others had gone away.

"Chance, dumb unadulterated damn luck—I was on my way to the Middle East, had my tickets in my hand . . . "

I drained off my beer and pointed to the empty bottle.

"Barman! Damned if I didn't just turn around, halfway to the plane and everything, tore up my ticket right in front of her . . . "

My jacket was drying on the stool next to me. I had stopped shivering hours ago, just after he bought me my first boilermaker. I had felt a little self-conscious coming in, but the second one took care of that. Now even the fear of a beating, or even getting killed, was subsiding. I lit one of the cigars that lay on the bar.

" . . . picked up my fishing gear and drove away!"

"You won't have much luck here," I said.

"What? Fish?"

"You won't have much luck here."

"Caught a mess of them yesterday."

"But there are no fish around here."

"Pike—three of them over five pounds. Caught one big northern in Minnesota that ran over thirty."

"That was Minnesota. That wasn't here. You'd be lucky to catch a cold here."

"Caught some nice little rainbows too. Pan size."

"There aren't any rainbows."

He looked at me. He was a big man, soft and healthy, like a baby. He combed his gray hair straight back, so that his red-veined nose seemed too big for his face.

"Tell you what—" He snorted into his hand. "I'll take you out with me tomorrow and if we don't catch any fish, I'll buy you the biggest steak in —where are we?—Malta! You have an outfit?"

"At home—but that's fifty miles away."

"No problem. I've got a spinning rig you can use. Furthermore, I'll use my fly rod and if I don't catch more fish than you, you can have both outfits. Now you can't beat that deal."

I calculated how much both outfits would be worth. "What if neither one of us catches any fish?"

"I'll throw in the biggest steak in Kalamazoo."

"There are no fish in the river," I said confidently. "Not even a sucker."

"Hell . . . " He winked at the bartender, who had been listening, then ordered another boilermaker for me and a double Scotch for himself. "Get one for yourself," he called after the bartender.

Two men in suits opened the door. Then, as though they realized this was the wrong place, they hesitated. After a short conversation, they came in, moving down the bar like cows on slick ice, their eyes not yet adjusted to the dimness of the small blue lights in the ceiling. As they passed me, I smelled the wet wool of their suits. One of them giggled.

The bartender followed them down the other side of the bar as though he were stalking them. He was a skinny man. His red vest and black string tie made him look like a frontier gambler. But he knew all the baseball scores and had been to New York once.

Standing a few feet away from me, a barmaid leaned on her tray. She poked the ice cubes in her Coke with her finger and glared at herself in the mirror. Although I couldn't see a cigarette near her, she was blowing smoke rings.

The two men sat down on the other side of the man who had torn up his airplane ticket.

"What do you think—Shall I ask them?"

"About the fish?"

"What else? What else were we talking about? Or would you rather admit you made a mistake?"

I shook my head. "You said you caught a mess of goldeyes?"

"Did I say that? But you're mistaken—There aren't any goldeyes in this river. I've never even heard of goldeyes." He turned to the men in suits. "This man says there are no fish around here."

The two suits looked up. One had a red tie.

"He says there are no fish around here," he repeated.

"Why, that's false," the first suit said. "There are pike in the reservoir south of town. Just the other day I caught a nice bunch."

"In the reservoir south of town," the second suit said.

"Ah, you see," said the man who had torn up his airplane ticket.

"But not in the river. It is too muddy and the fish can't see your bait."

"Not likely. It's clear and cold and the fish are firm."

"Yes," said the second suit. "Just the other day my wife and her girl friend fished in the river and they said it was clear and cold."

"I have often remarked on the clarity of the water. It isn't muddy like the reservoir south of town." First suit tasted his drink. He fished out a cherry and nibbled at it. "No matter—no fish there anyway."

"In the reservoir?" I asked.

"Hell no," said the man who had torn up his airplane ticket. "In the creek west of here. The reservoir is full of sunfish."

Second suit, who had finished his drink, ordered another round. He lifted his replenished glass to the mirror and said: "I don't understand these people around here."

"Neither do I," said the man who had torn up his airplane ticket. "Hell—it's uncanny."

I began to feel the effects of the boilermakers. I winked at myself in the mirror and the barmaid, who had returned, glared back.

"I don't understand the people around here—like that man down there." I pointed down the bar to second suit. He was fiddling with a camera.

"I wouldn't know—I'm new here." She blew more smoke rings. There was still no cigarette near her.

"Wait a minute, just a minute here." The man who had torn up his airplane ticket looked past me at the girl. "Don't I know you from someplace?"

"How should I know?"

"But I've seen you before, somewhere else. My memory is like a steel trap." He narrowed his eyes. "Bismarck? North Dakota?"

She shook her head.

"Minneapolis?"

She blew a smoke ring at the mirror.

"That's funny. You sure it wasn't Chicago?"

"I've never been there. I might be from the West Coast."

"That's it! Seattle!" His elbow bounced off my ribs. "Ha, you see?"

"Seattle?" I asked.

"I wouldn't be from Seattle for all the rice in China." She counted some coins on her tray. "Now, Portland might be different—they've got roses there."

"My mother raises morning glories," I said.

"Los Angeles?"

"I hate morning glories. I hate anything to do with morning."

"But that's just the name. They bloom in the evening too—even at night I can smell them outside my window. Our cat used to lie in them because it was cool."

"Our cat smothered my baby sister. He lay on her face one night and she couldn't breathe. She would have looked just like me, only she had a birthmark right here." She pressed her finger into the side of the neck. She leaned closer, still without looking at me, and whispered: "That's why he thinks he knows me. He remembers my sister's birthmark."

"But why doesn't he remember you?"

"San Francisco?"

"Oh, he will. Can't you see he's trying right now?"

"San Francisco?"

"I used to dance all the time. That's why he doesn't remember me, because I was always dancing and the faster I danced the less he saw of me."

"But he's from New York," I said.

"He used to pay me. There's why I hated it. He use to pay me a dollar to dance for him." She laughed. "It was such fun, twirling around the room, faster and faster until I must have been a blur. That's why he forgets my face."

"San Francisco? Santa Rosa! My wife was from Santa Rosa but she's dead now."

"I could just tell him who I am. Do you think I should?"

"No," I said. "Let him guess."

"I suppose . . . but it might make him mad. That's one thing you learn about men—you don't joke with them unless you mean business." She picked up her tray and walked back to the booths.

The two suits watched her.

"Nice little twitch," said the first suit. His red necktie had worked its way out of his coat.

"Yes," said the second suit. "I wouldn't mind a little bit of that myself."

"Ah, but she would wear you out. You can tell by the hips."

"My wife has hips like that and it's all I can do to stay in bed with her."

"My wife has hips like that," I said, "but she has smaller breasts."

"Small breasts are best," said second suit. "My wife has big breasts and they just get in the way. What you can't get in your mouth is wasted anyway."

"My wife has breasts that hang down to her knees and her nipples are too dark."

"Pink nipples are easily the best," I said.

"My wife is dead," said the man who had torn up his airplane ticket.

The bartender brought us a round of drinks on the house and recited some baseball scores. The airplane man continued to name places, but the barmaid wasn't there. Second suit fumbled with his camera. He had the insides out and the film was hanging down over the counter.

My leg had gone numb, as though waterlogged by the boilermakers. At least it didn't ache.

When the barmaid returned, I looked at her breasts. They were not as large as I had thought; her white blouse was a little small, stretched tight across them, straining the button between them.

The airplane man jerked his thumb at me and said: "This man doesn't believe there are goldeyes in the river."

"Of course there are," she said. "I caught seven of them just this morning."

"You can't mean it."

"Positively."

The airplane man glared at her. Suddenly he jerked upright and roared—I thought first suit had stuck a knife in his back—then rushed her, arms extended as if to hug or strangle her. At the last instant, he swerved and hit the door, plunging into the night.

The barmaid smiled at me. "It's still raining."

"You should have danced for him," I said.

"No." She shook her head sadly. "It wouldn't be the same."

Thomas King

(b. 1943) Cherokee

Thomas King was born in 1943. He was raised by his mother in California, a mixedblood of Cherokee, Greek, and German descent. He studied at California State University at Chico and the University of Utah. He has taught in the Native Studies Department at the University of Lethbridge in Alberta and in American Studies at the University of Minnesota. **Medicine River**, his first novel, was published in 1990. "A lovely book. Thomas King is off to a wonderful start," wrote Tony Hillerman. **Green Grass, Running Water**, his second comic novel, was published in 1993.

The comic characters and scenes in his stories count on the common representation of the trickster as coyote, the cosmopolitan coyote of popular culture. Many tribes have trickster stories, and the trickster takes various human and animal forms, as there is no distinction between animate and inanimate in imagination and natural reason. The code of coyote is the most familiar representation of the trickster in stories.

"My responsibilities are to the story and to the people from whom I get some of the stories," King told Jace Weaver in **Publishers Weekly**. "I like to hear my characters talking. I like to hear their voices. Although I greatly admire writers like N. Scott Momaday, who can go for pages and never have anyone say anything, I'd go nuts if I couldn't hear my characters speak."

Medicine River is located in a fictional town near the Blood Reserve in Alberta, Canada. A Canadian reserve is similar to a reservation in the United States. "Like the protagonists of many twentieth-century American Indian novels," wrote LaVonne Ruoff in **American Indian Literatures**,

> "King's hero, Will, is a passive mixed-blood who flies to learn more about himself, his family" [and the natives of his hometown.].... A classic distancer at the beginning of the novel, Will, the son of an Indian mother, becomes increasingly involved with the people of Medicine River....
>
> Harlen is full of enterprises that never quite come off, misguided advice for Will, and rambling stories. King creates accurate portraits of life in an off reservation town and on the reserve, as well as a memorable character in the farcical but lovable Harlen.

Maydean Joe and Harlen Bigbear are comic characters in the basement scenes in **Medicine River**. Harlen "was like the prairie wind. You never knew when he was coming or when he was going to leave." Maydean was backward, tenacious, and a trickster chance in the literature of survivance. Indeed, she outwitted the wiser boys in their own basement.

Maydean Joe

Maydean Joe was retarded. She lived in the apartment building next door to ours, and every so often, Maydean would wander into our basement. We played in that basement in the winter, when it was too cold to go out, and in the summer, when it was too hot to stay out. I guess we figured we owned that basement.

When Maydean first showed up, we didn't know what to do. Henry Goodrider told her it was our basement, and that if she wanted to play in it, she would have to pay. Maydean just stood and looked at Henry with her mouth hanging open. Her arms hung in the air at funny angles, and every so often, they would jump as though someone had pulled on a set of strings. She sort of frightened me, her arms jumping about and her head jerking as if she couldn't control it. I think she frightened Henry, too.

We tried to play a couple of tricks on her. One day, James and Henry and me pretended we couldn't hear Maydean or see her. We walked around the basement, as though she wasn't there. We talked to each other as though she didn't exist. It was a joke, but all of a sudden, Maydean let out a scream and rushed Henry and pushed him into some boxes that were stacked in the corner near the washers and the large commercial dryer. He wasn't hurt, but he was angry as hell, and he got up and pushed Maydean. She fell down, and then she got up and pushed Henry, and Henry pushed her back, and then she pushed me. We all started pushing each other, and then we started laughing, and after that, Maydean was okay.

I don't mean she got better or anything like that. She was still retarded. She liked to hug us, and that was embarrassing. She'd run over in that staggering, falling, loose-limbed way she had of moving, and grab Henry or James or me. She was strong, and she liked to squeeze us as hard as she could.

The other kids didn't like her much. Lena Oswald called her Little Miss Moron, and Bat Brain, and Slobberdean, because Maydean drooled a little when she got excited. Vicki Wright and her sister Robin started drawing pictures and writing things like "Will loves Maydean" or "James loves Maydean" or "Henry loves Maydean" on the basement walls with chalk they stole from school. Vicki said if you hung around retards like Maydean and let them slobber all over you, you would become a retard, too.

The kids said all those things out loud in front of Maydean, as if she couldn't hear or didn't care. One day, she sort of went wild in the basement and started scrubbing at a picture Vicki had drawn. Maydean tried to erase it with her bare hands, and she got most of it off, but not before she cut her hands on the concrete. They didn't bleed much, but you could see the faint fan of blood on the wall.

Harlen had told me the story of David Plume. As soon as the Indians took over Wounded Knee, David and Kevin Longbird and Amos Morley piled into Kevin's van and headed for South Dakota. They got stopped in Fargo and were thrown in jail there. After they got out, Kevin and Amos Morley turned back and came home.

Ray Little Buffalo figured that David was bullshitting everyone. "Once the feds closed down the highways and the secondary roads around Wounded Knee, no one got in. Plume probably just hung out in town and tried to convince the whores he was some big hero. Probably got that jacket at a surplus store."

According to Harlen, after Wounded Knee ended, David got himself arrested for aggravated assault in Lincoln and spent fourteen months in jail. When he came home, he had the jacket.

The photograph could have been taken inside Wounded Knee. But it could have been taken at someone's house, too, or in a bus depot.

"I can fix it," I said. "It won't be as good as new, and I can't print a poster-size copy. How about an eight-by-ten and some wallet size?"

"Kinda like something bigger. It's a historic picture."

"Don't have the equipment to do real big stuff. There might be some places in Calgary that can do that."

"It was taken the morning the cops really started shooting at us," David said. "This jacket has power. You had to have been there."

It was Henry's idea that we put Maydean in the dryer. James wanted to be the one, but Henry said that he might bang his head as the dryer went around, and that if Maydean banged her head, it probably wouldn't hurt.

We'd put Maydean in the dryer and wait until my mother came down to put the wash in the dryer and just before she turned it on, we'd say, "Hey, isn't that Maydean?" or something like that. That was the idea.

But Maydean wouldn't get in the dryer. She got as far as the door, but she wouldn't get in.

"Come on, Maydean. It'll be fun."

"No," said Maydean.

"Look, tell you what. We won't let her turn it on."

"No."

"Maydean," said Henry. "If you want to play with us and be our pal, you got to get in the dryer."

Maydean didn't get in the dryer. She was stubborn sometimes, and this was one of those times. So we were stuck with James. Henry borrowed his brother's hockey helmet and a pair of gloves because, he said, you can't be too safe. James looked like one of those astronauts climbing into a spaceship. He pressed his nose against the glass and stuck out his tongue. Maydean stood in front of the dryer jerking her head around and laughing, while James made fish faces behind the glass.

When we heard Mom coming down the stairs, we told James to be quiet, and we shut the door. Maydean stood in front of the dryer, and she wouldn't move. We thought she'd give the whole thing away. "You mess this up, Maydean, and you can just find some other basement."

Henry and me went and stood by the washers and tried to look casual. "We'll help you, Mom," I said as soon as she came through the door. Henry opened the washer, and we began carrying the wet clothes to the dryer.

My mother didn't say anything. She just watched us. Maydean started to laugh and sway.

"You kids break something?"

We got all the clothes from the washer into the dryer, and my mother took her coin purse out of her apron pocket.

"Maybe you should take a look to see that we put them in right."

"Don't know of a wrong way to do it."

"We may have made a mistake, you know."

My mother opened the purse and took out two quarters, but as she closed the purse, it slipped out of her hand and fell, the coins scattering across the floor.

Henry and me leaped on the quarters and the dimes and the nickels. Some of the coins ran under the washer. Others rolled to the far side of the room. We chased them all down, pouncing on them like hawks on field mice.

I was just starting to count my coins, when I heard a klunking sound and Maydean's crazy laugh.

"What's wrong with this dryer?" my mother was saying. "What'd you kids put in here?"

I made some coffee. David sat in the easy chair. He sat with his legs sprawled out in front of him as though he had walked a long distance and was tired.

"You ever been shot at?"

It was a casual question. David might have asked me if I'd flown in a plane or if I liked sushi or if I had ever been to Yellowknife.

"It's weird, you know. At night, you can see the flash and the tracers coming in. Every so often, you'd hear the bullets hitting something."

"There's a poster company in Calgary. I could make a negative and send it to them. They'll blow it up to any size you want."

"I was never scared at Wounded Knee. Most of the time we just sat around and talked. Most of the time we sat and waited. Most days, it was boring as hell. You know the cops killed Frank Clearwater while he was sleeping?"

I was trying to think of something sympathetic to say when David got out of the chair and tucked the tail of his shirt back in his pants. "You get close to guys when someone's trying to kill you. You know what I mean? Me and Dennis Banks were like that."

I nodded and started moving towards the door, hoping David would follow. "Give me a couple of days," I said. "I'll shoot a negative, touch it up and print a couple of wallet-size photos. I'll look up that address in Calgary."

"He gave me this jacket," David said, and he turned so I could see the letters on the back. "Harlen says you were in Toronto when we took Wounded Knee."

"That's right," I said. "I thought about going."

"Lots of people thought about going."

David walked back to the chair and sat down. I watched the window hoping Harlen would drop in. We talked about Wounded Knee. We talked about Medicine River and the reserve. David's parents lived in Cardston. They were both Mormons, and he didn't see much of them. It was a friendly conversation full of anecdotes and humour, but as he talked, his gestures became laboured and jerky as though springs were slipping inside, and his voice plunged and thrashed like someone dying in water. I wasn't sorry when he finally left.

I caught Harlen at the Friendship Centre. "David shows everyone that picture," Harlen told me. "He doesn't mean to make people feel bad, you know. He's the only one who went to Wounded Knee from around here. Kevin and Amos went with him, but they didn't stay."

"He didn't make me feel bad."

"That's good. Some of the boys don't like him. Ray figures David likes to show off. Those two almost got into a fight at the American a few weeks back. Things would be easier if he didn't wear that jacket all the time."

"You think that's the problem?"

"Sure. Jimmy Bruised Head went to law school, and Louise's cousin Alice got two or three degrees and went to teach at that university in Saskatoon. You and Louise own your own businesses."

"So?"

"So, none of you went to Wounded Knee."

"So?"

"David did. You can see how it all makes sense."

Henry and me got James out of the dryer. His nose was bleeding, and the helmet was jammed down over his eyes. We took him over to the sink and got most of the blood off his face. He was trying not to cry. I knew Mom was looking at me.

"He wanted to do it. I told him no, but he did it anyway."

"That's right," said Henry. "It's Maydean's fault. She was supposed to do it, but she didn't want to because she's crazy."

My mother stood and looked at the three of us, Henry and me and James, who was trying to stop the blood with a corner of his shirt.

"Where's Maydean?" my mother said.

She wasn't in the basement, and at first, I thought she had left. But then I heard her popping laugh. She was in the dryer. She was lying in the dryer on her back, her knees drawn up against her stomach.

"Hey, get out of there. You're going to get those clothes dirty."

"Yeah," said Henry. "You didn't want to get in the dryer before and look what happened. Now it's too late." Henry reached in and grabbed Maydean's arm. She jerked the arm out of Henry's grasp, rolled over, kicked at Henry and began screaming. Henry snapped his arm back and banged it on the side of the dryer. "Damn," he shouted. "You gone and done it this time, Maydean Joe. Everyone's going to know you're crazy. Wanting to stay in a dryer is real nuts."

The following Wednesday, just before closing, David pulled up in front of the studio in Kevin Longbird's van. Kevin was in the driver's seat, and I could see Amos Morley in the back.

"We're on our way to Ottawa," David told me. "Government wants to cut the money for Indian education."

"They're always trying to do that."

"You should come along, Will. You could take pictures."

"I don't know why the government does that."

"I meet a lot of Indians, you know, who are sorry they didn't go to Wounded Knee. That's what they tell me. They feel like they got left out. It feels good to be part of something important."

"Yeah," I said. "I know what you mean."

We stood around the dryer. James's nose had stopped bleeding. Maydean was rolled up on her side with her face against the back of the dryer.

"Go on," my mother said. "Go play outside. She just wants to be like the rest of you."

Mom pulled up a chair next to the dryer and sat down and waited. "Go on," she said again. "Going to take a while to fix this foolishness."

Leslie Marmon Silko

(b. 1948) Laguna Pueblo

Leslie Marmon Silko was born in 1948. She is mixedblood Laguna and Mexican. She was raised on stories, a natural inheritance of a writer. Robert Gunn Marmon and other relatives were once prominent leaders at Laguna Pueblo. Silko studied at the University of New Mexico. She taught at Navajo Community College and the University of Arizona. In 1981 she received a grant from the MacArthur Fellows Program.

Laguna Woman *her first collection of poems, was published in 1974.* **Ceremony**, *published three years later, is her first and most celebrated novel.* **Storyteller**, *a collection of autobiographical notes and poetry, was published in 1986.* **Almanac of the Dead**, *her second novel, was published in 1991.*

"At the core of **Ceremony** *is the author's attempt to find a particular strength within what has almost universally been treated as the 'tragic' fact of mixedblood existence," wrote Louis Owens in* **Other Destinies**. *"The central lesson of this novel is that through the dynamism, adaptability, and syncretism inherent in Native American cultures, both individuals and the cultures within which individuals find significance and identity are able to survive, grow, and evade the deadly traps of stasis and sterility."*

LaVonne Ruoff pointed out in **American Indian Literatures** *that the "veteran as the hero" and the "ritual quest" are the central themes in* **Ceremony**. *"Silko demonstrates the healing power of tribal ritual and storytelling by reuniting her mixedblood hero with his tribe at the end of the novel."*

Tayo, the main mixedblood character, wondered what ceremonies could heal the sickness of war and lies. Betonie, the post-Indian healer,

> *shook his head. "That is the trickery of the witchcraft," he said. "They want us to believe all evil resides with white people. Then we will look no further to see what is really happening. They want us to separate ourselves from white people, to be ignorant and helpless as we watch our own destruction." The witches manipulate white people. Betonie said he could deal with white people. "We can because we invented white people; it was Indian witchery that made white people in the first place."*

He had heard the stories that whites were created in a contest of native witches. This scene is a clever narrative resistance to the common binaries based on the codes of racialism. Once created, and once the stories are told, no one can call that story back.

Call That Story Back

Note on Bear People and Witches

Don't confuse those who go to the bears with the witch people. Human beings who live with the bears do not wear bear skins. They are naked and not conscious of being different from their bear relatives. Witches crawl into skins of dead animals, but they can do nothing but play around with objects and bodies. Living animals are terrified of witches. They smell the death. That's why witches can't get close to them. That's why people keep dogs around their hogans. Dogs howl with fear when witch animals come around.

The wind came up and fanned the fire. Tayo watched a red flame crawl out from under the white coals; he reached down for a piece of juniper and tossed it in. The fire caught. He rubbed pitch from the wood between his fingers and looked down at Gallup.

"I never told you about Emo," he said, "I never told you what happened to Rocky." He pointed at the lights below. "Something about the lights down there, something about the cars and the neon signs which reminds me of both of them."

"Yes," the old man said, "my grandmother would not leave this hill. She said the whole world could be seen from here."

"Rocky wanted to get away from the reservation; he wanted to make something of himself. In a city somewhere."

"They are down there. Ones like your brother. They are down there."

"He didn't make it though. I was supposed to help him, so he'd make it back. They were counting on him. They were proud of him. I owed them that much. After everything that happened. I owed it to them." He looked at the old man, but he was staring at the lights down below, following the headlights from the west until they were taillights disappearing in the east. He didn't seem to be listening.

"There are no limits to this thing," Betonie said. "When it was set loose, it ranged everywhere, from the mountains and plains to the towns and cities; rivers and oceans never stopped it." The wind was blowing steadily and the old man's voice was almost lost in it.

"Emo plays with these teeth—human teeth—and he says the Indians have nothing compared to white people. He talks about their cities and all the machines and food they have. He says the land is not good, and we must go after what they have, and take it from them." Tayo coughed and tried to clear the tightness from his throat.

"Well, I don't know how to say this but it seems that way. All you have to do is look around. And so I wonder," he said, feeling the tightness in his throat squeeze out the tears, "I wonder what good Indian ceremonies can do against the sickness which comes from their ward, their bombs, their lies?"

The old man shook his head. "That is the trickery of the witchcraft," he said. "They want us to believe all evil resides with white people. Then we will look no further to see what is really happening. They want us to separate ourselves from white people, to be ignorant and helpless as we watch our own destruction. But white people are only tools that the witchery manipulates; and I tell you, we can deal with white people, with their machines and their beliefs. We can because we invented white people; it was Indian witchery that made white people in the first place.

Long time ago
in the beginning
there were no white people in this world
there was nothing European.
And this world might have gone on like that
except for one thing;
witchery.
This world was already complete
even without white people.
There was everything
including witchery.

Then it happened.
These witch people got together.
Some came from far far away
across oceans
across mountains.
Some had slanty eyes
others had black skin.
They all got together for a contest
the way people have baseball tournaments nowadays
except this was a contest
in dark things.

So anyway
they all got together
witch people from all directions

witches from all the Pueblos
and all the tribes.
They had Navajo witches there,
some from Hopi, and a few from Zuni.
They were having a witches' conference,
that's what it was.
Way up in the lava rock hills
north of Cañoncito
they got together
to fool around in caves
with their animal skins.
Fox, badger, bobcat, and wolf
they circled the fire
and on the fourth time
they jumped into that animal's skin.

But this time it wasn't enough
and one of them
maybe a Sioux or some Eskimos
started showing off.
"That wasn't anything,
watch this."

The contest started like that.
Then some of them lifted the lids
on their big cooking pots,
calling the rest of them over
to take a look:
dead babies simmering in blood
circles of skull cut away
all the brains sucked out.
Witch medicine
to dry and grind into powder
for new victims.

Others untied skin bundles of disgusting objects:
dark flints, cinders from burned hogans where the dead lay
Whorls of skin

cut from fingertips
sliced from the penis end and clitoris tip.

Finally there was only one
who hadn't shown off charms or powers.
The witch stood in the shadows beyond the fire
and no one ever knew where this witch came from
which tribe
or if it was a woman or a man.
But the important thing was
this witch didn't show off any dark thunder charcoals
or red ant-hill beads.
This one just told them to listen:
"What I have is a story."

At first they all laughed
but this witch said
Okay
go ahead
laugh if you want to
but as I tell the story
it will begin to happen.

Set in motion now
set in motion by our witchery
to work for us.

Caves across the ocean
in caves of dark hills
white skin people
like the belly of a fish
covered with hair.

Then they grow away from the earth
then they grow away from the sun
then they grow away from the plants and animals.
They see no life
When they look

they see only objects.
The world is a dead thing for them
the trees and rivers are not alive
the mountains and stones are not alive.
The deer and bear are objects
They see no life.

They fear
They fear the world.
They destroy what they fear.
They fear themselves.

The wind will blow them across the ocean
thousands of them in giant boats
swarming like larva
out of crushed ant hill.

They will carry objects
which can shoot death
faster than the eye can see.

They will kill the things they fear
all the animals
the people will starve.

They will poison the water
they will spin the water away
and there will be drought
the people will starve.

They will fear what they find
They will fear the people
They kill what they fear.

Entire villages will be wiped out
They will slaughter whole tribes.

Corpses for us

Blood for us
Killing killing killing killing.
And those they do not kill
will die anyway
at the destruction they see
at the loss
at the loss of the children
the loss will destroy the rest.

Stolen rivers and mountains
the stolen land will eat their hearts
and jerk their mouths from the Mother.
The people will starve.

They will bring terrible diseases
the people have never known.
Entire tribes will die out
covered with festered sores
shitting blood
vomiting blood.
Corpses for our work

Set in motion now
set in motion by our witchery
set in motion
to work for us.

They will take this world from ocean to ocean
they will turn on each other
they will destroy each other
Up here
in these hills
they will find the rocks,
rocks with veins of green and yellow and black.
They will lay the final pattern with these rocks
they will lay it across the world
and explode everything.

Set in motion now
set in motion
To destroy
To kill
Objects to work for us
objects to act for us
Performing the witchery
for suffering
for torment
for the still-born
the deformed
the sterile
the dead.

Whirling
whirling
whirling
whirling
set into motion now
set into motion.

So the other witches said
"Okay you win; you take the prize,
but what you said just now—
it isn't so funny
It doesn't sound so good.
We are doing okay without it
we can get along without that kind of thing.
Take it back.
Call that story back."

But the witch just shook its head
at the others in their stinking animal skins, fur and feathers.
It's already turned loose.
It's already coming.
It can't be called back.

Louis Owens

(b. 1948) Choctaw/Cherokee

Louis Owens was born in 1948. He traces his descent from Choctaw, Cherokee, and Irish ancestors, and was raised in Mississippi and California. He is a professor of literature and creative writing at the University of New Mexico.

Owens is the author of numerous critical essays and short stories and three novels. **Wolfsong**, *his first novel, a native resistance to the destruction of the wilderness and land rights, was published in 1991.* **The Sharpest Sight** *was published in 1992.* **The Bone Game**, *his third novel, was published two years later by the University of Oklahoma Press in the American Indian Literature and Critical Studies series. "Ghosts walk and spirits talk in* **The Bone Game**," *a reviewer noted in* the **New York Times**, *calling it a metaphysical novel "that is eerie enough to be read aloud around a campfire."*

"The Last Stand" is a cautionary caricature story about a dog named Custer. The narrative style is direct, laconic, and ironic. "The pound people said he didn't have a name before. His owner was a crack dealer who just called him Dog. He had a deprived upbringing."

The Last Stand

Cole was splitting firewood when he heard the car. By the time he had walked around to the front of the house, Alex was there with the rear of the Volvo open. He held a heavy rope attached to something inside the car and was leaning back on the heels of his boots. Two thick, tawny legs protruded from the car.

Alex waved with his free hand, glancing at Cole but keeping his eyes on the car. "Hey, Cole."

Cole tried to peer into the Volvo. "Good afternoon, Alex. What is it?"

Abby stood on the path to the house, watching. Behind Abby, Onatima looked on with eyes squinted and arms crossed.

"Dog." Alex pulled on the rope, and an immense yellow-brown animal tumbled onto the gravel, snarling.

"Sit!" Alex yelled and jumped backwards at the same time.

The dog sat, its drooping black eyes fixed grimly on the hand at the end of the rope.

"Don't worry." Alex waved a hand at Cole. "He always sits when you tell him to. He likes to sit."

"What is he?" Cole asked.

"Bull mastiff. A beauty, huh? Hundred and forty pounds if he's an ounce."

A profound growl rumbled out of the mastiff's broad chest, and the head swung toward Cole.

"He's gorgeous," Abby said, moving up to stand beside her father. "Can I pet him?"

Alex shook his head. "I think maybe you'd better let him get used to his new home first. I think he's a little bit nervous."

"New home?" Cole said. "What do you mean, new home?"

"He's for you. I was thinking about the trouble Abby had the other day, and I decided you needed a guard dog, so I went to the pound. He's a housewarming present for you."

"I've lived in this house eight months, Alex. It's already warm."

"Well, I felt bad because I never held a giveaway for you, or a blessing ceremony or something. This will make up for it."

"You don't have to make up for it, Alex. I told you I don't want a dog."

"Indians and dogs go together, Cole. It's an ancient, honorable alliance. A good dog warms the lodge during those hard winters and warns when the stealthy enemy approaches. And Custer's a sweet dog; look at that face. He's just a little nervous right now. That's a bumpy road you have, and he probably misses his former home."

"Custer?" Cole and Abby spoke at the same time.

"You named him Custer?" Abby's voice rose to a higher pitch.

"Well, I didn't. The cop did."

"Cop?"

"The one who arrested his owner."

"Custer?" Cole looked at the dog's enormous head, with jaws big enough to snap a small oak, and the neck and chest that didn't seem distinguishable. "Why?"

"Well, I don't know, but the cop was a Lakota guy over in San Jose. A lot of Indian cops around, you know. Maybe it's his hair. It's golden, like General George Armstrong Custer's—you know, Yellowhair. The pound people said he didn't have a name before. His owner was a crack dealer who just called him Dog. He had a deprived upbringing—a dog with no name, guarding a crack house—and I figured I could kill two birds with one stone, so to speak, by getting him for you. He's a professional guard dog. They said it took five animal control people with nets to get him out of that house. The Lakota cop said they wanted to shoot him. He must have really felt like Custer, seeing all those guys coming. But he needs a regular home environment like you have here. It'll straighten him out, like therapy. You can keep him in the house for a while, and once he's used to the place, you can let him patrol outside, and nobody will bother you. Custer will protect you from attack."

Custer swivelled his head to look at Cole, the growl rumbling in a deeper note.

"I appreciate your thoughtfulness, Alex, but we don't need a killer to protect us from killers."

Alex glanced up, seeing the old lady for the first time, and waved, saying, "Good morning, Grandmother."

Cole looked at Onatima and then back toward Custer. "Alex, this is my grandmother, Onatima Blue Wood." He turned toward the old lady. "Grandmother, this is one of my colleagues from the university. He's a crazy Navajo transvestite."

"Come on, Cole. That's no way to introduce me to such a distinguished person as your grandmother. Besides, look at my wardrobe." Alex smiled at Onatima. "I've told him transvestite is not the technically correct term. It is an honor to meet you. Cole's told me splendid things about you."

Onatima nodded, watching with obvious amusement.

Abby stepped closer. "Oh, Dad, can't we keep him? Look how he's sitting there. He's well behaved. And if Alex takes him back to the pound, they may put him to sleep."

"That's what they would do for sure. The gas chamber. Don't you hate those white-man euphemisms? It's hard to believe people wouldn't snap up a pet like this, but they said I was his last hope, his stay of execution. He's my gift to your family. I already paid the animal control people for him, for shots and license and that stuff, and I won't get my money back. He'll be a sweet dog once he gets used to you." He took a step toward the dog, holding a hand out and crooning, "Good boy, Custer."

The growl rose in intensity and the dog snarled, saliva flying. Alex jerked his hand back. "Why don't you take him into the house and start getting him used to his new home?" He looked around at the clearing and the ridge to the west. "You know, this is the perfect place for a dog like Custer. A clean, wholesome environment, lots of room to stretch his legs. Reminds me of home."

"You have redwoods at Chinle?"

"Please, Dad? We could just try him for a while."

"Abby, that dog is antisocial, probably a social psychopath. Probably damaged by drugs."

The dog braced its front feet and sat back on its haunches.

"I'm very pleased to meet you," Onatima said, walking toward the car.

As she approached, Alex looked at the old lady with interest.

"Let me have the rope." Onatima held out her hand, and when he handed her the rope she held it loosely, stepping close to the dog. The growl turned into a snarl again.

"Stop that nonsense," she said, bending slightly to look the dog in the face. "A dog with a name like Custer can't afford to alienate anyone. You'd better stop. Now come with me."

Custer stood up, unfolding to amazing height on his long legs, and followed her into the house.

Inside, she led the dog to a braided rug in the center of the living room. "Sit," she said, and Custer sat.

"Where would you like him?" She smiled at Cole, and it was the same smile he'd first seen twenty years before in Luther's cabin when his brother's ghost had stepped from the corner. The joke was on him, and she was enjoying it.

"Right there, I guess. Maybe you could tell him to lie down on the rug."

Onatima unhooked the rope from the dog's collar. "Lie down," she said.

Custer looked at her and walked to the couch, climbing clumsily onto the cushions and stretching full length on his side. With his head horizontal on a cushion, the accordion lips folded and salivating, he glared at them for a moment and then his eyes fluttered and closed. He began to breathe in deep, painful gasps that fell quickly to a wheezy snoring.

"Can you make him get down?" Cole asked, "That's my bed, remember? He's already slimed it."

Onatima shook her head. "I don't think so. Custer is not a particularly bright dog, Grandson, and he is certainly not a happy one. We should probably let him rest for now."

"Looks like he's asleep," Alex said. "They told me they found him on the couch in the crack house. He's probably used to a couch." He smiled expansively at the dog. "Isn't he a magnificent animal? Look at those shoulders. Maybe you should feed him. That way he'll bond faster."

He stepped to the door. "I have to get back to a class. Enjoy Custer."

"Could I catch a ride down with you, Alex?" Abby asked. "I hate to leave Custer, but there's an evening class I've been auditing."

"You're leaving us with this dog?" Cole looked from the mastiff to his daughter.

"Give him some meat or frybread or something. He'll love you." Alex backed toward the door. "Oh, I almost forgot. You'll need these." He pulled a bottle out of his pocket. "Custer's thyroid pills."

"Thyroid pills?" Cole looked at the dog, whose massive side rose and fell with slow regularity.

"Mastiffs have this thing about their thyroids. You have to give him eight of these every day. The human dose is one, but that's a very big animal you have. He'll sleep a lot. Those thyroid pills really slow him down. But don't worry; he's a killer when he's awake."

He tossed the bottle to Cole and started out the door before pausing once more. "Come to think of it, you'd better not let him have any frybread. The pound folks told me that mastiffs need a very precise diet. Human food gives them diarrhea. Could be a real mess."

Cole watched Alex and Abby leave and then turned to Onatima. The old lady's thin lips were pressed tightly together, and her eyes glistened.

"You think this is funny?" Cole said.

She glanced at the dog and back to Cole, the corners of her mouth moving toward a smile. "It's good to see you have friends," she said at last.

Betty Louise Bell

(b. 1949) Cherokee

Betty Louise Bell was born in Oklahoma in 1949. She is mixedblood Cherokee. She earned her doctorate at Ohio State University and teaches literature at the University of Michigan at Ann Arbor. **Faces in the Moon,** *her first novel, was published in the American Indian Literature and Critical Studies series in 1994.*

"I was raised on the voices of women," she wrote in the first chapter of **Faces in the Moon**.

> *Indian women. The kitchen table was first a place of remembering, a place where women came and drew their lives from each other. The table was covered with an oilcloth in a floral pattern, large pink and red roses, the edges of the petals rubbed away by elbows.*

"In the Hour of the Wolf" is a selection from her novel; the memories and humorous stories could be heard at the kitchen table. The narrator remembers her mother and visits to hospitals.

> *In the middle of a waiting room, there had been a large chart: HOW TO DRESS WHEN COMING TO SEE THE DOCTOR. I studied the chart, I wanted to dress right, and any piece of information was appreciated. Over a picture of a man and woman in very fancy dress there was a large X; over a picture of a man and woman in pajamas there was a large X. I looked around, there was not one person in the room in fancy dress or pajamas. But the sign had said nothing about cowboys boots, so I tucked the boots Lizzie had given me under my chair....*
>
> *I stood over her bed and waited.... I took her cold hands in mine and ran my fingers over her arthritic joints. All those years of picking cotton and hard living, she said.* "I was pickin cotton when ya was born. Twelve hours a day in that Oklahoma sun. Without nobody a help but you Auney. And she needed help herself."

In the Hour of the Wolf

Some parents believe children have no memories. They hold their stories and lives until they are ready to return them, with full chronology and interpretation. History is written in this complicity, an infinite regression of children forgetting and remembering. It takes a long time to remember, it takes generations, sometimes nations, to make a story. And sometimes it takes a call in the night before the story is known.

Now, a lifetime later, when the phone rang at four in the morning, I pulled myself out of a strong sleep, knowing the voice over the phone before I heard it.

"How're you, Mabel? How's the girls and the grandkids?"

"Fine. They're just fine. Thank the Lord. Lucie Marie?" I heard a voice in the background and the quick muffling sound of a hand placed over the phone. From far away Mabel's voice called to someone, "She ain't got no idear." Then Mabel returned to the phone, "Sugar? Maybe I need to talk to your husband? Is your husband there, sugar?"

"I'm a single woman now, Mabel."

"I'm sorry to hear that, sugar."

"It happens."

"Doncha have no one to help ya?"

"What is it?" Suddenly I remembered it was four in the morning. I remembered Mabel was not a friend, she had been my mother's landlady for over thirty years, and I had not spoken to her for over five years.

"Is something wrong? Has something happened?"

"Are you sittin down, sugar?"

"I'm in bed."

"It's your momma. She just kinda fainted away."

"Is she alive?"

"Oh, my! Now there ain't no cause to be talking that way."

"Is she in the hospital?"

"That's it, sugar. She's in the hospital." Having delivered the bad news, she now relaxed into the easy chatter of a woman who had known me most of my life. "Johnnie called the ambulance, and they took her to the hospital."

"Who's Johnnie?"

"You know, Sam Bevis's boy." Sam Bevis was in his nineties; Johnnie was probably in his seventies. "Your momma's been seeing Johnnie for a good stretch of time now. Must be ... they started dating just after Valentine's Day ... no, that ain't right. I do believe your momma was with him 'fore that. That's right, I recall Johnnie bringin over a quart of Johnnie Walker on New Year's Eve. He's a good man. He'd give you the shirt right off his back and never take no notice. Why, when P. T. and Dale left for California, he lent them his Ford. Ya know, the one he was so proud of?"

"I don't think I remember Johnnie Bevis."

"Oh, sure you do, sugar. He used to go with that Indian girl Delores. Over in El Reno. They had some good-lookin half-breed kids, all thems grown up by now. Delores made sure them kids went to college. Just the other day I went down to the social security office to get my check and there, just as big as you please, was one a them kids sitting 'hind this big old desk."

"I remember Delores."

"Then you gotta member Johnnie."

"He has a taste for Indian women?"

"Now ya sound just like your momma in one a her black moods. Ain't nothing wrong with a man likin his meat on the dark side."

Mabel was going on, "He's been in and outta town all his life. He did spend some time down in Clinton, ya know, the penitentiary down there. But he got out and got him that Ford and he only been back once or twice."

"Momma. Do they know what happened to her?"

"I ain't no doctor, sugar. But Johnnie called me from the hospital, and he said they're a reckoning on a stroke."

"A stroke!"

"Now, there ain't no need to go a-scaring yourself. My Uncle Bailey had one a them things. Ya member my Uncle Bailey? He sure was fond a ya. Used to say, ya minded him of Jackie Kennedy. He had one a the purdiest funerals I ever seen. His whole family came. Even his daughter out in Californee. Ya run into her out there?"

"It's a big state, Mabel."

"Ain't that the truth. When he passed on, we had the durnest time getting a her. He went so fast, didn't nobody suspect … maybe y'all should come on down. Shoot, it couldn't hurt nothing."

The Oklahoma State Indian Hospital was the newest and biggest Indian hospital in the state. It was tucked in the corner of the mammoth health complex, miles and miles of hospitals and clinics and research laboratories quarantined in the northwest corner with the state capitol and government offices. What, I wondered, came first: the government men or the sickness? I couldn't imagine a better Indian joke, placing the contagions together and hoping they would kill each other off.

The Indian hospital covered almost a square mile of prairie at the junction of two interstate highways. At night travelers were pulled toward the white light of a gigantic cross emblazoned across the full six stories of the main building. From the back seat of the cab I saw it appear at the end of the flat and endless highway and knew the sight would have pleased Momma. The cab pulled to a stop under the cross, and I stepped out into the heat of a thousand lights.

Las Vegas. Arriving at night, momma at the wheel of our old Chevrolet and me on the passenger side, face pressed against the window, as we entered the city from the black surrounding desert. Suddenly, there was the glare of a powerful electric sun. "They say you can't tell night from day," momma said, and I knew why we had come: We came to see the miracle of something from nothing.

Comprised of large, blocked interconnecting buildings, the hospital was modern and efficiently planned, with narrow mazelike corridors and directories placed every hundred feet. It was a far cry from the Indian hospitals I had gone to as a child, with their sullen white doctors and their angel-of-mercy sisters giving you the privilege of their time and sympathy, driving each patient further into sickness with gratitude. The hospitals had been army barracks, their walls a pale government green, and the only Indians in the place were in the waiting room, some coughing blood, others dazed by the long wait, even the children hung lifeless from a lap or an arm. In the middle of a waiting room, there had been a large chart: HOW TO DRESS WHEN COMING TO SEE THE DOCTOR. I studied the chart, I wanted to dress right, and any piece of information was appreciated. Over a picture of a man and woman in very fancy dress there was a large X; over a picture of a man and woman in pajamas there was a large X. I looked around, there was not one person in the room in fancy dress or pajamas. But the sign had said nothing about cowboy boots, so I tucked the boots Lizzie had given me under my chair.

But the smell was the same. Not just the smell of disease and antiseptic, it was the funky smell of sweat, urine, excrement, and fear, mostly fear. "The smell of white people," Lizzie had said, "the smell of people who drank too much milk." The smell, I held my breath, of rotting spirits.

A little woman approached me from the end of the corridor. I watched her come, down the green hall, her steps soundless and her face silent. The width of the face and her sallow skin told me she was Indian. Cherokee, maybe. She paused next to me and whispered.

"Are they still killing Indians here?"

"Excuse me?"

The woman slipped passed.

"I'm sorry?" I turned and looked for the woman.

But she had already vanished down another sick green corridor. I caught the sound of a chant, monotonous and repetitive, fading into the hallways of the building.

"Crazy Indians!"

At the Intensive Care desk a nurse pointed to a plaque on the opposite wall and said, "Them there are the visiting hours, from one to three and from seven to nine. Visiting hours have been over for almost two hours. You'll have to come back tomorrow."

"But I've just arrived. I haven't seen my mother since ... this happened. I came all the way from California. I'd just like to let her know I'm here."

"I'm sorry. We have to live by the rules."

"Can you tell me how she is? Gracie Khatib?"

The nurse picked up a handful of manila folders and thumbed through them. "How're ya spelling that last name?"

"K... h ... a ... t ... i ... b."

"I don't find anyone here under that name."

"Evers. Do you have a Gracie Evers?"

"Yep. Room 310, just around the corner. But," she touched my shoulder with the file, "your momma's not going to know if you're here or not. Whyn't you just go on and get some sleep and come back tomorrow?"

"I'd like her to know I'm here."

"I imagine the good Lord has taken care of that."

"Please?"

"Alright. But don't make any noise. You can stay for fifteen or twenty minutes, longer if you sit still."

With the file she motioned for me to follow her down the corridor. All the doors on either side were open. I heard the beep, beep, beep, and crank of machines, but no sounds of the living. I tried to look inside the rooms but could see only the ends of hospital beds and televisions hanging from the ceiling. In a few rooms the pale light of the television flickered. Now and then, I thought I saw a bundle near the foot of the bed, a few bones wrapped in white sheets. At a door near the end of the corridor, the nurse waited for me.

"Now, don't try to disturb her. She can't hear you."

Slowly I approached the woman in the bed. Red lights from the machines over her head pulsated across the dark room. I watched her body disappear into darkness, and then resurrect in a luminous red glow. Here, gone, here, gone. Dizziness and nausea threatened, the room spun. Here, gone, here, gone. I closed my eyes and stepped outside. I took a deep breath and reentered. The woman had my mother's dyed yellow hair and heavy body, my mother's pert nose and swollen arthritic hands, but the face was different. I had never seen the face without animation, without laughter, anger, or dream. I had never seen the lips so limp and thin. From moment to moment, they had shaped words and emotion. Even when she became lost in her own stories, when her face and mind went slack with the past, her eyes burned across the silence.

Unconscious, Gracie Evers was not an attractive woman. The wrinkles laid heavier in their folds, the eyes sunk in their bags, and without her teeth, the cheeks collapsed into a moist crevice. Sometimes, if there were no men around, Gracie took out her teeth and smoked cigarette after cigarette, her gums locked hard around the filter and her wide smile stretching from gum to gum.

But there was something else, something besides the teeth missing. And then I knew. She was not snoring, that was it. My mother snored like an infantryman, the rasping wide big-mouthed buzz of the very, very tired. She stood twelve hours behind the cafeteria counter and when she came home, she soaked her feet and passed into sleep. Her boyfriends complained they were unable to sleep, most did not spend a second night. Now, only the machinery, breathing and beeping, filled the room with sound. Hypnotically, the bellows next to the bed expanded and collapsed with perfect and silent air, the fluids ticked into her nose and wrist, and the monitors above the bed pulsed the red glow through the room.

I was mesmerized by the machines, her breathing slowed to the bellows, her heart beat to the strobing red light, her body surrendered to the mechanics, the monotony of sustaining and registering life. I watched the bubbles of clear liquid travel through the plastic tubing into Gracie's arm, watched the final suspended drop pause before it fell, carrying sugared water into an inert body. Somehow my loud and vulgar mother had been subdued and sacrificed to this steady drip of fluids.

Beat the drum slowly ... don't ... stop ... too ... fast.

I watched, her body flashing and disappearing, hearing only the suck and gasp of machines. Here, death would not be the performance she had rehearsed again and again. Here, she was outside the story, simply a heavy prop in death's solo act. Here, there would be no stories of pain endured and fear conquered, only the data of life ending as it had ended billions of times before. For my mother, for whom everything was personal, this was not personal. I watched, unable to turn my eyes from the flickering final drop as it teetered just outside the enlarged bruised vein, then the nausea rose, and I fled the room.

"Lizzie wouldn't go to the Indian sanitarium in Talihina. She said, those were places for dying. For white dying, not Indian dying. And she stayed right there. Coughing up handkerchiefs of blood. The TB had her real bad."

Auney hacked on a long smoker's cough.

"But she wouldn't leave. She went to see Alice Sixkiller, that medicine woman over in Muskogee. That one she took you to when you had that turrible diarrhea. Alice Sixkiller saved your life many times, girlie, so don't you go acting like we're a bunch a dumb Indians and yer Miss Perfect. Hear?"

"I don't think she meant that, Grace."

"I saw that smirk."

"I was laughing about the diarrhea. How can anyone die of diarrhea?"

"Why don't you ask them doctors at the Indian hospital? You believe them. And they couldn't do no more than wring their hands." My mother wagged her finger at me. *"Sister, someday you're gonna be too smart for your own good. Someday, you member my words. Someday, ya gonna understand what I'm talking about."*

Le Anne Howe

(b. 1951) Choctaw

*Le Anne Howe was born in 1951. She is a Choctaw from Oklahoma and studied at Oklahoma State University. She has worked as a journalist and later sold bonds, an experience that became the subject of the comic short story published here. Howe has published several short stories in journals and anthologies. "Danse d'Amour, Danse de Mort," for instance, was published in **Earth Song, Sky Spirit** edited by Clifford Trafzer.*

"Actually, when you're Indian, you learn people are always telling you how Indians feel about everything," wrote Howe.

> *Priscilla Davis, this really nice white teacher I met while on vacation, told me that she taught on the Pine Ridge Reservation. She said that Indians don't talk much, but that when we say something it's always profound and fraught with meaning. I just looked at her.*

Le Anne Howe writes with that same sense of irony.

Moccasins Don't Have High Heels

Okay, like it was a day like any other day in the bond business. Everyone had been spitting up blood, eating, or talking to out-of-state buddies when an official from a state agency phoned in and wanted to blow out of 10 million treasuries.

Suddenly I looked around the room and I was alone. Everyone had stepped away.

I picked up the open telephone to our Houston trading desk.

"Edward." (I have changed the names to insure artistic exaggeration.)

"Bid 10 million 8 3/4 Nov. 98s."

"Ed," I continued. "I need a bid."

"98 to the buck, darlin'."

I go back to the client with 97 30/32.

Everyone is still cordial. She wants to do it.

"Ed, I'll sell you 10MM 8 3/4 Nov 98 at 98."

"Hold on, darlin'," he said. "97 28. The market's moving."

I check back with her. There is a screaming and gnashing of teeth, but, she wants to do it.

Okay, I'll sell 10MM Nov. 8 3/4 at 97 28."

"It's falling, darlin'," he said, "97 26."

I go back to her with 97 24.

A loud scream comes from the phone. Suddenly I'm a mother fucker. I start to sweat cannonballs. More screaming into my ear and I can just barely make out this low roar, "Yes. Get me out!" More screaming. I put the phone down.

My trader says, "97 22."

I holler. "Do it."

He comes back with, "97 18."

"Do it. Do it. Do it!"

He confirms, "You're done darlin', 97 and a half."

I start screaming. "You got to me, you cocksucker! You got to me, you mother fucker, cock-sucking pig...."

"Hello, Ma'am. You're done at 97 14."

More shrieking into my receiver.

She says she's sending an Iranian hit squad to our office. She tells me she'll never do business with me again. She says she's putting a curse on our unborn children. She threatens to catch the next plane to Dallas and come into town and rip off my tits.

"Yes. Yes. I am sorry. The market was falling and we were the best bidder on the street. My trader said there is a rumor the Japanese are going to.... Hello?

"No way did I get to you. There's no way I'd do that. I am telling the truth. Really. I'll call your assistant with figures. Don't worry about a thing. I'll take care of you. Listen, let me send you some theatre tickets in New York. We've been meaning to get you a couple to your favorite Broadway show. Yes, that's right. Anytime you say. We'll even meet you in New York, too. Whenever you say. Don't worry about a thing. Right, after all it's not our money? Yes, yes, it's gonna be okay." (Click.) "Hello?"

Ah, fuck it. I quit.

Actually I didn't quit. I always said I was quitting everyday of the week for four and one-half years, but to tell you the truth, I loved it.

After the crash of 1987, our home office eventually consolidated the bond department, and on a cold February morning we shut down the Dallas office and left one by one. Since I was the last one to turn out the light, I took one final look around.

Lying on top of the desk was a golf putter, the whoopee cushion from a co-worker's operation, a broken telephone cord, an orange nerf ball that had traveled with us from office to office, a political button that said, "If God So loved America, why did he create Democrats?" a couple of plastic handguns and an incredible view of the Dallas skyline. I had brought the guns in, and in mock Harry Kallahan-style, slaughtered my co-workers on a daily basis. They shrugged it off saying, "Aa-a-ah, it's the Tells and Kills in her."

So as a gesture of the passage of time and the memories, I symbolically put the golf putter in my boss's chair, gave the chair a spin, watched it silently go-around-and-around-and-around, just like I imagine the circle in which we live goes. Eventually the chair stood still. I took one last look and walked out the door alone.

That got to me.

For months I had nightmares. Each night I would dream I was back in the bond business, only this time my friends and I sat in grade school desks, all in a row. We are working for, like, this drive-in bank in a shopping center. In my dream our bond trader is in the same room with us watching *I Love Lucy*.

I am working for minimum wage and sell Indian beads, real estate and, of all things, ice cream to supplement our income to passersby who wander in off the street.

Suddenly a bomb explodes in the trading room. The glass case that holds the Indian beads blows apart. Glass beads blow across the bond room. The ice cream turns to water. We pull a white sheet over the body of our bond trader. We know he's dead. Lady Luck has left us forever. Man, she got to us.

When I left the business this time, I wasn't leaving my job, I was leaving my bond family probably for good. I was getting rid of my high heels and putting on my moccasins. I had to get away. Everything was getting to me, man. You may ask why I stayed with it? Why I did it? The money. The money got to me.

I took a few months off and a driving tour of Wyoming. Carla, a long time friend, and I did the Wild West trip.

We drove the corduroy roads of the Oregon trail. We saw Fort La'Ramee and sang "Oh Beautiful for Spacious Skies" as we crossed The Great Divide.

The Wyoming lands are lousy with antelope. Their white tails glisten in the sun. They are easy to see but hard to hit unless you're in a Ford Bronco driving forty miles an hour down a mountain road. For the most part there are no cars, no houses, no people, no nuclear power plants. It's an isolationist's dream. Hey, maybe it's a developer's dream. When asked about clear-cutting our national forests, former President Reagan once quipped, "Well, once you've seen one redwood, you've seen 'em all." So I figure maybe big business with the help of the big government will get to them, too.

However there is evidence of humanity in the national forests already. At 9,000 feet elevation we found plastic diet pill dispensers, beer cans. Silver bullets.

Eventually we made our way back to Jackson Hole. It was Old West Days and Alta, a friend of Carla's from Dallas, had flown in for the Old West.

When a band of Shoshoni began dancing a round dance and playing the drum and asking everyone to join in for friendship, Alta got nervous. She said she had been scalped by me in a previous lifetime and Indian drums got to her.

"Le Anne, what are those drums saying? Do they make you want to go to war? Does that sound make you want to start scalping people? Is that drumbeat getting to you the way it's getting to me? How does it feel?"

"Yeah, it's gettin' to me. You're gettin' to me, again, Alta. Maybe you should go inside, Alta, before I reach for my knife and hey, you know what happened last time."

Carla dragged Alta away by coaxing her into another rock shop. Alta looked back to see if I was serious, which I was, but knowing Alta, what she really wanted was more crystals. Crystals talk to Alta and tell her what to do. Who she's been. Who we've been. Where she's going. Where we're going. What's getting to her. What's gettin' to me.

But like, who am I to quibble with success? They say God lives in the Crystal Cathedral. (California, right?)

Actually, when you're Indian, you learn people are always telling you how Indians feel about everything.

"Don't you Indians, like ah-h, see yourselves, ah-h, as just transcending this time, space continuum thing? Yeah, like ah-h, you all practiced this kind of Indian-Zen thing? Right?

"Indian huh? Didn't you used to be white?

"Indians. Hey you're human too. You don't really feel any different than the rest of us. You put your pants on one leg at a time, Missy, so just stop that nonsense. It's just like, all in your head.

"Indians, I thought you were all dead?"

Priscilla David, this really nice white teacher I met while on vacation, told me that she taught on the Pine Ridge Reservation. She said that Indians don't talk much, but that when we say something it's always profound and fraught with meaning.

I just looked at her.

"Oh yeah," she said. "Did you know that Indian women are very jealous of their men?"

I deadpan. "White woman speak truth!"

Don't you get it?

I recently came back from an archaeologist conference in South Dakota on the Ethical Treatment of the Dead and Indians.

I listened to dozens of archaeologists tell us how we felt about the time, space continuum thing. About what diseases got to us.

About how back in the old days, say, one hundred years ago, Indians had small gene pools so we must have practiced incest. But by grinding our skeletons and sawing our skulls apart for analysis they didn't find any evidence of incest. Dr. Jekkell, a physical anthropologist who has spent his life dissolving our skeletal remains, said that while their facts were inconclusive they were going to keep on looking. Keep on cutting. Keep on trying. Keep on digging us up. He was gonna get to us somehow.

Am I gettin' to you?

I myself like what Edward Galeano said. "Throughout America, from north to south, the dominant culture acknowledges Indians as objects of study, but denies them as subjects of history. Indians have folklore, not culture, they practice superstitions, not religion, they speak dialects, not languages, they make crafts not arts...."

Doesn't it get to you, somehow?

In 1971 in Iowa a road crew unearthed a cemetery. Twenty-six of the bodies were white. They also found one Indian woman and her baby. The whites were placed in new coffins and reburied. The Indian and her baby were boxed up and sent to Iowa City for study.

They got to her, all right. Am I getting to you?

It seems it wasn't enough that the aliens wanted to capture our souls for a once-a-week alien God. They wanted to own our physical bodies. That's why in 1989 Governor Bill Clements of Texas vetoed a bill which would have protected unmarked Indian graves in the Lone Star State. The collectors and grave robbers from Dallas can still get to Indian graves in Texas without being charged with a crime. Ironically Governor Bill told listeners at a state archaeologist meeting that his fantasy profession was to be an archaeologist. But, like ah-h, he went into politics, instead. . . .

He got to us, all right. Am I getting to you?

Does it get to you, somehow?

Probably if I had to think of only one thing Indians represented in our collective histories, it would be that we were the first environmentalists. The first environmental advocates.

We made heap big speeches to Great White Father. "As long as sky blue, grass green and rivers flow."

Hey, that shit didn't fly and the grass ain't green, the sky ain't blue, and the rivers are full of trash. We didn't want to leave this place—this time, space continuum thing to you—but you wanted it. You got it. Now fix it!

Someone said once that lost causes were the only ones worth fighting for, worth dying for. They got to us, all right. But the poisons, man, they're gettin' to you, too.

Am I gettin' to you?

Is it gettin' to you, too?

I will get you, too.

Because, my country (this is my country)

'tis of me, tis of thee. First. Last. And Forever.

Am I gettin' to you, somehow?

I will get to you. Somehow.

Because, together,

man, woman, child, all that exists,

Together, we can

GET IT

Together.

Evelina Zuni Lucero

(b. 1953) Isleta Pueblo

Evelina Zuni Lucero was born in Albuquerque, New Mexico, in 1953. She lives with her husband and four children in Isleta Pueblo. Evelina is a graduate of Stanford University and the University of New Mexico.

Her short stories have been published in several journals and anthologies, including the **Northeast Indian Quarterly**, **Blue Mesa Review**, **Women and Hunting**, *and* **Returning the Gift**. *She has completed a novel entitled* **Fancy Dancer**.

"Deer Dance" is a redoubled story of wise and ironic remembrance. That handsome man at the Watering Hole wore leather boots, but he might be the same stranger at a wedding dance in another story. Trini danced with the stranger and remembered the tribal story about the man with feet like a deer. "Later, his deer tracks were found beneath all the windows of the hall."

Deer Dance

Trini had been told not to come because nothing good ever happened at the bar. Grandma, Old Auntie Lena, all the aunts, and her mother stretched thin lips when the bar's name, the Watering Hole, was mentioned.

Now here she was in reckless disregard dancing at the Watering Hole with Reynard with his cool, distant air, and the half-moon curve of his smile. Drop-dead handsome, she thought.

The thought almost stopped her in her tracks as she remembered the Deer Man.

Trini smiled when she caught herself looking at Reynard's feet. His gleaming leather boots were as fancy as the rest of him. Cross-stitched thunderbirds stretched their wings across the front yokes of his shirt, a crisp, black and white checkered print neatly tucked into his blue jeans. A large silver buckle sat atop his firm belly, threading a leather tooled belt which blazed REYNARD on the back. Like a buck, he was sleek and full, well muscled, surefooted, his neck smooth and graceful, his skin an even bronze tone. He possessed an easy smile that flashed like a lightning bolt, illuminating his face and sparking movement behind his photogreys.

Yes, he was good-looking enough to fit the story that Auntie Rosalee liked to spook them with as children:

The tall, handsome stranger strode into a wedding dance, commanding attention with his silent entrance, looking neither to the left or right. No one knew who he was though he looked vaguely familiar, like someone's cousin's cousin. The bride's family thought he must be the guest of the groom's family, and the groom's family assumed he was known by the bride's side. He carried himself with grace and sureness, head erect, meeting all questioning eyes and answering them with careful indifference. Large turquoise stones, conspicuously old and heavy, dangled from his earlobes. His long hair was pulled back in an oldtime style. He leaned against the wall, smoking a cigarette, a glint of amusement in his dark, slanted eyes.

All the young, single women and even the restless married ones watched, ready to catch his eye, hoping to be the one he'd ask to dance. After a long time, when the dance was almost over, he asked the prettiest girl to dance. The other women sighed, tossed their heads and pretended they didn't care, but they watched enviously, seeing how he tenderly gazed into the depths of her eyes, and how he smoothly spun her across the room. He was light on his feet and she moved easily with him. Other women crossed their arms and shook their heads in disapproval at her reckless laughter.

The girl forgot who she came with, forgot that her sweetheart might have meant something to her, that he stood in the corner sulking. A woman letting her hair down, she danced on with the stranger, yielding to him. The songs became soft sighs, each dance a yearning. The stranger held her tighter and tighter till her boyfriend rushed forward, his eyes narrow slits. Before he could reach her, as the song was ending, screams and shouts filled the air. The band stopped. The crowd parted. The young girl lay lifeless on the floor.

In the confusion of the moment, the stranger almost slipped away, but he was stopped at the door by belligerent, red-eyed young men. Something about his movement as he stepped back from them caused one young man to look down at the stranger's feet. The young man's eyes widened, causing others to follow his gaze. Once again, terrified screams broke loose, paralyzing the crowd. In the sudden hush that came upon the room, someone cried out, "Look! Look at his feet! He has the feet of a deer!" The stranger smiled, brazen and fearless. He pushed his way to the door unchallenged and walked out.

Later, his deer tracks were found beneath all the windows of the hall.

Auntie Rosalee heard the story from the Indian matrons at the Indian School who insisted that it was true, that two-legged deer tracks were still to be found in the snow on winter mornings. During the deer hunting season, Rosalee and other women would joke, saying, "Now that the men are gone, let's go on a hunt of our own for a two-legged *dear.*" It took years before Trini caught the pun. She used to wonder why they'd want to look for the Deer Man and risk being danced to death.

Only in a place like this could that happen.

Reynard smiled at her.

She looked away.

Louise Erdrich

(b. 1954) Anishinaabe

Louise Erdrich was born in Little Falls, Minnesota, in 1954. She was raised in Wahpeton, North Dakota, where her parents were teachers at the Bureau of Indian Affairs School. Her mother is Chippewa and her father is of German descent. Erdrich is a member of the Turtle Mountain Reservation. She is married to the author Michael Dorris.

Erdrich studied at Dartmouth College and earned a master's degree in creative writing at Johns Hopkins University. She is the author of four novels. **Love Medicine** *was first published in 1984,* **The Beet Queen** *in 1986,* **Tracks** *in 1988, and* **The Bingo Palace** *in 1994.* **Love Medicine** *won the National Book Critics Circle Award and the* **Los Angeles Times** *Book Award in 1985.*

Erdrich and Dorris are the authors of **The Crown of Columbus**, *a novel published in 1991. The authors have also published stories "for popular consumption" under the pen name of Milou North. "So actually we write some less serious things together," wrote Erdrich.*

Louis Owens wrote in **Other Destinies** *that*

> **Love Medicine** *is an episodic story of three inextricably tangled generations of Chippewa and mixedblood families: the Kashpaws, Morrisseys, Lamartines, and Lazarres. In fourteen chapters, seven narrators weave their many stories into a single story that becomes, very gradually, a coherent fabric of community—a recovered center. This "recovered center" is the worth of native remembrance.*

Laura Coltelli, in an interview published in **Winged Words**, *asked Erdrich about the major influences on her writing. Michael Dorris, her husband, she told Coltelli,*

> *has been a major influence. He really is. I am indebted to him for organizing and making the book into a novel. I tended to be a person who thought in terms of stories and poems and short things. He came one day and said pretty much, "Oh, this is a novel," and you know, we began to write it in that way.*

"Michael and I are truly collaborators in all aspects of writing and life," she told Joseph Bruchac in **Survival This Way**. *"It's very hard to separate the writing and the family life and Michael and I as.... I really think neither of us would write what we do unless we were together."*

Dorris told Coltelli that "Lipsha, the character in **Love Medicine** *is Mitchif bastardization for* le petit chou, *the French expression of endearment, 'my little cabbage,' and that's where the name comes from." Mitchif is not a debased colonial language or a native oral language, but a trade language of the metis, a dialect of Cree with words borrowed from French. Richard Rhodes noted in "Algonquian Trade Languages" that on "the Turtle Mountain Reservation there are numerous anecdotes about the relative status of high prestige Mitchif over low prestige Ojibwa, further strengthening the position that a trade language system existed there."*

Alan Velie noted in **The Lightning Within** *that the "hero" in the story "Lipsha Morrissey" from* **Love Medicine**

*is a bumbling but lovable idiot.... The mixture of pathos and humor in the story is
very effective. Great comic authors are often moving as well as funny, but only the
greatest—Shakespeare and Faulkner, for instance—are both at once. It may
sound hyperbolic to include Erdrich in that company, but her account of the
way Lipsha and his grandmother accidentally kill Nector Kashpaw is
reminiscent of Shakespeare's account of the death of Falstaff in the way it
combines humor and pathos.*

Velie is magnanimous and openhanded as a critic, but the three authors and their
characters are not comparable in time, text, or nature. Indeed, the substance of his notion
is an overstatement. Shakespeare is no Chippewa, Falstaff is no Grandpa Kashpaw, and
Faulkner is no Erdrich. The wise and comic creator of stories with turkey hearts as love
medicine is not enriched by a mere canon endorsement.

"I'm getting into my second childhood," said Grandpa Kashpaw. He shouted at church
services, ate too much sugar, and teased his memories of whoopee. "And you got no more
whoopee to pitch anymore anyhow!" said Grandma. Lipsha hunted for goose hearts and
ended with turkey parts. "I finally convinced myself that the real actual power to the love
medicine was not the goose heart itself but the faith in the cure." Grandpa "stuck his tongue
out with the heart on it" and then he choked. "He choked real bad," said Lipsha.

Shakespeare's Falstaff is one of the most noted comic characters in dramatic literature.
He is lecherous and unscrupulous, a man of common veneries and curious wisdom, more
sound than substance, more phenomenon than character, and banished in the end. Falstaff
is created in an orotund language; in the metrical prose and verse of dramatic literature at
the time.

Grandpa Kashpaw is created in an understated, literary vernacular of a rural
character, in the first-person voice of Lipsha. He is ironic, incidental, and answerable to the
elders. "I got to be honest about the love medicine," he told Grandma. "I told her about the
turkey hearts and how I had them blessed. I told her what I used as love medicine was
purely a fake." There is no anticipation of a theatrical performance.

Shakespeare considered it "important to make the verse spoken by characters ... sound
like speech as well as like verse," wrote George Wright in **Shakespeare's Metrical Art**. "The
speech may be elevated, grand in its diction, noble in its periods, but its tones and rhythms
must not stray too far from the familiar ones of everyday experience."

Falstaff belongs to the "carnivalesque, the satiric comedy of the people," wrote Terry
Eagleton in **William Shakespeare**.

> *Falstaff can turn the brute materiality of the body against the airy abstractions of
> ruling-class rhetoric.... But he is himself one of Shakespeare's most shameless
> verbal mystifiers, divorcing word from deed in his pathological boasting,
> recklessly erasing distinctions in his metaphorical excess.*

Falstaff and Grandpa Kashpaw, the theatrical bombaster and the man who choked on a
turkey heart, could become a new situational comedy, a post-Indian duologue in native
trickster stories.

Nanabozho or naanabozho *and* boosho or boozhoo *are words in the oral language of the
Chippewa or Anishinaabe:* naanabozho *is the name of the trickster, the transformational*

figure in native stories; boozho *is derived from* bonjour, *a greeting, one of the few words borrowed from the French.*

" 'Booshoo, Father,' I said. 'I got a slight request to make of you ... Would you bless this package?' I held out the hankie with the hearts tied inside it." The priest looked at the package. 'It's turkey hearts,' I honestly had to reply."

Lipsha Morrissey

I never really done much with my life, I suppose. I never had a television. Grandma Kashpaw had one inside her apartment at the Senior Citizens, so I used to go there and watch my favorite show. For a while she used to call me the biggest waste on the reservation and hark back to how she saved me from my own mother, who wanted to tie me in a potato sack and throw me in a slough. Sure, I was grateful to Grandma Kashpaw for saving me like that, for raising me, but gratitude gets old. After a while, stale. I had to stop thanking her. One day I told her I had paid her back in full by staying at her beck and call. I'd do anything for Grandma. She knew that. Besides, I took care of Grandpa like nobody else could, on account of what a handful he'd gotten to be.

But that was nothing. I know the tricks of mind and body inside out without ever having trained for it, because I got the touch. It's a thing you got to be born with. I got secrets in my hands that nobody ever knew to ask. Take Grandma Kashpaw with her tired veins all knotted up in her legs like clumps of blue snails. I take my fingers and I snap them on the knots. The medicine flows out of me. The touch. I run my fingers up the maps of those rivers of veins or I knock very gentle above their hearts or I make a circle motion on their stomachs, and it helps them. They feel much better. Such women pay me five dollars.

I couldn't do the touch for Grandpa, though. He was a hard nut. You know, some people fall right through the hole in their lives. It's invisible, but they come to it after time, never knowing where. There is this woman here, Lulu Lamartine, who always had a thing for Grandpa. She loved him since she was a girl and always said he was a genius. Now she says that his mind got so full it exploded.

How can I doubt that? I know the feeling when your mental power builds up too far. I always used to say that's why the Indians got drunk. Even statistically we're the smartest people on the earth. Anyhow with Grandpa I couldn't hardly believe it, because all my youth he stood out as a hero to me. When he started getting toward second childhood he went through different moods. He would stand in the woods and cry at the top of his shirt. It scared me, scared everyone, Grandma worst of all.

Yet he was so smart—do you believe it?—that he *knew* he was getting foolish.

He said so. He told me that December I failed school and come back on the train to Hoopdance. I didn't have nowhere else to go. He picked me up there and he said it straight out: "I'm getting into my second childhood." And then he said something else I still remember: "I been chosen for it. I couldn't say no." So I figure that a man so smart all his life—tribal chairman and the star of movies and even pictured in the statehouse and on cans of snuff—would know what he's doing by saying yes. I think he was called to second childhood like anybody else gets a call for the priesthood or the army or whatever. So I really did not listen too hard when the doctor said this was some kind of disease old people got eating too much sugar. You just can't tell me that a man who went to Washington and gave them bureaucrats what for could lose his mind from eating too much Milky Way. No, he put second childhood on himself.

Behind those songs he sings out in the middle of Mass, and back of those stories that everybody knows by heart, Grandpa is thinking hard about life. I know the feeling. Sometimes I'll throw up a smokescreen to think behind. I'll hitch up to Winnipeg and play the Space Invaders for six hours, but all the time there and back I will be thinking some fairly deep thoughts that surprise even me, and I'm used to it. As for him, if it was just the thoughts there wouldn't be no problem. Smokescreen is what irritates the social structure, see, and Grandpa has done things that just distract people to the point they want to throw him in the cookie jar where they keep the mentally insane. He's far from that, I know for sure, but even Grandma had trouble keeping her patience once he started sneaking off to Lamartine's place. He's not supposed to have his candy, and Lulu feeds it to him. That's *one* of the reasons why he goes.

Grandma tried to get me to put the touch on Grandpa soon after he began stepping out. I didn't want to, but before Grandma started telling me again what a bad state my bare behind was in when she first took me home, I thought I should at least pretend.

I put my hands on either side of Grandpa's head. You wouldn't look at him and say he was crazy. He's a fine figure of a man, as Lamartine would say, with all his hair and half his teeth, a beak like a hawk, and cheeks like the blades of a hatchet. They put his picture on all the tourist guides to North Dakota and even copied his face for artistic paintings. I guess you could call him a monument all of himself. He started grinning when I put my hands on his templates, and I knew right then he knew how come I touched him. I knew the smokescreen was going to fall.

And I was right: just for a moment it fell.

"Let's pitch whoopee," he said across my shoulder to Grandma.

They don't use that expression much around here anymore, but for damn sure it must have meant something. It got her goat right quick.

She threw my hands off his head herself and stood in front of him, overmatching him pound for pound, and taller too, for she had a growth spurt in middle age while he had shrunk, so now the length and breadth of her surpassed him. She glared up and spoke her piece into his face about how he was off at all hours tomcatting and chasing Lamartine again and making a damn old fool of himself.

"And you got no more whoopee to pitch anymore anyhow!" she yelled at last, surprising me so my jaw just dropped, for us kids all had pretended for so long that those rustling sounds we heard from their side of the room at night never happened. She sure had pretended it, up till now, anyway. I saw that tears were in her eyes. And that's when I saw how much grief and love she felt for him. And it gave me a real shock to the system. You see I thought love got easier over the years so it didn't hurt so bad when it hurt, or feel so good when it felt good. I thought it smoothed out and old people hardly noticed it. I thought it curled up and died, I guess. Now I saw it rear up like a whip and lash.

She loved him. She was jealous. She mourned him like the dead.

And he just smiled into the air, trapped in the seams of his mind.

So I didn't know what to do. I was in a laundry then. They was like parents to me, the way they had took me home and reared me. I could see her point for wanting to get him back the way he was so at least she could argue with him, sleep with him, not be shamed out by Lamartine. She'd always love him. That hit me like a ton of bricks. For one whole day I felt this odd feeling that cramped my hands. When you have the touch, that's where longing gets you. I never loved like that. It made me feel all inspired to see them fight, and I wanted to go out and find a woman who I would love until one of us died or went crazy. But I'm not like that really. From time to time I heal a person all up good inside, however when it comes to the long shot I doubt that I got staying power.

And you need that, staying power, going out to love somebody. I knew this quality was not going to jump on me with no effort. So I turned my thoughts back to Grandma and Grandpa. I felt her side of it with my hands and my tangled guts, and I felt his side of it within the stretch of my mentality. He had gone out to lunch one day and never came back. He was fishing in the middle of Lake Turcot. And there was big thoughts on his line, and he kept throwing them back for even bigger ones that would explain to him, say, the meaning of how we go here and why we have to leave so soon. All in all, I could not see myself treating Grandpa with the touch, bringing him back, when the real part of him had chose to be off thinking somewhere. It was only the rest of him that stayed around causing trouble, after all, and we could handle most of it without any problem.

Beside, it was hard to argue with his reasons for doing some things. Take Holy Mass. I used to go there just every so often, when I got frustrated mostly, because even though I know the Higher Power dwells every place, there's something very calming about the cool greenish inside of our mission. Or so I thought, anyway. Grandpa was the one who stripped off my delusions in this matter, for it was he who busted right through what Father Upsala calls the sacred serenity of the place.

We filed in that time. Me and Grandpa. We sat down in our pews. Then the rosary got started up pre-Mass and that's when Grandpa filled up his chest and opened his mouth and belted out them words.

HAIL MARIE FULL OF GRACE.

He had a powerful set of lungs.

And he kept on like that. He did not let up. He hollered and he yelled them prayers, and I guess people was used to him by now, because they only muttered theirs and did not quit and gawk like I did. I was getting red-faced, I admit. I give him the elbow once or twice, but that wasn't nothing to him. He kept on. He shrieked to heaven and he pleaded like an overactor and he pounded his chest like Tarzan in the Lord I Am Not Worthies. I thought he might hurt himself. Then after a while I guess I got used to it, and that's when I wondered: how come?

So afterwards I out and asked him. "How come? How come you yelled?"

"God don't hear me otherwise," said Grandpa Kashpaw.

I sweat. I broke right into a little cold sweat at my hairline because I knew this was perfectly right and for years not one damn other person had noticed it. God's been going deaf. Since the Old Testament, God's been deafening up on us. I read, see. Besides the dictionary, which I'm constantly in use of, I had this Bible once. I read it. I found there was discrepancies between then and now. It struck me. Here God used to raineth bread from clouds, smite the Phillipines, sling fire down on red-light districts where people got stabbed. He even appeared in person every once in a while. God used to pay attention, is what I'm saying.

Now there's your God in the Old Testament and there are Chippewa gods as well. Indian gods, good and bad, like tricky Nanabozho or the water monster, Missepeshu, who lives over in Lake Turcot. That water monster was the last God I ever heard to appear. It had a weakness for young girls and grabbed one of the Blues off her rowboat. She got to shore all right, but only after this monster had its way with her. She's an old lady now. Old Lady Blue. She still won't let her family fish that lake.

Our gods aren't perfect, is what I'm saying, but at least they come around. They'll do a favor if you ask them right. You don't have to yell. But you do have to know, like I said, how to ask in the right way. That makes problems, because to ask proper was an art that was lost to the Chippewas once the Catholics gained ground. Even now, I have to wonder if Higher Power turned it back, if we got to yell, or if we just don't speak its language.

I looked around me. How else could I explain what all I had seen in my short life—King smashing his fist in things. Gordie drinking himself down to the Bismarck hospitals, or Aunt June left by a white man to wander off in the snow. How else to explain the times my touch don't work, and farther back, the old-time Indians who were swept away in the outright germ warfare and dirty-dog killing of the whites. In those times, us Indians was so much kindlier than now.

We took them in.

On yes. I'm bitter as an old cutworm just thinking of how they done to us and doing still.

So Grandpa Kashpaw just opened my eyes a little there. Was there any sense relying on a God whose ears was stopped? Just like the government? I says then, right off, maybe we got nothing by ourselves. And that's not much, just personally speaking. I know I don't got the cold hard potatoes it takes to understand everything. Still, there's things I'd like to do. For instance, I'd like to help some people like my Grandpa and Grandma Kashpaw get back some happiness within the tail ends of their lives.

I told you once before I couldn't see my way clear to putting the direct touch on Grandpa's mind, and I kept my moral there, but something soon happened to make me think a little bit of mental adjustment wouldn't do him and the rest of us no harm.

It was after we saw him one afternoon in the sunshine courtyard of the Senior Citizens with Lulu Lamartine. Grandpa used to like to dig there. He had his little dandelion fork out, and he was prying up them dandelions right and left while Lamartine watched him.

"He's scratching up the dirt, all right," said Grandma, watching Lamartine watch Grandpa out the window.

Now Lamartine was about half the considerable size of Grandma, but you would never think of sizes anyway. They were different in an even more noticeable way. It was the difference between a house fixed up with paint and picky fence, and a house left to weather away into the soft earth, is what I'm saying. Lamartine was jacked up, latticed, shuttered, and vinyl sided, while Grandma sagged to bulged on her slipped foundations and let her hair go the silver gray of rain-dried lumber. Right now, she eyed the Lamartine's pert flowery dress with such a look it despaired me. I knew what this could lead to with Grandma. Alternating tongue storms and rock-hard silences was hard on a man, even one who didn't notice, like Grandpa. So I went fetching him.

But he was gone when I popped through the little screen door that let out on the courtyard. There was nobody out there either, to point which way they went. Just the dandelion fork quibbling upright in the ground. That gave me an idea. I snookered over to the Lamartine's door and I listened in first, then knocked. But nobody. So I went walking through the lounges and around the card tables. Still nobody. Finally it was my touch that led me to the laundry room. I cracked the door. I went in. There they were. And he was really loving her up good, boy, and she was going hell for leather. Sheets was flapping on the lines above, and washcloths, pillowcases, shirts was also flying through the air, for they was trying to clear out a place for themselves in a high-heaped but shallow laundry cart. The washers and the dryers was all on, chock full of quarters, shaking and moaning. I couldn't hear what Grandpa and the Lamartine was billing and cooing, and they couldn't hear me.

I didn't know what to do, so I went inside and shut the door.

The Lamartine wore a big curly light-brown wig. Looked like one of them squeaky little white-people dogs. Poodles they call them. Anyway, that wig is what saved us from the worse. For I could hardly shout and tell them I was in there, no more could I try and grab him. I was trapped where I was. There was nothing I could really do but hold the door shut. I was scared of somebody else upsetting in and really getting an eyeful. Turned out though, in the heat of the clinch, as I was trying to avert my eyes you see, the Lamartine's curly wig jumped off her head. And if you ever been in the midst of something and had a big change occur in the someone, you can't help know how it devastates your basic urges. Not only that, but her wig was almost with a life of its own. Grandpa's eyes were bugging at the change already, and swear to God if the thing didn't rear up and pop him in the face like it was going to start something. He scrambled up, Grandpa did, and the Lamartine jumped up after him all addled looking. They just stared at each other, huffing and puffing, with quizzical expression. The surprise seemed to drive all sense completely out of Grandpa's mind.

"The letter was what started the fire," he said. "I never would have done it."

"What letter?" said the Lamartine. She was stiff-necked now, and elegant, even bald, like some alien queen. I gave her back the wig. The Lamartine replaced it on her head, and whenever I saw her after that, I couldn't help thinking of her bald, with special powers, as if from another planet.

"That was a close call," I said to Grandpa after she had left.

But I think he had already forgot the incident. He just stood there all quiet and thoughtful. You really wouldn't think he was crazy. He looked like he was just about to say something important, explaining himself. He said something, all right, but it didn't have nothing to do with anything that made sense.

He wondered where the heck he put his dandelion fork. That's when I decided about the mental adjustment.

Now what was mostly our problem was not so much that he was not all there, but that what was there of him often hankered after Lamartine. If we could put a stop to that, I thought, we might be getting someplace. But here, see, my touch was of no use. For what could I snap my fingers at to make him faithful to Grandma? Like the quality of staying power, this faithfulness was invisible. I know it's something that you got to acquire, but I never known where from. Maybe there's no rhyme or reason to it, like my getting the touch, and then again maybe it's a kind of magic.

It was Grandma Kashpaw who thought of it in the end. She knows things. Although she will not admit she has a scrap of Indian blood in her, there's no doubt in my mind she's got some Chippewa. How else would you explain the way she'll be sitting there, in front of her TV story, rocking in her armchair and suddenly she turns on me, her brown eyes hard as lake-bed flint.

"Lipsha Morrissey," she'll say, "you went out last night and got drunk."

How did she know that? I'll hardly remember it myself. Then she'll say she just had a feeling or ache in the scar of her hand or a creak in her shoulder. She is constantly being told things by little aggravations in her joints or by her household appliances. One time she told Gordie never to ride with a crazy Lamartine boy. She had seen something in the polished-up tin of her bread toaster. So he didn't. Sure enough, the time came we heard how Lyman and Henry went out of control in their car, ending up in the river. Lyman swam to the top, but Henry never made it.

Thanks to Grandma's toaster, Gordie was probably spared.

Someplace in the blood Grandma Kashpaw knows things. She also remembers things, I found. She keeps things filed away. She's got a memory like them video games that don't forget your score. One reason she remembers so many details about the trouble I gave her in early life is so she can flash back her total when she needs to.

Like now. Take the love medicine. I don't know where she remembered that from. It came tumbling from her mind like an asteroid off the corner of the screen.

Of course she starts out by mentioning the time I had this accident in church and did she leave me there with wet overhalls? No she didn't. And ain't I glad? Yes I am. Now what you want now, Grandma?

But when she mentions them love medicines, I feel my back prickle at the danger. These love medicines is something of an old Chippewa specialty. No other tribe has got them down so well. But love medicines is not for the layman to handle. You don't just go out and get one without paying for it. Before you get one, even, you should go through one hell of a lot of mental condensation. You got to think it over. Choose the right one. You could really mess up your life grinding up the wrong little thing.

So anyhow, I said to Grandma I'd give this love medicine some thought. I knew the best thing was to go ask a specialist like Old Man Pillager, who lives up in a tangle of bush and never shows himself. But the truth is I was afraid of him, like everyone else. He was known for putting the twisted mouth on people, seizing up their hearts. Old Man Pillager was serious business, and I have always thought it best to steer clear of that whenever I could. That's why I took the powers in my own hands. That's why I did what I could.

I put my whole mentality to it, nothing held back. After a while I started to remember things I'd heard gossiped over.

I heard of this person once who carried a charm of seeds that looked like baby pearls. They was attracted to a metal knife, which made them powerful. But I didn't know where them seeds grew. Another love charm I heard about I couldn't go along with, because how was I suppose to catch frogs in the act, which it required. Them little creatures is slippery and fast. And then the powerfullest of all, the most extreme, involved nail clips and such. I wasn't anywhere near asking Grandma to provide me all the little body bits that this last love recipe called for. I went walking around for days just trying to think up something that would work.

Well I got it. If it hadn't been the early fall of the year, I never would have got it. But I was sitting underneath a tree one day down near the school just watching people's feet go by when something tells me, look up! Look up! So I look up, and I see two honkers, Canada geese, the kind with little masks on their faces, a bird what mates for life. I see them flying right over my head naturally preparing to land in some slough on the reservation, which they certainly won't get off of alive.

It hits me, anyway. Them geese, they mate for life. And I think to myself, just what if I went out and got a pair? And just what if I fed some part—say the goose heart—of the female to Grandma and Grandpa ate the other heart? Wouldn't that work? Maybe it's all invisible, and then maybe again it's magic. Love is a stony road. We know that for sure. If it's true that the higher feelings of devotion get lodged in the heart like people say, then we'd be home free. If not, eating goose heart couldn't harm nobody anyway. I thought it was worth my effort, and Grandma Kashpaw thought so, too. She had always known a good idea when she heard one. She borrowed me Grandpa's gun.

So I went out to this particular slough, maybe the exact same slough I never got thrown in by my mother, thanks to Grandma Kashpaw, and I hunched down in a good comfortable pile of rushes. I got my gun loaded up. I ate a few of these soft baloney sandwiches Grandma made me for lunch, and then I waited. The cattails blown back and forth above my head. Them stringy blue herons was spearing up their prey. The thing I know how to do best in this world, the thing I been training for all my life, is to wait. Sitting there and sitting there was no hardship on me. I got to thinking about some funny things that happened. There was this one time that Lulu Lamartine's little blue tweety bird, a paraclete, I guess you'd call it, flown up inside her dress and got lost within there. I recalled her running out into the hallway trying to yell something, shaking. She was doing a right good jig there, cutting the rug for sure, and the thing is it *never* flown out. To this day people speculate where it went. They fear she might perhaps of crushed it in her corsets. It sure hasn't ever yet been seen alive. I thought of funny things for a while, but then I used them up, and strange things that happened started weaseling their way into my mind.

I got to thinking quite naturally of the Lamartine's cousin named Wristwatch. I never knew what his real name was. They called him Wristwatch, because he got his father's broken wristwatch as a young boy when his father passed on. Never in his whole life did Wristwatch take his father's watch off. He didn't care if it worked, although after a while he got sensitive when people asked what time it was, teasing him. He often put it to his ear like he was listening to the tick. But it was broken for good and forever, people said so, at least that's what they thought.

Well I saw Wristwatch smoking in his pickup one afternoon and by nine that evening he was dead.

He died sitting at the Lamartine's table, too. As she told it. Wristwatch had just eaten himself a good-size dinner and she said would he take seconds on the hot dish when he fell over to the floor. They turnt him over. He was gone. But here's the strange thing: When the Senior Citizens orderly took the pulse he noticed that the wristwatch Wristwatch wore was now working. The moment he died the wristwatch started keeping perfect time. They buried him with the watch still ticking on his arm.

I got to thinking. What if some gravediggers dug up Wristwatch's casket in two hundred years and that watch was still going? I thought what question they would ask and it was this: Whose hand wound it?

I started shaking like a piece of grass at just the thought.

Not to get off the subject or nothing. I was still hunkered in the slough. It was passing late into the afternoon and still no honkers had touched down. Now I don't need to tell you that the waiting did not get to me, it was the chill. The rushes was very soft, but damp. I was getting cold and debating to leave, when they landed. Two geese swimming here and there as big as life, looking deep into each other's little pinhole eyes. Just the ones I was looking for. So I lifted Grandpa's gun to my shoulder and I aimed perfectly, and *blam*! *blam*! I delivered two accurate shots. But the thing is, them shots missed. I couldn't hardly believe it. Whether it was that the stock had warped or the barrel got bent someways, I don't quite know, but anyway them geese flown off into the dim sky, and Lipsha Morrissey was left there in the rushes with evening fallen and his two cold hands empty. He had before him just the prospect of another day of bone-cracking chill in them rushes, and the thought of it got him depressed.

Now it isn't my style, in no way, to get depressed.

So I said to myself, Lipsha Morrissey, you're a happy S.O.B. who could be covered up with weeds by now down at the bottom of this slough, but instead you're alive to tell the tale. You might have problems in life, but you still got the touch. You got the power, Lipsha Morrissey. Can't argue that. So put your mind to it and figure out how not to be depressed.

I took my advice. I put my mind to it. But I never saw at the time how my thoughts led me astray toward a tragic outcome none could have known. I ignored all the danger, all the limits, for I was tired of sitting in the slough and my feet were numb. My face was aching. I was chilled, so I played with fire. I told myself love medicine was simple. I told myself the old superstitions was just that—strange beliefs. I told myself to take the ten dollars Mary MacDonald had paid me for putting the touch on her arthritis joint, and the other five I hadn't spent yet from winning bingo last Thursday. I told myself to go down to the Red Owl store.

And here is what I did that made the medicine backfire. I took an evil shortcut. I looked at birds that was dead and froze.

All right. So now I guess you will say, "Slap a malpractice suit on Lipsha Morrissey."

I heard of those suits. I used to think it was a color clothing quack doctors had to wear so you could tell them from the good ones. Now I know better that it's law.

As I walked back from the Red Owl with the rock-hard, heavy turkeys, I argued to myself about malpractice. I thought of faith. I thought to myself that faith could be called belief against the odds and whether or not there's any proof. How does that sound? I thought how we might have to yell to be heard by Higher Power, but that's not saying it's not *there*. And that is faith for you. It's belief even when the goods don't deliver. Higher Power makes promises we all know they can't back up, but anybody ever go a slap an old malpractice suit on God? Or the U.S. government? No they don't. Faith might be stupid, but it gets us through. So what I'm heading at is this. I finally convinced myself that the real actual power to the love medicine was not the goose heart itself but the faith in the cure.

I didn't believe it, I knew it was wrong, but by then I had waded so far into my lie I was stuck there. And then I went one step further.

The next day, I cleaned the hearts away from the paper package of gizzards inside the turkeys. Then I wrapped them hearts with a clean hankie and brung them both to get blessed up at the mission. I wanted to get official blessings from the priest, but when Father answered the door to the rectory, wiping his hands on a little towel, I could tell he was a busy man.

"Booshoo, Father," I said. "I got a slight request to make of you this afternoon."

"What is it?" he said.

"Would you bless this package?" I held out the hankie with the hearts tied inside it.

He looked at the package, questioning it.

"It's turkey hearts," I honestly had to reply.

A look of annoyance crossed his face.

"Why don't you bring this matter over to Sister Martin," he said. "I have duties."

And so, although the blessing wouldn't be as powerful, I went over to the Sisters with the package.

I rung the bell, and they brought Sister Martin to the door. I had her as a music teacher, but I was always so shy then. I never talked out loud. Now, I had grown taller than Sister Martin. Looking down, I saw that she was not feeling up to snuff. Brown circles hung under her eyes.

"What's the matter?" she said, not noticing who I was.

"Remember me, sister?"

She squinted up at me.

"Oh yes," she said after a moment. "I'm sorry, you're the youngest of the Kashpaws. Gordie's brother."

Her face warmed up.

"Lipsha," I said, "that's my name."

"Well, Lipsha," she said, smiling broad at me now, "what can I do for you?"

They always said she was the kindest-hearted of the Sisters up the hill, and she was. She brought me back into their own kitchen and made me take a big yellow wedge of cake and a glass of milk.

"Now tell me," she said, nodding at my package. "What have you got wrapped up so carefully in those handkerchiefs?"

Like before, I answered honestly.

"Ah," said Sister Martin. "Turkey hearts." She waited.

"I hoped you could bless them."

She waited some more, smiling with her eyes. Kindhearted though she was, I began to sweat. A person could not pull the wool down over Sister Martin. I stumbled through my mind for an explanation, quick, that wouldn't scare her off.

"They're a present," I said, "for Saint Kateri's statue."

"She's not a saint yet."

"I know," I stuttered on, "in the hopes they will crown her."

"Lipsha," she said, "I never heard of such a thing."

So I told her. "Well the truth is," I said, "it's a kind of medicine."

"For what?"

"Love."

"Oh Lipsha," she said after a moment, "you don't need any medicine. I'm sure any girl would like you exactly the way you are."

I just sat there. I felt miserable, caught in my pack of lies.

"Tell you what," she said, seeing how bad I felt, "my blessing won't make any difference anyway. But there is something you can do."

I looked up at her, hopeless.

"Just be yourself."

I looked down at my plate. I knew I wasn't much to brag about right then, and I shortly became even less. For as I walked out the door I stuck my fingers in the cup of holy water that was sacred from their touches. I put my fingers in and blessed the hearts, quick, with my own hand.

I went back to Grandma and sat down in her little kitchen at the Senior Citizens. I unwrapped them hearts on the table, and her hard agate eyes went soft. She said she wasn't even going to cook those hearts up but eat them raw so their power would go down strong as possible.

I couldn't hardly watch when she munched hers. Now that's true love. I was worried about how she would get Grandpa to eat his, but she told me she'd think of something and don't worry. So I did not. I was supposed to hide off in her bedroom while she put dinner on a plate for Grandpa and fixed up the heart so he'd eat it. I caught a glint of the plate she was making for him. She put that heart smack on a piece of lettuce like in a restaurant and then attached to it a little heap of boiled peas.

He sat down. I was listening in the next room

She said, "why don't you have some mash potato?" So he had some mash potato. Then she gave him a little piece of boiled meat. He ate that. Then she said, "Why you didn't never touch your salad yet. See that heart? I'm feeding you it because the doctor said your blood needs building up."

I couldn't help it, at that point I peeked through a crack in the door.

I saw Grandpa picking at that heart on his plate with a certain look. He didn't look appetized at all, is what I'm saying. I doubted our plan was going to work. Grandma was getting worried, too. She told him one more time, loudly, that he had to eat that heart.

"Swallow it down," she said. "You'll hardly notice it."

He just looked at her straight on. The way he looked at her made me think I was going to see the smokescreen drop a second time, and sure enough it happened.

"What you want me to eat this for so bad?" he asked her uncannily.

Now Grandma knew the jig was up. She knew that he knew she was working medicine. He put his fork down. He rolled the heart around his saucer plate.

"I don't want to eat this," he said to Grandma. "It don't look good."

"Why it's fresh grade-A," she told him. "One hundred percent."

He didn't ask percent what, but his eyes took on an even more warier look.

"Just go on and try it," she said, taking the salt shaker up in her hand. She was getting annoyed. "Not tasty enough? You want me to salt it for you?" She waved the shaker over his plate.

"All right, skinny white girl!" She had got Grandpa mad. Oopsy-daisy, he popped the heart into his mouth. I was about to yawn loudly and come out of the bedroom. I was about ready for this crash of wills to be over, when I saw he was still up to his old tricks. First he rolled it into one side of his cheek. "Mmmmm," he said. Then he rolled it into the other side of his cheek. "Mmmmmmm," again. Then he stuck his tongue out with the heart on it and put it back, and there was no time to react. He had pulled Grandma's leg once too far. Her goat was got. She was so mad she hopped up quick as a wink and slugged him between the shoulderblades to make him swallow.

Only thing is, he choked.

He choked real bad. A person can choke to death. You ever sit down at a restaurant table and up above you there is a list of instructions what to do if something slides down the wrong pipe: It sure makes you chew slow, that's for damn sure. When Grandpa fell off his chair better believe me that little graphic illustrated poster fled into my mind. I jumped out the bedroom. I done everything within my power that I could do to unlodge what was choking him. I squeezed underneath his ribcage. I socked him in the back. I was desperate. But here's the factor of decision: he wasn't choking on the heart alone. There was more to it than that. It was other things that choked him as well. It didn't seem like he wanted to struggle or fight. Death came and tapped his chest, so he went just like that. I'm sorry all through my body at what I done to him with that heart, and there's those who will say Lipsha Morrissey is just excusing himself off the hook by giving song and dance about how Grandpa gave up.

Maybe I can't admit what I did. My touch had gone worthless, that is true. But here is what I seen while he lay in my arms.

You hear a person's life will flash before their eyes when they're in danger. It was him in danger, not me, but it was *his* life come over me. I saw him dying, and it was like someone pulled the shade down in a room. His eyes clouded over and squeezed shut, but just before that I looked in. He was still fishing in the middle of Lake Turcot. Big thoughts was on his line and he had half a case of beer in the boat. He waved at me, grinned, and then the bobber went under.

Grandma had gone out of the room crying for help. I bunched my force up in my hands and I had him. I was so wound up I couldn't even breathe. All the moments he had spent with me, all the times he had hoisted me on his shoulders or pointed into the leaves was concentrated in that moment. Time was flashing back and forth like a pinball machine. Lights blinked and balls hopped and rubber bands chirped, until suddenly I realized the last ball had gone down the drain and there was nothing. I felt his force leaving him, flowing out of Grandpa never to return. I felt his mind weakening. The bobber going under in the lake. And I felt the touch retreat back into the darkness inside my body, from where it came.

One time, long ago, both of us were fishing together. We caught a big old snapper what started towing us around like it was a motor. "This here fishline is pretty damn good," Grandpa said. "Let's keep this turtle on and see where he takes us." So we rode along behind that turtle, watching as from time to time it surfaced. The thing was just about the size of a washtub. It took us all around the lake twice, and as it was traveling, Grandpa said something as a joke. "Lipsha," he said, "we are glad your mother didn't want you because we was always looking for a boy like you who would tow us around the lake."

"I ain't no snapper. Snappers is so stupid they stay alive when their head's chopped off," I said.

"That ain't stupidity," said Grandpa. "Their brain's just in their heart, like yours is."

When I looked up, I knew the fuse had blown between my heart and my mind and that a terrible understanding was to be given. Grandma got back into the room and I saw her stumble. And then she went down too. It was like a house you can't hardly believe has stood so long, through years of record weather, suddenly goes down in the worst yet. It makes sense, is what I'm saying, but you still can't hardly believe it. You think a person you know has got through death and illness and being broke and living on commodity rice will get through anything. Then they fold and you see how fragile were the stones that underpinned them. You see how instantly the ground can shift you thought was solid. You see the stop signs and the yellow dividing markers of roads you traveled and all the instructions you had played according to vanish. You see how all the everyday things you counted on was just a dream you had been having by which you run your whole life. She had been over me, like a sheer overhang of rock dividing Lipsha Morrissey from outer space. And now she went underneath. It was as though the banks gave way on the shores of Lake Turcot, and where Grandpa's passing was just the house and the rock under it sliding after, sending half the lake splashing up to the clouds.

Where there was nothing.

You play them games never knowing what you see. When I fell into the dream alongside of both of them I saw that the dominions I had defended myself from anciently was but delusions of the screen. Blips of light. And I was scot-free now, whistling through space.

I don't know how I come back. I don't know from where. They was slapping my face when I arrived back at Senior Citizens and they was oxygenating her. I saw her chest move, almost unwilling. She sighed the way she would when somebody bothered her in the middle of a row of beads she was counting. I think it irritated her to no end that they brought her back. I knew from the way she looked after they took the mask off, she was not going to forgive them disturbing her restful peace. Nor was she forgiving Lipsha Morrissey. She had been stepping out onto the road of death, she told the children later at the funeral. I asked was there any stop signs or dividing markers on that road, but she clamped her lips in a vise the way she always done when she was mad.

Which didn't bother me. I knew when things had cleared out she wouldn't have no choice. I was not going to speculate where the blame was put for Grandpa's death. We was in it together. She had slugged him between the shoulders. My touch had failed him, never to return.

All the blood children and the took-ins, like me, came home from Minneapolis and Chicago, where they had relocated years ago. They stayed with friends on the reservation or with Aurelia or slept on Grandma's floor. They were struck down with grief and bereavement to be sure, every one of them. At the funeral I sat down in the back of the church with Albertine. She had gotten all skinny and ragged haired from cramming all her years of study into two or three. She had decided that to be a nurse was not enough for her so she was going to be a doctor. But the way she was straining her mind didn't look too hopeful. Her eyes were bloodshot from driving and crying. She took my hand. From the back we watched all the children and the mourners as they hunched over their prayers, their hands stuffed full of Kleenex. It was someplace in that long sad service that my vision shifted. I began to see things different, more clear. The family kneeling down turned to rocks in a field. It struck me how strong and reliable grief was, and death. Until the end of time, death would be our rock.

So I had perspective on it all, for death gives you that. All the Kashpaw children had done various things to me in their lives—shared their folks with me, loaned me cash, beat me up in secret—and I decided, because of death, then and there I'd call it quits. If I ever saw King again, I'd shake his hand. Forgiving somebody else made the whole thing easier to bear.

Everybody saw Grandpa off into the next world. And then the Kashpaws had to get back to their jobs, which was numerous and impressive. I had a few beers with them and I went back to Grandma, who had sort of got lost in the shuffle of everybody being sad about Grandpa and glad to see one another.

Zelda had sat beside her the whole time and was sitting with her now. I wanted to talk to Grandma, say how sorry I was, that it wasn't her fault, but only mine. I would have, but Zelda gave me one of her looks of strict warning as if to say, "I'll take care of Grandma. Don't horn in on the women."

If only Zelda knew, I thought, the sad realities would change her. But of course I couldn't tell the dark truth.

It was evening, late. Grandma's light was on underneath a crack in the door. About a week had passed since we buried Grandpa. I knocked first but there wasn't no answer, so I went right in. The door was unlocked. She was there but she didn't notice me at first. Her hands were tied up in her rosary, and her gaze was fully absorbed in the easy chair opposite her, the one that had always been Grandpa's favorite. I stood there, staring with her, at the little green nubs in the cloth and plastic armrest covers and the sad little hair-tonic stain he had made on the white doily where he laid his head. For the life of me I couldn't figure what she was staring at. Thin space. Then she turned.

"He ain't gone yet," she said.

Remember that chill I luckily didn't get from waiting in the slough? I got it now. I felt it start from the very center of me, where fear hides, waiting to attack. It spiraled outward so that in minutes my fingers and teeth were shaking and clattering. I knew she told the truth. She seen Grandpa. Whether or not he had been there is not the point. She has *seen* him, and that meant anybody else could see him, too. Not only that but, as is usually the case with these here ghosts, he had a certain uneasy reason to come back. And of course Grandma Kashpaw had scanned it out.

I sat down. We sat together on the couch watching his chair out of the corner of our eyes. She had found him sitting in his chair when she walked in the door.

"It's the love medicine, my Lipsha," she said. "It was stronger than we thought. He came back even after death to claim me to his side."

I was afraid. "We shouldn't have tampered with it," I said. She agreed. For a while we sat still. I don't know what she thought, but my head felt screwed on backward. I couldn't accurately consider the situation, so I told Grandma to go to bed. I would sleep on the couch keeping my eye on Grandpa's chair. Maybe he would come back and maybe he wouldn't. I guess I feared the one as much as the other, but I got to thinking, see, as I lay there in darkness, that perhaps even through my terrible mistakes some good might come. If Grandpa did come back, I thought he'd return in his right mind. I could talk with him. I could tell him it was all my fault for playing with power I did not understand. Maybe he'd forgive me and rest in peace. I hoped this. I calmed myself and waited for him all night.

He fooled me though. He knew what I was waiting for, and it wasn't what he was looking to hear. Come dawn I heard a blood-splitting cry from the bedroom and

I rushed in there. Grandma turnt the lights on. She was sitting on the edge of the bed and her face looked harsh, pinched-up gray.

"He was here," she said. "He came and laid down next to me in bed. And he touched me."

Her heart broke down. She cried. His touch was so cold. She laid back in bed after a while, as it was morning, and I went to the couch. As I lay there, falling asleep, I suddenly felt Grandpa's presence and the barrier between us like a swollen river. I felt how I had wronged him. How awful was the place where I had sent him. Behind the wall of death, he'd watched the living eat and cry and get drunk. He was lonesome, but I understood he meant no harm.

"Go back," I said to the dark, afraid and yet full of pity. "You got to be with your own kind now," I said. I felt him retreating, like a sigh, growing less. I felt his spirit as it shrunk back through the walls, the blinds, the brick courtyard of Senior Citizens. "Look up Aunt June," I whispered as he left.

I slept late the next morning, a good hard sleep allowing the sun to rise and warm the earth. It was past noon when I awoke. There is nothing, to my mind, like a long sleep to make those hard decisions that you neglect under stress of wakefulness. Soon as I woke up that morning, I saw exactly what I'd say to Grandma. I had gotten humble in the past week, not just losing the touch but getting jolted into the understanding that would prey on me from her on out. Your life feels different on you, once you greet death and understand your heart's position. You wear your life like a garment from the mission bundle sale ever after—lightly because you realize you never paid nothing for it, cherishing because you know you won't ever come by such a bargain again. Also you have the feeling someone wore it before you and someone will after. I can't explain that, not yet, but I'm putting my mind to it.

"Grandma," I said, "I got to be honest about the love medicine."

She listened. I knew from then on she would be listening to me the way I had listened to her before. I told her about the turkey hearts and how I had them blessed. I told her what I used as love medicine was purely a fake, and then I said to her what my understanding brought me.

"Love medicine ain't what brings him back to you, Grandma. No, it's something else. He loved you over time and distance, but he went off so quick he never got the chance to tell you how he loves you, how he doesn't blame you, how he understands. It's true feeling, not no magic. No supermarket heart could have brung him back."

She looked at me. She was seeing the years and days I had no way of knowing, and she didn't believe me. I could tell this. Yet a look came on her face. It was like the look of mothers drinking sweetness from their children's eyes. It was tenderness.

"Lipsha," she said, "you was always my favorite."

She took the beads off the bedpost, where she kept them to say at night, and she told me to put out my hand. When I did this, she shut the beads inside of my fist and held them there a long minute, tight, so my hand hurt. I almost cried when she did this. I don't really know why. Tears shot up behind my eyelids, and yet it was nothing. I didn't understand, except her hand was so strong, squeezing mine.

The earth was full of life and there were dandelions growing out the window, thick as thieves, already seeded, fat as big yellow plungers. She let my hand go. I got up. "I'll go out and dig a few dandelions," I told her.

Outside, the sun was hot and heavy as a hand on my back. I felt it flow down my arms, out my fingers, arrowing through the ends of the fork into the earth. With every root I prized up there was return, as if I was kin to its secret lesson. The touch got stronger as I worked through the grassy afternoon. Uncurling from me like a seed out of the blackness where I was lost, the touch spread. The spiked leaves full of bitter mother's milk. A buried root. A nuisance people dig up and throw in the sun to wither. A globe of frail seeds that's indestructible.

Kimberly Blaeser

(b. 1955) Anishinaabe

Kimberly Blaeser was born in Billings, Montana, in 1955. She is Anishinaabe and German and was raised in reservation communities. She is an enrolled member of the White Earth Reservation in Minnesota. She studied at the College of St. Catherine and the College of St. Benedict and earned her doctorate in literature at the University of Notre Dame. She was a research fellow at the Newberry Library in Chicago. Blaeser is now an associate professor of English at the University of Wisconsin in Milwaukee.

Trailing You, *her collection of poems, won the Diane Decora First Book Award in Poetry from the Native Writers' Circle of the Americas and was published in 1994. Her poetry and short stories have appeared in numerous journals and anthologies, including* **Dreams and Secrets**, **Returning the Gift, and Unsettling America: Race and Ethnicity in Contemporary American Poetry**. *"From Aboard the Night Train," a short story about dreams and remembrance, casinos, and the world in a window, was published in* **Earth Song, Sky Spirit**, *edited by Clifford Trafzer. Her essay, "Learning 'The Language the Presidents Speak': Images and Issues of Literary in American Indian Literature," was published in* **World Literature Today** *in 1992.*

"A Matter of Proportion" is a balance of remembrance and the dimensions of native chance on the roads not taken. Edna returns and she measures her return in conversations and the nostalgia of a "journey to lost beginnings."

Blaeser wrote, "There were endless comments on the decline of all things good, on her appearance, on the proper way to raise children." A certain crotchety manner haunted family scenes.

> *Edna blamed this inherited attraction to crotchetiness for landing her with a career in education; for making her the owner of a vintage house, vintage furniture, vintage car, vintage everything; for filling her house with misfit animals; and for her failed love life.*

The word mindawe *means* sullen *and* unsatisfied *in translation, and* omakakii *means* frog *in the oral language of the Anishinaabe.*

A Matter of Proportion

Edna had returned. Like a figure in a diorama, she stood stiffly, impassively gazing at the flowered linoleum of the living room floor. Suddenly she laughed out loud as she remembered and ran to the forbidden door. Another door to the outside, it had never been used except to catch an evening breeze or to launch her and the other children in secret parachute missions when the grown-ups were away. It was dangerous, an unfinished exit with no steps—one of the quirks of the house that everyone lived with and never bothered to change, the same way no one ever thought to change the contour of the land. Everyone knew which boards in the house would give slivers just like they knew where the potholes were in the yard or where sharp boulders jutted up along the trail—or they learned soon enough.

Like her smart aleck cousin Warren had learned about the "big drop" the day he tried to beat everyone to the best seat on the wagon by taking a shortcut out that door. "He doesn't listen to nothing nobody tells him," she and the other cousins proclaimed, shaking their heads and looking over in feigned sympathy where Warren lay on the cot with his swollen ankle propped up. It was true. Even though no one had actually *told* him about the door, he wouldn't have listened anyway.

Now as Edna strained to pull the door open and swing it inside, she felt the bottom scrape against the floor and stood looking at the familiar semi-circle worn on the linoleum by the path of the door. She imagined her marbles along that curve—cat's-eyes, purees, steelies all assembled in a colorful arc.

Lying on the floor with the cat beside her, young Edna had been rolling her marbles, tracing that half circle with the small globes, when her auntie spoke. "I like them crotchety," the old woman had said, "the more crotchety the better." Edna remembered laughing with all the womenfolk, but she was puzzled. And so she tucked the statement away as she did with all things that puzzled her about which she was too timid to ask. She heard it again later and again in the voice of her old auntie and wondered why Aunt Lydia had said it and what she meant.

It wasn't just a joke, she knew that; because the way the women laughed had that edge to it like when they laughed about getting old or about hauntings. She knew it wasn't funny in a real way, but funny in the way you felt if you got stuck in a tree because you climbed too high and were too afraid to put your foot down backwards to that first low branch. You laughed then, too, because you didn't want Harvard or Willie to see you cry and because somehow it made you a little braver and after awhile you could let Harvard climb up and pull your foot to the branch and make yourself believe—almost—that it was going to be there. Maybe that's why Edna remembered Aunt Lydia's voice talking about men, because it was a voice afraid of falling even though it sounded like the voice she used when she chased the animals out of the kitchen.

Later, Edna began to think that the old lady was right, not just about men in the way that the married women knew men, but right about crotchetiness in general. She thought of the big bull, the one that chased her and the other kids when they took the shortcut through the pasture. Mindewa Omakakii Uncle called it, because he said that bull had the disposition of a mad frog. But one morning when Edna had been up real early and down to the water trough to check on her goldfish, she saw Uncle petting that old bull and feeding him something by hand.

"You don't fool me, ol' boy, you like your sugar just as much as the next guy." She saw Mindewa rub against Uncle's arm and nuzzle his hand just like the cows all did. And she saw his great big tongue come out to take the food from Uncle's palm.

"Yeah, you're a tough old devil and you got the whole barnyard afraid of you. But you got an itch that needs scratching, too."

"Uncle," she whispered as she came up behind him. She was scared the bull might change back before she could touch him.

"It's okay, sister. Just come slow and say hello to his highness here." Uncle lifted her up with his right arm while with his left hand he kept scratching that bull's ears. And then she reached out and she touched the black rough coat. He made his loud bull noise and rolled his eyes at her a little, but he didn't run off and he didn't try to hurt her.

That moment seemed like the whole of childhood to her now: her uncle's arm around her waist holding her up, Mindewa on the other side of the fence blowing out of his nose while his tail moved rhythmically back and forth. Then suddenly Mindewa snorted for real, pawed the ground and ran off, raising little gusts of dust from the earth.

But after that, there was something between her and the bull. Even when he was ornery as all get out, she felt a strange love for that bull, more than for all the cows who had always let her pet them, feed them, and even ride on them. She often stood a safe distance and just looked at Mindewa and sometimes he would stop eating and look back, too. And then she would say something to him, something low so the others wouldn't hear, and after she would run off with a strange happy feeling inside.

It was the same with that old man who was their neighbor, who she once saw throwing tomatoes at his chickens when they got under foot in the garden. When she used to take him things from her mother and auntie, he would yell for her to wipe her feet and close the door. Then while he put the food away or tasted it, he would find something to criticize. "You tell your mother that meringue wouldn't pull away from the crust if she just used a little cream of tartar.... Wrapping that bread in plastic just spoils the crust. I like a nice hard crust on my bread. Next time store it in a paper bag. No need for those fancy plastic bags. Never had need of those in my day...."

There were endless comments on the decline of all things good, on her appearance, on the proper way to raise children. Finally he might ask her to sit with him and eat and, throughout the ritual he made of every bite, he would quiz and correct her. After, she would be required to help him wash, dry and put away. At first she stayed through all this because of what might come when the table was cleared: stories, a lesson in cards, the gift of a nickel, or a look at the browning photos, postcards, carved figures or other treasures he kept in the old cigar boxes. Later though, she knew for sure she'd inherited the family curse when she began to enjoy the haranguing itself, when a week didn't seem complete if she hadn't been witness to his mumbling complaints. When she outgrew the nickel, her thanks became a rough grasp of his hand when he walked her to the door.

Edna blamed this inherited attraction to crotchetiness for landing her with a career in education; for making her the owner of a vintage house, vintage furniture, vintage car, vintage everything; for filling her house with misfit animals; and for her failed love life. Pop-psychology books and her now-defunct relationship with a therapist had variously identified her problem as low self-esteem, a martyr complex, and co-dependency. She knew her superiors either celebrated or excused her oddities as manifestations of what, as scholars, they liked to call a hyphenated identity (even though American Indian wasn't hyphenated the way Asian-American, Hispanic-American or many of the other minority categories were).

Well maybe it had something to do with being Indian, but not in the way they meant. When Edna's Uncle was down in bed near the last, folks used to gather in the front room most days and keep him company if he woke up. One day when they thought Uncle was asleep behind the curtain, some of the ladies were talking about the hardships of mixedbloods and Indians on the reservation and someone was telling about Old Winthrop's family. "That man worked harder his whole life than any of the sheriff's kin and yet those people had it good for years and years spending our money and Old Win had just those few months at the end when that government check came for his grandson's death. Still remember how proud he was, walking to the store and buying food he had never tried in his whole life, paying cash for it, and laughing about those little salty fish, saying 'Hell, I been eating fish heads my whole life. If I'd a known white folks liked them so much, I would have traded mine for some beef.' "

Everyone was in a pretty pitiful mood, telling those sad stories, when Uncle's voice came from behind that curtain. "Yeah, white folks got years. But us Indians we got these moments. Best we don't tell them." And then he laughed in the dry sounding way that was in his voice those days.

Edna knew enough not to ask what he meant, because by then she'd learned that some things aren't to be explained. Still she thought of all the ways she could take those words and had chosen to take them just about every way possible through the years.

Now she was back again looking at the worn linoleum and listening for the old voices. A rusty water pail and dipper still stood on the counter in the kitchen and the walls were still covered with clippings, pieces of material, safety pins, and other odds and ends that no one had claimed. "Can't stay there now, Eddie Mae," her mother had said. "Nothing works at that place. Mice have been in there, might even be nests in the stovepipes. Not safe anyway at night." Edna thought about the streets of the city at night and wondered to herself what it was her mother considered unsafe about the old farm house at night. But she didn't argue. Instead she had come out for a quick look.

She walked through the barnyard, scolded furiously by the crows for her trespassing. The tool shed held the scent of skunk and Edna backed away from the doorway, laughing at her own cowardice. She scared up a couple of partridge that might be nesting in the old barn, and thought she saw a coyote pacing just at the tree line. Tempted to climb the windmill so she could see the surrounding land, she put her hood up and searched her pockets for gloves to cushion the cut of cold metal. But the wind still bit sharply at her face and her gloves, she remembered clearly now, had been left lying on her mother's counter. So she just stood there at the base of the windmill, watching while the blades were moved up and around, seeing all the Ednas she had been, caught between, trying to figure which one she was now.

That's what the whole visit was about really, she told herself—a cliché-riddled journey to lost beginnings. Although Edna was just cynical enough to know it wouldn't resolve anything, when the California job offer came last week her first instinct was to run home. Clarence from the tribal paper stopped by last night to interview her about the job—Indians at universities were big news back here. She surprised everyone even herself when she said she might not take the job, might decide to come back home and work in the tribal schools. She particularly knew by her mom's pan-banging that news wasn't well received.

When Clarence had polished off the last of the apple pie and rattled off in his vintage pickup, the inevitable argument had begun. "What the hell you got against success?" her mom demanded.

"I figure it's not part of our tradition," Edna responded with teasing in her voice. But she was only half joking. The thing that had been plaguing her was about the difference between success and happiness, and maybe that is what Uncle had been meaning that day long ago.

She thought she understood about moments and years and had tried once to explain to Ray, the therapist. He was angry at her for abandoning him at a posh ski hotel in Yosemite valley to spend the afternoon climbing with a girl friend. She told him about the steep icy trail, about the walking sticks they had fashioned, about the shaking of her legs from fatigue, the snow angels they had made, the snow they'd eaten to quench their thirst, and about the few precious moments they could spend at the top of Vernal Falls before they had to begin their descent, and about the race against the darkness on the way down. He hadn't understood. All that effort and danger for a ten-minute gaze from the top? It just proved to him all he had already guessed about Edna's flaws.

She was glad then that she'd never tried to explain to him about moments and men, or as old Aunt Lydia would have it, crotchetiness and men. For she did come to understand that, too. The first time she really understood, she was only eighteen and working for the school district during the summer, tutoring Pinto's two little girls. Pinto was a widower who did mostly seasonal labor like brushing, planting trees, ricing, logging, fishing and sugarbushing. He lived out a ways in Beaulieu township and Edna would stay three days each week. She was supposed to just teach the kids, but she liked it at Pinto's place and maybe her instincts took over a little, too, because she began mothering Frannie and Dawn, taking care of the meals and the house when she was there.

Pinto was quiet, gruff when he spoke at all to Edna, and he let her know clearly that he didn't believe in white schooling. But she saw how he was gentle in his handling of the little girls—washing, brushing, and braiding their long hair, holding their hands like delicate eggs as he clipped their nails. And, though there was a darkness about his eyes, to Edna, he was handsome in the most basic sort of way—not pretty like the colorful sumac, or shapely as a maple tree might be when it draws the sun equally, but handsome like a tall pine, sturdy like the pines she'd seen growing even out of rock.

One morning near the end of the summer, she brought him coffee and biscuits while he was milking in the barn. He usually ate when he came in, but that morning he'd been running late so she took him a plate and waited while he ate it. When he handed back the cup and plate and she turned to leave, he took hold of her arm just above the elbow and turned her to him. Nothing else happened or nothing that could be gossiped about. They simply stood and looked at one another until Edna's hand let go of the dishes and they fell with a dull thud to the straw. Then Pinto let her arm go, kicked over the milk bucket, and swore.

When she left for the last time that summer he stood up from the kitchen table and nodded his head as he spoke his name for her, "Girl…"

"Pinto." She tried the same restraint. It didn't work and she ended by going to him, kissing him on the cheek, and then running out the door.

But that single moment in the barn she had always kept as one of her finest memories. It was something Ray would never understand. He'd given her spa vacations and silk lingerie, but no moment like that with Pinto.

Edna knew that a romance writer could have a fine time with the plot of her life by bringing Pinto back into the story now on her return. But Pinto was gone the next year. He married a woman from Leech Lake and moved away.

No matter, really. Edna had another botched love affair to return to. Jones had been her companion summers when she was home from college and waitressing at one or another of the little lake resorts. He worked for the tribal conservation department. But Jones never asked anything of her straight out. He expected her to make choices they never spoke about. She damned him for it when she was alone and she damned herself for being unable somehow. One summer she just took a job away from home and that was that.

Back home tonight, everyone wanted to talk about her choices. Her mom had invited aunts and uncles and cousins and add-ons and they all worked on her over dinner. The dean of fine arts had called while she was at the farm—wondering if there were questions she had that he could help her with, wondering if she knew when she might make a decision, wondering if the offer was to her liking.

"What more could you ask for, Eddie Mae?"

"... moving money and faculty housing."

"Hey, now's your chance, Cousin! Pass the bread, wouldja?"

"... get out of that old house."

"People from that school took her out..."

"Eddie, think of how nice your life could be.

"... free lunches and dinners for two whole days."

"Teach a few classes a week..."

"These people talking about her work... You want some gravy with that?"

"... living away from all this snow!"

"Listen everybody, I appreciate this—really. No, no more potatoes, Auntie. But look, I came home to avoid thinking about this for a little while, you know? Besides are you all so anxious to get rid of me again?" It was the one thing Edna knew to say that would keep them quiet. Then of course, it became too damn quiet. "Hey, I heard there was snow softball on South Twin tonight. June Bug's coming by to pick me up. Any of you want to come with?"

Two of the younger cousins agreed to go, the conversation moved on to old games people remembered, and the three began digging out the layers of clothes they would need from the winter trunk. Who owned the assorted flannels, mittens, scarves, and hats had long since been forgotten. Edna remembered now how half the fun of winter dressing at the farm had been fighting for temporary possession and shaking out the stories each piece held.

"Let me have that one, I always liked it the best. It covers my ears but doesn't hang down around my eyes."

"That's cuz you got the ears to hold it back!"

"Your mother's second cousin from Ponsford knitted that hat the winter she stayed with us waiting for her baby to come. Everybody wanted the pattern, but she was selfish some and wouldn't show anybody how she made that rose pattern."

"You know, Grandma says that's why her little boy turned out like he did. You have to be careful of everything when you're in a family way."

"Any of you girls need to take notice?"

"Leave the poor girls in peace. They'll be late for their game."

Edna stepped out into the sharp night air. She was happy to hear it again, but happy, too, to close the door on the chatter of her family.

All but a thin layer of snow had been cleared from a patch of ice on the lake and dock lights illuminated the winter softball field. It was strange to see the diamond all white instead of green, gleaming as it reflected the light, with the winter gear of the players in vibrant colors against the white backdrop, seeming to leave color streams in their wake when they moved. The whole surreal scene came alive with the same field talk Edna remembered so vividly from the summer games. At night after tournaments, she used to hear the calling in her sleep: "Come on youse girls. Get ready.... This one's an out, easy out. I'm walkin' in.... No batter." Or from behind the plate: "Wait for your ball. Wait for your ball.... Jes' takes one.... Good eye.... Hey, back up." Sometimes, she remembered, a low chant would start up on the Indian teams and away-teams often got rattled by it.

Tonight the play was less serious. Edna was sliding into home base and the momentum and ice carried her right under the umpire who landed with a thump on top of her. They both lay there laughing hard, their breath steaming out in front of them, the ice beginning to penetrate their layers of clothing, and their bladders feeling dangerously full. Then Edna felt someone take her arm.

"Hey, need a handful. Don't you know you can get kicked out of a game for harassing the ump? God knows what the penalty is for upending 'em."

It was Jones. They both stood brushing her off and laughing, until suddenly conscious of the contact. June Bug arrived to say her car was full and could Jones take Edna, and then Edna remembered how all these things had always been arranged without either of them really deciding anything.

"You mind?"

"Not if you don't."

"We gotta walk over to the cabin first to get my truck."

And so they ended up at Jones's cabin drinking hot lemonade while he showed her the staircase and loft he built. It was a lovely cabin and she told him so. "Yeah, life's— getting kinda easy, ain't it? I heard you got a real job lined up." Then, in a tone she couldn't quite decipher, he added, "We both got pretty much all we need."

"Maybe we're getting old, Jones. Too lazy or too damned scared to make any changes."

This time his tone was clear; he was angry. "Is that why you come back? Or is this the long good-bye?"

"Let's not fight, Jones."

"I'm not. I'm talking like you always say you want to do."

For just a moment they face off before Edna notices Jones trying to suppress a smile. "Fine time to start too," she speaks with feigned annoyance, "the one time I don't have a damned thing to say." And then they're safe again she thinks—both laughing.

But just as suddenly they are embracing and she wants to close her eyes and let it all come easily, to have this because there is no reason she shouldn't.

Their awkwardness in the days that follow, however, is not that of two night lovers meeting again in the brightness of the day, but the awkwardness of indecision. They try hard to read each small sign from the other and yet to remain casual, not investing too much in what has not yet happened.

When she is to leave, he comes over to see her off. Folks have been stopping by all morning with advice or gifts. Jones helps her position everything for travel: fresh walleye stashed in a little Styrofoam ice chest, commodity peanuts, syrup from last year's sugarbush, venison sausage, new jellies, even garden carrots from someone's root cellar. Together they pack the foods carefully, all the things Old Winthrop must have needed and valued, too, through all the years of his life. Even at the last, Edna thought, when he decided to experiment with store bought foods, he knew enough not to take them too seriously. And when she drives off, she thinks of Old Winthrop's sardines and the story of how he had laughed that day about the puny size of the heads of those canned fish compared to the fish heads he had boiled up his whole life.

Gordon Henry, Jr.

(b. 1955) Anishinaabe

Gordon Henry, Jr., was born in Philadelphia, Pennsylvania, in 1955. He is an enrolled member of the White Earth Reservation. Gordon was raised on military bases in various parts of the world. His father served in the United States Navy. Joseph Vizenor, his maternal grandfather, was the tribal manager on the reservation.

Gordon studied at Michigan State University and earned his doctorate in literature at the University of North Dakota. He has taught at Ferris State University in Big Rapids, Michigan, and at Michigan State University.

The Light People, *his first novel, was published in the American Indian Literature and Critical Studies series by the University of Oklahoma Press in 1994.* **Outside White Earth**, *his first book of poems, was published by* **Blue Cloud Quarterly** *in 1988. His poems and stories have appeared in numerous journals and anthologies. "Sleeping in Rain" was published in* **Earth Power Coming**, *edited by Simon Ortiz. "The Prisoner of Haiku" was published in* **Earth Song, Sky Spirit**, *edited by Clifford Trafzer.*

Arthur Boozhoo, the main character in the story, was raised in the city. His father moved from the reservation on the federal relocation program and worked for a utility company. Arthur was ten when his father was "electrocuted on the spot." He did not return to the rez, or reservation, with his brothers and sisters. Instead, he worked in a candy factory. Later he studied drama and "got involved with a group of people who believed that everyone has a personal magic that they can ignore or use." So, he studied magic.

"I asked my grandfather about magic," Henry wrote about Boozhoo. Grandfather said

> *There are healers among us, men and women of gifts and visions. Some are relatives of light people. Sometimes their gifts can bring people back. Quite a few people have told us not to believe in those gifts, but with all the sickness around us and no cures by the white doctors, some people have returned to these descendants of the original teachers and bringers of light.*

The word boozhoo *is a greeting in the oral language of the Anishinaabe.* Meskwaa Geeshik *is a variation of* miskwaa *and means* it is red. *The second name is a variation of* giizhig *and means* day *or* sun. Oskinaway *is a variation of* oshkinawe *and means* young man. Minogeshig *or* minogiizhigad *means* a nice day. Shagonawshee *or* zhaaganaash *means* Englishman, *and* zhaaganaashiimo *means* speaks English. Bwanequah *or* bwaan *translates as* Dakota Indian, *and* ikwe *refers to* woman. Nawawzhee *is a variation or* naawakwe *or it is* noon.

Arthur Boozhoo On the Nature of Magic

I'm different, you may have noticed. I was raised far away in a city. My father went there under relocation to work for a utility company, electrical people. After a few years he died; he was falling, they say, and to save himself he reached up and grabbed at some wires and was electrocuted on the spot. I was ten. We moved around quite a bit after that. We lived with my aunties and uncles, but there were so many of us we caused hardship, so we didn't stay in one place long. About four years later, my mother met a man somewhere when she was out drinking with her sisters. They married, but the man didn't want anything to do with us, so they sent all the kids away to live with our grandparents. By then I was seventeen, and I made up my mind to stay in the city.

While my brothers and sisters returned to the rez, I got work part-time in a candy factory, and I was doing pretty good for a while. In a few months I bought a car and I could drive all over. I drove to see my mother once at a place in San Francisco, but the visit didn't seem to mean much to her so I left. After a year or so I got letters from my grandparents here asking me to come back, but I had already decided to go to college part-time. After I wrote back to tell them about my plans, they wrote and told me I could go to school full-time with tribal funding, at a school closer to the reservation. Instead I applied and got financial aid to attend college at San Jose State the next fall. At first I wanted to study everything, but after two or three terms, a counselor told me I should consider one field. I chose drama. I felt I could act, and that if I chose many different roles maybe I'd find the one I was closest to and live it. While I was taking the drama course work, I got involved with a group of people who believed that everyone has a personal magic that they can ignore or use. We'd all meet once a week to discuss those mystical concepts and study magic. By the end of the year all but two people had dropped out of the group. So there was just me and one woman. At our last meeting she told me the only reason she stayed in the group was because she loved me. I didn't know what she meant, and I told her I thought she was a very magical person, but I didn't think I loved her. That was the last I saw of her.

But I was in love with magic. So I quit school and I went around the city seeking out magicians and gathering an assortment of tricks and teachings from each one. I also studied magic books, every one I could find. In time I knew enough to make a living from magic, with illusion and memory tricks. But I wasn't sure about things. I kept getting letters from my grandparents and my brothers and sisters. They all wanted me to return to this place, the place of my grandparents, my ancestors. One letter brought me back. My youngest sister was sick. Doctors found no cure, and she was next to death. I got in my car and drove for two days straight.

When I got to my grandparents' house they took me into the room where the girl was dying. The light was such that her head was a shadow growing up from the bed with the floral print of the sheets.

I spoke to her: "Do you know who I am? Can you see me?"

The shadow turned from the window and became a face. I knew then her eyes didn't register. I was unrecognizable, so I moved closer. Grandmother tried to pull me back.

"It's catching, trachoma," she said. "Young people all over the reservation are dying."

But the child's voice moved me forward to the edge of the bed.

"Do you know magic?" she said. "Show me some magic, brother."

"Can you see me?" I said.

"No," she said, "I can't see you, but I remember seeing you."

"Then I can't do magic."

My sister turned her head to the window; sunlight surged out over her face, soaking into her skin, lighting her clearly, as I now see her in my mind.

"I can only see light," she said.

Two days later she died. In a week I came onto the same sickness. I could feel my sight going, but it was like the going had nothing to do with what I saw or what lived outside me. My sight was going from the inside, almost backward, like the memory of the operation of the eyes left out particulars and details, like my head was shoveling the inner light I needed to see into a great mound of expanding and hungry shadows.

I asked my grandfather about magic. "We have none here," he said, "at least not the kind you know, of the hand and the eye and memory games. But there are healers among us, men and women of gifts and visions. Some are relatives of light people. Sometimes their gifts can bring people back. Quite a few people have told us not to believe in those g⁻˚s, but with all the sickness around us and no cures by the white doctors, some people have returned to these descendants of the original teachers and bringers of light."

Then the old man took me to Jake Seed and he healed me. When I was well I went to Seed again and asked if he could teach me the magic he had. He told me to come every day and he would decide if he could teach me. I went to his place every day for about four years. Then he put me through a ceremony. After days of preparation and explanation of the meaning of the ceremony, he took me way back into the woods behind his place. We walked up a hill. I dug a hole; he prayed over it and put tobacco down. I stepped down into the hole and waited. Once again he prayed. Then he put a ring of tobacco around me and buried me up to my neck.

Darkness swelled out of the earth swallowing shadows, leaving only the light of animal's eyes and distant stars to compose the sights I saw. I was not there long when animals came shining low to the ground. They moved up to my face, scratching the earth, scratching dirt into my eyes. After a while, minutes, hours, a thousand blue blinks of stars, a hundred rustlings in the trees, animals sat in a circle around me, outside the ring of tobacco, growling and moaning. Then I understood their language and I felt fear for all of creation. My thoughts raced in the darkness to find the old man, but my body was still in the hole, nervous, shivering in the cold night dirt. There was no magic to match the feeling; no illusions could pull me from the ground. I waited for power and I sang like I always do when I'm nervous. The first song came out rough, a coarse melody, bent with fear, like a sapling resisting strong wind. The deeper I went into the song the more I felt the fear slacken into a strength of human sound mixing with air and elements. Soon the animals joined in, growling to long musical howls, introspective calls and silences. My own vocals hung on for a long time; note faded into note; song faded into song. There were words and there were no words; there were sounds and there were voices from the once fearful gut, grasping each musical moment. Then, when the songs grew longer, I knew no more of the source of the memorized and invented tones. The animals left. I felt their shadows slink back out of the circle and bolt away, skittering across dirt into the leaves, into the bush. In silence and solitude, I heard footsteps behind me; then laughter careened, in a strange dance. I finally caught sight, out of the corner of my eye, of a small person. At first, I thought he was a child, but as he drew closer I knew he was a little man. He had a small drum in his hand and he sang in laughter.

Red day coming
Red boy dreams
Red day coming
over the back of clouds

Eye of the Eagle
Swift and Swallow
Red day coming Red boy sings

Then the little man stopped, turned his back to me, and he wheeled back around. He held his enormous penis in his hands and pissed on the ground in front of me, close enough that I could see steam rising from the earth and smell and feel the sprinkle of his spray as he snickered. When he finished he abused me with gruff, untranslatable language, and he kicked dirt into my face. He swung his drumstick and struck the back of my neck with a force that astonished me with pain and the little man's power. I felt the sting of the blow vibrate in violent waves down to my feet. I rocked and twisted in the hole. I screamed, wailing anger. I cried, "Go away." I called to the spirit of god for mercy. But the little man stayed. He clubbed my ears, he crapped in front of me and danced with joy at my pain and degradation. Then I gave up. "Go ahead," I said, "do what you want, I surrender." Right then, in the middle of a wild raucous dance, in the middle of his ridiculing laughter, he stopped and sang again, a song of sorrow.

sees the fading stars
sees the northern lights
sees the eyes of animals
all in the face
all in the face
the face eats
the face speaks
boy and man
the faces love
the faces love the stars
the faces love the ghost lights
the animal faces
the faces eat
the boy and man
speak and eat
the faces they love

With that the man trudged off toward a huge stone, and walked around and vanished behind it. There the sky was coming onto day, and light shone red over and through the eastern trees.

Seed came up then, carrying a basket and a piece of red material. He sat down on the ground a short distance in front of me, took out a tobacco pouch and rolled up a smoke. For a long time he said nothing. Then he got up, reached into his basket, and brought out a plate of food. I smelled the boiled potatoes, and my eyes rested on the boiled meat as he set the plate in front of me. Next to the plate he set down a glass of water. "Let the eyes drink for you. Let the eyes eat for you," he said. Then he tied the material to a tree, toward the east, about fifty feet away from where I was buried.

That day the sun burned the memory of thirst and hunger into me. I grew angry at the sun, at Seed, at myself. I tried to sing again but my throat didn't work in the heat, in dryness. Then I cried. I cried for the rest of the day until the sun went down. At night I tried to sleep, but the animals returned, encircling me and keeping me awake. Just before dawn I heard laughter. I thought of the little man again, but I couldn't see anyone or anything in any direction. At last the sun pushed out red light, and I saw out in the east, on the tree where the tobacco was tied, a woodpecker, one of those big ones, pileated. The bird was laughing, driving its beak into the tree in the dawn light. Light streamed out from each place the woodpecker struck, as if the tree held its own sun inside and the bird conducted the light of that sun out. Time and again the bird backed off, lifted away from the tree, and landed on another part of the tree to peck and strike another place from which light flowed out. One final time the bird did this. Then the bird reached into the tree with its beak and extracted the light in a long bending waving string that followed the course of its flight to where it circled me. Then the woodpecker flew down over the hill out of my sight, with the long string of golden light trailing behind it. From there I saw Seed approaching, and after he dug me out I left the hole and the hill.

By the next spring it was clear that Seed had accepted me as his helper. Through him I learned to assist with ceremonials. At the same time, I continued practicing the magic I learned in the city, among the people of the reservation and the people of nearby communities. I ran ads in local news publications, and I posted my card on bulletin boards outside grocery stores, outside the tribal offices, all over. I got a few jobs but the work wasn't steady, so I started working part-time as a janitor at the Original Man School.

Things were going well for me. I was learning and I had work; I was surviving. Then in the fall I did my magic act for a children's birthday party in a town outside the reservation, in Detroit Lakes. I performed my most difficult tricks with the most success I'd ever had. One was a mentalist memory trick through which I heard, and recited back with my eyes closed, the names and details of clothing of every person at the party. For the other most difficult trick I had the birthday child rip up a piece of his parent's most important correspondence and put the ripped pieces into a fishbowl full of water. Then I threw my magic coat over the bowl and sang.

> Sleep, peels, angles of angels sing of sign, sword of words, elm smells concrete, encore on the corner, a northern ornithologist, jest in case, sends a letter which ends in ways to sway opinion to slice the union onion with a sword of words, without tears.

After that and the conventional magical smoke, the child retrieved the letter from the family mailbox and returned to show everyone that the ripped-up correspondence was whole and dry. Everyone was impressed; I was impressed; the children were impressed; the parents were impressed.

When I returned to the reservation to see Seed, to tell him about my success, a young woman met me at his door. She told me that she was Seed's daughter, Rose Meskwaa Geeshik, that the old man was sick. She had come to see him after a violent disturbing dream and found him sweating, fevered and weak. "He's been reciting names," she said. "Oskinaway, Minogeshig, Broken Tooth, Kubbemubbe, Shagonawshee, Bwanequay, Nawawzhee, Yellowhead, Abetung, Aishkonance. He repeats the names and shivers. I don't know what it means."

In the time I worked with Seed he never mentioned any living family or any children. She took me back to see the old man. I followed her to the back bedroom. Seed slept there, on the bed, wrapped in a star blanket. Sundown named the hour in the window of the room. The songs of faraway crows coruscated into the room in sundown angles. I spoke to him. "Seed," I said, "it's me, Boozhoo. How are you? Seed, wake up; I need to speak to you." For a long time there was no answer. Darkness worked into the room and only an occasional cigarette, the flare of a match, touched off any semblance of sight. After a time Rose asked me to pray with her for Seed. She called on grandfathers, the creator; she spoke of her love for the old man. Her eyes squeezed tight in the intensity of her thought.

> Creator bring him back to us
> he is far away now within the sight of ancestors
> their arms are open across the silver river
> there are giants and abysmal sorrows in the river
> Some of us will float over
> Some of us will find the water solid beneath our feet
> Some will step on the backs of the giants and slide away
> into an angry foam
> Some will sink straight down into a place
> where the river has no bottom.
> O creator do not take the man
> Dear ancestors sing a song that tells it is not time
> turn him back to us with your song
> Let Seed return to earth
> Let the skies drench him again
> Let him know again the fragrances of the great mother earth
> Let him draw his strength from the love that is here
> in my heart.

Rose prayed on and on, crying off and on between the words, at times screaming out into the darkness of the room, with a voice and a hope powerful enough to wake the most distant sleeping star. Still Seed didn't move; his face showed no change. Rose prayed on and on. I wanted to stay awake to help her, but only fear ever kept me from sleeping and at that time I felt no fear: maybe it was Rose's voice, maybe it was the strength I'd seen in Seed in times past, but I felt no fear.

Somehow I have come to sit on a log. After thinking I am asleep, I understand I am awake when a yellow dog crosses in front of me. Voices inside the log tell me I

must learn to fly. So I make a man out of tall grass and call him by my own name.
Then I throw him into the air and a whirlwind of leaves and human voices carries
the grass man away.

Rose woke me at dawn with a gentle hand on my shoulder. "Have some coffee," she said, offering me a yellow cup. "He'll be okay, now."

I took the coffee cup from her. "Where's the old man?" I said.

"Sleeping still, but he's okay. I think the fever is gone. He woke up for a few minutes, but he needs rest. You go wash up; I'll fix some breakfast. Then you can go home and get some rest. Come back later; he said he wants to speak to you."

"No," I said. "I'll stay for a while; I can watch him while you get some rest. He's been good to me, I'll stay."

Then I got up and went to the washbowl. There was no water, so I walked outside and worked the pump until water flowed out into the white bowl. When I came back inside Rose had breakfast ready. The table was set with eggs and fried potatoes, frybread, strawberry jam and honey. Rose poured another cup of coffee for me, and we both ate heartily. After breakfast I went out to the front porch to smoke. The sun had cleared the tallest trees of the reservation by then, and I could hear voices on the road to the church hall. As I lit a cigarette Rose came out and sat down beside me.

"Go inside," I said. "I'll watch the old man as soon as I'm done here."

She looked out into the trees as wisps of black hair licked the bones of her chin and grazed the flatness of her cheek. "I don't know if I can sleep," she said. "I keep hearing the voices out here, I keep thinking of my father, this whole place. You know, where we all come from."

POETRY

Mary TallMountain

(b. 1918) Athabaskan

Mary TallMountain was born in Nulato, Territory of Alaska, in 1918. She is Koyukon Athabaskan, and traces her descent to Russian, Scottish, and Irish ancestors. Her poetry and stories have been published in many anthologies. She lives in San Francisco. **There Is No Word for Goodbye**, her book of poems, was published by Blue Cloud Quarterly Press in 1982. The book was awarded a Pushcart Prize. "The Sinh of Niguudzagha," a short story, was published in **Earth Power Coming**, edited by Simon Ortiz.

"Alaska is my talisman, my strength, my spirit's home. Despite loss and disillusion, I count myself rich, fertile, and magical," she wrote in an autobiographical essay published in **I Tell You Now**. "I tell you now. You can go home again."

"The Yukon River was an unbearable sight," she wrote. The bush plane turned, and she closed her eyes. "There it was again, that sound I had been hearing for fifty years. At last I knew what it was. The river was speaking to me." She remembered the

> day in 1924 when I had left Nulato.... Like the shadows, it was gone now. All except these rare quick clips of vision. Yet there was a knowledge in me that I had been close to this certain earth in another life, far beyond childhood, an existence as old as the river....

> Mary Joe Demoski was Athabaskan and Russian, and the soldier Clem Stroup was my Irish and Scots father. They had ten years together and two children. The U.S. Army and the Catholic church would not let them marry. Mary Joe developed tuberculosis, as rampant and fatal as a plague. Doctor Randle ordered bed rest, and his wife Agnes took care of my little brother, Billy, and me. We were only two and three years old when we were told the Randles wanted us to be their children. Adoption of native children by Anglos was rare. Angrily, the village disputed the adoption, and the Anglos censured it. Relationships were embittered. Trying to yield to both factions, the village council said, "Girl go Outside with white doctor. Mary Joe keep Billy. Later he hunt and fish with his uncle." The separation would be the first of a series of calamities afflicting me during the coming years.

There Is No Word for Goodbye

Sokoya, I said, looking through
    the net of wrinkles into
    wise black pools
    of her eyes.

What do you say in Athabaskan
    when you leave each other?

What is the word
for goodbye?

A shade of feeling rippled
        the wind-tanned skin.
        Ah, nothing, she said,
        watching the river flash.

She looked at me close.
        We just say, Tlaa. That means,
        See you.
        We never leave each other.
        When does your mouth
        say goodbye to your heart?

She touched me light
        as a bluebell.
        You forget when you leave us;
        you're so small then.
        We don't use that word.

We always think you're coming back,
        but if you don't,
        we'll see you someplace else.
        You understand.
        There is no word for goodbye.

Maurice Kenny

(b. 1929) Mohawk

Maurice Kenny was born in Watertown, New York, in 1929. He is mixedblood and traces his descent to the Mohawk. His poems and stories have been published in many books and anthologies, including **From the Belly of the Shark**, edited by Walter Lowenfels; **The Remembered Earth**, edited by Geary Hobson; **Earth Power Coming**, edited by Simon Ortiz, **Words in the Blood**, edited by Jamake Highwater; and **Songs from This Earth on Turtle's Back**, *edited* by Joseph Bruchac.

Dancing Back Strong the Nation *was published by Blue Cloud Quarterly Press in 1979.* **Blackrobe**, *a collection of his poems, was published in 1982.* **The Mama Poems** *received the American Book Award in 1982.* **Rain and Other Fictions** *was published in 1985.* **Greyhounding This America** *was published the following year, and* **Between Two Rivers: Selected Poems** *was published in 1987. Kenny is the founder and editor of the Strawberry Press, which publishes poetry by Native Americans.*

"I have hunted not only words and images, metaphors, but, to my mother's relish, also song," *he wrote in an autobiographical essay in* **I Tell You Now**.

> I have heard the cedar sing, I have listened to the white pine, I have imitated white-tail deer and hawk and cocked an ear even to the more plain song of robin, a running brook, chicory weaving on summer....
>
> So where is this place that I write of? Is it the foothills of the Adirondacks, the Lake Ontario summer cabin, my aunt's farm on Fox Creek Road, the reservation on the St. Lawrence River; is it the woods or the fields growing strawberries so sweet to the tongue? Is it where I was born, where my first cry rent the night of that hot August; is it the Brooklyn apartment I share with my cat Sula: is it Kaherawaks, my surrogate granddaughter at Akwesasne; or is it a stuffy bus traveling the night highways across turtle's back? It is all of these places and things.

Kenny wrote in **I Tell You Now** *that he started the poem "Wild Strawberry" in the winter of 1978. He was ill at the time, living in Brooklyn Heights in New York City.*

> A close friend and nearby neighbor had the goodness of heart and thought to bring to my sick bed a basket of cultivated strawberries. Helene knew my fondness for the fruit and just how important the strawberry is to me and my poetry. The wild strawberry is not only the first natural fruit of the eastern spring, but it is the symbol of life to Iroquois people. The strawberry holds strong significance for all the people of the Six Nations and for me as a person, as a Mohawk writer, and as both editor and publisher. In 1976 I established Strawberry Press to be an exclusively Native American press to publish the poetry and art of Native.... The wild strawberry was given to us by the "little people" who live in a quarry, for the pleasure of eating and to be used in a healing ceremony.

Wild Strawberry

for Helene

And I rode the Greyhound down to Brooklyn
where I sit now eating woody strawberries
grown on the backs of Mexican farmers
imported from the fields of their hands,
juices without color or sweetness

      my wild blood berries of spring meadows
      sucked by June bees and protected by hawks
      have stained my face and honeyed
      my tongue ... healed the sorrow in my flesh

      vines crawl across the grassy floor
      of the north, scatter to the world
      seeking the light of the sun and innocent
      tap of the rain to feed the roots
      and bud small white flowers that in June
      will burst fruit and announce spring
      when wolf will drop winter fur
      and wrens will break the egg

      my blood, blood berries that brought laughter
      and the ache in the stooped back that vied
      with dandelions for the plucking,
      and the wines nourished our youth and heralded
      iris, corn and summer melon

      we fought bluebirds for the seeds
      armed against garter snakes, field mice;
      won the battle with the burning sun
      which blinded our eyes and froze our hands
      to the vines and the earth where knees knelt
      and we laughed in the morning dew like worms
      and grubs; we scented age and wisdom

my mother wrapped the wounds of the world
with a sassafras poultice and we ate
wild berries with their juices running
down the roots of our mouths and our joy

I sit here in Brooklyn eating Mexican
berries which I did no pick, nor do
I know the hands which did, nor their stories...
January snow falls, listen

Jim Barnes

(b. 1933) Choctaw

Jim Barnes was born near Summerfield in the hill country of eastern Oklahoma in 1933. He is Choctaw and was raised in Choctaw country, and traces some of his ancestors to the Welsh. He studied at Southeastern Oklahoma State University and earned his doctorate in literature from the University of Arkansas. He is a professor of comparative literature at Northeast Missouri State University in Kirksville. Barnes is founder and editor of the **Chariton Review**.

The American Book of the Dead, *an esteemed collection of poems, was published by the University of Illinois Press in 1982.* **A Season of Loss** *appeared three years later, and* **La Plata Cantata** *was published in 1989. His poems have appeared in many journals. Barnes won a National Endowment for the Arts Creative Writing Fellowship in Poetry in 1978, and a Translation Award from the Translation Center of Columbia University in 1980. He translated and published* **Summons and Signs: Poems of Dagmar Nick**.

LaVonne Ruoff wrote in **Native American Literatures** *that Barnes is one of the*

> *most highly polished.... [His poetry is characterized] by penetrating personal observations and a strong sense of place expressed in language of crystalline purity. Many of his poems are descriptive-reflective, celebrating what Wordsworth calls "spots of time" associated with specific places.*

"I was five years old the last time I heard the mountain lion scream," Barnes wrote in an autobiographical essay in **I Tell You Now**.

> *That was in Oklahoma, 1938, when times were hard and life was good—and sacred. But a year later the [Works Progress Administration] had done its work: roads were cut, burial mounds were dug, small concrete dams were blocking nearly every stream. The Government was caring for its people. Many were the make-work jobs. A man could eat again, while all about him the land suffered. The annual spring migration of that lone panther was no more. The riverbanks that had been his roads and way stations bore the scars of the times, the scars of loss.*

> *In my mind the rivers must always run free. But in truth today I do not recognize them. They are alien bodies on a flattening land where everything has been made safe, civilized into near extinction. Sounds of speedboats drown out the call of the remaining jays and crows. The din of highway traffic carries for miles now that the timber has fallen to chainsaw or chemical rot. Green silence in the heavy heat of summer afternoons is no more.*

Barnes was born near the Fourche Maline River,

> *on a meadow in a house that no longer stands. A lone clump of gnarled sassafras and oak rises out of the meadow a short mile northeast of Summerfield, in the hill country of eastern Oklahoma, where the land was once heavy with wood and*

game. Nobody knows why the clump of trees was not cut down when the land was first cleared for the plow. Once there was a house a few feet east of the trees....

I am proud of the Choctaw blood I carry, and I am equally proud of the Welsh blood in my veins. But I object to the term regional writer *or* ethnic writer *or even* Native American writer, *though it may apply to a number of us in a general sense. As a magazine editor and lover of good literature, I don't care who writes the poem, where it is written, or what it is written about. Whenever the universal grows out of the specific and vision is achieved, you can tell yourself here is art and it should be preserved.*

The Sawdust War

On the early summer days I lay with back
against the sawdust pile and felt the heat
of a thousand pines, oaks, elms, sycamores
flowing into my flesh, my nose alive
with that peculiar smell of death the trees
became. Odd to me then how the summer rain
made the heat even more intense. Digging
down the dust, I began to reshape a world
I hardly knew; the crumbly terrain became
theaters of the war. I was barely ten.

What I knew of the wide world and real war
came down the valley's road or flew over
the mountains I was caught between. Remote
I was nightly glued to the radio,
wondering at reports of a North African
campaign and Europe falling into chaos.
All daylight long I imitated what I
thought I heard, molding sawdust into hills,
roads, rivers, displacing troops of toys,
claiming ground by avalanche and mortar

fire, advancing bravely into black cities,
shrouding the fallen heroes with white bark.
I gained good ground against the Axis through
long summer days. Then one morning, dressed in

drab for hard work of war, I saw real smoke
rising from my battlefield. Crawling from
beneath the sawdust like vague spiderwebs,
claiming first the underground, then foxholes,
it spread like a wave of poison gas across
the woody hills I shaped with a mason's trowel.

I could not see the fire: it climbed from deep
within. No matter how I dug or shifted dust,
I could not find the source. My captured ground
nightly sank into itself. The gray smoke
hovered like owls under the slow stillness
of stars, until one night I woke to see,
at the center, a circle of smoldering sparks
turning to flame, ash spreading outward and down.
All night the pile glowed red, and I grew ashamed
for some fierce reason I could not then name.

Under the Tent

The traveling show stretched its canvas
over the bluegrass behind the store
when we were ten, the last picture
shows we'd get to see during the war

the Axis forced on us. We crouched
by the flapping tent. The summer wind
at night was mischief in our heads,
blowing wild thyme in our hair. Then

we were full of war, those of us
too young to go. We claimed to know
all battlegrounds through hell and back.
What we wanted to do was throw

enough of the dark upon our skins
to slip beneath all tents unseen,
as the night patrol did in the film
we saw that summer before the end.

We had to time it right: to roll
exactly under the tent the way
you roll away from quick danger
in your sleep. Or we'd have to play

the fool when the tentwalker caught
us by the neck. Our detailed plan
precise, we penetrated the held
blackness the exact moment when
all that I, soaring, had heard before. Numb
with the wild thrill of flight, that day I found
I had my war and rode the treetop down

through the tops of lesser trees to parachute
onto the alien earth that was my home.
My name would ride the sky filled with the drone
of planes. And I knew, when the night grew mute
with stars, part of me would still be up there,
loving the war, loving the dumbness of air.

The Cabin on Nanny Ridge

For days we felled the yellow pines
and shouldered them to the clearing we
had made at the rim of the ridge and swore
the way mountain men had done. Time
backed for us: we sang Cherokee
and Choctaw hymns, thatched the roof more

with words than limbs and needles from
the pines. We were innocent of all
that we surveyed. The world at war
was far enough away no bombs
that they told us fell could fall.
We lived without clock time, not sure

of the past we recreated or of
the squadrons daily overhead.
We lived the strategies we planned.

The days of summer when Europe
burned, we graved our dreamtime deeds
as runes below our small traced hands

on the stone north face of Nanny Ridge.
Forty years have grayed the glyphs,
and of the cabin nothing remains
but worms and a slow memory
of days we thought would never end—
before other wars changed our lives.

Diane Glancy

(b. 1941) Cherokee

Diane Glancy was born in Kansas City, Missouri, in 1941. She is Cherokee, and has maternal ancestors who are English and German. Glancy studied at the University of Missouri and at Central State University in Edmond, Oklahoma. She earned a master of fine arts degree at the University of Iowa, and now teaches creative writing at Macalester College in Saint Paul, Minnesota.

Glancy's poems and stories have been published in many anthologies. **Brown Wolf Leaves the Res**, her first collection of poems, was published by Blue Cloud Quarterly Press in 1984. Her poems appeared in **Songs from This Earth on Turtle's Back**, edited by Joseph Bruchac. **Trigger Dance**, her first collection of stories, won the Nilon Minority Fiction Award in 1990. **Lone Dog's Winter Count**, her fourth collection of poems, was published in 1991. **Claiming Breath**, autobiographical prose poems, won the North American Indian Prose Award and was published by the University of Nebraska Press in 1992. **Firesticks**, a collection of stories, was published in the American Indian Literature and Critical Studies series by the University of Oklahoma Press in 1993. "Lead Horse," a short story, was published in **Earth Song, Sky Spirit**, edited by Clifford Trafzer.

"I was raised by an English-German mother. My father, one-quarter Cherokee, was there also, but it was my mother who presented her white part of my heritage as a whole," she wrote in an autobiographical essay in **I Tell You Now**.

> When I was growing up, everything was done in order. It was the influence of my mother. My socks were folded and in their place in the chest of drawers, and my bed was made. Outwardly I was orderly, but inside I was Indian. I have a fierce shyness. I recognize the Great Spirit in all things. I speak to animals and rocks. And though the Cherokees are more sedentary than other tribes, I must travel now and then. In my spirit dreams, chevrons of geese and wild herds of striped antelope crawl up the back wall of my head.

> Still, I know little of my Indian heritage.... In my Christian faith, God is the Great Spirit, the Father. Jesus Christ is the son, the opening, the door. I see Christ standing on the prairie with his arms outstretched in love. A hole clear through his chest where his heart would be because this is what he lost when he was flesh in the world. When he was on earth, he was broken and fragmented like the Indian.

Glancy wrote in **Claiming Breath** that the

> direct line to my Indian heritage had been lost.... I often write about being in the middle ground between two cultures, not fully a part of either. I write with a split voice, often experimenting with language until the parts equal some sort of a whole....

> I think poetry evolves out of ordinary circumstance—the ideas I write about often come from the hardness of prairie life. Poetry is road maintenance for a fragmented world which seeks to be kept together.

SHEdonism

I have a poem called 'Dead Wood': 'At night I hear the breath of wolves \ Eee por tay. The limbs that whack my \ head. I chop the darkness for firewood.\ Dreams tug at my head. My father's \ death, my mother's illness, my son's \ surgeries, my husband's absences. It \ would make sense to let go. But when I \ wake in the night in a sweat, still \ driving the stage to Dead Wood, I think, \ this is what it's like to be a man.' It's a prose poem so the line breaks aren't that important. But what is, is the realization that without thinking I equate a responsible human being with the male gender. And even after I've done it, it doesn't bother me enough to make me change the poem. Let it be. It says what I felt when I wrote it.

I suppose it's because I'm from a generation whose mothers were homebound. It was my father who was the center of energy for the family. While he was at work and we were at school, my fretful, punctual mother waxed floors and baked cookies. She endured her isolation with complaint if I remember correctly. For most of those years she didn't have a car and even after she did and we were grown, she still stayed at home and felt uncomfortable with the freedom to be her own person. In fact, I don't think she ever made it to herself.

It was to my benefit to learn the agonies of that journey—that pulling off of adhesive that had been stuck there so long. In my case, it happened in the very beginning. Marriage was not the 'center' for my definition of self. It was painful. My husband traveled and drank a great deal. I received no comfort from him. I had the responsibility of keeping the house and family together and I did it for 19 years, most of which I wanted to leave. I also got my M.A. and taught writing during those years. Now I'm finally on my own. But it's not a woman's relationship to a man or the absence of that relationship that defines a woman. It's what the woman is to herself.

Being a minority also enlarged my difficulties. Maybe it's the reason I stayed married so long. I didn't know what else to do. In fact, it was all I could do for a while. I didn't fit into the structure of school. I always felt unworthy of what I wrote. It has taken YEARS to find my way. But my Native American heritage is also a strength (especially the images I get from it for writing). So my structure has always been one of conflict and ambivalence. Aren't all of us made of paradox and diversity, anger, hurt, hope, guilt, endurance? Aren't we all fragments of opposition, especially women? A composite for which we have to provide the connecting threads.

In an essay called 'Fragments \ Shards' (about the journey to the ani-yun-wiyu, or 'real people'), I called this existence, 'SHEdonism': the enjoyment of oneself as a woman. It includes the ability to sort through things and live with dichotomy, even in a world that has its own fragments and conflicts.

I think you can be your own person even in a situation you don't like. Many times I felt powerless at the moment as a woman with the responsibility of family and with the negative aspects of the Native American heritage, but inside, I dreamed and felt the presence of myself even when it was fretful, stressed and impatient. What I've ended up with over the years is myself as a friend.

I also learned independence as I taught writing. Isn't writing thinking? Aren't our lives made up of words? The ability to write clearly is the ability to think clearly. So I used exercises for both creative and essay or idea-transferring writing: thinking through the situation, organizing it, writing it clearly. Externalizing the thought process. Finding form for content. Using language for creative, expressive purposes. The revelation of words, their boldness, the imaginative impact of combined images, of seeing familiar in a new way. That's what writing is. That's what living is. That's probably what feminism is.

Simon Ortiz

(b. 1941) Acoma Pueblo

Simon Ortiz was born in Albuquerque, New Mexico, in 1941. He was raised in the Acoma Pueblo. As a child he attended St. Catherine's Indian School. He served in the military and graduated from the University of New Mexico and the writing program at the University of Iowa. He has taught creative writing and native literature at several institutions, including the Navajo Community College and Sinte Gleska College in South Dakota. His poems and short stories have appeared in numerous journals, and he has published many books. The voices in his poems and stories are visual, a natural inspiration of the oral tradition.

Joseph Bruchac asked him about language and writing in an interview published in **Survival This Way**. *Ortiz said that you learn language by*

> *listening as an experience. Listening not really to find any secrets or sudden enlightenment, but to be improved with that whole process and experience, that whole process and experience of language. That's the way we understand how we are, who we are, what we know, what we'll come to know. So, when I look at language in terms of writing, it's the language itself I'm concerned with, not that those symbols on a printed page have any meaning. What I try to be aware of is its core nature, the basic elements of language itself. So that writing is a furtherance or continuation of what is spoken, of what is emotion in terms of sound, meaning, magic, perception, reality.*

Ortiz kept a diary, "a journal of sorts," he said, when he left home and attended St. Catherine's Indian School. The journal was a secret, but it was his beginning as a writer. "Although my diary contained no more than inane items such as my adolescent yearnings, loneliness and my sorrows and joys, I became aware of literature and began to acquire a conscious awareness of what writing was."

Going for the Rain, *a collection of poems, was published in 1976.* **A Good Journey** *appeared in 1977,* **From Sand Creek** *in 1981, and* **Fightin': New and Collected Stories** *was published in 1983. Ortiz edited* **Earth Power Coming**, *an anthology of short fiction published by Navajo Community College Press in 1983.*

Ortiz wrote in an autobiographical essay in **I Tell You Now** *that he published his first poem in the Skull Valley School newsletter on the occasion of Mother's Day. He was in the fifth grade at the time.*

> *My love of language, which allowed me to deal with the world, to delve into it, to experiment and discover, held for me a vision of awe and wonder, and by then grammar teachers had noticed I was a good speller, used verbs and tenses correctly, and wrote complete sentences. Although I imagine that they might have surmised this as unusual for an Indian student whose original language was not English, I am grateful for their perception and attention.*

LaVonne Ruoff noted in **American Indian Literatures** *that*

> **From Sand Creek** *is an affecting collection of poems that commemorates the massacre of the peaceful Cheyenne and Arapaho at Sand Creek, Colorado, in*

1864. Balancing brief commentary with examples, Ortiz describes how the land and its native peoples have been destroyed or demoralized by the dominant society. He particularly memorializes the Indian veterans who suffer from physical and psychological wounds inflicted during America's wars.

A Story of How a Wall Stands

At Acu, there is a wall almost 400 years old which supports hundreds of tons of dirt and bones—it's a graveyard built on a steep incline—and it looks like it's about to fall down the incline but will not for a long time.

My father, who works with stone,
says, "that's just the part you see,
the stones which seem to be
just packed in on the outside,"
and with his hands puts the stone and mud
in place. "Underneath
what looks like loose stone,
there is stone woven together."
He ties one hand over the other,
fitting like the bones of his hands
and fingers. "That's what is
holding it together."

"It is built that carefully,"
he says, "the mud mixed
to a certain texture," patiently
"with the fingers," worked
in the palm of his hand. "So that
placed between the stones, they hold
together for a long, long time."

He tells me those things,
the story of them worked
with his fingers, in the palm
of his hands, working the stone
and the mud until they become
the wall that stands a long, long time.

My Father's Song

Wanting to say things,
I miss my father tonight.
His voice, the slight catch,
the depth from his thin chest,
the tremble of emotion
in something he has just said
to his son, his song:

We planted corn one spring at Acu—
we planted several times
but this one particular time
I remember the soft damp sand
in my hand.

My father had stopped at one point
to show me an overturned furrow,
the plowshare had unearthed
the burrow nest of a mouse
in the soft moist sand.

Very gently, he scooped tiny pink animals
into the palm of his hand
and told me to touch them.
We took them to the edge
of the field and put them in the shade
of a sand moist clod.

I remember the very softness
of cool and warm sand and tiny alive mice
and my father saying things.

[Grief]

Grief
memorizes this grass.
Raw
courage,
        believe it,
red-eyed and urgent,
stalking Denver.
Like stone,
like steel,
the hone and sheer gone,
just the brute
and perceptive angle left.

Like courage,

believe it,

left still;
the words from then
talk like that.

Believe it.

Linda Hogan

(b. 1947) Chickasaw

Linda Hogan is mixedblood Chickasaw, born in Denver, Colorado, in 1947. She was raised in Oklahoma, studied at the University of Colorado, and has taught at the University of Minnesota and the University of Colorado. Her poems and stories have been published in many journals and anthologies, and she has received many awards, including the Guggenheim, the National Endowment for the Arts, and the American Book Award.

Calling Myself Home, recollections of family and identity, was published in 1978. **Daughters, I Love You** appeared in 1981, **Eclipse** two years later, **Seeing Through the Sun** in 1985, and **Savings** in 1988. **Mean Spirit**, her first novel, was published in 1990. **The Book of Medicines** was published in 1993.

"Hogan often incorporates a feminist perspective in her verse through descriptions of women's lives and feelings," LaVonne Ruoff wrote in **American Indian Literatures.** "Many of her poems focus on the power and beauty of nature, which Hogan often uses as a metaphor for life."

"When I began to write," Hogan wrote in an autobiographical essay in **I Tell You Now,**

> I wrote partly to put this life in order, partly because I was too shy to speak. I was silent and the poems spoke first. I was ignorant and the poems educated me. When I realized that people were going to read the poems, I thought of the best ways to use words, how great was my responsibility to transmit words, ideas, and acts by which we could live with liberation, love, self-respect, good humor, and joy. In learning that, I also had to offer up our pain and grief and sorrow, because I know that denial and repression are the greatest hindrances to liberation and growth.

The New Apartment, Minneapolis

The floorboards creak.
The moon is on the wrong side of the building,

and burns remain
on the floor.

The house wants to fall down
the universe when earth turns.

It still holds the coughs of old men
and their canes tapping on the floor.

I think of Indian people here before me
and how last spring white merchants hung an elder
on a meat hook and beat him;
he was one of The People.

I remember this war
and all the wars

and relocation like putting the moon in prison
with no food and that moon was a crescent

but be warned, the moon grows full again
and the roofs of this town are all red

and we are looking through the walls of houses
at people suspended in air.

Some are baking, with flour on their hands,
or sleeping on floor three, or getting drunk.

I see the businessmen who hit their wives
and the men who are tender fathers.

There are women crying or making jokes.
Children are laughing under beds.

Girls in navy blue robes talk on the phone all night
and some Pawnee is singing 49s, drumming the table.

Inside the walls
world changes are planned, bosses overthrown.

If we had no coffee,
cigarettes or liquor,

says the woman in room 12,
they'd have a revolution on their hands.

Beyond walls are lakes and plains,
canyons and the universe;

the stars are the key
turning in the lock of night.

Turn the deadbolt and I am home.
I have walked to the dark earth,

opened a door to nights where there are no apartments,
just drumming and singing;

The Duck Song, The Snake Song,
The Drunk Song.

No one here remembers the city
or has ever lost the will to go on.

Hello aunt, hello brothers, hello trees
and deer walking quietly on the soft red earth.

The Truth Is

In my left pocket a Chickasaw hand
rests on the bone of the pelvis.
In my right pocket
a white hand. Don't worry. It's mine
and not some thief's.
It belongs to a woman who sleeps in a twin bed
even though she falls in love too easily,
and walks along with hands
in her own empty pockets
even though she has put them in others
for love not money.

About the hands, I'd like to say
I am a tree, grafted branches
bearing two kinds of fruit,

apricots maybe and pit cherries.
It's not that way. The truth is
we are crowded together
and knock against each other at night.
We want amnesty.

Linda, girl, I keep telling you
this is nonsense
about who loved who
and who killed who.

Here I am, taped together
like some old civilian conservation corps
passed by from the great depression
and my pockets are empty.
It's just as well since they are masks
for the soul, and since coins and keys
both have the sharp teeth of property.

Return: Buffalo

One man made a ladder
of stacked-up yellow bones
to climb the dead
toward his own salvation.
he wanted
light and fire, wanted
to reach and be close to his god.

But his god was the one
who opened his shirt
and revealed the scar of mortal climbing.

It is the scar
that lives in the house with me.
It goes to work with me.
It is the people I have loved
who fell

into the straight, unhealed
line of history.
It is a brother
who heard the bellowing cry of sacred hills
when nothing was there
but stories and rocks.

It was what ghost dancers heard
in their dream
of bringing buffalo down from the sky
as if song and prayer
were paths life would follow back
to land.

And the old women, they say,
would walk that land,
pick through bones for hide, marrow,
anything that could be used
or eaten.
Once they heard a terrible moan
and stood back,
and one was not dead
or it had come back from there,
walked out of the dark mountains
of rotted flesh and bony fur,
like a prophet
coming out from the hills
with a vision
too unholy to tell.

It must have traveled the endless journey
of fear,
returned from the far reaches
where men believed the world was flat
and they would fall over
its sharp edge
into pitiless fire,

and they must have thought
how life came together
was a casual matter,
war a righteous sin,
and betrayal
wasn't a round, naked thing
that would come back to them
one day.

Roberta Hill Whiteman

(b. 1947) Oneida

Roberta Hill Whiteman was born in 1947. She is Oneida and was raised near Green Bay, Wisconsin. She studied at the University of Wisconsin, the University of Montana, and the University of Minnesota. She teaches at the University of Wisconsin. She is married to the native artist Ernest Whiteman.

Star Quilt was published in 1984. Her poems have been published in many journals and anthologies. Whiteman has received numerous awards for her poetry, including a grant from the National Endowment for the Arts.

LaVonne Ruoff wrote in American Indian Literatures that Star Quilt is a "highly imaginative work" that demonstrates "a keen attention to detail and descriptive power." The images in her poems are delicate and empowered with lightning at the same time. She has a sure sense of nature in her poems.

Star Quilt

These are notes to lightning in my bedroom.
A star forged from linen thread and patches.
Purple, yellow, red like diamond suckers, children

of the star gleam on sweaty nights. The quilt unfolds
against sheets, moving, warm clouds of Chinook.
It covers my cuts, my red birch clusters under pine.

Under it your mouth begins a legend,
and wide as the plain, I hope Wisconsin marshes
promise your caress. The candle locks

us in forest smells, your cheek tattered
by shadow. Sweetened by wings, my mothlike heart
flies nightly among geraniums.

We know of land that looks lonely,
but isn't, of beef with hides of velveteen,
of sorrow, and eddy in blood.

Star quilt, sewn from dawn light by fingers
of flint, take away those touches
meant for noisier skins,

anoint us with grass and twilight air,
so we may embrace, two bitter roots
pushing back into the dust.

Wendy Rose

(b. 1948) Hopi/Miwok

Wendy Rose was born in Oakland, California, in 1948. She is a mighty, incisive poet with an invincible vision and sense of chance in native literature. Rose has published more than a dozen books of poetry. **Hopi Roadrunner Dancing** *was published by Greenfield Review Press in 1973.* **Lost Copper**, *a collection of poems, was published in 1980.* **The Halfbreed Chronicles** *was published by West End Press in 1985. Her poems have appeared in many anthologies, including* **Carriers of the Dream Wheel, The Remembered Earth,** *and* **Words in the Blood. Bone Dance: New and Selected Poems, 1965–1993**, *her most recent book, was published in the Sun Tracks American Indian Literacy series by the University of Arizona Press in 1994.*

Wendy Rose "creates both delicate lyrics and harsh protest poems," LaVonne Ruoff wrote in **American Indian Literatures**. *Many poems in the collection* **Lost Copper** *"deal with Hopi traditions or Rose's search for her Hopi roots."*

"Today I live about fifty miles from Bear Valley," California, she wrote in an autobiographical essay in **I Tell You Now**.

As I write, it is early August and the days are valley-hot, the nights thickly warm and filled with crickets. Although last winter was dry, this summer has found an explosion of toads in my yard. To uncover the memories, I have peeled back layers of scar tissue. I have invoked the ghosts and made them work for me. Is that the answer? To keep them busy? There is nothing authentic or nice about my past; I am sure that I would be a great disappointment to anthropologists....

My father told me ... that Hopi earth does contain my roots and I am, indeed, from that land. Because the roots are there, I will find them. But when I find them, he said, I must rebuild myself as a Hopi. I am not merely a conduit, but a participant. I am not a victim, but a woman.

I am building myself.
There are many roots.
I plant, I pick, I prune.
I consume....

Without a Hopi mother, I am not even part of a clan. Learning all of this had a great deal to do with my writing of poetry. How can you hope to speak if you have no voice? Neither castoffs, nor mongrels, nor assimilated sellouts, nor traditionalists, those who are like me are fulfilling in our own way a certain level of existence, a pattern in the prophecy. We must be here, though we cannot be soldiers or shields for those who are so much stronger than we are. We merely face the same enemy.

Why does the daughter of natives and strangers, gold miners and ranchers, write poetry? I can only mark certain times in my life when writing poetry was really

*the logical thing to do. For instance, there was a time when what I knew could
have burst from inside of me in other ways.*

To Some Few Hopi Ancestors

No longer the drifting
and falling of wind,
your songs have changed;
they have become
thin willow whispers
that take us by the ankle
and tangle us up
with red mesa stone,
that keep us turned
to the round sky,
that follow us down
to Winslow, to Sherman,
To Oakland, to all the spokes
that leave Earth's middle.
You have engraved yourself
with holy signs, encased yourself
in pumice, hammered on my bones
till you could no longer hear
the howl of the missions
slipping screams through your silence,
dropping dreams from your wings.
      Is this why
      you made me
      sing and weep
      for you?
Like butterflies
made to grow another way
this woman is chiseled
on the face of your world.
The badger-claw of her father
shows slightly in the stone
burrowed from her sight,
facing west from home.

Is It Crazy to Want to Unravel

like a dandelion gone to seed,
leaving nothing behind but a dent
or not even that to touch or burn
or remember. This is the way
winter begins—
        with the angry moth
        who grips the window screen
        and freezes into an opal.
        Well, that's one way to go—
        just get harder. Or I could dissolve
        as disobedient women do in the Bible
        their solemn salt hands still pointing
        to the pleasures of sin.
        I could evaporate or liquify
        or become dust or turn sideways
        before a funhouse mirror
        to become a needle
        becoming nothing.
I could scream so mightily
that only sound would survive.
I could cry myself dry,
be sifted by the desert wind
that burns my summer gold hills.
Or I could fly apart
        and watch my whirling blood
        form galaxies in the air,
        spatter on the men
        who hammer to death
        the trees and remark
        that a woman just
        was standing there
and now
poof she is gone.

For the White Poets
Who Would Be Indian

just once
just long enough
to snap up the words
fish-hooked
from our tongues.
You think of us now
when you kneel
on the earth,
turn holy
in a temporary tourism
of our souls.
With words
you paint your faces.
chew your doeskin,
touch breast to tree
as if sharing a mother
were all it takes,
could bring
instant and primal
of knowledge.
You think of us only
when your voice
wants for roots,
when you have sat back
on your heels
and become primitive.
You finish your poem
and go back.

Ray Young Bear

(b. 1950) Mesquakie

Ray Young Bear was born in Tama, Iowa, in 1950. He is a native speaker and member of the Mesquakie, or Sauk, and Fox. His poems have been published in numerous anthologies, including **Carriers of the Dream Wheel**, **Voices of the Rainbow**, *and* **The Remembered Earth**.

"In **Winter of the Salamander**, *the poet uses the tribal and contemporary influences on his life to examine the nature of humans and their relation to the landscape," LaVonne Ruoff wrote in* **American Indian Literatures**. *"His evocations of experiences and places are often combined with vision and dream so that the real and the unreal merge."*

Joseph Bruchac noted in **Survival This Way** *that*

> *Young Bear's poetry has a dual quality of powerful statement and mystery which seems to emanate from the earth itself. Perhaps this is because he is so involved in that Mesquakie community, long known for its closeness and its ties to traditional native culture.*

poem for viet nam

i will always miss the feeling
of friday on my mind.
the umbrella somewhere
in the dumps of south
viet nam. in exchange
for candy it will hide
the helicopter.
franco must be here
in a guy's heart. i've
heard so much about him.
the closer i got was when
i machine-gunned
the people waist deep
inside the brown speckled
swamp. the castle where we drank
the sweet wine from giant fish bowls
has come against us. we knew that
when we killed them they tasted
the blood of whoever stood
beside them. some of us

thought of our families.
the cactus warms in our
bodies. the old mansion
where his friend played
cards has murdered his
brother and we see the stabbing
right through the door. while
i ran i made a song from
my wind. i have not held
this god beside me. only
this rock that i've often
heard about stays and at times
feel it must be true. his words
are like my dreams. they are eating
balls of rice in front of us.
i heard them talking a couple
of yards ahead of us. the jets flew
in v formation and they reminded me
of the wild ducks back home. once,
when i looked down, my wrists opened
and i wiped the blood on a tree.
i can only sit there and imagine,
they were ear close. the next day
i wore their severed fingers
on my belt. my little brother
and i hunted while someone close
was being buried on the same hill
where we will end. we hardly knew him,
coming into his family twelve years
too late. it was a time when
strawberries came bearing
no actual meanings. the bright
color of our young clothes walks
out from the fog. a house speaks
through the mouth and mind
of the silversmith. we saw the red
sand on his boots. what do we
remember of him? i remember he
said good-bye that one fall.

it was on a sunday. he was slender.
the burns from a rifle barrel spotted
half his face. april black is somewhere.
i scratched his back knowing
of sacrifices. the children
growing up drunk.

coming back home

somewhere inside me
there is a memory
of my grandfathers stalking
and catching robins
in the night of early
spring for food.
the snow continues
to gather children
outside, and i think,
as long as they are moving.
the frost sets itself
on the window before
the old man's eye.
we sit together
and imagine designs
which will eventually
vanish when the room
and talk become warm.
he goes over the people
one by one and stops at one,
because he can't find any
answers as to why she took
the instrument and used it as if
she were one. they do not like
her much, he says, dancing barefoot
with tight clothes, taking the songs
into a small black machine.
it's how you breathe and space the song.
the same old crowd will be out
of jail soon, and then,

back again. the trees
will be running with sweetwater
and hard work is to be expected.
there is much error in the way
we carry our being and purpose.
we covered everything with his
conclusions and sometimes
he balanced his confusion
with a small gesture and said,
better to leave things like that
alone. nobody will understand.
i pressed my fingers
against the window, leaving
five clear answers of the day
before it left, barking
down the road.

winter of the salamander

i've waited through my wife's eyes
in the time of death. although we have peeled
the masks of summer away from our faces
we have each seen the badger encircle itself
to a star, knowing that a covenant with his spirit
is always too much to ask for.

unlike us, her birth-companions have gone before us,
resembling small jittery waterbugs who keep
bumping into each other, unable to perceive
the differences between the eyes of their
children, the light-colored seals
camouflaged with native tongue
and beaded outfits.

we'd like to understand why we breathe
the same air, why the dead grow
in number, the role i play in speaking
to mouths that darken blur with swollen
gunpowder burns, chapped lips, and alcohol.

we keep wondering whether or not we'll ever
leave in the form of eight sticks.
we have waited until morning to turn off
the lights, hoping to catch a glimpse
of light chasing light.

there was a man whose name was k.
there was another whose name was m.
they knew they shared the same father.
the car of their killer sits within
the fresh snow. their grandfather sits
within the thought of a hummingbird,
women arriving at his request,
the mistake in the deaths of his grandsons,
the spell that came back.

they say: the mixbloods know of one
chance to be a people.
some of us, knowing of little dispute
in our past, forget and we assume life
will go well for us, life after death
being automatic. they are told
to absorb themselves into religion,
to learn and to outdo some drunken
fullblood's life. and me: like a dim star
i shine on and off in the midst of many
who have sat repeatedly within this line
of seated men, singing into the ears of leaves,
fresh twigs of the fresh green bean.

alfred and pete are still godless.
the morning has shown itself through
the windows of their houses, dissolving
the peyote in their stomachs, mixing
into the meal of sweetened meat and coffee,
half-man, half-horse, the green shirt
and the lamb.

turning eagle and i sit in the roomlight
of the salamander's two houses.
within the third house the windows frost.
at the beginning and end of each winter
we sit here before a body the size of our hand.
we made ourselves believe that no one
was responsible. we took the sound it made
from its last breath and we imagined a dwarf
hanging from the rafters with a lighted
cigarette in his mouth, reminding us
of the midpoint in the day.

the black kettle in the corner changes
into my young wife and she walks over

Joy Harjo

(b. 1951) Creek

Joy Harjo was born in Tulsa, Oklahoma, in 1951. She is Creek, and a poet, musician, artist, television scriptwriter, and photographer. She studied at the Institute of American Indian Arts in Santa Fe and the University of New Mexico and earned a master's degree from the University of Iowa. She has taught creative writing at the University of Arizona, the University of Colorado, and the University of New Mexico.

The Last Song, *a collection of poems, was published in 1975.* **What Moon Drove Me to This?** *was published in 1980.* **She Had Some Horses** *was published by Thunder's Mouth Press in 1983.* **Secrets from the Center of the World**, *prose poems with photographs by Stephen Storm, was published in 1989, and* **In Mad Love and War**, *a collection of poems, appeared the following year. Her poetry has appeared in numerous anthologies.*

Harjo wrote in an autobiographical essay in **I Tell You Now** *that her mother was "mixed Cherokee and French." Her father was Creek*

> *who was then working as a mechanic for American Airlines. I don't think I was ever what they expected, but I am grateful that they made my life possible and honor them for it....*

> *When I first began writing, poetry was simply a way for me to speak. I was amazed that I could write anything down and have it come out a little more than coherently. Over the years the process has grown more complicated, more intricate, and the world within the poem more immense.*

Laura Coltelli, in an interview published in **Winged Words**, *asked Harjo how her Creek heritage affects her work as a poet. "It provides the underlying psychic structure, within which is a wealth of memory.... I know when I write there is an old Creek within me that often participates."*

Coltelli asked, "You said once, memory is like 'a delta in the skin,' so you are 'memory alive,' your poetry stems from memory always at work." Harjo responded,

> *It is Creek, and touches in on the larger tribal continental memory and the larger human memory, global. It's not something I consciously chose; I mean, I am not a full-blood, but it was something that chose me, that lives in me, and I cannot deny it. Sometimes I wish I could disappear into the crowds of the city and lose this responsibility, because it is a responsibility. But I can't.*

In **She Had Some Horses**, *Harjo "pays tribute to the survival of contemporary Indians, while acknowledging and casting off fear within herself," LaVonne Ruoff wrote in* **American Indian Literatures**.

> *In the title section of the volume, which uses traditional song structure, the metaphor of horses suggests the variety of personal responses of Indians to their environments.* She had some horses. She had horses who whispered in the dark, who were afraid to speak....

She Had Some Horses

She had some horses.

She had horses who were bodies of sand.
She had horses who were maps drawn of blood.
She had horses who were skins of ocean water.
She had horses who were the blue air of sky.

She had horses who were fur and teeth.
She had horses who were clay and would break.
She had horses who were splintered red cliff.

She had some horses.

She had horses with long, pointed breasts.
She had horses with full, brown thighs.
She had horses who laughed too much.
She had horses who threw rocks at glass houses.
She had horses who licked razor blades.

She had some horses.

She had horses who danced in their mothers' arms.
She had horses who thought they were the sun and their
bodies shone and burned like stars.
She had horses who waltzed nightly on the moon.
She had horses who were much too shy, and kept quiet
in stall of their own making.

She had some horses.

She had horses who liked Creek Stomp Dance songs.
She had horses who cried in their beer.
She had horses who spit at male queens who made
them afraid of themselves.
She had horses who said they weren't afraid.
She had horses who lied.

She had horses who told the truth, who were stripped
bare of their tongues.

She had some horses.

She had horses who called themselves, "horse."
She had horses who called themselves, "spirit," and kept
their voices secret and to themselves.
She had horses who had no names.
She had horses who had books of names.

She had some horses.

She had horses who whispered in the dark, who were afraid
to speak.
She had horses who screamed out of fear of the silence, who
carried knives to protect themselves from ghosts.
She had horses who waited for destruction.
She had horses who waited for resurrection.

She had some horses.

She had horses who got down on their knees for any savior.
She had horses who thought their high price had saved
them.
She had horses who tried to save her, who climbed in her
bed at night and prayed as they raped her.

She had some horses.

She had some horses she loved.
She had some horses she hated.

These were the same horses.

Luci Tapahonso

(b. 1953) Navajo

Luci Tapahonso was born in Shiprock, New Mexico, in 1953. She is Navajo and was raised three miles from town on the north mesa. She studied at the Navajo Methodist Mission, Shiprock High School, and the University of New Mexico.

Tapahonso has published several books and her poems have appeared in many anthologies. **One More Shiprock Night** *was published in 1981.* **Season Woman** *appeared the following year.* **A Breeze Swept Through** *was published in 1987.* **Sáanii Dahataal: The Women Are Singing**, *poems and stories, was published in the Sun Tracks American Indian Literary Series by the University of Arizona Press in 1994.*

"A lot of my poems are memory poems," Tapahonso told Joseph Bruchac in an interview published in **Survival This Way**.

> *Things that people have told me or memories from my own life, from my parents and from the stories they have told me. And I think that it is really important because the past determines what our present is or what our future will be. I don't think there is really a separation of the three.*

Tapahonso wrote in **Sáanii Dahataal** *that there*

> *is such a love of stories among Navajo people that it seems each time a group of more than two gather, the dialogue eventually evolves into sharing stories and memories, laughing, and teasing. To be included in this is a distinct way of showing affection and appreciation for each other. So it is true that daily conversations strengthen us as do the old stories of our ancestors that have been told since the beginning of the Navajo time.*

For Lori Tazbah

tonight it rained hard
the thunder cracked
my blood froze.
I caught my breath
and thought of you
you slept peacefully
your breathing gentle, soft
unaware of my sudden panic.

last year you memorized
the pledge of allegiance perfectly
you teacher proud of your perfect salute.

when she asked everyone
to sit "Indian style" and
you asked why sitting
cross-legged was Indian
when everyone could do it.

now you're six,
you've waited so long
to be in "regular school."
no more naps, snacks or color games.
you're impatient and want to
learn to read and do times.
the first day you went
I cried for hours.

Hills Brothers Coffee

My uncle is a small man.
In Navajo, we call him "shidáf,"
my mother's brother.

He doesn't know English,
but his name in the white way is Tom Jim.
He lives about a mile or so
down the road from our house.

One morning he sat in the kitchen,
drinking coffee.
I just came over, he said.
The store is where I'm going to.

He tells me about how my mother seems to be gone
every time he comes over.
Maybe she sees me coming
then runs and jumps in her car
and speeds away!
he says smiling.

We both laugh—just to think of my mother
jumping in her car and speeding.

I pour him more coffee
and he spoons in sugar and cream
until it looks almost like a chocolate shake.
Then he sees the coffee can.

Oh, that's that coffee with the man in a dress,
like a church man.
Ah-h, that's the one that does it for me.
Very good coffee.

I sit down again and he tells me.
Some coffee has no kick.
But this one is the one.
It does it good for me.

I pour us both a cup
and while we wait for my mother,
his eyes crinkle with the smile and he says,
Yes, ah yes. This is the very one
(putting in more sugar and cream).

So I usually buy Hills Brothers Coffee.
Once or sometimes twice a day,
I drink a hot coffee and

it sure does it for me.

Louise Erdrich

(b. 1954) Anishinaabe

Louise Erdrich was born in Little Falls, Minnesota, in 1954. She was raised in Wahpeton, North Dakota, where her parents were teachers at the Bureau of Indian Affairs School. Erdrich is a member of the Turtle Mountain Reservation. She is married to the author Michael Dorris.

Erdrich is the author of four novels and coauthor of a fifth novel with her husband. She is an esteemed novelist and poet. **Jacklight**, poems and narratives, was published in 1984. The poem "Indian Boarding School: The Runaways" is one of the most incisive poems in the collection. LaVonne Ruoff in **American Indian Literatures** noted that "Erdrich poignantly portrays the desperate homesickness of these children: 'Home's the place we head for in our sleep. / Boxcars stumbling north in dreams / don't wait for us. We catch them on the run.'" **Baptism of Desire**, poems of ecstasies and visions, was published in 1989.

Indian Boarding School:
the Runaways

Home's the place we head for in our sleep.
Boxcars stumbling north in dreams
don't wait for us. We catch them on the run.
The rails, old lacerations that we love,
shoot parallel across the face and break
just under Turtle Mountains. Riding scars
you can't get lost. Home is the place they cross.

The lame guard strikes a match and makes the dark
less tolerant. We watch through cracks in boards
as the land starts rolling, rolling till it hurts
to be here, cold in regulation clothes.
We know the sheriff's waiting at midrun
to take us back. His car is dumb and warm.
The highway doesn't rock, it only hums
like a wing of long insults. The worn-down welts
of ancient punishments lead back and forth.

All runaways wore dresses, long green ones,
the color you would think shame was. We scrub
the sidewalks down because it's shameful work.
Our brushes cut the stone in watered arcs
and in the soak frail outlines shiver clear

a moment, things us kids pressed on the dark
face before it hardened, pale, remembering
delicate old injuries, the spines of names and leaves.

Turtle Mountain Reservation

The heron makes a cross
flying low over the marsh.
Its heart is an old compass
pointing off in four directions.
It drags the world along,
the world it becomes.

My face surfaces in the green
beveled glass above the washstand.
My handprint in thick black powder
on the bedroom shade.
Home I could drink like thin fire
that gathers
like lead in my veins,
heart's armor, the coffee stains.

In the dust of the double hollyhock,
Theresa, one frail flame eating wind.
One slim candle
that snaps in the dry grass.
Ascending tall ladders
that walk to the edge of dusk.
Riding a blue cricket
through the tumult of the falling dawn.

At dusk the gray owl walks the length of the roof,
sharpening its talons on the shingles,
Grandpa leans back
between spoonfuls of canned soup
and repeats to himself a word
that belongs to a world
no one else can remember.
The day has not come

when from sloughs, the great salamander
lumbers through snow, salt, and fire
to be with him, throws the hatchet
of its head through the door of the three-room house
and eats the blue roses that are peeling off the walls.

Uncle Ray, drunk for three days
behind the jagged window
of a new government box,
drapes himself in fallen curtains, and dreams that the odd
beast seen near Cannonball, North Dakota,
crouches moaning at the door to his body. The latch
is the small hook and eye

of religion. Twenty nuns
fall through clouds to park their butts
on the metal hasp. Surely that
would be considered miraculous almost anyplace,

but here in the Turtle Mountains
it is no more than common fact.
Raymond wakes,
but he can't shrug them off. He is looking up
dark tunnels of their sleeves,
and into their frozen armpits,
or is it heaven? He counts the points
of their hairs like stars.

One by one they blink out,
and Theresa comes forth
clothed in the lovely hair
she has been washing all day. She smells
like a hayfield, drifting pollen
of birch trees.
Her hair steals across her shoulders
like a postcard sunset.

All the boys tonight, goaded from below,
will approach her in The Blazer, The Tomahawk,
The White Roach Bar where everyone

gets up to cut the rug, wagging everything they got,
as the one bass drum of The Holy Greaseballs
lights a depth
charge through the smoke.

Grandpa leans closer to the bingo.
The small fortune his heart pumps for
is hidden in the stained, dancing numbers.
The Ping-Pong balls rise through colored lights,
brief as sparrows
God is in the sleight of the woman's hand.

He walks from Saint Ann's, limp and crazy
as the loon that calls its children
across the lake
in this broke, knowing laughter.
Hitchhiking home from the Mission, if he sings,
it is a loud, rasping wail
that saws through the spine
of Ira Comes Last, at the wheel.

Drawn up through the neck ropes,
drawn out of his stomach
by the spirit of the stones that line
the road and speak
to him only in their old agreement.
Ira knows the old man is nuts.
Lets him out at the road that leads up
over stars and the skulls of white cranes.

And through the soft explosions of cattail
and the scattering of seeds on still water,
walks Grandpa, all the time that there is in his hands
that have grown to be the twisted doubles
of the burrows of mole and badger,
that have come to be the absence
of birds in a nest.
Hands of earth, of this clay
I'm also made from.

Sherman Alexie

(b. 1966) Coeur D'Alene

Sherman Alexie was born in 1966. He is a Spokane, Coeur D'Alene Indian from Wellpinit, Washington, on the Spokane Indian Reservation. His poems and stories have been published in **Caliban, New York Ouarterly, Zyzzyva**, *and many other journals. "The Approximate Size of My Favorite Tumor" was published in* **Earth Song, Sky Spirit**, *edited by Clifford Trafzer.*

The Business of Fancydancing, *his first collection of poems and stories, was selected by the* **New York Times Book Review** *as one of the Notable Books of the Year in 1992.* **First Indian on the Moon** *was published in 1993.*

"Thomas Builds-the-Fire told his story to every other Skin on the Spokane Indian Reservation before he was twelve years old," Alexie wrote in **Fancydancing**. *"By the time he was twenty, Thomas had told his story so many times all the other Indians hid when they saw him coming, transformed themselves into picnic benches, small mongrel dogs, a 1965 Malibu with no windshield."*

The Lone Ranger and Tonto Fistfight in Heaven, *a collection of stories, was published in 1992. Alexie, in "Jesus Christ's Half-Brother Is Alive and Well on the Spokane Indian Reservation," wrote that*

> *Rosemary MorningDove gave birth to a boy today and seeing as how it was nearly Christmas and she kept telling everyone she was still a virgin even though Frank Many Horses said it was his we all just figured it was an accident. Anyhow she gave birth to him but he came out all blue and they couldn't get him to breathe for a long time but he finally did and Rosemary MorningDove named him ——— which is unpronounceable in Indian and English but it means:* He Who Crawls Silently Through the Grass with a Small Bow and One Bad Arrow Hunting for Enough Deer to Feed the Whole Tribe. *We just called him James.*

Alexie is a natural in the business of native humor. His poems and stories are direct and laconic, and common situations are brushed with reservation chance. Tricksters and their sudden presence in comic names are never heard as heroes. Even the termination of reservations is not an end, but a mere turn and transformation of memories in stories. The native ironies and twists of histories in his stories are the traplights of a new trickster.

Before We Knew about Mirrors

Disappearing Coins

Black Star, the hunchback magician, lived on the Reservation in a one-room house near the Catholic church. He was the man who could make his fingers disappear, transport quarters into the back pockets of Indian Boys who suddenly believed in everything.

A quarter could be anything then: a jawbreaker, a piece of deer jerky from some grandmother, a coke, a slice of the heart. But, did Black Star pull those quarters from the air behind our hearts, just to prove what we possessed in our chest, or did he take them from his own heart? Piece by piece, coin by coin, did he make himself, his dreams, less, every time a braided boy reached into his pocket?

I still have one of those quarters at the bottom of my coin jar, distinct and frightening in a sea of lesser pennies, nickels, dimes. What can I do to reach it? Spend, spend, find the smallest possible treasures in the dime stores, the garage sales, Goodwill? After I fill my small room with all that I've bought, will that quarter bring me any answers?

Pick a Card, Any Card

Indian Boys always find some way to die. The faces I see in my mirror look the same: U.S. Government glasses, fractured nose, braids like wild ponies, eyes like mine and his and his and yours.

Everything we own, everything we want to own, is just that flat. Like slapping an open hand onto a table. Like pressing tightly against the walls. Like shuffling a deck of cards. But every card is the same, all face cards with the same face.

When an Indian stranger sees another Indian stranger, they both stare. They have the same eyes, mirrors, reflecting what they have witnessed; understanding the distance pain creates between past and present, they move to random consolations.

So, if someone hands us a card, calls it a dream, and asks if it is the correct one, what can we answer? Would we have time to baptize it, give it a Christian name, an education, the keys to a fast car? Will it be able to fancydance, anticipate the beating of drums, begin the message?

Black Star, the hunchback magician, drank more than any of the Indians on their Reservation. Assimilation, he called it, and meant it. Many mornings, we would find him passed out on the roadside, in a doorway, everywhere, and we would carry him home. Every morning, we would pull him up from the hole he threw himself down the night before. Every morning, we would follow him down as he recanted years of life.

"Indians can never live in the city."

"White women will break your heart."

"Money ain't worth shit."

"Never fall in love."

Black Star, you alcoholic wise man, none of your Indian Boys ever fell in love.

Sawing Beautiful Women into Halves

Black Star, the hunchback magician, always said it was the only revenge he ever had.

Levitation

Black Star, the hunchback magician, named us by the defects we possessed. I was Little Man, in town hat and hair, his favored assistant, gathering scarves, rings, coins, dreams.

I was the one levitating, supported by a single broomstick, always prepared to fall in some simple way.

I would close my eyes and dream of something strong, dream of horses exploding, rising into the air, their hearts beating survive, survive, survive.

Vanishing

The last time I saw Black Star, the hunchback magician, he was loading up a truck with everything he owned. All the boxes, rings, gimmicks, closets, where he kept all of our futures hidden.

"When you coming back?" I asked him.

"Never," he said and was gone.

Days later, we rummaged through his house, searching for answers. I found a book he left behind: HOW TO FOOL AND AMAZE YOUR FRIENDS: 101 GREAT TRICKS OF THE MASTER MAGICIANS.

Black Star, you bastard, I know how you did them all. I know everything.

Crazy Horse Speaks

1.
I discovered the evidence
in a vault of The Mormon Church
3,000 skeletons of my cousins
in a silence so great
I built four walls around it
and gave it a name.
I called it Custer
and he came to me
again in a dream.
He forgave all my sins.

2.
Little Big Horn
Little Big Horn does not belong to me.
I was there
my horse exploded under me.
I searched for Long Hair
the man you call Custer
the man I call My Father.
But it wasn't me who killed him
it was_____
who cut off his head
and left the body for proof.
I dream of him
and search doorways and alleys
for his grave.
General George Armstrong Custer
my heart is beating
· survive   survive   survive.

3.
I wear the color of my skin
like a brown paper bag
wrapped around a bottle.
Sleeping between
the pages of dictionaries
your language cuts
tears holes in my tongue
until I do not have strength
to use the word "love."
What could it mean
in this city where everyone is
Afraid-of-Horses?

4.
There are places I cannot leave.
Rooms without doors or windows
the eternal ribcage.

I sat across the fire
from Sitting Bull
shared smoke and eyes.
We both saw the same thing
our futures tight and small
an $8\frac{1}{2}$ by 11 dream
called the reservation.
We had no alternatives
but to fight again and again
live our lives on horseback.
After The Civil War
the number of Indian warriors
in The West doubled
tripled the number of soldiers
but Indians never have shared
the exact skin
never the same home.

5.
History.
History is never the truth.
So much can happen
in the space between
touching and becoming.
I dream custer
walking along the hills
of Little Big Horn
counting blades of grass
trying to find some measurement
of why he fell.
I tell him the exact number
and the story
about the grandmother
the mother and the daughter
who did the counting
each growing larger
and larger with every word.

6.
I am the mirror
practicing masks
and definitions.
I have always wanted to be anonymous
instead of the crazy skin
who rode his horse backwards
and laid down alone.
It was never easy
to be frightened
by the sound of a color.
I can still hear white
it is the sound
of glass shattering.

7.
I hear the verdict
in the museum in New York
where five Eskimo were flown in
to be a living exhibit.
Three died within days
lacking natural immunity
their hearts miles
and miles of thin ice.
The three dead Eskimo
were stuffed and mounted
hunched over a fishing hole
next to the two living
who held their thin hands
close to their chests
mortal and sinless.

8.
Whenever it all begins again
I will be waiting.

Robert DeNiro

I used to think he lived on my reservation in that green house on the hill, near the water tower. Not because I ever saw him or even imagined I saw him. Only because every light in the house was always on and the car that sat in the driveway moved so gradually that it took me a calendar to realize it. Like a clock, the car pointed north, pointed toward twelve at the beginning of the year. By the time summer ended, the car pointed south toward six. At Christmas, it was nearly twelve again. I knew only Robert DeNiro could get away with something that crazy and exact. I knew only Robert DeNiro could test my tribe's edges like that and not push us completely over. I knew only Robert DeNiro could afford the electricity bill.

DRAMA

Gerald Vizenor

(b. 1934) Anishinaabe

Gerald Vizenor has published five novels, narrative histories, and several collections of short stories and essays. He wrote the screenplay for **Harold of Orange**, *which was released as a short fiction film in 1983.* **Ishi and the Wood Ducks** *is based on events surrounding the life and death of the tribal man named Ishi. Alfred Kroeber, the anthropologist, arranged for Ishi to live and work at the Museum of Anthropology at the University of California between 1911 and his death in 1916.*

"Postindian Trickster Comedies," the subtitle of the play, refers to the humorous transformations of native tricksters and the postindian time after the invention of the "Indian" by Christopher Columbus. Ishi is present in the prologue and four acts of the play. The first scene is situated in the museum; in the remaining three acts Ishi is a character in the story of his life after his death. He is an artist and cannot prove that he is a native person under the provisions of the Indian Arts and Crafts Act.

Ishi and the Wood Ducks: Postindian Trickster Comedies

Historical Production

Sheriff Webber secured "a pathetic figure crouched upon the floor," the *Oroville Register* reported on August 29, 1911. "The canvas from which his outer shirt was made had been roughly sewed together. His undershirt had evidently been stolen in a raid upon some cabin. His feet were almost as wide as they were long, showing plainly that he had never worn either moccasins or shoes. In his ears were rings made of buckskin thongs." The sheriff "removed the cartridges from his revolver" and "gave the weapon to the Indian. The aborigine showed no evidence that he knew anything regarding its use. A cigarette was offered to him, and while it was very evident that he knew what tobacco was, he had never smoked it in that form, and had to be taught the art."

Alfred Kroeber, the anthropologist, read the newspaper report and contacted the sheriff who "had put the Indian in jail not knowing what else to do with him since no one around town could understand his speech or he theirs," wrote Theodora Kroeber in *Alfred Kroeber: A Personal Configuration*. "Within a few days the Department of Indian Affairs authorized the sheriff to release the wild man to the custody of Kroeber and the museum staff...."

Ishi lived and worked in a museum, housed in comfortable rooms furnished by the patron Phoebe Apperson Hearst. She had created the first Department and Museum of Anthropology at the University of California.

"He was the last of his tribe," wrote Mary Ashe Miller in the San Francisco *Call* on September 6, 1911. He "feared people" and "wandered alone, like a hunted animal."

This "man is as aboriginal in his mode of life as though he inhabited the heart of an African jungle, all of his methods are those of primitive peoples."

Professor Kroeber, however, pointed out that "he has perceptive powers far keener than those of highly educated white men. He reasons well, grasps an idea quickly, has a keen sense of humor, is gentle, thoughtful, and courteous and has a higher type of mentality than most Indians."

Thomas Waterman, the linguist at the museum, administered psychological tests at the time and concluded in a newspaper interview that "this wild man has a better head on him than a good many college men."

Ishi, who never revealed his sacred name, has become one of the most memorable names of tribal survivance in the world. Even so, he has seldom been heard as a real person who loved to tease his friends with stories. He "looked upon us as sophisticated children," wrote the medical doctor Saxton Pope. "We knew many things, and much that is false. He knew nature, which is always true," and his "soul was that of a child, his mind that of a philosopher."

Ishi was born about 1860 in the area of the Southern Yana. He lived near Deer Creek in Tehama County in northern California. Abraham Lincoln won the presidential election that year. The first Beadle Dime Novel, *A Tale of Two Cities* by Charles Dickens, and *Origin of Species* by Charles Darwin were published about the same time.

Saxton Pope wrote that he once took Ishi to see Buffalo Bill's Wild West Show. Ishi

always enjoyed the circus, horseback feats, clowns, and similar performances. While at the show we were watching some Plains Indians dress for their performance. A very dignified warrior, bedecked in all his paint and feathers, approached us. The two Indians looked at each other in absolute silence for several minutes. The Sioux then spoke in perfect English, saying: 'What tribe of Indian is this?' I answered, 'Yana, from Northern California.' The Sioux then gently picked up a bit of Ishi's hair, rolled it between his fingers, looked critically into his face, and said, 'He is a very high grade of Indian.' As we left, I asked Ishi what he thought of the Sioux. Ishi said, 'Him's a big chiep [chief].' Apparently their estimates were equally complimentary.

Doctor Pope wrote in a medical report that Ishi was at his best two years before his death.

On a trip to Tehama County he was undoubtedly in prime health. His stature is magnificent. Although he has lost the typical Indian litheness, there is grace and strength in every contour. For a year he was absolutely perfect. He worked, hunted, played, and enjoyed life.

Then a gradual change overcame him. His energy waned. He no longer was keen to shoot at targets with the bow. His skin became darker. He contracted another cold. He lost weight and wanted to rest most of the time. There were periods of slight improvement and we had hope that a return to his primitive mode of life might benefit him.

But as his malady increased, his cough became more distressing, fever consumed him, and eating became impossible. Our city water did not taste good to him, and he asked me to get him fresh spring water—'sweet water' he called it. We made a special effort to do this for him.

Although starving, racked with hiccough or coughing, and in more or less constant distress, he never complained. He never spoke of his suffering; never referred to death.... Ishi died of tuberculosis on March 25, 1916.

"Ishi, the man primeval, is dead," reported the *Chico Record*.

He could not stand the rigors of civilization, and tuberculosis, that arch-enemy of those who live in the simplicity of nature and then abandon that life, claimed him. Ishi was supposed to be the last of a tribe that flourished in California long before the white man reached these shores. He could make a fire with sticks, fashion arrowheads out of flint, and was familiar with other arts long lost to civilization. He furnished amusement and study to the savants at the University of California for a number of years, and doubtless much of ancient Indian lore was learned from him, but we do not believe he was the marvel that the professors would have the public believe. He was just a starved-out Indian from the wilds of Deer Creek who, by hiding in its fastness, was able to long escape the white man's pursuit. And the white man with his food and clothing and shelter finally killed the Indian just as effectually as he would have killed him with a rifle.

Ishi's "body was carried to the undertakers, where it was embalmed," wrote Saxton Pope.

No funeral services were held. Professor T. T. Waterman, Mr. E. W. Gifford, Mr. A. Warburton, Mr. L. L. Loud, of the Museum of Anthropology, and I visited the parlor, and reverently placed in his coffin his bow, a quiver full of arrows, ten pieces of dentalia or Indian money, some dried venison, some acorn meal, his fire sticks, and a small quantity of tobacco. We then accompanied the body to Laurel Hill cemetery near San Francisco, where it was cremated. The ashes were placed in a small Indian pottery jar on the outside of which is inscribed: 'Ishi, the last Yahi Indian, died March 1916.'

The black pottery jar with the ashes of this native philosopher are now secured in a niche in the columbarium at Mount Olivet Cemetery near San Francisco.

Characters

Ishi and Boots Story, an old woman, are characters in the prologue and four acts of the play. He wears a fashionable but oversized suit and tie. He wears shoes in the opening of the prologue and at the end of the last act. His hair is parted in the center. Boots wears a floral print dress with white boots and bold accessories.

Ishi
Boots Story
Alfred Kroeber
Thomas Waterman
Saxton Pope
Ashe Miller
Prince Chamber
Zero Larkin
Angel Day
Trope Browne

The actors and names of the characters are the same in the prologue and four acts of the play. The sense of time, manifest manners, and historical contradictions are redoubled and enhanced by the mutations of identities in the same characters. Ashe Miller, for instance, is a newspaper reporter in the first and second acts, a professor in the third act, and a federal prosecutor in the last act. Prince Chamber is a photographer in the first act, a video maker in the second act, a professor of visual arts in the third act, and a court clerk in the last act. Trope Browne is an attendant at the columbarium in the second act and a professor in the third act. Saxton Pope is a medical doctor in the first act and defense counsel in the last act.

Prologue

Ishi and Boots, an old woman, are seated on a wide polished bench outside a federal courtroom. The bench is framed in a slant of warm light. Ishi wears an oversized suit and tie and carries a leather briefcase. Slowly he removes his shoes and socks, turns the cuffs of his trousers, and then inserts leather thongs in his ears. Boots preens in a hand mirror; she turns the mirror to watch the man on the other end of the bench.

ISHI: Have you ever heard the wood duck stories?
BOOTS: Wood ducks?
ISHI *(Wavering voice):* Winotay, winotay, winotay...

BOOTS: What are you singing?
ISHI: They named me Ishi.
BOOTS: The wood ducks?
ISHI: No, the anthropologists.
BOOTS: Never heard that one.
ISHI: Ishi is my museum name, not my real name.
BOOTS: Same with me.

Boots notices his new shoes on the bench and laughs.

ISHI: Do you have a sacred name?
BOOTS: Boots, the boys teased me about my boots.

She moves her head to a silent rhythm, raises her wide dress just above her fancy white cowboy boots, and dances in place. Ishi place his shoes and sock in the briefcase.

ISHI: Ishi is my nickname.
BOOTS: Boots is my sacred name.
ISHI: No one has ever heard my sacred name.
BOOTS: No one has ever heard my real name.
ISHI: Alfred Kroeber gave me a museum name.
BOOTS: My husband lied to me about our name.
ISHI *(To the audience)*: Kroeber was an anthropologist and got me out of
    jail to live in a museum *(Pause),* he was one of my very first friends.
BOOTS: *(Loud voice):* Raider, my husband, he brought me here, but we were
    never married, and even my birth records were lost in the war.

Boots is nervous, puckers her mouth, and looks out to the audience.

ISHI: Kroeber named me *(Pause),* in my own language, he named me the
    last man of the stone age.
BOOTS: What, a mountain man?
ISHI: The primitive, a stone breaker.
BOOTS: Why would he do that?
ISHI: He was a museum man, but we named each other.
BOOTS: Who are you talking about?
ISHI: Ishi, me *(Points to himself),* and he was my Big Chiep.
BOOTS: You can say that again Mister Stone.
ISHI: Big Chiep, that was my best version of big chief at the time.
BOOTS: Raider was so cheep he never even gave me his real name.
ISHI: Big Chiep was lonesome, a museum talker, and he wanted to be like
    me, with stories out of the mountains.

BOOTS: Stone breakers?

ISHI: Anthropologists never hear their own stories.

BOOTS: Raider *(Pause)*, he was a great dancer.

She moves her head and boots as in a dance, and then she looks over at his bare feet and smiles.

ISHI: Big Chiep never told his own stories.

BOOTS: My Raider was a story, he dropped dead right over an expensive dinner, that bastard, and left me with the bill.

ISHI: Big Chiep outlived me in the museum, and then, when they forgot me they named a building after him at the university.

BOOTS: You only need one name on buildings.

ISHI: He named me the last, the last of my tribe, but he was the end of anthropology.

BOOTS: Raider painted my name on the side of his car.

ISHI: They named it Big Chiep Hall.

BOOTS: Raider left me with nothing, not even a real name.

Silence.

ISHI: Nothing?

BOOTS: Nothing *(Pause, she looks down at her boots)*, nothing but my boots.

ISHI: So, why are you here in federal court?

BOOTS: I need a real name, or the judge said he would send me back home, an old woman without a country.

ISHI: So, where is home?

BOOTS: Everywhere, nowhere, we were Gypsies.

She pouts, moves closer, with one hand on the bench between them, studies the thongs in his ears, and moves back to the end of the bench.

ISHI: How about a reservation?

BOOTS: Why, do you need one?

ISHI: The government offered me a reservation once, a reservation of my choice, but at the time the museum was a better place to live.

BOOTS: That would be nice.

ISHI: What, a reservation with a choice?

BOOTS: No, no, choosers are too much when you never get what you want, no *(Pause),* but home in a museum with a real name, now that would be real nice.

ISHI: Choose a name, any name, and start your own museum.

BOOTS: No, no *(Pause)*, what sort of museum?

ISHI: Any kind, you name the objects.

> *Boots is suspicious and looks to the audience.*

BOOTS: You are a very strange person with your bare feet and that leather in your ears, and all this talk about museums.

ISHI: How about a museum of stories?

BOOTS: Who can remember stories anymore?

ISHI: That's why you need your own museum.

BOOTS: No, no, who could start a museum without stories?

ISHI: Everybody does.

BOOTS: Show me then, show me your museum.

ISHI: My home is an anthropology museum.

BOOTS: What kind of story is that?

ISHI: Lonesome anthropologists love museums with no stories.

BOOTS: Never been to one myself.

ISHI: Anthropologists never had their own stories *(Pause),* that's why they started so many museums.

BOOTS: So what's the story?

ISHI: Names without stories are the end.

BOOTS: That's for me, real names without the trouble.

ISHI: Real names are like museums.

BOOTS: Not in my big book.

ISHI: That leaves museums with stolen stories.

BOOTS *(Loud voice)*: Never mind the stories.

ISHI: No stories, no reservations.

BOOTS: No, no, stories are too much for me to remember, but listen, you can show me the way to that museum, the one that needs a good cleaning you know *(Pause),* floors, sinks, cases, and things.

ISHI: Wait *(Laughs),* how about the museum of lost shoes?

BOOTS: Don't you ever make fun of my boots.

ISHI: Never *(Pause),* would you dance with me?

> *He stands, holds out his hands, and she looks down at his bare feet.*

BOOTS: Not now, they want me in court.

> *Boots dances to the courtroom with her dress held above her white boots.*

ISHI *(Shouts):* Boots, tell them you run a museum with stories.

ACT ONE

Ishi sits at the entrance to a wickiup, a tribal house, in the Museum of Anthropology at the University of California. He cracks stones into arrowheads with a flaker. BOOTS pushes a wide duster on the floor and then leans on a display case to watch the scene. SAXTON POPE, the medical doctor, enters the museum; he is casual, with a sense of ironic humor.

POPE: Ishi, my patients in the women's ward are delighted when you visit the hospital.

ISHI: Must be my wood duck stories?

POPE: The women want to hear you sing.

Boots raises her eyebrows and looks to the audience.

ISHI: How could they understand my songs?

POPE: They understand your manner, the natural healer *(Pause)*, why must my patients understand the words in your songs?

ISHI: Because, then they could sing for themselves.

POPE: My friend, you tease my nature *(Pause)*. Have you ever seen one of these, a police whistle?

Saxton Pope blows the police whistle. Ishi is hesitant but learns how to use the whistle.

ISHI: No animal would make such a sound.

POPE: The police ... *(Sound of the whistle)*.

ISHI: This could chase the savages away.

POPE: Don't be so sure.

Pope checks the time on his pocket watch. Boots leans closer to see. Ishi is pleased to show his own gold pocket watch.

ISHI: What time on your watch?

POPE: Three, but you never set the time.

Ishi listens to his pocket watch and turns to the arrowheads.

ISHI: These arrowheads are for your son.

Pope examines each of the arrowheads; he runs his finger on the sharp edges, and then holds them up to the bright light one by one as he speaks. Boots is curious and moves closer to see. She drops the handle of the duster on the floor.

POPE: Obsidian?

ISHI: Yes, very sharp.

POPE: This one is green.

ISHI: Broken bottle.

POPE: Ishi, you must reconsider our invitation, we want you to show us your home in the mountains *(Pause),* especially my son, he would be honored if you taught him how to hunt and fish with a bow and arrow, and how to make arrowheads out of broken bottles.

ISHI *(Turns to the audience)*: The mountains are dangerous.

> Silence.

POPE: Nonsense, what could happen?

ISHl *(Whispers):* The savages, the savages.

POPE: Savages? Which savages?

ISHl: The gold miners.

POPE: No need to worry about them anymore.

ISHI: They have no stories.

POPE: Who, the savages?

ISHI: The miners are dead voices, no songs, no stories.

POPE: Sounds like my bankers.

ISHI: They have no culture.

POPE: My son says the same thing about bankers.

> *Saxton Pope checks his watch again. Boots pushes the duster past the doctor and then returns to the display case. Alfred Kroeber enters the museum; he is formal and serious.*

KROEBER: Ishi, the photographer and reporters are on their way.

ISHI: To the mountains?

POPE *(Laughs):* We were talking about the trip.

KROEBER: Of course, the photographer wants to take your picture, here in the museum, with your crafts.

> *Boots dusts the display cases.*

ISHI: Those men have my picture.

POPE: You were not at your best in the first pictures.

ISHI: Pictures are not my best.

KROEBER: The only photographs we have of you were taken in jail.

POPE: My friend, you look like an immigrant in your own country.

ISHI: Pictures are never me.

KROEBER: Ishi, we need a professional photograph of you, a museum portrait for posterity.

ISHI: Dead shadows that were never me.

POPE: Pictures are the play of light, not fate.

ISHI: Cameras are dead stories.

KROEBER: Ishi, why do you worry so much about cameras?

ISHI: My stories are lost in pictures.

Boots touches her cheeks with her hands. She is moved by his resistance to the cameras.

POPE: Listen, photographers are the ones lost behind the camera.

KROEBER: Ishi, the shadows are the stories, as the shadows of an eagle hover and land on the earth, so lands a photograph.

ISHI: Shadows never hover, shadows are the seasons....

KROEBER: Yes, very good point.

ISHI: Savages land in your pictures.

POPE: Indeed, my son does have a savage pose *(Pause),* especially with his bow and arrows.

KROEBER: Ishi, the newspaper reporter may ask you questions about your life in the mountains and about your work in the museum.

ISHI: Has she heard my wood duck stories?

POPE: The ducks are too much for this interview.

KROEBER: Ishi, you could sing a hunting song.

ISHI: Hunting for the newspapers...

POPE: Not exactly, but one of your songs.

ISHI *(Wavering voice):* Winotay, winotay, winotay....

POPE: Yes, love songs, as you do in the hospital, but not for hours.

ISHI: Newspapers are dead stories.

KROEBER: Newspapers?

Boots waits over the duster. Kroeber and Pope look to each other for an answer. Ishi raises his arms and as he moves a slant of light creates a shadow of light.

ISHI: No one listens.

POPE: Not so, we record your stories.

ISHI: My stories are heard in a museum.

POPE: The women in the hospital listen to your songs and stories.

Ishi smiles and moves in flight with his shadow around the museum and then enters the wickiup. Kroeber and Pope continue their conversation.

KROEBER: Ishi spends too much time in the women's ward, you must do something about that before there are complaints.

POPE: Quite the opposite, my friend, his songs and stories have a very positive effect on the women in the ward.

KROEBER: In what way?

POPE: The women are amused, he is a natural healer.

KROEBER: Nevertheless, we must be cautious.

POPE: Cautious about what, his stories?

KROEBER: Ishi is our ward *(Pause)*, and we are responsible for the way in which the public sees him in the museum.

Ashe Miller, the reporter, and Prince Chambers, the photographer, enter the museum and are introduced. Prince searches for the best light and then he sets an enormous camera on a tripod.

MILLER: So, where have you hidden the primitive?

KROEBER: Perhaps we could discuss the situation in my office.

MILLER: Why, is he dangerous?

POPE: Ishi is neither primitive nor dangerous.

MILLER: What is he then?

POPE: Ishi is a natural philosopher.

MILLER: Naturally, he's a stone age theologian with no name who lives alone in a museum.

Boots pushes the duster into the reporter. Ishi is inside the wickiup. Kroeber moves to the entrance. The reporter writes in a notebook.

POPE: Ishi is his name.

MILLER: But not his real name.

POPE: Miss Miller, his real name is sacred.

MILLER: Of course, so is mine.

KROEBER: Ishi is our name *(Pause)*, and the name is a common word in his language that means "man" or "one of the people."

MILLER: One of the people, is that his first or surname?

KROEBER: Ishi, you might say, is a nickname.

MILLER: His surname is a nickname?

KROEBER: You might say that, as he must have a name.

POPE: Miller, is that a surname or a gristmill operator?

Pope is dominant, but he smiles, an invitation to the pleasure of ironies. Miller laughs, she is not troubled. Kroeber is worried.

KROEBER: Miss Miller, we were very concerned that he be known by a name in his own language.

MILLER: Mister Ishi Ishi, the natural philosopher, has vanished with a double name.

KROEBER: Ishi, please come out to meet the reporter.

MILLER: Ishi Ishi, my name is Ashe Miller.

POPE *(Smiles):* Miss Miller Miller.

Silence.

MILLER: Doctor, dare we double your name?

Miller moves closer to the wickiup.

POPE: Fear not, crawl right in and introduce yourself.

MILLER: Why not?

POPE: Ishi is a natural healer.

MILLER: Of course, what else?

POPE: He sings to women patients in the hospital.

Kroeber is worried and directs the reporter to the entrance. Miller smiles and leans closer, examines the bows and arrows. Mysterious shadows move around the museum. The light is blue at the entrance to the wickiup. Boots is worried, hides behind the display case.

MILLER: Ishi, come out and show me your arrowheads.

POPE: Miss Miller, this is a hickory bow.

Pope raises a bow and draws the string.

MILLER: And this is a broken bottle.

Miller holds the green arrowhead up to the light.

POPE: Ishi is an artist, he can make arrowheads out of anything, obsidian or green glass.

MILLER: Really, you know so much about bows and arrowheads.

POPE: Ishi is my teacher.

MILLER: Why does a surgeon turn to archery?

POPE: Indeed *(Pause),* curiosity.

Pope shows his obsidian arrowheads. He holds the arrowheads to the light and as she looks at them, her cheek is close to his hand.

MILLER: The wild man vanished, as the doctor counted arrowheads.

POPE: Miller Miller, your wild manner has not vanished.

KROEBER: Ishi, please show the reporter your hickory bows.

Silence.

MILLER: Ishi, are you playing hide and seek with me?
KROEBER: Perhaps you could show your face at the entrance.

Miller moves on hands and knees closer to the entrance. She whistles, looks back once, and then crawls into the wickiup without hesitation.

KROEBER *(Shouts):* Ashe Miller writes stories for the newspapers.

Silence.

POPE *(Shouts):* Ishi, she has never heard the wood duck stories.

Silence.

KROEBER: Ishi, remember to show her your pocket watch.

Kroeber and Pope look to each other and then wait to hear the voice of the reporter in the wickiup. Kroeber paces with his hands behind his back. Pope examines a bow and several arrows.

MILLER: Ishi, where shall we begin?

Silence.

MILLER: Or *when* shall we begin?
ISHI: Hullo.
MILLER: Hullo, hullo, now that's a good start.

Pope laughs and checks his pocket watch. Prince paces around his camera. Boots leans on the duster. Thomas Waterman, the linguist, enters the museum. He wears a suit and thick glasses and has a mustache. Kroeber touches his lips, motions to be silent, and then points to the wickiup.

MILLER: Professor Kroeber said you were the find of a lifetime.
ISHI: Hims Big Chiep.
MILLER: Big Chiep?
ISHI: Hims good Chiep.
MILLER: The Big Chiep said you were the only man in America who knows
          no Christmas, is that true?
ISHI: How much money tee.
MILLER: For what?
ISHI: Hullo, hullo, hullo.

Pope mocks the salutation and then laughs. Kroeber and Waterman smile in silence. Prince is bored and leans on his camera.

MILLER: Have you been contaminated by civilization?
ISHI: I all a time smoke.
MILLER: Big Chiep said you come from a "puny native civilization," and that
        you are "unspeakably ignorant" *(Pause)*. Do you know anything?
ISHI: Too much pina.
MILLER: What does "pina" mean?
ISHI: Too much pina.

Waterman rushes to the entrance of the wickiup and shouts inside.

WATERMAN: Pain, he means pain.

Kroeber turns with embarrassment; he brushes the sleeves of his coat.

MILLER: Would you like to be an anthropologist?
ISHI: Hims lazy boy.

Pope waves his finger at the anthropologist. Kroeber doubles over in laughter, holds his stomach. Boots is very serious. Prince sits on the floor with his back against the tripod.

MILLER: Doctor Pope said he learned the lost art of archery from you, but
        did he ever teach you how to shoot a gun?
ISHI: Hims lazy boy.

Kroeber waves his finger at the doctor. Boots frowns.

MILLER: Why do you say hims *(Pause),* he is lazy?
ISHI: How much money tee.
MILLER: Never mind.

Silence.

MILLER: What is your name?

Silence.

MILLER: How old are you?

Silence.

MILLER: Are you married?

Silence.

MILLER: Do you fear menstruating women?

Silence.

MILLER: Are you the loneliest man on the earth?
ISHI: Candy tee, soda wata.
MILLER: Do you like candy?
ISHI: You go pretty soon.

Pope and the others are very amused and pace around the museum. Prince closes his eyes in boredom.

MILLER: Doctor Pope said you never learned how to say "thank you."

Pope waves his hands and turns his head from side to side.

ISHI: What's a matter tee.
MILLER: Nothing, just a few more questions.
ISHI: Hims lazy boy.
MILLER: Doctor Pope said you are modest and cover your genitalia when
      changing clothes, is that true?
ISHI: Hims lazy boy.

Pope covers his crotch with his hands and then doubles over with laughter. Kroeber points at the doctor and waves his finger once more. Boots is disgusted and turns toward the audience.

MILLER: Why don't you wear shoes?

Silence.

MILLER: Would you rather live on a reservation than in a museum?
ISHI: You go pretty soon.
MILLER: Doctor Pope said you heal women in the hospital.
ISHI: Evelybody hoppy.
MILLER: Do you heal women?
ISHI: Evelybody, evelybody hoppy.
MILLER: Edward Sapir, the linguist, said you were gentle....

Ishi blows the police whistle in the wickiup.

ISHI: Evelybody hoppy.

Ishi blows the whistle until the reporter leaves the wickiup.

MILLER: Who gave him the police whistle?

Miller frowns and covers her ears.

KROEBER: Doctor Pope.

POPE: Evelybody hoppy.

Pope and the others laugh and then mock the expression to each other several times. Ishi comes out of the wickiup and laughs with them. Prince is awakened by the laughter.

KROEBER: Professor Waterman, have you met Ashe Miller, reporter for the San Francisco *Call*?
WATERMAN: Thomas Waterman.

Waterman bows, he is formal and distant. Prince sets up the camera. Ishi is curious about the camera, ducks under the shroud, but resists any pose. The others are talking near the display case.

MILLER: Were you the first person to visit Ishi in jail?
WATERMAN: Yes, from the museum.
MILLER: What were your first impressions?
WATERMAN: Delighted that we could speak a few words.
MILLER: What words?
WATERMAN: Maeela.
MILLER: What does "maeela" mean?

Ishi turns when he hears the word "maeela."

WATERMAN: Ishi is here, ask him.
ISHI: Coyote stole the fire....
MILLER: Wait a minute, is this another coyote story?
WATERMAN: When asked about his wife he tells coyote stories.
MILLER: So, that's what "maeela" means?
WATERMAN: Ishi evades direct questions.
MILLER: But you said he was smarter than many college students.
WATERMAN: Yes, he is remarkable, a very lovable man.
MILLER: What other words?
WATERMAN: Ulisi.
MILLER: Ulisi, what does "ulisi" mean?

Ishi turns and smiles when he hears the word "ulisi."

WATERMAN: I don't understand.
MILLER: How could you not understand "ulisi"?
ISHI: Don't understand.
WATERMAN: "Ulisi" means not to understand.
MILLER: I understand.

Ishi and Waterman are very pleased with the discussion. Miller writes in her notebook. Ishi leaves the reporter with another word.

ISHI: Hansi saltu.
MILLER: So, what does that mean?
WATERMAN: Many white people.

Prince motions that he is ready. Waterman turns to the camera.

MILLER: Wait, one last question, what are the wood duck stories?

Silence.

KROEBER: Please, come closer to the camera.
POPE: Ishi, we are with you in name and picture.
ISHI: I am alone, and my name is not a picture.
POPE: True, no one has a picture for a name.
PRINCE: Ishi, stand here, lean on the display case.

Prince places a black pottery funeral urn on the display case. Boots dusts the camera.

MILLER: Ishi, what are the wood duck stories?
KROEBER: Perhaps he could tell you later.
POPE: Yes, later, when he takes his wood ducks to the hospital.

Prince is under the black shroud at the back of the camera. He prances in place and mutters.

ISHI: Hims lazy boy.
PRINCE: Ishi, look into the camera.
MILLER: His name is on the black pot.
POPE: So it is.
PRINCE *(Shouts)*: Ishi, remove your coat and shirt.

Ishi leaves the display case. In silence he looks around the museum, notices each person, and then smiles at the photographer.

ISHI: I will live like the white people from now on *(Pause)*. I want to stay
      where I am *(Pause)*. I will grow old here, and die in this house.
PRINCE: Ishi, bare your chest, the light is good.

Ishi whispers to Kroeber.

KROEBER: Ishi say he not see any other people go without them, without
      clothes *(Pause),* and he say he never take them off no more.

ACT 2

Mount Olivet Cemetery columbarium, a bunch of flowers in an urn, and funeral music. Ishi died seventy years earlier and his ashes are in a black pottery urn placed in a niche. Zero Larkin, a sculptor, is inspired by the remains of Ishi. Prince, the photographer, and Ashe Miller, the reporter, are there to record the moment of inspiration. Trope Browne, the attendant at the columbarium, opens the niche. Angel Day, the manager of the cemetery association, is an officious expert on tribal histories. Ishi and Boots are seated on a bench unseen at the side of the columbarium and comment on the scene.

ZERO: Zero Larkin, native sculptor with a vision.

Zero holds out his hand to Trope. Firm and energetic handshake.

TROPE: Trope...
ZERO: What's your name?
TROPE *(Shouts)*: Trope.
ZERO: Trope, are you a brother?
TROPE: That depends...
ZERO: On what?
TROPE: How much money you want.
ZERO: Brother, when was this niche last opened?
TROPE: Seventy years ago.
ZERO: No, someone's been here since then.
TROPE: I clean it, nobody else.

Trope unlocks the glass door on the niche. The funeral music stops. Silence, and then the sound of a rattle. Prince moves closer to record the event with a video camera. Zero gestures to the camera.

ZERO: Stand back.
TROPE: Zero...
ZERO: What, what's wrong?
TROPE: Wait a minute.
ZERO: Why, something wrong here?
TROPE: Do you want to make a rubbing first?
ZERO: Yeah, good idea, where's the paper?

Trope looks around and finds a roll of thick white paper. He tears a piece and tries to hold it in place against the writing on the jar in the niche.

TROPE: Don't push too hard.
ZERO: Trope, hold it, let me rub the name good.

Trope and Zero struggle to make a rubbing of the name on the jar. The paper is too thick and moves on the surface.

TROPE: The paper's too thick.
ZERO: It worked before.
TROPE: Not on round jars.
ZERO: Yeah, where's the thin paper, you got any?
TROPE: I got some flower tissue in the back.

Trope leaves for the paper. Zero stands by the niche. Angel moves closer and talks to the reporter.

ANGEL: Ishi, you see, made this, his own burial pot.
ASHE: Do you represent the columbarium?
ANGEL: Yes, Angel Day, manager of the cemetery.

Angel hands a business card to Ashe.

ASHE: What about the burial pot?
ANGEL: Ishi made it when he lived in the museum.
ASHE: You mean with his bows and arrowheads?
ANGEL: Precisely.
ASHE: Really, you mean he knew when he would die?
ANGEL: Yes, he was a shaman.
ASHE: Indeed, a shaman?

Ashe writes in a notebook. Angel waits until she has finished and then continues her officious comments on Ishi.

ANGEL: Not many people know this because it was sacred.
ASHE: Of course.
ANGEL: As a shaman he healed many women in the hospital.
ASHE: Why women?
ANGEL: Seventy years ago women were at the mercy of their male doctors
        and no one was worried that the last shaman was healing women.
ASHE: What did he do?
ANGEL: Well, he told the women stories about wood ducks.
ASHE: Wood ducks?
ANGEL: Yes, stories about wood ducks.
ASHE: Surely there is more to it than water birds?

ANGEL: Naturally, he chanted, touched the women with wood duck feathers, and then burned an incense made from duck feet, or some other duck parts.

ASHE: Sounds erotic to me.

ANGEL: Shamans are erotic healers.

ASHE: Whatever, but wood ducks have never inspired me.

ANGEL: Ishi was a natural healer.

ASHE: Naturally.

ANGEL: Natural and erotic.

Ishi and Boots are on the bench at the side of the niche; they are unseen by the others at the columbarium. She wears her floral dress and white boots. He wears a suit and tie, but no shoes. He laughs and then turns to Boots.

ISHI: I was never a shaman.

BOOTS: But you told those wood duck stories.

ISHI: Women listened to my wood duck stories in the hospital.

BOOTS: No one hears me.

ISHI: The women were better listeners than anthropologists.

BOOTS: What was so erotic?

ISHI: My hands, but that was eighty years ago.

Ishi holds out his hands. She examines his hands, turns them over several times.

BOOTS: You never told me you could write.

ISHI: I learned how to sign my name in the museum.

BOOTS: Angel said you made that black pot and then you wrote your name on it before you died, is that true?

ISHI: My family never made pottery, we made baskets.

BOOTS: Angel lied then.

ISHI: Not really, she's an expert on Indians.

BOOTS: That makes her a liar.

ISHI: Indians are inventions, so what's there to lie about?

BOOTS: But she said you wrote your own name.

ISHI: My signature, but if you look closely you can see that the letters on the black pot are printed *(Pause)*, very modern.

Boots walks over to the niche and examines the name on the black pot. She traces the letters with her finger. Then she raises the pot over her head with one hand. She is not noticed by the others.

BOOTS *(Shouts)*: You're right, this is not your signature.
ISHI: Ishi was never my name.
BOOTS: Angel is a liar, never mind the preventions.
ISHI: Indian inventions.

Trope returns with wide sheets of tissue paper. He tears the sheets into smaller pieces and holds one against the name on the jar. Zero raises the marker over his head, smiles at the video camera, and marks the paper.

ZERO: Ishi is a name with sacred power.
ASHE: I hear your name too.
ZERO: Ishi gives me my power as an artist.

Ishi turns to Boots on the bench and smiles.

BOOTS: Ishi was never your name.
ISHI: Zero is the same cipher either way.
BOOTS: Zero, Zero, and the cemetery liars.

Zero raises the rubbing of Ishi to the camera and the audience.

ZERO: Ishi is with me, our spirit is one in his sacred name.
ASHE: Zero, what are you going to do with the rubbing?
ZERO: I'm going to blast his sacred signature, right from this rubbing, at the bottom of my stone sculpture, my tribute to his power as an Indian.
ASHE: Have you finished the sculpture?
ZERO: Not yet, but with the inspiration of his name it won't take long.
ASHE: Does the sculpture have a home?
ZERO: Kroeber Hall, at the University of California, where he worked.
ASHE: You mean in the anthropology museum?
ZERO: Yeah, and he's going to be surrounded by children.
ASHE: Ishi never had children.
ANGEL: Indeed, but he would have had children if he had survived.
ZERO: Yeah, and we must think about the next generation.
ASHE: Generation of what?
ZERO: Indians, what else is this about?
ASHE: Zero, does it make a difference to anyone that you are not from the same tribe as Ishi?
ZERO: What's this now, an identity question?
ASHE: No, a tribal question.
ZERO: Ishi's my inspiration.
ASHE: Zero, say no more…

ZERO: We are both tribal artists, and that's our identity.
ASHE: I didn't know Ishi was a sculptor.
ZERO: He made this pot.

Zero reaches for the pot in the niche. Prince raises one hand and shouts.

PRINCE: Wait, wait, I want to start with a new tape.

Zero waits, a pose with his hands close to the jar in the niche.

ANGEL: Prince, this is one of those great documentary moments in life.
ASHE: Indeed, and death.
ANGEL: Somehow, even in the cemetery business, I never think about death.

Prince loads the videotape and shoulders the camera.

PRINCE: Zero, get ready, do your thing, man.

Ishi and Boots raise their hands and shout from the bench but no one hears them.

ISHI: Zero, do your inspiration thing with my pot.
BOOTS: Ishi never made that pot so that much is a zero.

Zero reaches into the niche and as he touches the pot with both hands he begins to tremble from his fingers on down to his feet.

ZERO: I can feel his spirit.
BOOTS: Zero, he's over here on the bench.
ISHI: Never mind, if he drops the pot we're both free.
ZERO: Ishi is with me, his spirit is coming through my fingers.
ASHE: What does it feel like?
ZERO: The greatest power of my life, the spirit of my people.
ASHE: Northern California?
ZERO: We are one as tribal people.

Zero trembles, and he smiles as the camera comes closer. Trope moves closer to be sure he does not drop the pot.

ASHE: Which one?
ANGEL: He means a universal tribal spirit.
ASHE *(ironically)*: That explains it then.
ZERO: Ishi is moving through my body.
PRINCE: Hang on my man.

Prince moves around and closer with the camera.

ZERO: He's taking over my body, from my fingers down to my toes.

Ishi moves his toes. Boots laughs, raises her dress, and dances near the bench in her white boots.

BOOTS: Nobody's trembled over my bones for a long time.
ISHI: Put yourself in a jar and see what happens.
BOOTS: Zero, Zero and the cemetery liars.
ISHI: Do you think they could hear my duck stories?

ACT THREE

Kroeber Hall, University of California, committee on names and spaces. The faculty is seated at a conference table to consider a proposal to rename the building "Ishi Hall." Angel Day, professor of anthropology, is chair of the committee. Other professors on the committee are Trope Browne, history, Ashe Miller, mass communication, and Prince Chamber, visual arts. Professor Alfred Kroeber initiated the proposal. Ishi and Boots are seated on a bench at the side unseen by the committee.

ANGEL: The Names Committee has considered this proposal three times.
TROPE: Why must we consider it again?
PRINCE: We have more important matters to consider.
ANGEL: Professor Kroeber is behind this, the third proposal.
TROPE: Why would he want to change his own name?
ANGEL: I have asked him to explain.

Kroeber enters and sits at the end of the conference table. He cleans his glasses, and then slowly explains his proposal to rename the building.

KROEBER: Ishi made my name...
TROPE: Forgive me professor, but this is not the case.
ANGEL: Trope, please, this is a proposal not an examination.
KROEBER: I remember that moment more than any other, at "eleven o'clock in the evening on Labor Day, 1911, there stepped off the ferry boat into the glare of electric lights, into the shouting of hotel runners, and the clanging of trolley cars on Market Street, San Francisco, Ishi, the last wild Indian in the United States."
PRINCE: Yes, we have heard that story many times.
KROEBER: Ishi's name is not genuine.
PRINCE: Once again, we understand the history.

KROEBER: "When the reporters swarmed out to the University Museum of Anthropology ... the morning after he arrived, their second inquiry was for his age, their first for his... To this day Ishi has never disclosed his real name." He has a strong sense of propriety.

ANGEL: And yet you would give up your honored name for his?

KROEBER: Not exactly.

ANGEL: Professor Kroeber, what, then, is the point of your proposal?

KROEBER: Ishi, we found, had "perceptive powers far keener than those of highly educated white men. He reasoned well, grasped an idea quickly," had a "keen sense of humor," was "gentle, thoughtful, and courteous" and had a "higher type of mentality that most Indians."

PRINCE: But you wrote at the time that because of what his, and I quote, "puny native civilization" made him, "he represents a stage through which our ancestors passed thousands of years ago."

KROEBER: Yes, at the time of his discovery.

PRINCE: Professor Kroeber, are you asking the committee to turn over the name of a building to a stone age escapee who would not reveal his own name?

KROEBER: Yes, but for the stone age, that would be exactly my proposal.

ANGEL: Several years ago, as you know, we received a proposal from an errant faculty member to change the name of Kroeber Hall to Big Chiep Hall *(Pause)*. Naturally, and in honor of your distinction as an anthropologist, we chose not to discuss the proposal.

KROEBER: What a pity.

PRINCE: Why on earth would you say that?

KROEBER: I supported that proposal.

ANGEL: Surely, professor, you are being facetious.

KROEBER: I am, but not in the sense of your gesture.

ANGEL: Please.

KROEBER: I am, indeed, the Big Chiep as much as he is Ishi.

Ishi smiles and moves from the bench to stand behind Kroeber. Ishi is seen and heard by no one but Boots. Ishi places his hands on Kroeber's shoulders.

ISHI: Big Chiep is my loyal friend.

BOOTS: Those professors need to hear the wood duck stories.

ISHI: The Big Chiep is on one of his name stories.

KROEBER: Ishi honored me with a nickname, in the same sense that we gave him his name *(Pause)*, the contradiction, of course, is that our name for him is romantic, while his name for me is a story.

TROPE: What is the story?

KROEBER: Ishi trusted me, an innocent in the politics of museum names, and he praised me with a nickname, his best pronunciation of chief.

ASHE: Surely mispronounced words are not suitable names for buildings?

KROEBER: No less than the names of immigrants.

TROPE: Professor Kroeber, as you know, building names are historical, but a nickname is, at best, ephemeral.

Ishi raises his hand and then stands up to speak. No one hears him.

ISHI: Indeed, our best stories and our best histories are nicknames.

BOOTS: I never had a name to mispronounce.

KROEBER: Ishi was the first native philosopher on campus, and he worked in the museum with distinction *(Pause)*. You see, he must be honored more than me because this man taught me, and others, our own discipline.

BOOTS: Kroeber said it, you are his anthropologist.

ISHI: Not a chance, he's the subject not the object.

BOOTS: Who are you then?

ISHI: The last object of their stone age.

ANGEL: Big Chiep Hall would not be acceptable to the administration.

KROEBER: Ishi, then, must replace my name.

ANGEL: Anything more to say before we discuss your proposal?

KROEBER: Ishi should have received the doctorate.

PRINCE: Forgive me professor, but that's ridiculous.

KROEBER: Ishi taught many anthropologists what they needed to know for promotion, and in that sense, the advanced degrees should be given to native philosophers.

PRINCE: Who would evaluate their knowledge?

BOOTS: Doctor Ishi, that sounds just fine to me.

ISHI: Kroeber has courage *(Pause)*, they must think he's lost his mind.

KROEBER: Professor Thomas Waterman noted in the results of psychological tests that Ishi had a "better head on him that a good many college men."

PRINCE: Actually, he said, "this wild man," did he not?

KROEBER: Professor Prince, you are well read for a man in the visual arts.

ISHI: He studies what he lost *(Pause)*, visual memories.

PRINCE: You also said that he was "unspeakably ignorant."

KROEBER: Saxton Pope, the medical doctor who spent the most time with him, said many times that Ishi was a natural healer *(Pause)*, and he wrote that "his temperament was philosophical, analytical, reserved, and cheerful. He probably looked upon us as extremely smart.

Ishi smiles and moves around the table. Boots joins him in a dance. They pause and read the notes of several faculty members on the committee.

BOOTS: Listen to this one, "over my dead body."
ISHI: How about this one, "who pays for the cost of new business cards?"
BOOTS: Listen to this, "Ishi sounds too much like icky."
KROEBER: "While we knew many things," Doctor Pope noted, "we had no knowledge of nature, no reserve; we were all busy-bodies. We were in fact sophisticated children."
ANGEL: Thank you professor for your generous instruction. We will meet in private to discuss your proposal and, of course, send you notice of our recommendation to the academic senate.
KROEBER: Ishi has given our lives a new measure of knowledge, we are the better for his kindness, and we must not lose this chance to honor him as a way to honor our own situational ethics as scholars.
ANGEL: Thank you.

The committee applauds Kroeber. The faculty rises to shake his hand as he leaves the room. Ishi and Boots move with Kroeber to the door, then sit at the seminar table for the discussion.

TROPE: Well, how are we to proceed with this romance?
ANGEL: Perhaps we could go around the room for comments.

The committee members look to each other in silence.

ASHE: Kroeber was a great anthropologist, and a very sensitive man.
BOOTS: That's right, and that's only the half of it.
PRINCE: Indeed, he was great *(Pause)*. Now, this sad romantic visitation.
TROPE: Romanticism, in fact, is not the issue here.
PRINCE: What is it then?
BOOTS: Yes, what is your problem?
TROPE: Established names are histories, not rumors, and these ridiculous nicknames are rumors, nothing more.
ISHl: Now there is a lonesome man with no stories.
BOOTS: Sounds like he's ready for the museum. *Ishi waves to Trope.*
ISHI: Call me Hearst.
BOOTS: Did you hear Trope, he's got a real name?
ISHI: Doctor Ishi Boaz Hearst.

Angel looks around the table.

ANGEL: Anything more before we vote.

ASHE: Actually, his name you know, sounds too much like icky.

PRINCE: Big Chiep, if we must, would be better than Icky Hall.

TROPE: Alas, who would pay the cost of printing new stationery and business cards if the building changes names?

ASHE: Good point.

ANGEL: Show of hands please, those in favor of the proposal to change Kroeber Hall to Ishi Hall.

Ishi and Boots raise their hands.

ANGEL: Those opposed to the proposal.

The four faculty members raise their hands.

ASHE: Professor Kroeber will be troubled by this, could we reach out to him in some way?

TROPE: Reach out, for what?

ANGEL: The vote was unanimous to oppose the proposal.

ASHE: He's one of the founders of anthropology.

TROPE: Histories are not founded, they are discovered.

ASHE: Indians were discovered....

TROPE: Indians were invented in a binary structure to counter the romance of those who favored noble savagism over civilization....

ANGEL: Trope, we got the point.

TROPE: Kroeber, with his liberal romance of the stone age and ridiculous names, would turn back the age of reason, the enlightenment, and a constitutional democracy.

ANGEL: Kroeber Hall shall remain so named.

BOOTS: I won't forget this, you did a real dumb thing here today.

Silence.

ISHI: Wait, before you leave, there is one more proposal to consider.

The faculty members gather their papers in silence, look up suddenly, and then pause to listen. They look around, not able to locate the voice.

ANGEL: Who said another proposal?

The faculty members look to each other in silence.

ASHE: I heard it too.

TROPE: What now, clairaudience proposals?
ISHI: Doctor Ishi Hearst proposes that no building on campus would bear
     the same name for more than two years at a time.
ASHE: Who is Ishi Hearst?

*Angel and Ashe, the women faculty members, hear the voice but no
one can hear or see Ishi or Boots at the table.*

ISHI: University of California buildings would be known by their nicknames
     and stories, and no building would hold even a nickname for more
     than two years.
BOOTS: Don't forget my nickname.
ANGEL: That voice sounds like my grandmother.
TROPE: Ishi Kroeber Hearst is even better *(Pause)*. Enough of this nonsense.

The male faculty members leave the table.

ISHI: Boots Hall, is that a better name?

ACT FOUR

*Federal Courtroom, a high bench, two tables, and metal folding chairs.
Attached to the back of chairs is a sign that reads First District Court of
Character. Ishi is the accused. Alfred Kroeber is the federal trial judge.*

*Ashe Miller is the federal attorney and prosecutor. Saxton Pope is the
court-appointed defense attorney. Angel Day is the bailiff. Prince Chamber
is the court clerk. Trope Browne, Zero Larkin, Thomas Waterman, and Boots
Story are seated in the courtroom as witnesses. Ishi places several bows,
arrows, arrowheads, and fire sticks on the defense table.*

ANGEL: Please rise, the First District Court of Character is now in session....

*Judge Kroeber enters the courtroom. He is dressed in an academic
robe and stands behind a high bench.*

ANGEL: The Honorable Alfred Kroeber presiding.
KROEBER: Characters here and the clerk be ready.

*Kroeber looks around the courtroom and the audience. Trope waves
to him but he does not respond.*

PRINCE: Ready for the judgment.
KROEBER: Character judgment.

PRINCE: How the times have changed.

KROEBER: Mister Ishi has been charged with seven counts of violating provisions of the Indian Arts and Crafts Act of 1990. He sold objects as tribal made, and could not prove that he was in fact a member of a tribe or recognized by a reservation government.

Prince hands the judge several sheets of paper.

PRINCE: Ishi was arrested at the Santa Fe Indian Market when other artists complained that he was not a real Indian.

KROEBER: Ashe Miller is the federal attorney this morning, is that correct?

ASHE: Yes, your honor, and the government is prepared to show that the man named Ishi sold seven works of art in violation of the Indian Arts and Crafts Act.

KROEBER: Now, is the government prepared to prove that Ishi is not an enrolled member of a recognized tribe?

ASHE: Yes, your honor.

KROEBER: His character, in fact, constitutes the reason for this hearing under the Minority Character and Judicial Reform Act.

ASHE: Yes, your honor, in the context of tribal enrollment.

KROEBER: Mister Ishi, are you repressed by counsel to answer these charges, that you are not an established tribal character?

ISHI: Hims good boy.

POPE: Saxton Pope, your honor, and we intend to prove that no one is more tribal than Ishi.

KROEBER: What tribal character does he intend to claim?

POPE: Yahi, of the Yana.

ASHE: The Yahi, your honor, is not a federally recognized tribe.

KROEBER: The Yahi, however, were studied by anthropologists.

POPE: Ishi, your honor, is the last of the Yahi.

KROEBER: Counsel agreed in chambers this morning not to romance the remains of the stone age, and we agreed to proceed with minimal formalities.

POPE: Indeed, your honor, but the defendant is the last of his tribe.

ASHE: The Yahi have been extinct for more than a century.

POPE: Your honor, that is cruel and inaccurate.

Ashe rises and reads from a yellow legal pad.

ASHE: The Yahi, your honor, were noted as extinct for forty years in a report published by the Bureau of American Ethnology in 1925.

POPE: That same report, written by a distinguished anthropologist, pointed out that the tribe was, and I quote, "believed extinct," but there was evidence of "aboriginal existence" at a much later date.

Kroeber searches in the pile of papers and reports on the bench.

KROEBER: I have a copy of that report (Pause), which, in fact, names the relator character of the Yahi as the southernmost division of the Yana.

ASHE: Yes, your honor.

Kroeber reads from the report and gestures with his hands.

KROEBER: The Yahi, "once resident on Mill and Deer Creeks, two eastern affluents of the Sacramento, are of a peculiar interest because of their rediscovery in recent years after they had been believed extinct for forty years."

POPE: Judge Kroeber, I move to dismiss, once more, the charges against my client who clearly is not now, and never has been, an extinct character.

KROEBER: Motion is denied *(Pause)*. The character of the defendant has not been established as tribal, we have heard only that the tribe he names may not be extinct.

POPE: Ishi, your honor, is an honorable name.

ASHE: Your honor, the defendant must prove that he is a member of both tribes, and that burden is more than a mere tribal nickname.

PRINCE: Counselor, what is that nickname?

ASHE: Ishi, the name of the defendant.

PRINCE: Ishi is not his surname, but a mere nickname?

POPE: Please, your honor, could we continue?

Kroeber stands at the bench and continues to read.

KROEBER: "The Yana are a people of fairly extensive territory but rather restricted numbers, concerning whom little general information has been extant, but to whom mystery of some kind has usually been made to attach...."

ASHE: Your honor, the defendant is charged with a felony not a mystery.

Kroeber ignores the comment and continues to read from the report. Ishi raises his arms as in flight. Angel drums her fingers on the table. Prince cleans his fingernails. Pope leans back in his chair and shivers. Boots dances in place, and the others in the courtroom show various gestures of boredom.

KROEBER: The Yana "were reputed of a marked physical type: their speech was not only distinctive but abnormally peculiar; in military prowess and cunning they far outshone all their neighbors; they had perhaps come from the far east. As usual, there is a thin sediment of fact to these fancies."

ASHE: Sediment, your honor, is a peculiar legal notion.

KROEBER: Indeed, is it the sense of residue or trash that bothers you the most?

ASHE: Sediment and trash, your honor, may establish character at the university or in a circus, but not according to the provisions of the Indian Arts and Crafts Act.

Boots turns to the spectators Trope and Waterman.

BOOTS: Ishi is a healer, what is this sediment?

TROPE: Nicknames and tribal fancies in character court.

BOOTS: Ishi should say something.

TROPE: Not yet.

BOOTS: Why not?

WATERMAN: Kroeber would never survive the wood duck stories.

BOOTS: You mean he's going to tell his stories?

WATERMAN: How else can he prove his character?

The bailiff motions to the spectators to be silent in court.

BOOTS: That same bailiff laughed when the judge told me to choose another name.

WATERMAN: What did you choose?

BOOTS: Boots Story.

TROPE: Great name, any relation to the jurists?

The bailiff frowns and moves toward the spectators.

POPE: Ishi has an established character.

KROEBER: Indeed, and how does he respond to the charges that he sold two hickory bows, four arrows with obsidian arrowheads, and one fire stick to federal undercover agents at the market in Santa Fe.

POPE: Ishi is that very person.

KROEBER: And the sale was in violation of the provision that the artist must prove a documented tribal character.

POPE: Ishi is that tribal artist.

KROEBER: How does he respond to the charges?

POPE: He made the bows, arrowheads, and the fire sticks that you see on the table, and he sold some of them to the agents for a very high price, but his tribal art is not a violation of any law, natural or otherwise.

Ishi raises a bow and draws the string. Pope taps an arrowhead on the table.

ASHE: Your honor, the defendant displayed and sold art and craft objects as an Indian, but he is not able to establish and prove his tribal character according to the provisions of the amended Indian Arts and Crafts Act.

POPE: Ishi was born Yahi.

ASHE: Moreover, your honor, the defendant was in violation of the provision that prohibits a tribe from imposing a fee in certifying an individual as an artisan.

KROEBER: What does that mean?

ASHE: He bought a certificate that said he was an Indian.

KROEBER: Why was this not mentioned in my chambers?

ASHE: I learned about this late, your honor, after our conference.

KROEBER: What is it that you learned?

POPE: Your honor, we can explain....

KROEBER: Miss Ashe, are these new charges?

ASHE: Your honor, we just learned that the defendant misrepresented his tribal character when he bought an enrollment document, in violation of the law, from the Dedicednu Indians of California.

There is a moment of silence, as the judge, the defense lawyer, the bailiff, the clerk, and the spectators in the courtroom smile and then burst into wild laughter. Ishi stands, waves his arms, and others double over with laughter. Prince turns and tumbles out of his chair. The bailiff shouts, laughs, pounds on the bench, and then wipes tears from her eyes. Ashe is unaware of the cause of the humor; she look around and forces a smile.

KROEBER: Now that was a character crime.

ASHE: Your honor, why the laughter?

KROEBER: What was the name of that tribe?

ASHE: The Dedicednu Indians.

Second round of laughter.

POPE: Indeed, but not at the moment.

KROEBER: Do you know what that means?

ASHE: Your honor, the certificate he purchased in violation of the law said the tribe was located in Laguna Beach, California.

KROEBER: The Dedicednus are the undecided spelled backwards.

Slow, third round of laughter.

POPE: Undecided, a condition of character courts.

ASHE: The Federal Bureau of Investigation, your honor, reported the evidence of misrepresentation by the defendant, and the government, notwithstanding the humor of the court, must institute a criminal action.

KROEBER: Proceed with your evidence.

ASHE: Your honor, we have recorded each criminal transaction with sound and two video cameras.

POPE: We stipulate that my client did indeed sell his bows and arrows to federal agents, and, we might add, for a very high price.

KROEBER: Get on with the rest then.

ASHE: Ishi is not a genuine name, and that has been established in numerous documents, and the defendant cannot under the law claim an extinct tribe as evidence to establish his character.

POPE: Your honor, we have identified seventeen official documents by doctors, attorneys, anthropologists, and journalists as evidence of his tribal character and identity.

ASHE: The government has studied these documents and nowhere is the defendant established by specific genealogical or communal evidence to the tribes named Yahi and Yana of California.

KROEBER: Counselor, are you twisting the tail of the arts and crafts amendment to the extreme?

ASHE: No, your honor, the government is protecting the genuine production and sale of tribal arts and crafts from criminal fraud and misrepresentation.

KROEBER: Ishi names a very remote tribe with no immediate evidence of his descent and that, clearly, is a burden under the provisions of the new law.

Ishi raises a bow and draws the sting.

ASHE: Your honor, the bows and arrows are evidence.

KROEBER: Ishi has stipulated that he willfully displayed and offered for sale certain bows and arrows, and other objects.

ASHE: Yes, your honor.

KROEBER: Now, is the federal attorney prepared to prove that the accused made and sold counterfeit objects by claiming a traditional association with a recognized tribe?

ASHE: Yes, your honor.

POPE: Nonsense, my client is more tribal than anyone in the country.

ASHE: Ishi sold counterfeit arrowheads made with broken bottles.

POPE: Yes, and to his credit as an artist, but he has never misrepresented such arrowheads as obsidian or anything other than broken glass.

ASHE: Counselor, the crime is his character not his arrowheads.

POPE: Ishi, your honor, has never been enrolled in a recognized tribe because he is the last of his tribe.

KROEBER: Do you have more character evidence to present?

POPE: Photographs, your honor, are the best evidence of his character.

ASHE: The photographic evidence is not dated and he could be a mere immigrant who later pretended to be tribal.

POPE: Your honor, consider the medical evidence....

KROEBER: What medical evidence?

POPE: His wide feet, the fact the he would rather not wear shoes, and the leather thongs in his ears.

Ishi raises his bare feet above the defense table.

KROEBER: Yes, wide feet so noted.

ASHE: My grandfather had wide feet, he was a farmer.

POPE: Ishi carries a pocket watch, but he never learned how to read the time.

ASHE: Neither has my son.

POPE: Ishi never lets dogs lick his hands.

KROEBER: What does that mean?

POPE: Something about disease.

ASHE: Would that be canine or a tribal character?

POPE: Ishi has trouble raising a window shade.

ASHE: So does my aunt.

POPE: Ishi never heard of Christmas.

ASHE: The absence is not a presence of character.

POPE: He is a natural archer....

ASHE: So what? He never took sweat baths.

POPE: "Archery is nearly a lost art."

ASHE: So is foot binding.

KROEBER: Ishi is a hunter with bow and arrows?

ASHE: Could he be in violation of federal game laws?

POPE: "Among civilized peoples archery survives only as a game, however, it is well known that even as late as two centuries ago the bow was a vigorous competitor with the flintlock in warfare."

KROEBER: The evidence is dramatic but the photographs, written documents, and stories, do not establish a clear connection to a tribal character, because the tribes he would claim, while they are secure in anthropology, have never been recognized by the federal government.

POPE: Your honor, did you earn the Order of the Arrow?

KROEBER: Counselor, my awards are not at issue here.

POPE: Your honor, forgive me, but the cultural contradiction is significant to my argument of character.

ASHE: Really, your honor, stories about the Boy Scouts...

KROEBER: Mister Pope, what is your point?

POPE: That while your character has been enhanced by the Order of the Arrow, the natural practices of a real tribal archer are denied as evidence of character under the provisions of the new arts act.

ASHE: Your honor, this is a deliberate obfuscation....

KROEBER: Prince, strike comments on the Order of the Arrow.

Ishi blows his police whistle. Kroeber motions to the bailiff.

KROEBER: Angel, remove that whistle.

Angel holds out her hand and the sound stops.

KROEBER: Prince, strike the whistle.

POPE: Your honor, have you ever heard the wood duck stories?

KROEBER: No, are they the same as the raven stories?

POPE: The wood duck stories are heard in one distinct tribe.

KROEBER: That would be oral literature?

ASHE: Oral stories, your honor, would be hearsay not evidence.

POPE: Yes, your honor, oral stories are none other than a real character, the character of tribal remembrance, the character that heard and remembered the wood duck stories.

ASHE: We are not here to hear stories, but to establish character.

KROEBER: Mister Pope, what is the point?

POPE: No one could ever fake the wood duck stories.

KROEBER: What exactly are these stories about?

POPE: Wood duck lives with his sisters and wants to get married.

ASHE: Your honor, these stories never end.

KROEBER: Ishi's character, then, is based on his performance of these stories, and that would be the prima facie case evidence of recognition as a tribal character?

POPE: Tribal character par excellence.

KROEBER: How long is the performance?

POPE: Well, your honor, there is no measured time of the stories.

KROEBER: How long was his last performance?

ASHE: Seven hours, your honor, the wood duck lasted seven hours.

Kroeber looks at his watch. Ashe holds her hands in prayer.

KROEBER: The wood duck has two minutes to be heard.

ISHI *(Wavering voice)*: Winotay, winotay, winotay...

KROEBER: Two minutes, no more.

POPE: Wood duck grew up and wanted a...

ASHE: Your honor, please...

Kroeber leans back and holds his chin. Ashe rests her head on the table.

POPE: So, early one morning he began to sing a love song. He sat up in bed and sang.

Pope gestures to Ishi.

ISHI *(Wavering voice)*: Winotay, winotay, winotay...

POPE: "Then wood duck stood up and turned to the four corners of the earth. As he turned he looked far, far away. When he had turned until he looked into the north he stopped and called in his two sisters..."

KROEBER: Seven hours?

POPE: Yes, your honor, but he cannot start now because he never starts the wood duck stories before dark.

KROEBER: What a pity.

ASHE: Your honor, the government would hear as evidence the one minute wood duck, but no more.

KROEBER: Clearly the performance of wood duck stories, no matter how great the audience response, does not establish tribal character or identity under the provisions of the Indian Arts and Crafts Act of 1990.

POPE: Your honor, the best stories can be ruined by a bad act.

Kroeber moves toward the audience. The others turn and move with him in silence. He speaks to the audience.

KROEBER: What would you do under the circumstances?

Gestures to the audience.

KROEBER: Would you decide in favor of the government *(Pause),* as if a federal agent could determine the meaning of criminal acts in the sale of tribal art and crafts, even in Santa Fe, New Mexico?

Kroeber moves closer to the audience.

KROEBER: The First District Court of Character hears thousands of cases that arise from cultural contradictions and misrepresentations *(Pause).* Now the court must decide if wood duck stories are enough to establish a tribal character....

Spectators in the court shout their responses.

BOOTS: Ishi heals women.

KROEBER: What is criminal in the imagination of a tribal artist?

TROPE: Portraits of the presidents.

KROEBER: Colonial inventions are criminal, not tribal survivance.

WATERMAN: Wait until you hear the wood duck stories.

KROEBER: Ishi was a native hunter in a museum *(Pause).* I ask you, are his bows and arrows more criminal as art objects under this new law?

POPE: The native hunter is the natural artist, and the natural has always been a threat to consumer artists.

KROEBER: Consumer fraud? Or is this a case of cultural romance?

PRINCE: Who knows the difference in Santa Fe?

KROEBER: Could the issue be cultural romance and legislative protectionism of tribal arts and crafts?

ASHE: The government protects the true Indian.

TROPE: Counselor you got that right.

KROEBER: Then the Indian, not the buyer, must beware.

Kroeber returns to the bench. The others turn and listen.

BAILIFF: Please rise to hear the wood duck stories.

ISHI *(Wavering voice)*: Winotay, winotay, winotay....

KROEBER: No, no, not the stories.

ASHE: Your honor, duck stories told so early in the day could be another violation of the Indian Arts and Crafts Act.

KROEBER: Ever so vigilant on behalf of the consumer.

ASHE: Thank you, your honor.

BAILIFF: Please rise.

KROEBER: The First District Court of Character cannot rule in favor of either side in this matter *(Pause)*. Ishi has not established evidence of his tribal character that satisfies provisions of the Indian Arts and Crafts Act. At the same time, he is a native artist and his bows and arrows are clearly not criminal...

Kroeber pauses and looks to the audience.

Ishi is real and the law is not. Therefore, my decision is to declare that the accused is his own tribe. Ishi is his own sovereign tribal nation, and this is clear and present evidence of his character...

Ishi, the man so named, has established a tribal character in a museum and in his endless wood duck stories...

Ishi, naturally, is a member of his own tribe, extinct or not. Clearly, he is an established tribal character and he has never been in violation of the Indian Arts and Crafts Act...

Ishi is an artist, he is our remembrance of justice, and that is his natural character.

Ishi puts on his shoes, ties them, waves to the judge, and then leaves the courtroom with Boots. The two walk down the aisle past the audience.

THE END

Hanay Geiogamah

(B. 1945) Kiowa

Hanay Geiogamah was born in Lawton, Oklahoma, in 1945. He is Kiowa. He studied journalism at the University of Oklahoma and theater and drama at Indiana University. He has taught at Colorado College, the University of Washington, and the University of California at Los Angeles. Geiogamah is a dramatist and director and one of the organizers of the American Indian Theater Ensemble. **Body Indian**, *his first play, was the premiere production that year.* **Foghorn** *was first presented at Theater im Reichskabarett, West Berlin, Germany, on October 18, 1973.*

Jeffrey Huntsman, in the introduction to **New Native American Drama: Three Plays**, *wrote that the "plays grew out of their author's desire to present Native Americans to Native Americans in ways that are vivid and compelling and free from the more pernicious of the Euro-American stereotypes of Indians." Geiogamah's* **Foghorn** *provides*

> *his audience an occasion to exorcise their own acceptance of the ancestral noble savage—dour, stoic, and dumb—or the contemporary welfare derelict—drunken, irresponsible, and shiftless. This purpose he accomplishes with unflagging good humor, classically exposing absurdity with teasing caricature....*

> *Geiogamah understands and uses the history and literary techniques and traditions of Native American peoples while avoiding lurching cavalcades of wooden figures. Above all, there is a dignity and integrity to these plays, a sense in which the works themselves, funny and fierce, stand as examples of the philosophical and political values they promote.*

LaVonne Ruoff wrote in **American Indian Literatures** *that "***Foghorn***, a multimedia satire, pokes fun at stereotypes of Indians from the arrival of Columbus to the 1973 confrontations at Wounded Knee; the title refers to the foghorns blasted at the Indians who occupied Alcatraz in 1969."*

"Almost all the characters in this play are stereotypes pushed to the point of absurdity," Geiogamah noted in **Foghorn**. *"The satire proceeds by playful mockery rather than bitter denunciation."*

Foghorn

Foghorn was first presented at Theater in Reichskabarett, West Berlin, Germany, on October 18, 1973, with the following cast:

Jane Lind
Bruce Miller
Marie Antoinette Rogers
Irene Toledo
Maggie Geiogamah

Phillip George
Charlie Hill
Denice Hernandez
Luis Romero
Carpio Bernal

Directed by John Vaccaro
Production Stage Manager, Kenn Hill
Sets by Joe Peroni and Larry Rutter
Costumes by Margo Lazzaro

The People of the Play

NARRATOR, a spokesman for the Indians
NUN
ALTAR BOY
SCHOOLTEACHER, circa 1900, in stars and stripes skirt
THE PRINCESS POCAHONTAS
POCAHONTAS'S handmaidens, three or four
LONE RANGER
TONTO
FIRST LADY OF THE UNITED STATES
U.S. GOVERNMENT SPY
VOICE OF THE SPY'S CONTACT, (can be acted)
BULL
GIRL (reading treaties)

Wild West Show

SHOW CARD GIRL
HEAD WARRIOR
TWO INDIAN BRAVES (Performing "hand-to-hand" combat)
TWO CHIEFS AND ASSORTED BRAVES (For Indian war council)
INDIAN INTERPRETER
LOVELY WHITE MAIDEN (Wearing bright blonde wig)
LECHEROUS INDIAN MAN (Who chases her)

Music

ELECTRONIC COMPOSITION FOR JOURNEY (4 or 5 minutes)
ZUNI SUNRISE CHANT

PLAINS INDIAN WAR DANCE SONG
VERY LOFTY CHURCH-ORGAN MUSIC (Nun Scene)
GOOD MORNING TO YOU (Schoolteacher Scene)
THE STAR SPANGLED BANNER (Schoolteacher Scene)
THE INDIAN LOVE CALL (Pocahontas Scene)
WILLIAM TELL OVERTURE ("Lone Ranger" Theme)
AMERICA THE BEAUTIFUL (First Lady Scene)
PASS THAT PEACE PIPE (AND BURY THAT HATCHET) (Special Arrangement)
WILD WEST SHOW ACCOMPANIMENT (Special composition on show organ or piano; mock drumming rhythms of Indian Council of War, Authentic Indian War Dance, and Savage Brutal Scalp Dance. Old-fashioned piano for chasing of Lovely White Maiden.)
THE AIM SONG ("Indian people will be free when we win at Wounded Knee")

Author's Note

Almost all the characters in this play are stereotypes pushed to the point of absurdity. The satire proceeds by playful mockery rather than bitter denunciation. A production should aim at a light, almost frivolous effect (the basic seriousness of the play will emerge all the more effectively if the heavy hand is avoided). The actors should never appear to be preaching, nor should they strive too much for laughs; they should simply let them occur.

It is vital that there be a minimum of delay between scenes. The drilling sounds and the visuals of earth being drilled form a bridge between scenes, but they should be kept brief.

The stage can be decorated to reflect a mixture of the prison yard on Alcatraz Island during the 1969–71 occupation; the terrain around Wounded Knee, South Dakota, during the 1973 incident; a composite Indian reservation; and various national monuments across the United states, such as Mount Rushmore and the Jefferson Memorial. The visuals are intended to counterpoint the action and to give a feeling that the audience is actually present yet not directly participating in the action of the play.

It is desirable that the actors know how to sing, for live performance of the songs makes for a much stronger production. Some of the songs, such as "Pass That Peace Pipe and Bury That Hatchet," can be recorded on tape and the performance synchronized with them. The Wild West Show composition should almost certainly be taped. All traditional drumming should be performed live if possible.

It is not important if the audience can see offstage into the wings or if other elements of the production are exposed. The actors should pay no attention to this informality and take any accidents that may occur in their stride.

There should be a lot of color, but not so riotous that it distracts the attention of the audience. Props should be of slapstick proportions in the Nun, Peace Pipe, and Wild West Show Scenes.

1

The opening section of the play, until the appearance of the religious personnel, is performed against a background of progressive electronic sound, one that evokes a journey through time and space, perhaps composed on a synthesizer or possibly with string instruments and percussion. The performing group follows a stylized choreography that is patterned to follow the electronic score. The "parts" are distributed among members of the performing group who form an ensemble for the production. They carry bundles of belongings, pull travois, and so forth. The costumes and movement should suggest a forced journeys, such as Trail of Tears, spanning the centuries from 1492 to the present and stretching geographically from the West Indies to Alcatraz Island. The delivery of the first six statements must be timed as a narration for the journey, and must convey an evolving attitude toward Indians. If enough performers are available, the company members can portray the Spanish sailor, senator, and others in spotlighted areas about the stage. Or the lines can be recorded on tape with the electronic score.

The stage is dark. Suddenly a large, painted Indian face appears, apparitionlike, moving slowly as it is projected about the stage, its eyes gazing toward the audience. The electronic music begins.

SPANISH SAILOR (*Very excited*): ¡Señor Capitan Columbus! ¡Mire! ¡Mire! ¡Mire! ¡Alla! ¡Mire! ¡Dios mio! ¡Estos hombres, cho-co-la-tes! ¡Los indios! ¡Los indios! ¡Ellos son los indios!

The face fades as lights come up dimly, revealing the performing group frozen in position onstage. They begin moving slowly as the electronic journey music resumes.

MALE SETTLER: You're only an Injun. Don't talk back! (*Now louder.*) You're only an Injun! Don't talk back!

Sounds of mixed gunfire: rifles, old muskets, and so forth, followed by a pause. Then more gunfire.

TWO WHITE MEN *(Voices colliding)*: Vermin! Varmits! Vermin! Varmits! Vermin! Varmits!

Electronic journey music, group movement.

FEMALE SETTLER: Filthy savages. Murderers! Scalpers!

Electronic journey music, group movement.

ANGRY MALE VIGILANTE: I say let's force 'em off the land! Move 'em with force, guns! Now!

Electronic journey music, group movement, mixed gunshots, high volume. Electronic journey music and group movement continue. More gunshots. Electronic journey music and group movement now becoming fragmented.

UNITED STATES SENATOR: The Indian problem is a matter for the courts and the Congress to deal with. We've been victorious over them on the battlefield, now they must settle on the reservations we have generously set aside for them. They have stood in the way of our great American Manifest Destiny long enough.

Electronic journey music concludes and performers exit.

2

The performing group returns to the stage one by one as a panoramic view of Alcatraz Island is projected onto the cyclorama or back wall of the playing area. Photographs of the occupation are seen in a dissolving sequence as the group sings the Zuni Sunrise Chant.

GROUP: *Following a leader, with respectful expressions*
　　　BAH HEY BA HO
　　　BAH HEY BA HO
　　　EYE YA NE NAH WAY
　　　EE I YA HO. I YA HO WAY.
　　　SHEY-NE NAH-WAY
　　　BAH HO. BA HEY.
　　　BA HO. BA HEY.
NARRATOR: Thanksgiving Day, 1969, Alcatraz Island, San Francisco Bay. We are discovered, again. It was the first time that we had taken back

land that already was ours. Indian people everywhere felt good about our having the island, about our determination.

The visuals continue, their projection punctured by the silhouettes of the performing group members, who stand attentively about the playing area.

We planned to develop the island, to build a cultural and spiritual center for all tribes, all people. Nineteen months. It was a good beginning.

Alcatraz fades. A gigantic map of the United States, blank except for delineations of the Indian reservations, comes into focus. The performing group now pantomimes boarding a boat, sailing across the bay. A low flute is heard. The players form a phalanx across the front of the stage as they disembark, and the narrator moves to downstage center.

NARRATOR: We, the Native Americans, reclaim this land, known as America, in the name of all American Indians, by right of discovery. We wish to be fair and honorable with the Caucasian inhabitants of this land, who as a majority wrongfully claim it as theirs, and hereby pledge that we shall give to the majority inhabitants of this country a portion of the land for their own, to be held in trust by the American Indian people—for as long as the sun shall rise and the rivers go down to the sea! We will further guide the majority inhabitants in the proper way of living. We will offer them our religion, our education, our way of life—in order to help them achieve our level of civilization and thus raise them and all their white brothers from their savage and unhappy state.

3

The performing group loudly sings and drums a Plains Indian War Dance song in celebration. When the singing ends, an organ blasts out church music, bringing on a Catholic nun and Indian altar boy, who carries a cross covered with paper money. Members of the performing group, wrapped in blankets and with poker-faced expressions, take places right and left of the nun and altar boy who are standing stage center, smiling.

NUN: *(As church music fades, she speaks first calmly, then gradually up to a frenzy.)* My blessed savages. Children of the unknown, of the wilderness. You are most fortunate that we have found you. You have

been smiled favorably upon by the holy father in Rome. He has seen fit to send us out to this New World to impart the divine wisdom of God to you. *(She pauses, fondles her book, then raises it in front of the Indians.)* This book contains all of His holy teachings. I am going to give His teachings to you. For no soul must be without knowledge of the Almighty. No soul must be allowed to wander in the darkness, as yours have for so long, and never know the Kingdom of God. You do not have religion! You do not have an all-forgiving father like ours. You are heathens. Pagans. Poor, miserable, ignorant, uncivilized, NAKED! *(She calms herself.)*
We are going to take you out of this darkness and show you His way. And you will be happy and grateful, forever, that we have found you. Our faith, our beautiful faith, that has been the salvation of so many millions of souls, will now be yours. For without faith in God, the one, true Christian God, you will never have the hope of becoming civilized, of knowing a way of life other than this pitiful existence of yours. And! If we did not find you, your souls would burn! Burn forever, for eternity! In HELL!

She and the altar boy, who has been raising and lowering the cross behind her as she is speaking, now stand triumphantly before the group. The Indians attack them as the church music blasts through the theater. Then a sharp drilling noise is heard, the lights flash, and action visuals of giant chunks of earth flying through space are projected on the playing area.

4

A clownish schoolteacher dances onstage, ringing a bell, carrying a bundle of small American flags, singing "Good Morning to You." She has been preceded by a group of very young Indian students who run onstage playfully, taking seats on two wooden benches. They respond to the teacher with awe, surprise, mild defiance, and fear. The teacher is snobbish, nervous, rude, feisty, and blusterous.

TEACHER: *(Very overdone, but with control)* Good morning, boys and girls, er, squaw and bucks. Good morning.

(She puts the bell down, fusses with her hair and dress. The students pay no attention. She becomes angry.)

G—ood morning, savages! (She busily arranges them in "order.") I see that this is going to be more difficult than they told me it would be. You are all totally ignorant. You might as well be deaf and dumb! Do any of you understand any English? Not a single one of you?
(To the audience) I wonder if the people in Washington really know what they're doing by trying to teach these savages how to speak English, how to live like civilized human beings. These stupid children should be left on their reservations and forgotten about. What a bunch of worthless things.

(She sees one of the girls gesture to one of the others, and pummels the girl, who pulls back wide-eyed with surprise.)

What are you doing there? What was that? Was that an Indian sign-language gesture I saw you making there? Was it? Was it sign language? Well, there won't be any more of that in this classroom, none of that! I'll rap your knuckles hard if you do that again. Do you hear me? Do you understand me? It'll be the dark room for you. *(Pause)* That's one step out of savagery for you.

(Suddenly, pinching her nose in broad gesture)

Ooooooooh, oooooh! What an odor! *(She lifts the blanket of a girl pupil.)* Ooooooohweeeeee, young lady, ooooohweeeee! You don't smell like a white woman! You smell like a... like... a ... Oh, my goodness, you are going to have to learn how to take a nice, civilized ladylike bath and keep your body clean. Do you hear me? That will be another step out of your darkness!
(Looking in one of the boys' hair) Oh, heavens alive! Oh, good heavens! Nits! Nits! Oh, and they're alive, they're real! Oh, oh! Live! How disgusting, how utterly disgusting! *(She scratches herself wildly.)* Well, this can be easily solved. Everyone of you, everyone of you will have your hair cut off tonight. Tonight! Girls and boys. We will not have a bunch of lousy Indians in this classroom! No, oh, no! *(After a short pause)* Sign language! Stinking bodies! Blankets! Deaf and dumb! How did these people ever get themselves in this condition?

The students are giggling again, she reestablishes order, continues.

You Indians are going to become educated, educated! That's spelled E-D-U-C-A-T-E-D, ed-u-ca-ted! Here in this school you are going to learn the English language. You are going to learn how to be Christians, how to worship God and live a clean, wholesome, decent life. You are going to learn how to be civilized people, civilized Indians, Indians who can earn an honest living, Indians that the American people can be proud of, not shamed by, so that we can hold our heads up high and say, "They are just like us, they are civilized. They aren't wild and on the warpath anymore. They are living the American way."

(She sings a line of "Star Spangled Banner," then sees the girl make the gesture again, lunges at her, yanks up the child, shouts directly into her face.)

This is not the reservation, child! This is not that awful place you came from where you all run around half naked, filthy, living in sin! This is a white man's schoolhouse. I told you not to do that again. I told you what I'd do. *(She shakes the child violently.)* You are going to be a lesson for the others. You, child, are going to be punished. *(She pulls out a bottle of castor oil and pours it down the struggling child's mouth.)* It's the dark room for you. *(She pushes the child into a dark closet space.)* You will stay in here all day. No food! No water! And no toilet! *(Turns to others)* She is a lesson for all of you to follow. I caught her doing a sign-language gesture. No more of that in this classroom, do you hear me? You are going to forget all of your Indian ways, all of them. You can start erasing them from your minds right now, right here, right this instant. No more of your disgusting sign language. No more of your savage tongue. No more greasy, lousy hair. No more blankets. You are going to learn the English language. That is what you were brought here for. *(Turning to the audience)* The English language. The most beautiful language in all the world. The language that has brought hope and civilization to people everywhere. The one true language, OUR language! *(Quickly turning her back to the students)* Now, listen to me carefully, very carefully. I am going to teach you your first word of English. Listen carefully, for it is the word, the one word, you must know first to become civilized. You must say this word to all of the white people you see, all of them, men and ladies. They'll be proud of you when they hear you say it, yes, proud, and when they hear you say it, they'll know that you are being relieved of your savage, uncivilized ways. They'll smile back at you and say the same thing. All right? Okay? Listen closely. The word is hell-o. Hell-o. H-E-L-L-O. Hello. Listen to the way I say it. Hello. Hell-o. It's the first word of the American way. The American way begins with hello. Say it, children, say it. Hell-O, Hell-O.

One of the pupils timidly tries the word and giggles as the others show amusement. The teacher hears her, yanks her to the front of the class with much flourish.

She said it! She said it! She said the word. She's on the road to the American way now! She said hello!

The teacher hands the girl a small American flag, then takes it back to demonstrate how to wave it while repeating hello. The girl clowns crudely with the flag in her hand as the teacher turns to coax the class one by one to say hello. The students ape the teacher with strong gestures as she continues to instruct the remaining students. The teacher soars on her success. The pupils form into a tight group, fists clenched, close in on her and attack. The lights fade on the drilling sound, earth visuals.

5

The Princess Pocahontas runs onstage carrying flowers and singing "The Indian Love Call." Her handmaidens follow, giggling. As Pocahontas flutters about, the handmaidens seat themselves in a semicircle for gossip.

HANDMAIDENS: *(Very eager)* How was it, Princess Pocahontas? How was it? Tell us.

POCAHONTAS: *(A languid smile on her face)* I couldn't take my eyes off him when I first saw him. He was so … so … ooh!

The handmaidens twitter excitedly, Pocahontas flutters back and forth.

HANDMAIDENS: So, so what, Pocahontas? Tell us, please.

POCAHONTAS: *(Gesturing with her hands)* He was so … big. Ooooooh, uuuh.

HANDMAIDENS: *(Puzzled)* Big? How do you mean, Pocahontas, big?

POCAHONTAS: *(Enjoying the handmaidens' curiosity)* He had such big legs. Such big, uh, arms, such big, uh, uh, chest. Such big, big head. Such big, big hands. Such big, big feet. Such big eyes. Such big mouth. Such big ears. Oooooh, aaahaaa.

HANDMAIDENS: And? And?

POCAHONTAS: And his hat was big. And his cape was big. And his boots and his sword and his... And all of the other white men with him were big. Ooooooh, uuuh.

The handmaidens squeal loudly as they pant for more details.

POCAHONTAS: *(Eyes becoming dreamy)* Be quiet and I will tell you about the big captain. The big, big captain.

The handmaidens calm down, move in closer to hear.

POCAHONTAS: First, first he took me to his dwelling and he seemed, uh, kind of, of nervous about me being with him. He told one of the other captains that nobody was to ... to come into the hut. This made me a little bit afraid at first, but he took hold of my hand and smiled at me. He kept smiling at me, and then he asked me, he asked me if I was a ... a ... vir-gin. When he said enough so that I knew what he was talking about, I ... I said to him, "Yes, yes ... I am a vir-gin." When I said this, he seemed to get kind of nervous, excited. He looked at me deeply ... in *luff* with me and he wanted me to ... to ... know his body and that he wanted to know, know my body too. Then he pulled me gently down on the bed and began to put his lips on mine. He did this several times, and each time his breathing became more, more nervous, like he was getting very warm. Then he began to kiss my neck and my cheeks. *(The handmaidens urge her on.)* And then he touched my breasts. And then he stood up, suddenly, and began to take off his clothes. He took off his boots, his shirt, his pants, all that he was wearing. He stood over me, his big, big, big body naked like one of the little children. There was so much hair on his body, it made me a little afraid. *(She giggles to herself.)*
HANDMAIDENS: *(Interrupting)* Did you ... did you take off...?
POCAHONTAS: Yes, I did, slowly, I didn't know what ... I was doing, but I felt happy and warm and...

One of the older handmaidens casts an unbelieving glance to one of her companions on the last remark.

HANDMAIDENS: Yes, Tell us all of it!
POCAHONTAS: And the big captain was standing above me, looking down at me, breathing like a boy after a footrace, and I saw that his ...

The handmaidens huddle closely with Pocahontas for the intimate details. One of them pops up, exclaiming "Pink?" Then Pocahontas rises above them, lifts her arms in a manner to suggest an erect phallus. The handmaidens gasp. Then a kazoo whistle indicates that the erection falls, quickly, and the handmaidens explode with laughter.

POCAHONTAS: *(Fighting for their attention)* He said to me, I love you, dear Pocahontas. I promise you it won't happen the next time. I promise, I promise, I promise.

The lights fade on the handmaidens squealing with laughter. Drilling sound, earth visuals.

6

Tonto and the Lone Ranger enter with horse-riding pantomime as a piano thumps out familiar Lone Ranger *theme. Piano stops and starts, giving Tonto an opportunity to make mocking gestures toward the Lone Ranger. Entrance music ends; they dismount. Lone Ranger takes a seat, exhales, motions to Tonto to shine his boots.*

LONE RANGER: *(Worried)* You know, Tonto, I've been thinking.

TONTO: *(Impassively)* Kemo Sabay.

LONE RANGER: I've been thinking, Tonto. The way you always bail me out of the crisis right at the last minute with your clever thinking sure doesn't look too good for me. You know what I mean? It looks maybe like I'm not too smart having to rely on an illiterate Injun like you to do all the clever thinking, and even outsmarting the white man.

TONTO: *(Briskly shining the boots)* Kemo Sabay.

LONE RANGER: Tonto, can you think of any way that I can come to your rescue and save you from the hands of death? Just one, Tonto? I'm really feeling insecure about this, old partner. You always come up with something good.

TONTO: Kemo Sabay.

LONE RANGER: People might start losing faith in me if they keep seeing you doing all the smart stuff. It's bad for business, Tonto.

TONTO: *(Shifting to Lone Ranger's other boot)* Kemo Sabay.

LONE RANGER: *(Inspired)* I got it! I got it! *(Piano interlude suggestion wickedness, villainy)* Tonto, you get shot, real badly, right smack in the chest by a no-good Injun varmit who says you stole his squaw. You're about to die, and I find you. I get you to a friendly rancher's house, one where they'll let me bring my Injun friend inside, and do an operation on you to remove the bullet. How's that, Tonto?

TONTO: Kemo Sabay.

LONE RANGER: *(Excited)* You're just about to bleed to death, and I know all this doctor's learning about surgery. Your life is fast slipping away. I'm trying hard to save you, me in my mask and my doctor's outfit and my scalpel and other tools, and suddenly you rise up to tell me which aorta in your heart to bypass, and the shock from this kills you instantly, and you fall back, dead. And, and, and I say: "I did what I could for my Injun friend, I tried to save him. I almost did, but he killed himself before I could finish the operation." How's that? Huh, Tonto, how's that? That'll show I'm not so reliant on you, right? It'd be the end of the Lone Ranger and Tonto, his faithful Injun companion. Then, there'd by just the Lone Ranger. How's that, Tonto? Sound like it'll work to you?

The Lone Ranger stands staring out toward the audience, caught up in the story. Tonto rises from the floor, taps him lightly on the shoulder, he turns, and Tonto cuts his throat with a knife. Drilling sound on tape, earth visuals, lights out fast.

7

The performing group becomes an audience for a dedication ceremony. "America the Beautiful" is heard, then scattered applause, all on tape.

DEEP MALE VOICE: *(Velvety and awestruck, on tape)* Ladies and gentlemen, I give you, the First Lay—dee of the United States.

Thunderous applause.

FIRST LADY: *(A bit daffy and with fluttery happiness "to be here.")* Thank you. Thank yooou. I want to say right away that I have never seen such lovely, stoic faces as those of you Indian friends here with us today. Just look at those beautiful facial lines, those high cheekbones, those wonderfully well-rounded lips, those big dark eyes. And their costumes. Aren't they simply tooo beautiful? Let's-give-them-a-big-hand-ladies-and-gentlemen, let's-give-them-a-big-hand. *(The Indians applaud, rib each other.)* Their radiance has made this day truly one to remember.

(She clears her throat, quickly checks her makeup.) I know, I just know they are going to be wonderful assets to the new national recreational park which I am here with you today to dedicate. In the next few years, there will be hundreds-of-pretty-pictures-of-these-colorful, uh Indian natives, taken-here-in-this-neeyew park of ours, adding the excitement of a great outdoors vacation in the great American West to family photo albums in homes all across our land. Isn't-that-wonderful?

Applause cut short on tape, she fidgets nervously, smiles widely, hurries on with her speech.

The idea for this new park came directly from my husband, the pres-i-dent, and his assistant, the secretary of the interior. The three of us were having tea and ladyfingers in my sitting room in the family quarters of the White House, discussing ways to beautify America, and the secretary said to the pres-i-dent, "Mr. Pres-i-dent, I have a great idea. As you know sir, some of nature's most spectacular scenery is located right on many of the Indian reservations out West. Why don't we declare one of these reservations a national park? *(Pause)* It'll be a first." *(There is a stir in the Indian group.)* "The Indians get very little use of them anyway." The pres-i-dent said he thought it was a great idea, and time an entire Indian reservation be made a nation park.

INDIAN: *(With prop camera in hand, interrupting)* Hey, First Lady, would you smile for me?

FIRST LADY: Why, why I'd be mighty happy to.

She strikes a lavish pose as the Indian clicks his shutter. A puff of smoke, sparks fly, the First Lady lets out a very ladylike scream. The Indians break up. Drilling sound, lights out, earth visuals.

8

The lights reveal an isolated telephone booth at corner stage left. Flashes of light pepper the distant background. A racing siren wails faintly. A suggestion of the Washington Monument can also be seen in the shadowy background. A man comes on, wrapped in an Indian blanket, and anxiously enters the telephone booth.

SPY: *(Dialing furtively)* My God! Those damned Indians are crazier than the Afghans, the Congolese, the...

His call number goes through, the sound of the telephone clicking musically comes on tape.

VOICE: Hell ... o. White ... uh, excuse me I mean, thank you for calling, and how is the weather today?

SPY: I'm not worried about the weather, pal. Who is this? Dwight? Gordon? Bob? Who? Which one of you guys am I talking with?

VOICE: You ... you know better than to refer directly to ... uh, uh, the names of the innocent, oh, excuse me, I mean, certain individuals. Haven't we warned you enough times about doing that?

SPY: Be serious. Who would dare listen in on a direct call to the White House? How could anybody be smart enough to tape, I mean tap, this call box? *(Confusion)* Wait a minute. I'm not calling to argue about that, my friend, you know I'm here on assignment. The Indians are going to blow the hell out of the Bureau of Indian Affairs building any time now. They have every kind of revolutionary armament and defensive device you can think of in that place. The entire joint is wired. I managed to infiltrate by wrapping a blanket around myself and putting on a braided wig. I look pretty convincing.

VOICE: What tribe were you passing for? Oh, never mind!

SPY: *(Pleased) As* a matter of fact, I thought I looked like a Sioux *(Pronounces it "Si-ox")* or an Apache.

VOICE: And what is your reading of the situation? The boss has no time to devote to this matter just now. You know the election is just two days away. It cannot be blown. Do you understand that?

SPY: Yes, yes, yes! You know I understand. I'm just trying to be helpful, that's all. Helpful as long as you pay me, goddammit!

VOICE: Please, don't use profanity on this line!

SPY: Oh, excuse me, I forgot I was talking to the White ... oh!

VOICE: Don't say it!

SPY: Okay! Okay! Now listen, the only way we can save the building and prevent a bloody massacre of all those Indians and head off an explosive situation which could turn into an extremely embarrassing mess for the administration in the eyes of the world is to...

VOICE: Yes, we're waiting.

SPY: Is to bribe 'em, buy 'em off! *(He looks around to see if he is being watched)*

VOICE: How do you mean that? With beads, blankets, and whiskey?

SPY: No, hell no, dammit!

VOICE: Stop cursing, please!

SPY: No, no, we pay them cash, cold, hard cash. You know what that is, don't you? I know you do.

VOICE: How much?

SPY: I managed to do some figuring while I was inside the building. If my figures are correct, Indians are about two-thirds of one percent of the total population of the country, right? So, give them something like, uh, $66,500. Say to the press it's for travel expenses, to get the Indians back to their reservations. The public'll be impressed that even the poor old Indians are getting a little of the dole from Washington. Deliver the money to them in a briefcase. Or two if it all won't fit into one. Get it in and get out quick.

VOICE: *(Indignant)* Hush money?

SPY: No, perfectly legal. Travel expenses. They're all government consultants. You can put it down as that.

VOICE: And yourself, how much for you?

SPY: My fee for this national security operation will be $250,000, in cold, cold, hard, hard cash, of course.

VOICE: *(Disbelief)* Two hundred and fifty ...

SPY: *(Cutting him off)* You heard me, $250,000, in cold, hard cash!

VOICE: If we had to we could raise that, no problem. But we, we could use troops and tear gas to get those redskins out; why pay them? This is an unnecessary extravagance, highway robbery, plain old extortion.

SPY: Who says so?

VOICE: Well, you're getting more than the Indians will get, if this outrageously expensive transaction is approved.

SPY: This is dangerous work. I could have been scalped or killed if I had been caught in my disguise. And besides, the election will be in two days. You don't want a big bloody mess over here to foul things up, do you?

VOICE: Hang up now. I'll have to check this out with the Committee to Re
   … oh, pardon me, please. I need to consult my superiors. We'll be
   right back to you.

SPY: Don't take all night. This is an explosive situation over here. The
   specters of death and disaster are everywhere in the air. Have you
   ever been in the middle of a wild mob of hot-blooded warriors, buddy?

VOICE: Thank you so much for the weather report, Mr. Smith, uh, Jones.

   Spy hangs up, looks again to see if he is watched. Phone rings intermittently.

SPY: This is Neptune. The fish are running.

VOICE: What kind of fish?

SPY: Red snappers.

VOICE: The word is go. We'll make the arrangements on this end to get
   the money to the Indians. It will look very proper. The public knows
   how money-happy all Indians are, so miserable and poor, and our
   most isolated minority. They'll do anything to get their hands on
   some. Giving them money is a wonderful way to show them and
   the voters how much this administration cares. How do we get
   yours to you?

SPY: The usual way.

VOICE: Thank you for this weather report.

SPY: Sure, any time

   He hangs up, steps outside the booth, is showered with money. Drilling sound,
earth visuals. Lights out.

9

   The performing group lines up in a choreographed pattern as the piano begins
"Pass That Peace Pipe." Between each of the stanzas of the song, delivered as a wild
production number, an actor wearing a bull's head is spotlighted with a pretty girl
in pigtails, who reads from a giant roll of toilet tissue. The bull also holds a roll, and
unwinds enough tissue to wipe his behind each time a treaty is called out.

CHORUS: IF YOUR TEMPER'S GETTIN' THE TOP HAND ALL YOU GOTTA DO IS
   JUST STOP AND PASS THAT PEACE PIPE AND BURY THAT HATCHET LIKE
   THE CHOCTAWS, CHICKASAWS, CHATTAHOOCHIES, CHIPPEWAS DO!

GIRL: *(Leading the bull to front of stage)* THE TREATY OF ATOKA!

(Action)

    THE TREATY OF NEW ECHOTA!

(Action)

    THE TREATY OF DANCING RABBIT CREEK.

(Action)

    THE TREATY OF 1851.

Action)

CHORUS: IF YOU'RE FEELIN' MAD AS A WET HEN
        MAD AS YOU CAN POSSIBLY GET,
        THEN PASS THAT PEACE PIPE AND BURY THAT TOMAHAWK
        LIKE THOSE CHICHIMECS, CHEROKEES, CHEPULTEPECS,
        TOO!
GIRL: THE TREATY OF MEDICINE LODGE CREEK!

(Action)

    THE TREATY OF PORT ELLIOTT!

(Action)

    THE TREATY OF THE LITTLE ARKANSAS!

(Action)

    THE TREATY OF FORT WISE!

Action)

CHORUS: DON'T BE CRANKY, TRY TO USE A LITTLE RESTRAINT
        FOLD THAT HANKY, AND WIPE OFF ALL OF THAT WAR PAINT!
        AND IF YOU FIND YOURSELF IN A FURY, BE YOUR
        OWN JUDGE AND YOUR OWN JURY!
        PASS THAT PEACE PIPE AND BURY THAT HATCHET
        LIKE THE CHOCTAWS, CHICKASAWS, CHATTAHOOCHIES,
        CHIPPEWAS, DO!
GIRL: THE TREATY OF FORT LARAMIE!

(Action)

    THE TREATY OF MEDICINE LODGE!

(Action)

THE TREATY OF FORT KLAMATH!

(Action)

AND THE TREATY OF POINT NO POINT!

(Action)

CHORUS: WRITE THAT APOLOGY, AND DISPATCH IT,
WHEN YOU'VE QUARRELED, IT'S BETTER TO PATCH IT.
PASS THAT PEACE PIPE AND BURY THAT HATCHET
LIKE THE CHOCTAWS, CHICKASAWS, CHATTAHOOCHIES,
CHIPPEWAS,
AND THOSE CHICHIMECS, CHEROKEES, CHEPULTEPECS,
AND THOSE CHICUTIMEES, CHEPECHETS AND
CHICAPEES,
CHO-CHOS, CHANGOS, CHATTANOOGAS, CHEECAROWS,
DO!

Drilling sound, earth visuals, lights.

10

The choreography and music for this Wild West Show sequence provides the performing group members wide latitude for clowning. A girl in flimsy costume runs onstage with a show card to announce each scene. (The show cards will read: WILD APACHES; INDIAN COUNCIL OF WAR: LOVELY WHITE MAIDEN; SCALP DANCE; and TRIUMPH OF THE WHITES.) The Indians wear fake war bonnets, ride stick horses and yelp war whoops.

ANNOUNCER'S VOICE: *(On tape) coming* SOON! COMING SOON! TO THE
OLYMPIC THEATER! DIRECTLY FROM THEIR HOMES IN THE WILD,
WILD, WEST!! THE   WI—LD APACHES OF ARIZONA!
(Music up, Indians ride onstage.) Stalwart Braves and Squaws,
Without Doubt the Finest Specimens of the Aborigines Ever Seen in
this City in a Live Show of this Kind!
THIS ENTERTAINMENT WILL CONSIST OF A SERIES OF STIRRING
TABLEAUX, INTENSELY AND ACCURATELY ILLUSTRATIVE OF
INDIAN MODES AND CUSTOMS, NEVER BEFORE SO FAITHFULLY
SET FORTH!!

(Music up)

See Unbelievable, Breathtaking Scenes of Thrilling Hand-To-Hand Combat. A True-To-Life Indian Council of War! Featuring Speeches in the Actual Indian Tongues, By the Noted Chiefs and Braves. The Breaking of the Arrow!

(Music up)

An original, authentic WAAARRR DANCE!

Music and drumming create transition: all performers exit for entrance of Lovely White Maiden.

See the Lovely White Maiden! The surprise! The chase! The taking of the scalp! A savage, brutal SCALP DANCE! THE TRIUMPH OF THE WHITES!

Loud drumbeat for shotgun blast ends scalp dance and knocks the Indians dead on stage floor.

These, as well as many other fascinating true-to-life scenes of this vanishing specimen of primitive mankind.

Piano now fading. Show-card girl tiptoes among the Indian bodies with her final card.

ANNOUNCER: Special matinees of this fantastic spectacle will be given on Saturdays and Sundays, as well as all national and civic holidays.

Show-card girl flits off. With the bodies on the floor, the drilling sound and earth slides are now more intense than before. In an instant they change to rifle fire and vistas of the terrain around Wounded Knee, South Dakota. The visuals stop on a single picture of a marshal peering through a rifle scope that is aimed toward the performers and the audience.

11

The performing group members now rise from the floor and form a semicircle around the drummer, who is bare-chested. He drums and sings The AIM Song, building to a spirited pitch. A single rifle shot rings out and the drummer falls forward, his body taut, glistening in the lights. The helicopters, armored cars, and more gunfire are heard. The picture of the marshal switches to a sequence of action shots of the siege of Wounded Knee in 1973.

MARSHAL'S VOICE: *(Mixed with sounds of siege on tape)* May I please have your attention! I am the United States District Marshal from Rapid City, and I am at the head of a force of 500 federal officers and deputies. We have the entire area surrounded. You cannot escape.

The performers lift the drummer's body, raise it above their heads, and begin a slow procession offstage.

It is my duty to inform you that you are all under arrest on the charge of unlawfully trespassing on private property. Warrants for your arrest have been issued in federal district court. I must caution all of you not to make any sudden moves. We are armed and are prepared to take any necessary defensive action. All of you who do not surrender without resistance are hereby warned that additional charges will be filed against you for resisting arrest.
Your hands must be held high above your heads until the handcuffs are placed on you.
Again, I warn you, do not make any sudden moves.
Your cooperation will help to speed this procedure. Move forward, stay at absolute arm's length.

The siege visuals end as the performing group files back on the darkened stage in a funeral procession, led by a drummer who sounds a single heavy beat. The men carry the body of the dead drummer covered by a star blanket. A series of visuals showing the hands of the performing group members being handcuffed are projected as they file off. Then, one by one, they return to the stage, handcuffed, with their arms raised above their heads. The narrator steps to the front of the group.

NARRATOR: We move on. To a courtroom in Rapid City, South Dakota. To a courtroom in Sioux Falls, Iowa.
PERFORMER: *(Moving out from the group, he thrusts his hands toward audience.)* I am Pawnee.
NARRATOR: We move on.
PERFORMER: *(Repeating the action)* I am Creek.
NARRATOR: Back to our homes, our people.
PERFORMER: I am Winnebago.
NARRATOR: We move on.
PERFORMER: I am Sioux.
NARRATOR: To the land.
PERFORMER: I am Apache.
NARRATOR: To the sky.

PERFORMER: I am Ojibwa.

The lights dim as the apparition of the Indian face again appears on the stage backside and moves slowly around the playing area.

VOICE OF SPANISH SAILOR: *(on tape)*¡ Capitan! ¡Capitan! ¡Dios mio! ¡Muchas gracias! ¡Madre mia! ¡Los indios! ¡Los indios! ¡India! ¡Ellos son los indios!

NARRATOR: *(Very compassionately)* I am ... NOT GUILTY!

Lights fade slowly. Performing group exits.

THE END

Alternate Table of Contents by Theme

LANGUAGE

Selected Bibliography

H. David Brumble, *American Indian Autobiography.* University of California Press, 1988.

Ward Churchill, *Indians are Us?* Common Courage Press, Monroe, Maine, 1994.

Tom Colonnese and Louis Owens, *American Indian Novelists: An Annotated Critical Bibliography.* Garland Publishing, 1985.

Laura Coltelli, *Winged Words: American Indian Writers Speak.* University of Nebraska Press, 1990.

Vine Deloria, Jr., *Custer Died for Your Sins.* University of Oklahoma Press, 1988.

_____, *God is Red.* Grosset and Dunlap, 1973.

_____, *Behind the Trail of Broken Treaties.* Dell, 1974.

Henry Dobyns, *Native American Historical Demography.* Indiana University Press, 1976.

Richard Drinnon, *Facing West: The Metaphysics of Indian-Hating and Empire Building.* University of Minnesota Press, 1980.

Richard Fleck, editor, *Critical Perspectives on Native American Fiction.* Three Continents Press, 1993.

Sam Gill, *Mother Earth: An American Story.* The University of Chicago Press, 1987.

_____, *Native American Religions: An Introduction.* Wadsworth, 1982.

William Hagan, *American Indians.* The University of Chicago Press, 1979.

Frederick Hoxie, editor, *Indians in American History,* Harlan Davidson, 1988.

Ake Hultkrantz, *Native Religions of North America,* Harper & Row, 1987.

_____, *The Religions of the American Indians.* University of California Press, 1967.

Dorothy Jones, *License for Empire: Colonialism by Treaty in Early America.* The University of Chicago Press, 1982.

Thomas King, editor, *All My Relations: An Anthology of Contemporary Canadian Native Fiction.* University of Oklahoma Press, 1992.

Arnold Krupat, *For Those Who Come After: A Study of Native American Autobiography.* University of California Press, 1985.

K. Tsianina Lomawaima, *The Story of Chilocco Indian School: They Called it Prairie Light.* University of Nebraska Press, 1994.

Hartmut Lutz, *Contemporary Challenges: Conversations with Canadian Native Authors.* Fifth House Publishers, 1991.

L. G. Moses and Raymond Wilson, editors, *Indian Lives: Essays on Nineteenth- and Twentieth-Century Native American Leaders*. University of New Mexico Press, 1985.

Duane Niatum, editor, *Harper's Anthology of 20th Century Native American Poetry*. Harper & Row, 1988.

_____, editor, *Carriers of the Dream Wheel: Contemporary Native American Poetry*. Harper & Row, 1975.

Sharon O'Brien, *American Indian Tribal Government*. University of Oklahoma Press, 1989.

Barry O'Connell, *On Our Own Ground: The Complete Writings of William Apess, A Pequot*. University of Massachusetts Press, 1992.

Simon Ortiz, editor, *Earth Power Coming: Short Fiction in Native American Literature*. Navajo Community College Press, 1983.

Louis Owens, *Other Destinies: Understanding the American Indian Novel*. University of Oklahoma Press, 1992.

Dorothy Parker, *Singing an Indian Song: A Biography of D'Arcy McNickle*. University of Nebraska Press, 1992.

Roy Harvey Pearce, *Savagism and Civilization: A Study of the Indian and the American Mind*. University of California Press, 1988.

Bernard Peyer, *The Singing Spirit: Early Short Stories by North American Indians*. University of Arizona Press, 1989.

Kenneth Roemer, editor, *Approaches to Teaching Momaday's The Way to Rainy Mountain*. The Modern Language Association of America, 1988.

Kenneth Rosen, *The Man to Send Rain Clouds: Contemporary Stories by American Indians*. Viking, 1974.

A. LaVonne Brown Ruoff, *American Indian Literatures*. The Modern Language Association of America, 1990.

Susan Scarberry-Garcia, *Landmarks of Healing: A Study of House Made of Dawn*. University of New Mexico Press, 1990.

Jane Smith and Robert Kvasnicka, editors, *Indian-White Relations: A Persistent Paradox*. Howard University Press, 1976.

Brian Swann, editor, *Smoothing the Ground: Essays on Native American Oral Literature*. University of California, 1983.

_____ and Arnold Krupat, editors, *I Tell You Now*. University of Nebraska Press, 1987.

_____ and Arnold Krupat, editors, *Recovering the Word: Essays on Native American Literature*. University of California Press, 1987.

Margaret Connell Szasz, editor, *Between Indian and White Worlds*. University of Oklahoma Press, 1994.

Dennis Tedlock, *The Spoken Word and the Work of Interpretations*. University of Pennsylvania Press, 1983.

Clifford Trafzer, editor, *Earth Song, Sky Spirit: Short Stories of the Contemporary Native American Experience*. Doubleday, 1992.

Alan Velie, editor, *American Indian Literature: An Anthology*. University of Oklahoma Press, 1991.

Gerald Vizenor, *Crossbloods: Bone Courts Bingo and Other Reports*. University of Minnesota Press, 1990.

_____, *Manifest Manners: Postindian Warriors of Survivance*. Wesleyan University Press, 1994.

_____, editor, *Narrative Chance: Postmodern Discourse on Native American Literatures*. University of Oklahoma Press, 1993.

_____, editor, *Touchwood: A Collection of Ojibway Prose*. New Rivers Press, 1987.

Virgil Vogel, *American Indian Medicine*. University of Oklahoma Press, 1970.

John Wunder, *Retained by the People*. Oxford University Press, 1994.

Index of Author Names, Titles and First Lines of Poems

Acknowledgments

Sherman Alexie. "Before We Knew about Mirrors" and "Crazy Horse Speaks" from <u>Caliban</u>, 1990. "Robert DeNiro" from <u>Caliban</u>, #13, 1993. Reprinted by permission from <u>Caliban</u>.

Paula Gunn Allen. "Someday Soon" from <u>Grandmothers of the Light</u> by Paula Gunn Allen. Copyright © 1991 by Paula Gunn Allen. Reprinted by permission of Beacon Press.

William Apess. "A Son of the Forest" from <u>On Our Own Ground: The Complete Writings of William Apess, a Pequot</u> (Amherst: University of Massachusetts Press, 1992).

Jim Barnes. "The Sawdust War," "Under the Tent," and "The Cabin on Nanny Ridge" from <u>The Sawdust War</u> by Jim Barnes. Copyright © 1992 by Jim Barnes. Reprinted by permission of the University of Illinois Press.

Betty Louise Bell. "In the Hour of the Wolf" From <u>Faces in the Moon</u> by Betty Louise Bell. Copyright © 1994 by Betty Louise Bell. Reprinted by permission of the University of Oklahoma Press.

Kimberly Blaeser. "A Matter of Proportion" Copyright ©1995 by Kimberly Blaeser. Used by permission of the author.

Maria Campbell. "The Little People," reprinted from <u>Halfbreed</u> by Maria Campbell, by permission of the University of Nebraska Press and the Canadian Publishers, McClelland & Stewart, Toronto. Copyright © 1973 by Maria Campbell.

Elizabeth Cook-Lynn. "A Good Chance" from <u>The Power of Horses and Other Stories</u> by Elizabeth Cook-Lynn (Arcade Publishing). Copyright © 1990 by Elizabeth Cook-Lynn. Reprinted by permission of the author.

Louise Erdrich. "Lipsha Morrissey" from <u>Love Medicine, New and Expanded Version</u> by Louise Erdrich. Copyright © 1984, 1993 by Louise Erdrich. Reprinted by permission of Henry Holt and Company, Inc. "Indian Boarding School: The Runaways" and "Turtle Mountain Reservation" from <u>Jacklight</u> by Louise Erdrich. Copyright © 1984 by Louise Erdrich. Reprinted by permission of Henry Holt and Company, Inc.

Hanay Geiogamah. "Foghorn" from <u>New Native American Drama: Three Plays by Hanay Geiogamah</u>. Copyright © 1980 by the University of Oklahoma Press. Reprinted by permission of the publisher.

N. Scott Momaday. "The Way to Rainy Mountain." First published in The Reporter, 26 January 1967. Reprinted from The Way to Rainy Mountain, Copyright © 1969, The University of New Mexico Press, by permission of the publisher. "The Names" excerpted from The Names, Copyright © 1976 by N. Scott Momaday, by permission of the author. "Rise of the Song" from House Made of Dawn by N. Scott Momaday. Copyright © 1966, 1967, 1968 by N. Scott Momaday. Reprinted by permission of HarperCollins Publishers, Inc.

Simon J. Ortiz. "A Story of How a Wall Stands," "My Father's Song," and "From Sand Creek" from the book From Sand Creek by Simon Ortiz. Copyright © 1981 by Simon J. Ortiz. Used by permission of the publisher, Thunder's Mouth Press.

Louis Owens. "The Last Stand" From Bone Game by Louis Owens. Copyright © 1994 by Louis Owens. Reprinted by permission of the University of Oklahoma Press. "Motion of Fire and Form." Copyright © 1995 by Louis Owens. Used by permission of the author.

John Rogers. "Return to White Earth" From Red World and White: Memories of a Chippewa Boyhood by John Rogers (Chief Snow Cloud). Copyright © 1957 as A Chippewa Speaks by John Rogers. Copyright assigned to the University of Oklahoma Press, 1973. Reprinted by permission of the publisher.

Wendy Rose. "Neon Scars." Reprinted from I Tell You Now: Autobiographical Essays by Native American Writers, edited by Brian Swann and Arnold Krupat, by permission of the University of Nebraska Press. Copyright © 1987 by the University of Nebraska Press. "To Some Few Hopi Ancestors," "Is It Crazy to Want to Unravel," and "For the White Poets Who Would Be Indian" from Bone Dance: New and Selected Poems, 1965–1993 by Wendy Rose. Copyright © 1994 Arizona Board of Regents. Reprinted by permission of the University of Arizona Press.

Leslie Marmon Silko. "Call That Story Back" from Ceremony by Leslie Marmon Silko. Copyright © 1977 by Leslie Silko. Used by permission of Viking Penguin, a division of Penguin Books USA Inc.

Luther Standing Bear. "First Days at Carlisle" from My People, the Sioux by Luther Standing Bear (University of Nebraska Press, 1975).

Mary TallMountain. "There Is No Word for Goodbye" from There Is No Word for Goodbye by Mary TallMountain. Copyright © 1982 by Mary TallMountain. Reprinted by permission of the author's literary estate.

Luci Tapahonso. "For Lori Tazbah" from Geary Hobson, ed., The Remembered Earth (University of New Mexico Press). Copyright © 1979 by Luci Tapahonso. Reprinted